Total
Productivity
MANAGEMENT

*A Systemic and Quantitative
Approach to Compete in
Quality, Price, and Time*

David J. Sumanth, Ph.D.

S^t_L

St. Lucie Press
Boca Raton, Florida

Library of Congress Cataloging-in-Publication Data

Catalog information may be obtained from the Library of Congress

© 1998 by CRC Press LLC
St. Lucie Press is an imprint of CRC Press LLC

No claim to original U.S. Government works
International Standard Book Number 1-57444-057-8
Printed in the United States of America 1 2 3 4 5 6 7 8 9 0
Printed on acid-free paper

To my beloved wife, Chaya,
for her inspiration and dedication in this effort.

CONTENTS

PREFACE

Up to the 1950s, managers in general, and American managers in particular, emphasized the *manufacturing* function; in the 1960s, *marketing* became a main strategy. In the 1970s and early 1980s, corporate acquisitions and mergers heavily relied on the power of *finance*. In the latter half of the 1980s and the early 1990s, management began to realize the importance of *quality* and *participative management*. The second half of the 1990s and the first decade of the 21st century will see a balanced approach to managing three strategic variables: *quality*, *technology,* and *total productivity.* The necessity to mitigate the problems caused by exclusive and/or excessive emphasis on the traditional labor productivity concept and the need to balance these three strategic variables form the basis for *Total Productivity Management* (TPmgt™) thinking. This concept was first proposed by the author in 1981, and many of its elements have been demonstrated in more than 60 different types of enterprises, ranging from computer manufacturing and space-shuttle payload processing to hospitals, mass transit operations, banks, insurance companies, and utilities.

Total productivity management, as defined in this author's earlier work, is:

> a formal management process that follows the four phases of the "Productivity Cycle", so as to increase *total productivity* and to reduce the *total unit costs* of products or services at the highest *quality* possible.

The *productivity cycle,* developed by this author in 1979, with a focus on total productivity, is the central framework for TPmgt in that it recognizes the importance of four ongoing activities: productivity measurement, productivity evaluation, productivity planning, and productivity improvement.

Productivity measurement is the critical first phase of the productivity process. The *Total Productivity Model* (TPM©) is the main measurement tool in this phase. This model, which plays a central role in TPmgt, is presented in Chapter 3.

Productivity evaluation is a comparison of actual productivity levels achieved against planned values and actual values for previous periods. It is a comparative process. Purely quantitative as well as semi-subjective models have been developed to do this comparative analysis; they are powerful benchmarking tools.

Productivity planning deals with the determination of target levels of productivity. Both short-term (less than one year) and long-term (more than one year) productivity planning are necessary in order to manage total productivity and profitability in a systematic manner.

The fourth phase, productivity improvement, deals with a rational and systematic approach to achieving the target levels of total productivity set in the productivity planning phase.

The key to practicing the TPmgt concept is maintaining as close to a "relevantly optimal" level of total productivity as possible. The total productivity value reflects the change in output produced due to the simultaneous impact of all the input resources. Thus, it is a more accurate representation of reality than are partial productivity measures. For example, if human productivity were to improve for a particular time period, the total productivity value would be examined first to see if it also improved. If it did not, the reasons could be analyzed by determining the magnitude and direction of change in all five partial productivities (human, material, capital, energy, and other expense productivities).

This book takes the position that every organizational entity can and must train its management and employees or "associates" to be quality competitive, price competitive, and time competitive—all simultaneously. With TPmgt, everyone is a "winner," because this management concept is based on optimizing total productivity instead of just labor productivity. The total unit cost of producing a product or service is reduced by increasing total productivity. This translates into benefits for customers, employees, management, stockholders, and suppliers—in effect, the entire society!

As an example to illustrate this management concept, suppose a company that manufactures computers increases its total productivity such that the unit cost per computer drops from $1,200 to $1,000 for the same quality level(s). Prior to this improvement in total productivity, the company had been selling its computers for $1,600, with a profit of $400 on each computer. With costs down by $200, the company is able to lower the selling price for the computer by $100. As you might expect, more delighted customers rush to buy the computer, which now costs $100 less for the same quality product The demand for the computer goes up, and the company hires more people. Stockholders are happy as profits soar by 25%. The employees and management receive bonuses, and the suppliers get paid sooner as the company's cash flow improves. Every stakeholder is a winner! A similar scenario can be applied to a bank, hospital, insurance firm, fast-food restaurant, retail store, grocery store, university, consulting firm, construction contractor, local government agency—in effect, any entity that offers a product or a service.

The effectiveness of any "new" claim must be evaluated based on a set of longitudinal observations. The TPmgt philosophy, concept, and methodology have been tested and proven to be innovative, relevant, and long-lasting over the last 17 years on every continent. TPmgt has been found not to be culture-biased and is not affected by a company's size or type of business. It works anywhere, because it integrates the human approach to treating people with the technical approach to managing all resources under an overarching umbrella of systems thinking.

ACKNOWLEDGMENTS

This book has been in the making for ten years. It is based on my research, consulting, training, and observations during the past 27 years in many diversified industries, enterprises, and cultural settings in 45 countries around the world. This work also evolved considerably from the worldwide implementation experiences of theories presented in my first book, *Productivity Engineering and Management* (McGraw-Hill, 1984, 1985, 1990, and 1994). I owe a great deal to the hundreds of academic scholars, corporate CEOs and managers, consultants, government officials, and the many thousands who have attended my keynote addresses, seminars, short courses, and lectures and have shaped the theme and content of this book directly and indirectly. I am indebted to the more than 3,000 former students who have taken my courses since 1973. They have been a source of encouragement and friendly critique to constantly refine my thinking. A thank-you also to my former students Laura Castrillo, Fausto Izurieta, Lila Parrales, and Jessica Rodriguez for their assistance in Chapter 5.

Since 1968, my firsthand observations of international companies such as the Shriram Group in India; Rimoldi in Italy; Pfaff in Germany; Mitsubishi in Japan; Lincoln Electric, IBM, AT&T, Westinghouse, and General Electric in the United States; Dunlop in Malaysia; the Occidente Group in Guatemala; the Kodela Group in Curaçao; and many other companies have given me a unique depth and breadth of practical insights to confidently propose what I do in this book. My sincere thanks to all these companies for giving me an opportunity to learn from them.

I am also grateful to my colleagues at the University of Miami, who, during the last 17 years, have helped directly and indirectly with their support and constructive critique. My special thanks to Dr. Norman G. Einspruch, Chairman, IE Department; Dr. M. Lewis Temares, Dean, College of Engineering; Dr. Luis Glaser, Executive Vice President and Provost; and Dr. Edward T. Foote II, President, who continue to believe in my work.

I am greatly indebted to Dennis Buda and Dennis McClellan of St. Lucie Press for keenly pursuing, supporting, and marketing this work. My very special thanks to Sandy Pearlman of St. Lucie Press, whose tireless effort and dedication have been responsible for the excellent editing, design, and production of this book. My sincere gratitude also to the initial reviewers of this manuscript— whose insights have been most valuable.

If there is one person who has been responsible for this book finally coming out in print, it is my life-partner and wife, Chaya. In addition to her steadfast inspiration to me, she tenaciously typed all of the manuscript, including the figures and tables! I dedicate this book to her most gratefully. Special thanks also goes out to my eldest son, John, who not only assisted in the typing of this book, but who also serves as my "intellectual partner." I am also grateful to my second son, Paul, whose cheerful disposition always perked me up during the long working hours, and to my mother, Nancy, whose constant prayers kept me encouraged.

Everyone has a significant mentor in their life. Mine during the last 50 years has been Jesus Christ, my Lord, my Guide, and my Master, whose daily guidance and teachings have had a profound impact in shaping my treatment of my fellow human beings around the world and in my applying many of His concepts from classrooms to boardrooms.

David J. Sumanth

ABOUT THE AUTHOR

Dr. David J. Sumanth, Ph.D., is Professor and Founding Director (since 1979) of the Productivity Research Group at the University of Miami. In 1979, he introduced Productivity Engineering as a Master's concentration in Industrial Engineering at the University of Miami, making it the first U.S. university to offer such a program. He founded the International Conference Series on Productivity & Quality Research and chaired the first five conferences from 1987 to 1995 and is co-chairing the seventh one in 1998. He also founded the International Society for Productivity and Quality Research in 1993 and serves as chairman of its board.

His book *Productivity Engineering and Management* (published by McGraw-Hill, New York, 1984; Singapore, 1985; Mexico, 1990; India, 1990, New York, 1994) has become a "classic"; it has influenced "productivity engineering" thinking in 25 countries and has helped initiate new courses on the subject. He is the author/co-author/editor of 20 books, monographs, and video courses and more than 100 publications. His research is focused on his "Total Productivity Management," engineering management, quality, competitiveness, reengineering, measurement and improvement of excellence, and continuous improvement approaches, including TQM, benchmarking, quality function deployment, and problem-solving tools. For 25 years, he has advised many prestigious organizations around the world where his concepts have been implemented.

He is a Senior Member of the (American) Institute of Industrial Engineers (IIE), as well as past president and past director (Miami Chapter). He is also a Charter Member of the American Society for Engineering Management, a member of The Institute of Management Sciences, and a past member of the Operations Research Society of America and the American Association for the Advancement of Science. Since 1984, he has served as Assistant Director of Productivity Management and Chairman for Research in the Management Division of IIE; he also served on the special Productivity Committee of IIE. Under his leadership, the University of Miami became one of the five Founding Members of the Sterling Council, which administers the Governor's Florida Sterling Award for quality and productivity. As a Governor's appointee, he has served as a Judge and Senior Judge for this award since its inception in 1992.

Dr. Sumanth earned his B.E. (Mechanical Engineering) and M.E. (Production Engineering) degrees from Osmania University and M.S. and Ph.D. degrees in Industrial Engineering from the Illinois Institute of Technology, Chicago. He is a frequent national and international speaker in the United States, Europe, the Far East, and Latin America and is the recipient of more than 60 honors and awards, including the *YMCA Educational Achievement Gold Medal* (1969), *Outstanding Industrial Engineer of the Year Award* (1983, 1984), *George Washington Honor Medal for Excellence in Economic Education* (1987), and *Fellow of the World Academy of Productivity Science* (1989) for his contributions to productivity education. His biographical listings include *World Researchers of the 1980's, Who's Who in the South and Southwest, Who's Who in Finance and Industry, Men of Achievement, Community Leaders of America, Personalities of America, Directory of Distinguished Americans, Two Thousand Notable American Men, Who's Who in America, Who's Who in the World, Who's Who in Science and Engineering, International Who's Who of Contemporary Achievement, International Leaders in Achievement,* and *5000 Personalities of the World.*

Most importantly, he likes to motivate, encourage, and "build people up," for "we all have the same color of blood!"

1 INTRODUCTION

A country's *level* and *rate* of *productivity* growth have a significant bearing on its standard of living, inflation, unemployment rate, and general economic well-being. Today, productivity and quality have become the national concern of both the developing and the developed economies. However, efforts to improve a country's productivity level and growth rate have to begin with its basic economic units, namely, companies/enterprises. Dr. John Kendrick, one of the well-respected contemporary authorities on productivity, puts it best: "Companies with higher productivity than the industry average tend to have higher profit margins. Moreover if productivity is growing faster than that of competitors, the margins will rise. Conversely, below-average levels and rates of growth of productivity will ultimately lead to bankruptcy."[1] Therefore, the focus of this book is to show proven, practical concepts and methodologies to improve the competitiveness of companies/enterprises. But first things first.

1.1 MISCONCEPTIONS ABOUT QUALITY, TECHNOLOGY, AND PRODUCTIVITY

Part of the motivation to propose "total productivity management" stems from the awareness of many misconceptions about quality, technology, productivity, and the problems with the partial productivity perspective.

Misconceptions About Quality

"The typical factory invests a staggering 20 to 25% of its operating budget in finding and fixing mistakes."[2] In fact, "most experts on the 'cost of quality' said losses are more in the range of 20 percent to 30 percent for defective or unsatisfactory products. For example, a company with $1 billion in sales might lose up to $200 million annually as a result of poor quality."[3]

Quality is a difficult term to define, because it is subjective in that it has an emotional connotation. The historical introduction to quality in Appendix A is based on my research for the University of Miami's Institute of Studies in Quality (UMISQ). From this, we see that a number of major achievements have been made in developing the field of quality, but ironically, there is no interdisciplinary or interfunctional definition of the term. The UMISQ, under Dr. Howard Gitlow's direction, has undertaken research projects to develop a cohesive quality theory from a holistic viewpoint.

One of the commonly accepted descriptions of quality is through Dr. Juran's three dimensions: *quality of design, quality of conformance,* and *quality of performance.*

Quality of design refers to the level at which specifications are "fixed" into the design of a product or service. *Quality of conformance* refers to the extent to which these specifications are achieved while manufacturing a product or delivering a service. *Quality of performance*, also known as reliability, refers to the extent to which a product functions at any given time, that is, the probability of a product or service functioning at any given time. To understand this quality concept, let's use a cardiac pacemaker as an example. A cardiac pacemaker is an intricate medical device embedded into a human body to monitor heart function. Needless to say, the quality of design here must be extremely high! Therefore, when engineers and scientists design it, they make sure that the specifications are stringent while manufacturing this pacemaker. Extreme care is exercised to ensure that those specifications built into the product at the time of the design are indeed achieved. Finally, when the product is made, it is tested and retested to make sure that it will function reliably in a human body. After all, if you were to wear a pacemaker, you certainly would want the reliability of this product to be 100%, wouldn't you?

Among General Electric's many products, the dishwasher is one of the most well-known household appliances. When GE dramatically improved the quality of performance (reliability) of this product by 45%, labor productivity improved by 42%.

When one or more of the three dimensions of quality improves, there may or may not be an effect on labor productivity, but there will always be some systemic effect on product quality, process quality, and/or service quality. Contrary to common myth that productivity suffers because of quality improvement, *total productivity* actually improves in the long run when quality improves. Thus,

- Quality improvement does not have to be at the expense of productivity.
- Quality and "total productivity" are sides of the same coin, or two rails of the same track.

Misconceptions About Technology

Most people think of technology as computers, machines, or gadgets. Technology, as broadly defined, is any means to accomplish an objective or task. There are four basic types of technologies: product technology, process technology, information technology, and managerial technology.[4] Process technology has a significant impact on the operational efficiencies of a plant. For example, a study reported in 1983 by Roger Schmenner indicated that the number one reason for plant closures was inefficient or outdated process technology.[5]

Process technology is certainly *one* of the four available technologies to improve productivity in any enterprise. Another study (Table 1.1) indicated the major benefits of advanced manufacturing technologies on machine cycle time, reliability, inventory, labor, flexibility, and quality.[6] However, it is important to recognize that not all technologies are appropriate and relevant at all times; their effect on productivity is not always in the positive direction. For example, when new automatic toll booths were installed on a busy highway in Miami, traffic delays seemed to actually increase! It took more time for the mechanical arm of the automated coin collectors to rise and allow drivers through than it did for a human to accept payment.[7] The common myth that technology *always* improves

TABLE 1.1   Major Benefits of Advanced Manufacturing Technologies

Advanced Manufacturing Technology: Survey of Vendors and Users			
Benefit	*Expecting Benefit*	*Disappointed*	*Satisfied*
Faster machine cycle time	70%	31%	69%
Greater reliability	76	46	56
Reduced work-in-process inventory	74	36	64
Direct labor savings	80	39	61
Greater flexibility	74	29	71
Improved quality	83	34	66

Source: Uzumi, V. and Sanderson, S.W., "Buying Advanced Manufacturing Technology—An Exclusive Survey of Vendors and Users," *Manufacturing Engineering,* Vol. 105, No. 2, Aug. 1990. Published by SME, One SME Drive, Dearborn, MI 48121.

productivity must be replaced by the reality that managing technology is a much more complex issue for decision makers.

Misconceptions About Productivity

The word "productivity" has been in existence for more than 200 years (Table 1.2). When we distill the well-known literature on the subject, we see an interesting evolution of this concept.

The term *productivity* was probably first mentioned by the French mathematician Quesnay in an article in 1766. In 1883, another Frenchman, Littre, defined productivity as the "faculty to produce." In 1950, the Organization for European Economic Cooperation (OEEC), one of the oldest organizations espousing productivity enhancement, particularly in the Europe, issued a formal definition:[8]

> Productivity is the quotient obtained by dividing output by one of the factors of production. In this way it is possible to speak of the productivity of capital, investment, or raw materials, according to whether output is being considered in relation to capital, investment or raw materials, etc.

Dr. John Kendrick and Daniel Creamer, in their classic work, offered definitions of productivity from an economist's viewpoint. In the late 1970s and

TABLE 1.2   History of Productivity Definitions

Productivity Definitions	
Quesnay	1766
Littre	1883
OEEC	1950
Davis	1955
Kendrick and Creamer	1965
Siegel	1976
Sumanth	1979
APC	1979
Sumanth	1987

Basic Types of Productivity Measures

- Partial Productivity (PP)
- Total Factor Productivity (TFP)
- Total Productivity (TP)
- Comprehensive Total Productivity (CTP)

early 1980s, the then American Productivity Center (APC) popularized its definition: Profitability = Productivity × Price Recovery.

In 1979, and later in 1984, this author offered the first three (and in 1987 the fourth) basic definitions[9] of productivity, particularly as relevant to companies/enterprises:

- **Partial productivity** is the ratio of output to one class of input. For example, output per man-hour (a labor productivity measure) is a partial productivity concept. So are output per ton of material (a material productivity ratio) and interest revenue generated per dollar of capital (a capital productivity ratio) and so on.

- **Total factor productivity** is the ratio of net output to the sum of associated labor and capital (factor) inputs. The net output here is sometimes called *value-added output*. In this ratio, we explicitly consider only the labor and capital input factors in the denominator. Since materials account for as much as 65% of product costs in consumer goods such as TVs, VCRs, and computers, this measure is not the best one in most cases.

- **Total productivity** is the ratio of *total* output to the sum of all input factors. This is a holistic measure which takes into consideration the joint and simultaneous impact of *all* the input resources on the output, such as manpower, materials, machines, capital, energy, etc. This measure has received much attention over the past ten years, as evidenced by many papers and case studies.[10] Another term used in recent years is multifactor productivity, which considers more than one input factor in the denominator of the productivity ratio, but is not necessarily a total factor or total productivity measure.

- **Comprehensive total productivity** index is the total productivity index multiplied by the intangible factor index. This is the most sophisticated measure that extends the total productivity measure to include any user-defined qualitative factors—as many as are relevant to a company—ranging from product quality and process quality to timeliness, market share, community attitude, etc. This measure is discussed in Chapter 3.

Earlier research showed that about 80% of the indicators companies use (thinking that they are measuring productivity) are really non-standard in that they do *not* belong to one of the above first four *basic* productivity definitions: partial productivity, total factor productivity, total productivity, and comprehensive total productivity.[11]

A detailed treatment of various productivity definitions and models is presented in this author's earlier work.[12] This author's Total Productivity Model

(TPM©), discussed in Chapter 3, is based on total productivity, a set of partial productivities, and the unique *break-even concept of total productivity*. The advantages and limitations of each of the four basic productivity concepts are summarized in Table 1.3.

Historically, for almost a century, the U.S. Bureau of Labor Statistics (BLS) has been measuring, maintaining, and analyzing measures of productivity. Jerome Mark[13] of the BLS points out that "these measures have ranged from plant level productivity indexes to those for industries, major economic sectors and the total private business economy. They have included single factor productivity measures such as output per hour and in the last decade multifactor productivity indexes including inputs of labor, capital, energy, and materials."

In the 1970s and early 1980s, he used to include a disclaimer and caution in the BLS publication on labor productivity indexes to warn readers that the labor productivity measure does not represent the contribution of only labor. He correctly recognizes that the "increased globalization of industries with emphasis

TABLE 1.3   Advantages and Limitations of Using the Basic Types of Productivity Measures in Companies

Advantages	*Limitations*
Partial Productivity Measures	
1. Easy to understand	1. If used *alone,* can be very misleading and may lead to costly mistakes
2. Easy to obtain the data	
3. Easy to compute the productivity indices	2. Do not have the ability to explain overall cost increases
4. Easy to sell to management because of the above three advantages	3. Tend to shift the blame to the wrong areas of management control
5. Some partial productivity indicator data (e.g., output per man-hour) is available industry-wide	4. Profit control through partial productivity measures can be a hit-and-miss approach
6. Good diagnostic tools to pinpoint areas for productivity improvement, if used along with total productivity indicators	
Total Factor Productivity Measure	
1. The data from company records are relatively easy to obtain	1. Does not directly capture the impact of materials and energy inputs

TABLE 1.3   Advantages and Limitations of Using the Basic Types of Productivity Measures in Companies (continued)

Advantages	*Limitations*
Total Factor Productivity Measures (continued)	
2. Usually appealing from a corporate economist's viewpoint	2. The value-added approach to defining the output is not very appropriate in a company setting
	3. Not appropriate when material costs form a sizeable portion of total product costs
	4. Only labor and capital inputs are considered in the total factor input
	5. Data for comparison purposes are relatively difficult to obtain, although for some specific industries and specific time periods, the indices have been published
Total Productivity Measure	
1. Considers all quantifiable output and input factors; therefore, is a more accurate representation of the real economic picture of a company	1. Data for computations are relatively difficult to obtain at product and customer levels, unless data collection systems are designed for this purpose
2. Profit control through the use of total productivity indices is a tremendous benefit to top management	2. Like the partial and total factor measures, does not consider intangible factors of output and input in a direct sense
3. If used in conjunction with partial measures *can direct* management attention in an effective manner	
4. Sensitivity analysis is easier to perform	
5. Easily related to total costs	
Comprehensive Total Productivity Measure	
1. Considers *all* the *tangible* as well as *intangible* factors	1. Though the benefits of this measure far outweigh its limitations, it requires the input of a few more indicators into the measurement model

TABLE 1.3 Advantages and Limitations of Using the Basic Types of
Productivity Measures in Companies (continued)

Advantages	Limitations
Comprehensive Total Productivity Measure (continued)	
2. All the factors, particularly the intangible ones, are user-definable; therefore, any number of them can be accommodated in the measure	2. Requires a consensus or majority agreement on the "ranks" and "weights" in the model
3. The measure provides a quantitative approach to link *everything* from product quality to process timeliness to customer satisfaction to dozens of other critical performance indicators to profitability	
4. Helps management at any level to factor out the various effects of quality, costs, time, etc.	
5. This measure is indeed the most comprehensive productivity measure	
6. Decision makers can easily study the effect of technology on total productivity and profitability	
7. This measure makes it possible, for the first time, to link technology strategy to business strategy	

on competitiveness will lead to more pressure for better and more comprehensive measures of productivity."[14] In this book, we do have such comprehensive measures—the Total Productivity Model (TPM©) and the Comprehensive Total Productivity Model (CTPM©)—both a backbone of total productivity management, as we shall see in Chapter 3.

In the meantime, let's look at some of the labor productivity trends in the United States and other countries for which data are often assembled regularly for comparative purposes. Table 1.4 shows that in the manufacturing sector, the United States registered a 2.8% per year growth rate in labor productivity (value added per manufacturing employee) between 1985 and 1992. In terms of labor productivity, the United States is surpassed by Japan in the steel, car parts, metal, automotive, and consumer electronics industries (Figure 1.1).

TABLE 1.4 Labor Productivity in Manufacturing

	Level	*Trend*
	Value Added/ Worker,[a] 1989 (Index: U.S. = 100)	*Output/Hour %/Year 1985–92*
Japan	135	3.4
France	115	2.7
Canada	109	0.8
Germany	105	1.6
Italy	101	3.1
U.S.	100	2.8
Netherlands	97	1.6
U.K.	64	4.5

[a] If this measure were value added per employee per hour, Japan's lead would be cut in half due to longer hours worked in Japan.

Source: *Perspectives '94,* p. 18. ©American Productivity & Quality Center, Houston, Texas. Data from World Competitiveness Report (IMD), Bureau of Labor Statistics. Used with permission.

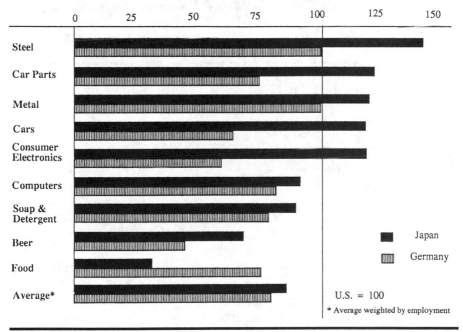

FIGURE 1.1 Labor productivity in selected industries, 1990. (Source: McKinsey, *Economist* and *Perspectives '94,* p. 18. ©American Productivity & Quality Center. Used with permission.)

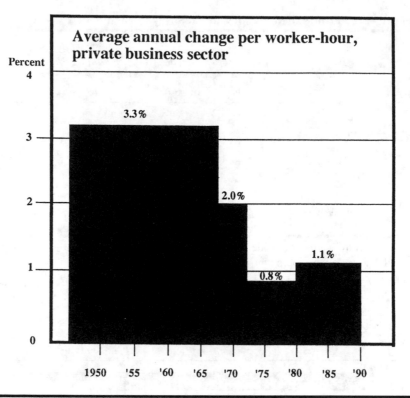

FIGURE 1.2   Labor productivity growth in the United States. (Source: U.S. Bureau of Labor Statistics. See Fiedler,[15] p. 1-3.3.)

In his recent work, Edgar Fiedler[15] of the Conference Board analyzed the labor productivity picture for the United States during the last four decades. He shows an interesting situation (Figure 1.2). Fiedler concludes from his analysis that "in the aggregate, we are still tracking a very weak long-term productivity trend."[16]

The American Productivity and Quality Center[17] analyzed the labor productivity trend during the more recent 25-year period from 1968 to 1993, and its results show that labor productivity growth in the service sector has been virtually stagnant. Despite nearly the 4.0% growth in 1993 in the manufacturing sector, the overall growth rate for the private business sector has been only 2.0%. This is a far cry from the more than 3% growth rate experienced in the United States in the post-war period through 1967.

While interpreting these productivity trends, we should also be cognizant of the system dynamics. Dr. Jay Forrester of the MIT Sloan School of Management points out that "productivity does not increase at a constant rate," and he sees "rise in productivity as accelerating and decelerating in response to a long sweep of economic change." His position is that the period of the 1980s, extending into the 1990s, is showing social pressures and growing economic uncertainty. He argues that for corporate strategy to be effective, "it must recognize the shifting environment within which productivity must be sought."[18]

It must also be pointed out here that the thrust of this book is at the company level, not the industry, sector, or national level. Also, this work limits the labor productivity perspective only within the total productivity and comprehensive productivity context. That is, the fundamental focus in this book is on total productivity, and as along as labor productivity is measured, monitored, and rewarded within the much broader, holistic comprehensive productivity concept, there is no harm done. Labor productivity must not be a primary focus, as has been the tradition for nearly a century. It is still an important measure but should be of secondary significance, while the total productivity and comprehensive productivity measures must take on a primary role to manage the productivity of enterprises.

Now, in spite of the common use, and possibly misuse, of the word productivity, many misconceptions prevail. Let's review them briefly. The following truths are antonyms of these misconceptions.

***Production* improvement does not necessarily mean productivity improvement.** Production is essentially the output generated, but productivity is a ratio of that output to some input(s) consumed (Figure 1.3).

Suppose a bank processed 1,000 checks yesterday, using 20 hours of labor. Let's say that the same bank processed 1,200 checks today, using 24 hours. Production has increased by 20%, from 1,000 to 1,200 checks. However, the labor productivity for this operation is unchanged, because 1,000 checks divided by 20 labor hours is 50 checks per hour yesterday, and 1,200 checks divided by 24 labor hours is also 50 checks per labor hour. Thus, improvement in production may not necessarily generate improvement in labor productivity. Yet, 80 to 85% of companies do not usually understand this fact.

***Efficiency* improvement does not guarantee productivity improvement.** People often think that if you improve efficiency, you are more productive. Efficiency is a *necessary* but not a *sufficient* condition for productivity. In fact, both effectiveness and efficiency are necessary in order to be productive.

PRODUCTION

PRODUCTIVITY

Production   is concerned with the activity of producing goods and services

Productivity   is concerned with the efficiency and effectiveness with which
these goods and services are produced

FIGURE 1.3   Production does not necessarily imply productivity. (©1980, D.J. Sumanth.)

Efficiency is the ratio of actual output generated to the expected (or standard) output prescribed. Effectiveness, on the other hand, is the degree to which the relevant goals or objectives are achieved (Figure 1.4).

Effectiveness involves determining the relevant (right) goals or objectives first and then achieving them. If, for example, nine out of ten relevant objectives are achieved, effectiveness is 90%. One can be very efficient and still not be productive. For example, suppose a doctor amputates a patient's leg in half the usual time and boasts to the nurses, "I have been twice as efficient as I have been in the past." The nurses, who view the situation differently, say, "What a disaster—the doctor amputated the wrong leg!" Here, the doctor's effectiveness was zero because he did not achieve the relevant goal, even though his efficiency improved by 100%. Clearly, the doctor was anything but productive! To be productive, one must be effective as well as efficient—in that order (Figure 1.5).

***Improvement* in sales revenue does not necessarily ensure productivity improvement.** If a company increases its revenues, does that automatically imply it is productive as well (Figure 1.6)?

Virtually every company in the world sets targets for sales revenues. In fact, companies seem to be infatuated with discussing sales revenues on a monthly, weekly, sometimes even a daily basis. Yet, they rarely have a similar passion for

PRODUCTIVITY

$$\text{Efficiency} = \frac{\text{Actual Output}}{\text{Standard Output}} \qquad \text{Productivity} = \frac{\text{Actual Output}}{\text{"Some" Input Factors}}$$

E.g. Actual Production = 80 units

Standard Production = 100 units

$$\text{Efficiency} = \frac{80}{100} = 80\% \qquad \text{Productivity} = \frac{80 \text{ units}}{\text{Inputs Consumed}}$$

FIGURE 1.4   Efficiency does not necessarily imply productivity. (©1980, D.J. Sumanth.)

PRODUCTIVITY

→

BOTH

√   **Effectiveness**

and

√   **Efficiency**

FIGURE 1.5   Productivity requires both effectiveness and efficiency. (©1980, D.J. Sumanth.)

FIGURE 1.6 Revenues do not necessarily imply productivity. (©1980, D.J. Sumanth.)

monitoring productivity. A multibillion-dollar Midwestern company steadily increased its sales about 10% per year from 1970 to 1979 (Figure 1.7), but its total productivity hardly increased during that period. In fact, the company laid off thousands of employees in the early 1980s, causing a social disaster in the local community.

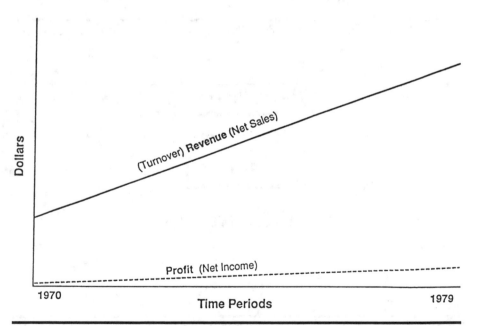

FIGURE 1.7 Typical revenue and profit curves for ABC Company (manufacturer of heavy equipment). (©1980, D.J. Sumanth.)

Quality improvement does not have to be at the expense of productivity. Matsushita, based in Japan, is one of the largest consumer electronics firms in the world. One of its products is microphones. When Matsushita improved service quality and reliability of its microphones considerably, the company increased (labor) productivity by 25% and, as a result, reduced the unit labor cost and unit total cost to such an extent that the selling price of the microphones dropped by 27%! Clearly, quality improvement here was not at the expense of productivity; rather, productivity actually improved when product quality improved.

Therefore, when talking about productivity and quality, it is important not to use the terms loosely or interchangeably. We can prematurely pat ourselves on the back if we do not clearly understand the meaning of these terms.

1.2 PROBLEMS WITH THE "PARTIAL PRODUCTIVITY PERSPECTIVE"

Partial productivity, as stated before, is a ratio of output to one type of input. Labor productivity, expressed as output per man-hour, is the most commonly used measure in this category. Frederick Taylor's scientific management popularized this measure in the early 1900s. Work study specialists, methods engineers, and industrial engineers have continued to place great emphasis on the output-per-man-hour measure, as part of work measurement efforts to set up time standards, to prepare labor efficiency reports, and to do manpower planning and unit labor costing.

In the preface of this book, I discussed some problems of the *partial* productivity mentality, to justify focusing the theme of the book on *total* productivity. *Exclusive emphasis on partial productivity measures, such as labor productivity, must be replaced by an emphasis only in the context of the total productivity measure,* as reinforced by this author's 27 years of observations, research, and consulting experience with hundreds of enterprises throughout the world.

Several problems arise from an exclusive partial productivity emphasis, particularly the labor productivity measure, as discussed next.

Neglecting the Impact of Other Resources

In the labor productivity measure, only labor input, generally in man-hours, is considered. In reality, however, output produced is not just due to labor contribution, but rather is from many other inputs—materials, machinery, working capital, energy, and so on. By ignoring all these other input resources in the labor productivity concept, a company is "looking only at the trees and not the forest."

Many companies continue to face problems of price competitiveness because of their exclusive reliance on this partial productivity measure. In some cases, the labor productivity level continuously improves, but the total unit cost keeps rising! In today's rapidly changing technological environment, new machinery that incorporates advanced technologies can dramatically increase labor productivity, but *fixed capital productivity* might actually decrease because of a proportionately larger increase in depreciation expenses on new machinery and equipment—and total unit costs generally rise in the short run. What good is it to claim with false pride, "Oh, my company's labor is very productive," but then have a tough time rationalizing the increase in total unit cost, the consequent price increases, and the resulting drop in market share?

Labor: The Winner or Loser?

Depending on the circumstances, direct labor has sometimes been rewarded for labor productivity improvements, but has been treated poorly at other times through layoffs.

In union-controlled environments, where collective bargaining agreements are based primarily on labor productivity gains, the union membership has been a "winner," but if other resources have not been utilized productively, the company passes on *additional costs* to consumers. Conversely, with no labor productivity gains, wage increases may be modest, if any, and the union membership comes out a "loser." In reality, the former situation may have been equivalent to giving credit where it is not due entirely; in the latter, it may have been the path of least resistance for management to place blame on the workers. In either case, this is a financially dangerous scenario, particularly in an oligopoly market, where profit margins are thin and a small incremental increase in *total unit costs* could mean losing large chunks of market share. Companies that use labor productivity gains as the basis for collective bargaining are "playing with fire."

Poor Linkage with Quality

One great challenge facing a "productivity specialist" is erasing the erroneous perception that productivity improvement means sacrificing quality. This is because of the difficulty in linking labor productivity with quality. For example, if labor productivity in an assembly line increases by 20% but the finished product rejection rate increases by 10%, this certainly will be perceived as improved productivity at the expense of quality. But if a *total productivity measure* had been used, there would have been a short-term *drop* in that measure, indicating problems perhaps with incoming quality of materials and parts, lack of training with new assembly tools, etc. The labor productivity measure does not offer a *systemic* view of variables. Quality and total productivity are indeed interlinked, and their mutual dependence can be rationalized much more readily in the *total productivity perspective*, whereas it is extremely difficult to do so with labor productivity.

Justifying New Technologies

As we steer through the 1990s, we face challenges in the management of technology. Fierce competitiveness in the global arena is forcing out many that have not integrated their technology strategy and manufacturing strategy with their business strategy. Some recent technologies like robotics, computer-integrated manufacturing, laser technology, and fiber optics have not found ready acceptance even in multibillion-dollar companies, partly because payback periods exceed three years. Interestingly, many companies still use the traditional labor productivity savings to justify new technologies and equipment. The partial productivity perspective is so deep-rooted in management thinking and in industrial engineers' training that we see many companies lose opportunities to upgrade their technologies and facilities because of the traditional economic justification models. Also, partly at fault are traditional accounting concepts that do not adapt to the introduction of fast-changing technologies. The activity-based costing approach, which is slowly taking hold now, will at least help in more relevant justification methods, although not entirely satisfactorily.

Inability to Link with Profits

The term productivity has continued to have negative connotations for many. A major reason for the inability of productivity consultants and specialists to "sell" the concept to management has been the absence of a quantifiable mechanism to link labor productivity to profitability. On the other hand, the total productivity concept lends itself to a mathematical linkage with profit margin, as we shall see in Chapter 3.

Inability to Measure Non-Direct Labor

While it is relatively straightforward to measure labor productivity of blue-collar employees at the shop-floor or operations level, the same is not true for clerical staff (white-collar employees) and professional staff, such as engineers and managers (knowledge workers). The inability of the output-per-man-hour concept of labor productivity to measure the white-collar and knowledge work areas is a major challenge for productivity specialists. How can we measure the thinking and creative activity of knowledge workers by the labor hour, particularly when there is a big time lapse between the time such creative activity or thinking occurs and the time a measurable output is identified?

Stumbling Block to Teamwork

By setting up labor productivity standards, a company can measure and *control* labor efficiencies, but it loses sight of major advantages at the expense of this perceived management control. For example, if management sees a $100,000 reduction in labor costs by instituting labor productivity standards, it might be very satisfied. However, management may have overlooked the increases in clerical and professional staff costs to the extent of $250,000 simply because no control was exercised in these costs. On the other hand, if a teamwork concept involved a common target of cost reduction for *all* employees as a group, the company may have realized much better results, even without the labor standards.

Time standards are essential to establish "ballpark" figures for manpower, machinery, and facility requirements, but if they become an end in themselves, they limit the full, creative potential of employees to constantly improve quality and total productivity. Further, accountability is merely shifted to direct labor when, in fact, all employees, including management, must be held responsible. Many participation techniques such as quality circles and employee participation groups have not been as successful as they could have been partly because of this narrow emphasis on labor productivity.

Unfortunately, time standards are rarely updated on time when methods change. Even if they are, workers seem to outsmart time study analysts, and the rating factor in time studies is still a controversial issue. Of course, mature industrial engineers everywhere, particularly in Japan, know how to use time standards for the right purposes—in manpower planning, capacity requirements planning, line balancing, project management, and other important functions—but not to "drive workers with a whip"!

Labor: A Minor Portion of the Cost of Many Products

In a majority of industries, particularly manufacturing and process-type industries, labor accounts for a minor portion of the total resources when compared to other resources such as machinery, capital, energy, and materials. For example, "IBM's direct labour cost is (only) about 4 percent, and at Apple Macintosh plant, it is 1 percent."[19] Therefore, in such industries, exclusive emphasis on labor productivity alone is not going to ensure that all other resources are equally well attended to in monitoring their usage effectively and efficiently.

The problems with the traditional labor productivity concept can be summarized as follows:

1. Output produced is a result of the joint and simultaneous impact of *all* resources, not just labor.
2. Companies that show high labor productivity growth rates are still not always competitive in their markets.
3. Organizations with collective bargaining agreements based only on labor productivity tend to reduce the *unit labor* cost but not necessarily the *total unit* cost.
4. It is extremely difficult to implement team concepts of management when performance measurement is focused only on labor productivity.
5. Organizational structures tend to be less flexible when emphasis is on control of labor productivity rather than total productivity.
6. Traditionally, companies/enterprises have devoted enormous time, energy, and effort to establishing time standards and labor productivity ratios, without always updating them on a timely basis when methods change. These suboptimizing ratios have often become ends in themselves rather than means. It is difficult to infuse "improve-the-improved" thinking in such settings.
7. It is difficult to directly relate labor productivity to profits.
8. In a majority of manufacturing and process-type industries, labor accounts for a much smaller percentage of costs than machinery, capital, energy, and materials. Overemphasis on labor productivity in such industries is being "penny-wise and pound-foolish."

This author certainly recognizes the fact that a wealth of management talent exists in each country, based on the experience of many generations. After nearly a quarter century of managerial experience, the author still considers himself a student, eager and open-minded to learn new but relevant perspectives in management theory and practice. After all, as the philosopher Vivekananda once pointed out:

Education is the manifestation of perfection already in man.

Experience is important, but in spite of our long experience in management, we cannot blame the competition for outwitting us. That would be like the defense one lawyer offered in representing his client who was accused in a hit-and-run case:

> "Your Honor, that man who was injured must have been careless. My client is an experienced driver of more than 20 years." The other attorney, defending the injured man argued: "Well, if experience is the issue here, Your Honor, my client has been walking for 50 years!"

The point is clear. While we give due credit and respect to all those who provide us various perspectives in management, we have to select and apply management philosophies and methodologies *relevant* to our times. This book presents a philosophy of management which is non-traditional, but one which is relevant to today's enterprises that must function in a world rapidly changing politically, economically, culturally, ideologically, and environmentally.

The role of managers in managing productivity has been emphasized by many, including Peter Drucker, who pointed out that "making resources productive is the specific job of Management as distinct from the other jobs of the 'manager': Entrepreneurship and Administration."[20]

"Productivity is the ultimate responsibility of the manager."[21] Yet, the task is not an easy one. There has to be a conscious effort on the part of enterprises to develop the necessary philosophy and strategy that could integrate the total productivity factor into the existing decision-making processes.

1.3 MANAGERIAL TECHNIQUES COMMONLY USED IN DECISION MAKING

Analytical managerial techniques often used by managers can be categorized into three groups:[22]

- Managerial economics
- Managerial accounting
- Management science

Managerial economics is the managerial application of economic principles in the decision-making process. The most common tools for this include:

- Break-even analysis
- Demand analysis

Managerial accounting, which is based on the accounting discipline, primarily uses:

- Financial ratio analysis
- Funds analysis
- Tailored cost analysis

The *management science* approach provides managers with a conceptual framework and analytical techniques based on quantitative concepts. In implementing such analytical aids, a manager usually has a choice of the following:

- Deterministic models
- Probabilistic models
- Simulation

1.4 ORGANIZATIONAL GOALS FOR MANAGERIAL DECISION MAKING

Vision, goals, and objectives give direction to an organization and are a basis for assessing its performance. Therefore, they must be specified clearly for decision making—preferably with help from any of the above-mentioned analytical aids where practically feasible. Management needs to make sure that the company objectives have been stated and understood *clearly* before it can achieve them effectively and efficiently. "Objectives are, or ought to be, integral to the organization's entire process."[23]

Over the years, many experts have identified objectives that a company should strive to meet. Management guru Peter Drucker[24] emphasizes eight objectives as important to be achieved by a company:

- Market share
- Innovation
- *Productivity*
- Physical and financial resources
- Profitability
- Manager performance and development
- Worker performance and attitude
- Public responsibility

Another expert, Ericson,[25] identifies six goals as important to business organizations:

- *High productivity*
- Industrial leadership
- Organizational stability

- Profit maximization
- Organization efficiency
- Organization growth

England,[26] another management expert, prescribed four levels of organizational goals based on behavioral importance and content:

1. Maximization criteria
   - ***High productivity***
   - Profit maximization
2. Associate status goals
   - Organizational growth
   - Industry leadership
   - Organizational stability
3. Intended goals
   - Employee welfare
4. Low relevance goals
   - Social welfare

Even though all the above-mentioned experts emphasized productivity as a desirable goal to be pursued, Shetty's[27] survey indicated that American companies were using the following three as their main goals:

- Profit
- Growth
- Market share

This survey was conducted among 193 companies from *Business Week's* list of the largest industrial and non-industrial firms. They were divided into four basic industrial groups: chemicals and drugs, packaging materials (containers and papers), electrical and electronics, and food processing. The results of the survey, based on 82 responding companies, showed that *efficiency* appeared as a goal only in the packaging materials industry when the five most frequently cited goals of corporations are listed by industrial group. Further, the results compiled by company size indicated that *productivity* did not appear in the five most frequently cited goals of corporations for which sales exceeded one billion dollars! This showed that the large, multibillion-dollar companies did not have productivity as a strategic variable, even though management experts considered it to be so.

Individual corporations may place emphasis on productivity as an objective, but the fact that it did not appear in the group as a whole is an important observation to be noted here.

1.5 IMPORTANCE OF MANAGEMENT'S ROLE IN INCREASING PRODUCTIVITY

In 1980, Peter Drucker had warned that in the previous 10 to 15 years, productivity of all resources had actually decreased in all major developed countries.[28] Productivity, he pointed out, is one of the major responsibilities of management. As stated earlier, the number one corporate goal in most companies is *profitability*, followed by *growth*. These goals have led to the development strategies that stimulate growth and profit without taking into account how the productivity of a firm is being affected.[29] It seems safe to say that Drucker's statements have the same validity today as they did 15 years ago!

Two important aspects of management's role often contribute to low productivity. The first is the reward system, which encourages short-term performance and penalizes long-term investment. The second is executives who, being mostly finance and law oriented, tolerate and even encourage production systems which are designed to meet growing market demands and financial goals rather than meet the requirements for the highest possible quality and productivity improvements.[29] Also, causal variables that have a direct impact on an organization's performance and over which management has control have been identified. These causal variables are structural, process, and leadership. However, management has often failed to recognize its control over these variables.[30] No matter what the traditional emphases have been, the importance of productivity cannot be overstated, as has been pointed out by experts in management theory.

1.6 PROPOSED APPROACH TO MANAGEMENT DECISION MAKING

In view of management's critical role in improving productivity, it is necessary to have a management style that takes into consideration, to a great extent, productivity as a primary goal. A formal approach to productivity management is suggested here as a supplement, or even as an alternative, to currently popular management decision-making approaches.

Total Productivity Management (TPmgt™) is a proactive, pragmatic, innovative, and unique concept, management philosophy, and systematic process, based on an integration of industrial engineering and behavioral sciences. Because of its systemic nature, TPmgt is truly *total,* both conceptually and analytically. It emphasizes an explicit relationship between quality and total productivity. Quality and total productivity are considered two performance sides of the same coin or two performing rails of the same track. They are inseparable conceptually and quantitatively. The concept is generic; it is easily adapted to *any* type of organization or enterprise, as has been demonstrated during the last 17 years in many countries around the world.

One of the best practical advantages of the total productivity approach to a company is that it can determine the level of total productivity needed to obtain a certain level of profit and vice versa.[31-33] A firm can objectively plan its profits based on its ability to reach certain preestablished targets of total productivity. Of course, we shall see the power of this approach as we go through the remaining chapters of this book.

1.7 RELATIONSHIP BETWEEN TOTAL PRODUCTIVITY AND OTHER MANAGEMENT GOALS

Figure 1.8 shows how traditional management goals can be achieved by controlling *total productivity*. An increase in total productivity of a firm results in improved product quality and service, decreased production costs, and improved market share and profit. Greater market share translates into sales growth, which in turn leads to a multinational level of operations. As the profit margin becomes larger, money available for research and development becomes greater, which in turn helps to improve production systems and procedures and encourages development of new technologies and new products. The creation and production of new products helps diversify the company. Further, an increased profit margin leads to better financial stability and improved welfare of employees, whose jobs not only become more stable but also command higher wages and salaries. Better utilization and conservation of resources is just one of the results of improved total productivity, and this, along with improved employee welfare, will help a company meet its social responsibilities much more readily.

Management should include improvement of total productivity as one of the firm's primary goals; by attaining this goal, several other goals are automatically achieved. Total productivity should be the concern of everyone in a company— at all levels. Even though this is more easily said than done, it is extremely important for management to create and sustain an atmosphere where the concern for total productivity becomes as natural as breathing. In Chapter 4, we shall discuss a specific practical strategy to create this common concern.

Management can and should take a total productivity approach to decision making in addition to managerial economics, managerial accounting, and management science. As the rest of the book unfolds, we shall see that the concepts

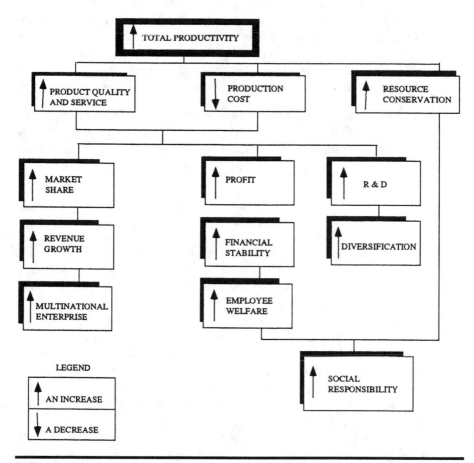

FIGURE 1.8 Relationship between total productivity and other organizational goals.

used in the total productivity approach are comprehensive and pragmatic. If implemented correctly, the approach would provide a common direction to achieve *multiple* goals, including *market share, innovation, profitability, efficiency, effectiveness, growth, stability,* and *social welfare.*

Important benefits derived from using a total productivity approach are discussed in detail in Chapter 8 but for now can be summarized as follows:

1. Multiple goals can be achieved simultaneously by increasing the *total productivity* of a company.
2. Using the relationship between profit and total productivity, a firm can objectively *plan* its *profit* level, based on its ability to reach a certain total productivity level.

3. Using the concept of *break-even point of total productivity*, a firm can determine if its total productivity level is in the region that yields profits.
4. Management is forced into a long-term and simultaneous emphasis on quality, profitability, market share, growth, and best value to stakeholders.

Incorporating total productivity as a major corporate criterion of success helps companies/organizations to compete better in today's complex and competitive market environment. The total productivity approach to managerial decision making is a viable complement or alternative to current practices.

QUESTIONS TO PONDER

1.1 Why is productivity an important organizational goal in today's enterprises—private, public, and/or government? Analyze newspaper and magazines articles published during the last year to determine the extent to which productivity has been highlighted as a major factor to improve competitiveness.

1.2 What are Peter Drucker's eight objectives that a company should strive to meet? Explain briefly how these objectives are interrelated. Are they relevant today in your particular enterprise? If so, how; if not, why not?

1.3 The Japanese have emphasized *market share* as a primary strategic variable. In the Western world, *profit* and *revenue growth* have been more dominant organizational priorities. Discuss the reasons for the difference in these emphases between the Japanese and non-Japanese approaches. Is there evidence in recent years to show that the traditional Japanese management style is changing to mimic the Western style—in particular the American style? Discuss the ramifications of this trend, if it does exist, for Japanese competitiveness into the 21st century.

1.4 Do an in-depth study of one of the references, and comment on the fundamental issues raised in that work.

1.5 List at least three research dimensions that can be explored from your reading.

1.6 Do a content analysis (of the last five years) to determine the five most crucial business issues facing companies or enterprises.

1.7 What is the extent of partial productivity thinking in your enterprise? Can you think of some specific examples where a labor productivity mentality landed you in trouble with product line profitability?

1.8 If your enterprise has been applying total quality management in recent times, what has been your experience? Has it worked well? If so, what were the chief factors contributing to its success? If not, why?

1.9 How has your thinking changed (after reading this chapter) about quality, technology, and productivity—particularly with reference to their meanings?

REFERENCES AND NOTES

1. Kendrick, J.W., "Productivity—Why It Matters—How It's Measured," in Christopher, W.F. and Thor, C.G. (eds.), *Handbook for Productivity Measurement and Improvement,* Productivity Press, Portland, OR, 1993, p. 1-1.4.
2. Denton, D.K., "Enhance Competitiveness and Customer Satisfaction—Here's One Approach," *Industrial Engineering,* p. 24, May 1990.
3. Skrzycki, C., "Making Quality a Priority," *The Washington Post,* pp. K1–K4, Oct. 11, 1987.
4. Sumanth, D.J., "A Total Systems Approach to Technology Management," in Khalil et al. (eds.), *Technology Management Frontiers—I,* Inderscience Publishers, Switzerland, 1988.
5. Schmenner, Roger W., "Every Factory Has a Life Cycle," *Harvard Business Review*, pp. 121–129, March–April 1983.
6. Uzumi, V. and Swanson, S.W., "Buying Advanced Manufacturing Technology—An Exclusive Survey of Vendors and Users," *Manufacturing Engineering*, Vol. 105, No. 2, Aug. 1990.
7. Chardy, Alfonso, "Technology Looks Like the Culprit in Toll-Plaza Delays," *The Miami Herald,* pp. 1A and 26A, Nov. 10, 1995.
8. OEEC, *Terminology of Productivity,* Par. 2, 2, rue Andre-Pascal, Paris-16, 1950.
9. Sumanth, D.J., *Productivity Engineering and Management,* McGraw-Hill, New York, 1984, p. 7.
10. Sumanth, D.J. et al. (eds.), *Productivity & Quality Management Frontiers III, IV, and V,* IIE Press, Atlanta, 1991, 1993, and 1995.
11. Sumanth, D.J. and Einspruch, N.G., "Productivity Awareness in the U.S.: A Survey of Some Major Corporations," *Industrial Engineering,* pp. 84–90, Oct. 1980.
12. Sumanth, D.J., *Productivity Engineering and Management,* McGraw-Hill, New York, 1984, Chapter 7; Sumanth, D.J., The "Comprehensive Total Productivity Model" (CTPM), ©1987–1996. This is an extension of Sumanth's "Total Productivity Model" (TPM), ©1979, 1984.
13. Mark, Jerome A., "A Brief History of Productivity Measurement," in Christopher, W.F. and Thor, C.G. (eds.), *Handbook for Productivity Measurement and Improvement,* Productivity Press, Portland, OR, 1993, p. 3-2.1.

14. Ibid., p. 3-2.7.

15. Fiedler, Edgar R., "Worries," in Christopher, W.F. and Thor, C.G. (eds.)., *Handbook for Productivity Measurement and Improvement,* Productivity Press, Portland, OR, 1993, p. 1-3.3

16. Ibid., p. 1-3.5.

17. See the American Productivity & Quality Center's 1994 yearly publication *Perspectives '94,* p. 6.

18. Forrester, Jay W., "Low Productivity: Is It the Problem, or Merely a Symptom?" in Christopher, W.F. and Thor, C.G. (eds.)., *Handbook for Productivity Measurement and Improvement,* Productivity Press, Portland, OR, 1993, pp. 1-6.1–1-6.2.

19. Gould, L., "Computers Run the Factory," *Electronics Week*, p. 57, March 1985.

20. Drucker, P.F., *Managing in Turbulent Times,* Harper & Row, New York, 1980, p. 14.

21. Shetty, Y.K., "Management's Role in Declining Productivity," *California Management Review,* Vol. 25, No. 1, pp. 33–47, 1982.

22. Massie, J. and Douglas, J., *Managing—A Contemporary Introduction,* Prentice Hall, Englewood Cliffs, NJ, 1977.

23. Oxenfeldt, A.R., Miller, D.W., and Dickinson, R.A., *A Basic Approach to Executive Decision Making,* AMACOM, New York, 1978, p. 14.

24. Drucker, P.F., *The Practice of Management*, Harper & Row, New York, 1954, p. 63.

25. Ericson, R.F., "The Impact of Cybernetic Information Technology on Management Value Systems," *Management Science*, Vol. 16, p. B-48, Oct. 1969.

26. England, G.W., "Organizational Goals and Expected Behavior of American Managers," *Academy of Management Journal,* Vol. 10, pp. 107–117, 1967.

27. Shetty, Y.K., "New Look at Corporate Goals," *California Management Review*, Vol. 22, No. 2, pp. 71–79, 1979.

28. Drucker, P.F., *Managing in Turbulent Times*, Harper & Row, New York, 1980, p. 18.

29. Shetty, Y.K. "Management's Role in Declining Productivity," *California Management Review*, Vol. 25, No. 1, p. 37, 1982.

30. English, J. and Marchione, R.A., "Productivity: A New Perspective," *California Management Review*, Vol. 25, No. 2, pp. 57–66, 1983.

31. Sumanth, D.J., "Productivity Management—A Challenge for the 80's," *ASEM Proceedings, First Annual Conference*, 1980, pp. 37–42.

32. Sumanth, D.J., Productivity Measurement and Evaluation Models for Manufacturing Companies, Ph.D. dissertation, Department of Industrial Engineering, I.I.T., Chicago (published by University Microfilms International, Ann Arbor, MI, #80-03, 665), 1979.

33. Sumanth, D.J., *Productivity Engineering and Management*, McGraw-Hill, New York, 1994, Chapter 8.

2

THE NEED FOR TOTAL PRODUCTIVITY MANAGEMENT

In this chapter, we will articulate the need for another management philosophy, concept, and methodology to go beyond the currently known ones. As total quality management (TQM) has pervaded the thinking of many enterprises around the world, it becomes necessary to look at the potential for improving TQM theory even further. This chapter is intended to rationalize the need for Total Productivity Management (TPmgt™), as we shall refer to it hereafter.

From a content analysis done in 1991, it was a significant surprise to find that of the top five major contemporary issues, the largest proportion (46.31%) dealt with business issues, followed by political issues (21.11%), social issues (12.0%), and family issues (7.11%), as shown in Figure 2.1.

This points to the significance of business in shaping world dynamics not only in the 1990s but into the early part of the 21st century. Clearly, management of business enterprises, and even non-business enterprises, will be our focus for the benefit of world economics, societal welfare, and even human freedom.

The world's economic, political, and social climate changed most dramatically in the late 1980s and continues to change in the second half of the 1990s. Who expected the U.S. stock market crash of October 19, 1987? Who could have dared to predict the fall of the Berlin Wall, the reunification of Germany, the unprecedented democratization of the former Soviet Union and other Eastern European countries, or the peace treaty between Israel and the PLO and the latter's establishment as a freely governed political entity in Israel? Who could have predicted the four- and five-digit inflation figures in countries like Peru, Argentina, and

Issue, Percentage and Number of Occurrences

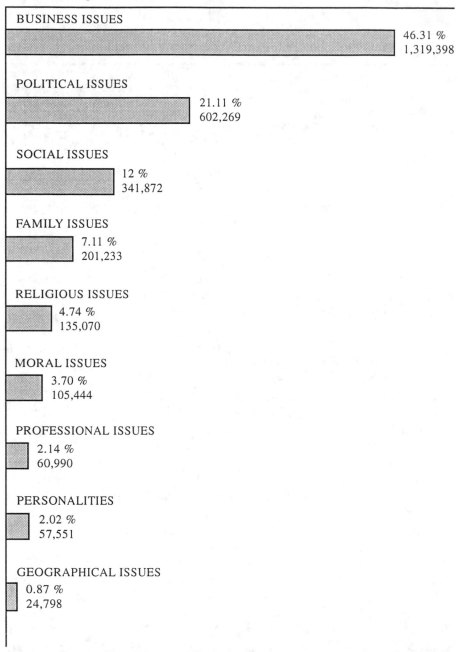

BUSINESS ISSUES

46.31 %
1,319,398

POLITICAL ISSUES

21.11 %
602,269

SOCIAL ISSUES

12 %
341,872

FAMILY ISSUES

7.11 %
201,233

RELIGIOUS ISSUES

4.74 %
135,070

MORAL ISSUES

3.70 %
105,444

PROFESSIONAL ISSUES

2.14 %
60,990

PERSONALITIES

2.02 %
57,551

GEOGRAPHICAL ISSUES

0.87 %
24,798

FIGURE 2.1   Pareto chart listings for contemporary issues. (©1991, D.J. Sumanth.)

Bolivia in the late 1980s and early 1990s? Unfortunately, more startling events seem to be coming as we approach the year 2000. The "Europe 1992" plan already has dramatically changed the way some Europeans now travel, trade, and conduct their political, economic, social, and business affairs. The North American Free Trade Agreement (NAFTA) with Mexico has opened up significant doors for the United States and Canada to trade as a monolithic economic bloc. Economic and social values are so volatile today that it is difficult to predict what awaits us in the coming years. A recent best-selling author even predicted the collapse of capitalism by the turn of the century, although that prediction is controversial.

2.1 UNIQUE FACTORS AFFECTING ENTERPRISES

Some of the forces impacting the way enterprises have to operate today did not matter as recently as just a decade ago, but they are significant today and include:

- Interconnected and interdependent world
- Shifts in economic demographics
- The global market arena
- Ecological concerns and a sustainable future

Their importance requires some elaboration.

Interconnected and Interdependent World

Our world today, as viewed by more than five billion people, is vastly different from the one we knew just five years ago or even five minutes ago! We never know what major event is making its way as a story to one of the major international news stations. Electronic communication has totally changed the way we think, observe, work, worship, negotiate, play, shop, invest, entertain, and live today.

High-Speed Global Communication—Technology in general, and information technology in particular, are growing and changing people's lives dramatically all over the world. There are both advantages and perils to high-speed global communication. On the one hand, most if not all of us on this planet are being networked together through satellite communication capabilities. For example, the news reported daily makes us all aware of the opportunities available and challenges we face, but at the same time puts considerable pressure on enterprises—business and non-business alike—to respond to these rapidly changing conditions. Just three years ago, the Internet, World Wide Web, and Gopher sounded sophisticated to even technically knowledgeable people. Today, not only are these words part of our everyday vocabulary, but thousands of companies and individuals are doing business on the Internet. It is impossible to keep track of the new users browsing cyberspace every hour. Today, at least 30 million computers are connected to the Internet, and the number is growing by about 30,000 per day!

The Paradox of Cooperation and Competitiveness—Today, there seems to be a strange paradox of cooperation and competitiveness among companies and countries. Because of high-speed information technology, companies can cooperate more easily within their own divisions and subsidiaries and even with their competitors. However, political, legal, and intellectual property issues require that a constant competitive edge be maintained.

Complexity and Uncertainty—The complexity and uncertainty of world dynamics are so enormous that management models of yesterday can rapidly become obsolete. For example, the cultural diversity among employees in a multinational company in the United States can impact the quality of products and services in many countries around the world. Similarly, the quality of software produced in Malaysia, Singapore, or India can affect the quality of communication devices produced by a leading telecommunications company in the United States. Many problems associated with such organizations are extremely complex. The Berkana Institute[1] in Provo, Utah, has been sponsoring dialogues on this subject since 1993. It asks the basic question: "What can 20th century science teach us about the design of 21st century organizations?" The institute believes that the new sciences of chaos theory, complexity, and self-organizing systems have much to teach us about control, autonomy, information, values, participation, planning, and prediction.

Shifts and Economic Demographics

Until the 1970s, the economic power base was in the United States. The inflation rate in the United States hit double-digit figures in the late 1970s and early 1980s. Of course, these figures are mild when compared to the 1989 inflation rates in some Latin American and European countries—Peru (3,398%), Argentina (3,079%), Brazil (1,287%), the then Yugoslavia (1,239%), and Poland (244.5).[2] While many U.S. banks had bad debts from some Latin American countries in the 1980s, the 1990s brought a more difficult situation. U.S. investments and stock investments were $9 billion and $8.5 billion, respectively, in 1990. These numbers were expected to shoot up to $20 billion and $17 billion in 1996.[3] Beginning in the latter part of the 1970s, the economic power base shifted to Japan, which continues to have a trade surplus with the United States. While politicians argue about the fairness of the Japanese not allowing American goods into their country, the reality of the matter is that Japan has increased the market share of its many targeted products, such as automobiles, consumer electronic products, and other high-tech items. "For the first time, a vehicle with a foreign nameplate has become the year's best-seller in the United States....Americans bought more Honda Accords in 1989 than any other automobile." To be exact, the top sellers for 1989 in the United States were:[4]

1. Honda Accord   362,707
2. Ford Taurus   348,061
3. Ford Escort   333,535
4. Chevrolet Corsica and Beretta   326,006
5. Chevrolet Cavalier   295,715

In the 1970s, when Matsushita took over the Motorola TV plant in Franklin, Illinois, it was a major shock. In the 1980s, Japanese management in the United States became common. A few examples of Japan's presence in the United States include:

- GM–Toyota plant in Fremont, California
- Kawasaki plant in Lincoln, Nebraska
- Sony plant in San Diego, California
- Honda plant in Marysville, Ohio
- Nissan plant in Smyrna, Tennessee

In 1990, the Japanese had 837 manufacturing operations across the United States (with 8 in Florida).[5]

The J.D. Power & Associates' 1990 New Car Initial Quality Survey was startling in that it declared that seven of the top ten in the selected class of cars were Japanese, with the only American car among the top ten (Buick) rated number five.[6] The managerial philosophies of American companies must at least match the merit of those in Japan and Europe for them to be equally and continuously competitive.

Table 2.1 compares the performance characteristics of automotive plants in Japan, Europe, and the United States. In general, Japanese plants in Japan have the best performance figures, and Japanese plants in the United States are the next best, although the latter have not yet been able to reduce their stocks very well. The American-owned U.S. plants are quite similar. The European producers do more training and have fewer job classifications but have very little team structure; interestingly, their productivity is significantly worse.

TABLE 2.1   Auto Assembly Differences

Auto Assembly Plant Characteristics[a]			
	Japanese in Japan	*Japanese in America*	*Americans in America*	*European Producers*
---	---	---	---	---
Productivity (hours per vehicle)	16.8	21.2	25.1	36.2
Assembly defects per 100 vehicles	60.0	65.0	82.0	97.0
Repair area (% of assembly space)	4.1	4.9	12.9	14.4
Stock (days)[b]	0.2	1.6	2.9	2.0
Work force in a team (%)	69.3	71.3	17.3	0.6
Number of job classifications	12.0	9.0	67.0	15.0
Training of new workers (hours)	380.0	370.0	46.0	173.0
Absenteeism (%)	5.0	4.8	11.7	12.1
Welding	86.2	85.0	76.2	76.6
Painting	54.6	40.7	33.6	38.2
Assembly	1.7	1.1	1.2	3.1

[a] Averages for plants in each region, 1989.
[b] For eight sample parts.

Source: *The Economist,* MIT, J.D. Power.

The Global Market Arena

Playing the corporate game in the global arena has become extremely important, as evidenced by the growing body of literature in global operations management.[7]

International Players—As privatization has spread from the United States and Canada to Europe, Latin America, and the Far East, the number of international players in the business game has been rapidly rising. In 1981, there were two major personal computer manufacturers competing with each other in the United States—IBM and Apple. Today, that number is more like 110 and includes Epson, Compaq, NEC, Packard Bell, and Dell, just to name a few. The concept of benchmarking is an absolute necessity for maintaining international competitiveness in today's world, whereas ten years ago, very few companies took benchmarking seriously.

Selective Customers—Today's customers do not have as much brand loyalty as they used to. What they want is value for their money, even if they have to pay a little more. They also want prompt, attentive, and courteous service. One small business owner recently canceled a contract worth more than $100,000 with a leading computer company, because it would not respond immediately to his request for service. He substituted this leading company with a smaller competitor. Today, time responsiveness is becoming extremely critical for customers who are more educated and selective. Exorbitant healthcare costs have forced even hospitals and healthcare service organizations to compete for patients—just to keep their facilities from being shut down. There is intense competition everywhere because of the educated consumer. Even the traditionally bureaucratic governments are realizing the importance of efficient and effective operations, lest the taxpayers take action to curtail government funds.

Deregulation—In late 1970s, the airline industry was deregulated in the United States. As a result, competition became and continues to be severe. Braniff went out of business, Continental Airlines was reorganized, Eastern Airlines folded, and Pan Am met the same fate, although it reopened just recently. In the 1980s, the banking industry in the United States was also deregulated. Profit margins have steadily shrunk for most of the banks. About 15 years ago, in terms of total assets, nine of the top ten banks in the world were American. In 1989, all the top ten banks in the world were Japanese. Citicorp was ranked twelfth. Today, not one American bank ranks in the top ten. Citicorp, which is still the largest bank in the United States, is only ranked in the second half of the top 20.[8]

With the deregulation of the telephone industry, you and I can now go out and buy a telephone for as little as ten dollars and can shop around for long-distance service among several companies. AT&T, the biggest provider, has had to respond through drastic changes in its organization, administration, operations, and marketing.

Shrinking Product Life Cycles—Due to rapid technological developments and adaptation of concurrent engineering approaches, design cycles for products are dramatically shrinking. In the 1970s, a typical automobile took seven years to produce from the time it was conceived to the time a consumer drove it out of the showroom. Today, that time has been dramatically slashed to less than half! For example, the product development cycle for Saturn is 24 to 36 months.[9] This challenge has been unbelievable, particularly in the electronics and computer companies. Large, well-established electronics and computer firms have slipped in sales per employee and profits per employee (Figure 2.2) for many reasons, including the inability to cope with rapidly shrinking product life cycles and to design products to meet customers' true needs. Clearly, managing technology discontinuities as a result of shrinking product life cycles has become a major challenge for most companies.

Today's technologies are changing so rapidly that the challenge becomes even greater as enterprises have to keep pace at both the product level and the production process level. Consider, for example, the personal computer. In the late 1970s, when the first personal computer (TRS-80 by Tandy Corp.) came out, the product life cycle was about four to five years. In 1984, the IBM PC XT, which had been introduced only three years earlier, became obsolete as the new PS/2 systems came onto the market. The average shelf life of personal computers was about two years in the late 1980s and is just about one year today! Imagine the dynamics of change for a typical manufacturer of personal computers. By the time the product is designed, pilot tested, sourced out to vendors for parts, assembled, and marketed with a decent advertising program, the competition is already in the "cloning mode," ready to threaten with new product entries. Global satellite communication has made it possible to access vital information on a worldwide basis at unprecedented speed. Gone are the days when a computer manufacturer could think that it would make all its money in the first three or four years after releasing a new model, because in that time a product is usually no longer state-of-the-art and might even become obsolete. Honda and other world-class manufacturers clearly recognize that the new, continually shrinking product life cycles can no longer support the lengthy design processes typical of most contemporary engineering. To win in today's marketplace, manufacturers must design and introduce new products rapidly to beat the competition.[10]

Ecological Concern and Sustainable Future

Following the 1992 summit in Brazil on ecological concerns, we have seen a rapid shift toward reusable and recyclable materials. McDonald's, Burger King, Wendy's and many other American fast-food chains have switched from styrofoam to biodegradable packaging materials. Freon-12, used in refrigeration systems, particularly automobiles, is fast disappearing.

After four years of negotiations by 43 countries, a "revolutionary" environmental management system specification—ISO 14001—was published in late 1996. Joseph Cascio, chairman of the U.S. Technical Advisory Group and the lead U.S. delegate to the International Organization for Standardization's Technical Committee 207, says that this is quite different from ISO 9000, which does

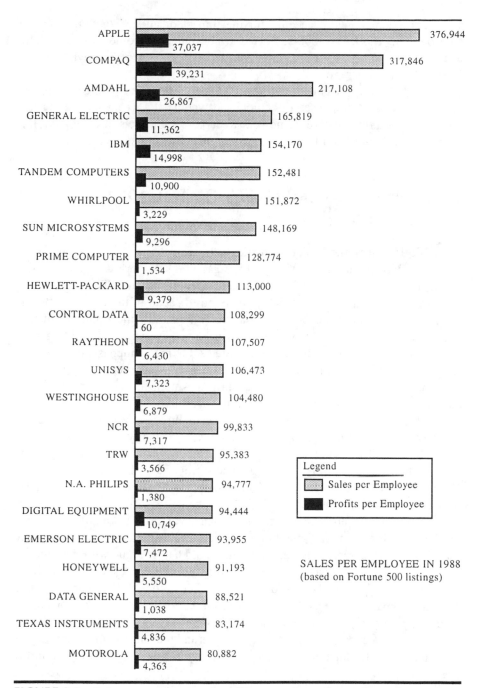

FIGURE 2.2 Sales per employee and profit per employee figures for major computer and electronic companies. (©1991, D.J. Sumanth.)

not require companies to account for the impact of all their activities on the environment. The ISO 14000 standards are designed to provide companies the direction to manage, measure, improve, and communicate the environmental aspects of their operations.[11]

The accounting systems of the past 100 years have to be changed to reflect the social costs of responses to ecological awareness. Present managerial approaches lack a quantitative framework to capture the effects of ecological factors while designing and building products or delivering services.

2.2 CONFUSED EMPHASES OF THE 1970s AND 1980s

After World War II, the Japanese and the Germans began to rebuild their economies meticulously and aggressively. They gave highest priority to their educational, industrial, and social infrastructures. Quality "gurus" like Dr. Deming and Dr. Juran from the United States traveled to Japan in the early 1950s and educated Japanese executives and managers in the basic philosophies of quality management. The U.S. Marshall Plan also helped in rapidly rebuilding both Japan and West Germany. In the United States, the main emphasis in the 1950s and 1960s was on creating a consumer economic boom and enjoying it without any notable competition from other countries. American managers were concerned with short-term profits and earnings per share.

With the oil embargo in 1973, the U.S. economy received a sudden jolt— a sort of mild economic earthquake—which caused energy prices to jump dramatically and inflation to rise unlike anything before. The American auto industry was the first to be affected, as Japanese imports rushed in from Toyota, Nissan, and Mazda. All of a sudden, Americans began to discover to their pleasant amazement that they could buy a Japanese car for about $1,500 less than an American equivalent in the same category. Critics were quick to blame the Japanese for "dumping" their cars at prices below cost. While the Japanese trade policy was perceived to be unfair, one could hardly argue with the superior quality of their cars. Still, complacency among U.S. automakers did not diminish until the late 1970s. In 1979, Ford desperately began to look for a car that could help the company regain its then dwindling market share. Millions of consumers who had previously owned U.S.-made cars were buying Japanese automobiles because the perceived quality was much better and the energy consumption was significantly better than an American counterpart at that time. In addition, the trade-in value of Japanese cars was much higher; it was not unusual to recover a large portion of the original investment! As a result, people began to seriously analyze the reasons why the Japanese were so successful. The 1980 NBC White Paper[12] entitled "If Japan Can, Why Can't We?" challenged American management, perhaps like never before.

While Chrysler was rebuilding itself with Lee Iacocca's vision, Ford came out with its best-selling Taurus, and in 1982 GM was planning Saturn with its "Team of 99." The educational, industrial, and social infrastructures in these companies were being redesigned, reformed, and adapted. In the meantime, the Japanese and the Germans were building trade surpluses with their cars, machine tools, and everything else. For example, the Japanese were spending almost $7.5 billion on machine tools, while the United States spent only $4.4 billion—less than even the former Soviet Union, which spent nearly $6 billion on machinery and equipment.[13] The Japanese were number one in total tool production, while the United States was a distant sixth.

These are clear indications that the Japanese and the Germans have steadily emphasized building a strong manufacturing base, whereas in the United States, it was not fashionable to be manufacturing oriented in the 1970s and early 1980s. Many books that point out the inevitable shift toward services hastened American management's move into the service industry. With revitalized emphasis on manufacturing engineering education, Americans are beginning to recognize training youngsters to become manufacturing managers and operations managers, as opposed to facilitators of corporate acquisitions, mergers, and leveraged buyouts. The United States still has a long way to go to catch up with the Japanese but finally seems to be heading in the right direction.

Conflicting Extremes

The second half of the 1980s and the early part of the 1990s can perhaps be characterized as the period of "customer sensitization." The TQM phenomenon pervaded this period to refocus our attention on customer satisfaction, both internally and externally. To achieve this, quality and value became significant prerequisites to survive, sustain, and increase market share, but the United States and Japan have significantly different emphases when it comes to key objectives (Table 2.2).

As reflected in Table 2.2, U.S. companies place more emphasis on return on investment and capital gain for stockholders, while Japanese counterparts concentrate on increasing market share, new product ratio, company image, and quality of working conditions.

TABLE 2.2   Objectives of the United States and Japan

Goals	United States	Japan
1. Return on investment	2.43	1.24[a]
2. Capital gain for stockholders	1.14	0.02[a]
3. Increase in market share	0.73	1.43[a]
4. Improvement of product portfolio	0.50	0.68
5. Efficiency of logistic activities	0.46	0.71[b]
6. Equity/debt ratio	0.38	0.59
7. New product ratio	0.21	1.06[a]
8. Public image of the company	0.05	0.20[b]
9. Quality of working conditions	0.04	0.09[b]

[a] Significant at 0.001 level by the *t*-test of means.
[b] Significant at 0.01 level by the *t*-test of means.

Note: Means sum of importance (3 points for most important goal, 2 points for second, 1 point for third, 0 points for others).

Source: Kagona, T., Nonaka, I., Sakakibara, K., and Okumura, A., *Strategies vs. Evolutionary Management*, North-Holland, New York, 1985.

Today's enterprises have to deal with a unique set of *conflicting* objectives (Table 2.3)—an extraordinary challenge by any stretch of the imagination. Today's management problems stem from the fact that even TQM and reengineering have not been able to address these conflicting objectives in a systemic manner.

Clearly, many, if not most, of these objectives are conflicting in nature. For example, companies want a loyal work force, but they do not mind laying people off—even by the hundreds or thousands. Companies want to produce ecologically sensitive products, but the additional cost is passed on to consumers. Employees are asked to operate in a participative environment, but people are becoming more assertive of their individual rights. Essentially, the legal framework often prevents conformance at any cost. At a macro level, there is a major conflicting extreme. In one sense, globalization is creating wonderful opportunities for economic explosion throughout the world, as corporations have unlimited growth potential through the electronic business world. However, in another sense, the global economy has become like a malignant cancer, as Dr. David Korten, a former faculty member at Harvard University Graduate School of Business, forcefully argues in his recent book in which he exposes the harmful effects that economic globalization is having on all areas of life because of powerful corporations.[14]

TABLE 2.3   Conflicting Objectives Companies Are Facing Today

1. Highest customer satisfaction possible, both internally and externally, but at competitive prices
2. Lowest manufacturing cycle times possible, but with limited financial capital
3. Minimal fixed capital investment at shortest payback periods possible
4. The best possible human resources development in spite of ill-trained and untrained work force
5. High aspirations but highly legal societies
6. High system reliability to ensure low warranty costs and high repeat customer rates, but low total unit costs
7. High ecological sensitivity, but low unit costs
8. Unmanageable organizational growth, yet without a well-defined mission
9. High employee loyalty in spite of high job insecurity

Simply put, companies want to be globally optimal, but they are doing so with suboptimal thinking and suboptimal actions.

Shifts in Management Focus

In the 1950s, with latent demand for products suddenly unleashed after World War II, managers had to be concerned with *production* and *distribution*. In the 1960s, managers began to focus on *marketing*; they needed to find ways to attract new markets for existing products while doing market research for new ones. With the oil crisis in 1973, managers desperately turned toward energy conservation and means to conserve resources. *Productivity* became a buzzword in the 1970s. Managers by the thousands attended seminars and conferences on productivity by the thousands from the mid 1970s to early 1980s. Then, management's focus shifted to finance—everything from financial leverage through acquisitions and mergers to debt financing and buyouts. *Quality* became the buzzword in corporate America and elsewhere in the world beginning around 1981, and through the end of the 1980s managers lined up for seminars by W. Edwards Deming, Philip Crosby, and other quality experts. The primary management focus in the 1980s was quality, in particular TQM. During the late 1980s and early 1990s, everyone from quality experts to media reporters shied away from the word productivity and latched onto quality! Consultants dropped and added buzzwords to suit their clients' moods and tastes. With the popularization of the IBM personal computer in 1981 and the introduction of the Apple

Macintosh in 1984, the 1980s changed forever the landscape of personal computing, publishing, database management, and the business environment in general. We went from individual PCs to workstations to local area networks (LANs) to supercomputers and the Information Superhighway—all in just a 10- to 15-year period. The focus of managers in the late 1980s was significantly different from what it had been in the early 1950s. What a change in just 40 years!

While these tumultuous changes were taking place, political and social upheaval continued to dominate the 1980s. The net result was that senior managers who were trained in concepts of management relevant to the 1950s and 1960s now had to become experts at managing an exploding set of challenging and conflicting objectives (see Table 2.3). Decisions made by managers seemed suboptimal more than most would like to admit. In short, U.S. managers were asked to shift their focus from:

- Short-term to long-term *results*
- Domestic to global *markets*
- Operational to strategic *activities*
- Practical actions to strategic *visions*
- Internal employees to external *stakeholders*
- Productivity to *quality*
- Individualism to *participation*

2.3 CONTINUED CHAOS OF THE 1990s

Unfortunately, the suboptimal thinking of the 1980s continued into the 1990s, only to get worse. The information revolution that began in the 1980s has been accelerating so rapidly in the 1990s, and will continue into the 21st century, that we may even have to redefine the concept of an enterprise. Companies and even individuals are able to go from being national to international, multinational to global, and probably soon from global to universal.

Concurrent Extremes

Despite the U.S. domination of the world economy, the so-called "human development index" indicated a surprising situation. The United States ranked 19th, while Japan, Sweden, and Switzerland ranked 1st, 2nd, and 3rd, respectively. The average number of hours worked per week by an employee in Japan was almost 47 compared to 40 in the United States.[15] This can be viewed positively or negatively, depending upon one's cultural perspective. The "proof of the pudding" is in Japan's ability to keep increasing its export/import ratio (Figure 2.3).

International Trade Balances : 1989 and 1992 (in $ Billions)

Country	Exports 1989	1992	Imports 1989	1992	Exports/Imports Ratio 1989	1992	Percent Change (%)
Japan	270	331	193	198	1.40	1.67	19.29
Germany	326	406	248	374	1.31	1.08	(16.79)
Canada	121	134	116	125	1.04	1.07	2.88
Italy	140	178	142	175	0.99	1.02	3.03
France	172	226	183	224	0.94	1.01	7.45
U.K	151	187	189	212	0.80	0.88	10.00
U.S.A.	362	439	475	535	0.76	0.82	7.89

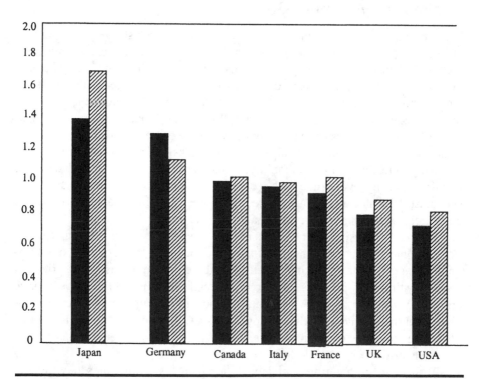

FIGURE 2.3 Export/import ratios for the G-7 countries. (Computed from *Perspectives '94*, p. 23, American Productivity and Quality Center, Houston, Feb. 1994. ©APQC. Used with permission.)

From 1989 to 1992, Japan's export/import ratio jumped 19%, while that of the United States rose only about 8%. In Germany, this ratio actually decreased from 1.31 to 1.09. In recent years, German auto giants Mercedes Benz and BMW have also faced tough competition from Toyota's Lexus series.

Japan is one of the few countries that has been able to operate in a "concurrent extremes" atmosphere wherein there is a challenge to concurrently optimize extreme goals. For example, Japanese companies are able to compete fiercely in domestic markets as well as in foreign ones. They appear to thrive on competition. For a country the size of the state of Indiana, with very few natural resources, it is a matter of necessity to produce and market quality products worldwide in order to pay for everything from oil to coal. For a country that is more racially homogeneous than most others, Japan has learned to balance national goals with internationalism, prosperity with peace, and automation without anarchy.

Minimizing Maximum Diversity

With the explosion of information technology during the last five years, particularly in the past two years, companies, as well as the rest of society, have been faced with constant and consistent information overload. This has created a very diversified set of options for companies to perceive. For example, with the Home Shopping Channel and QVC on virtually 24 hours a day, consumers can order dozens of items from the comfort of their homes in just a few minutes. Our level of expectation has risen to the point where we expect goods to be delivered within a matter of hours instead of days or weeks as it used to be. Yet for a company to respond to orders rapidly, it must have an organizational structure that is driven by cycle time and a delivery system that not only ensures the speediest delivery but also guarantees the highest customer satisfaction. Large corporations, which are not traditionally "lean and mean" and tend to be highly bureaucratic, are losing their customers to smaller, more responsive enterprises. For example, suppose you needed to replace the color monitor for your computer. You call the original manufacturer and are quoted a reasonable price but a delivery time of two weeks. You go to a local dealership and find a lower price and a delivery time of one week. Finally, you call a computer mail-order company, and the monitor is delivered by 10:00 A.M. the next morning. Here, two companies lost the opportunity for a sale; if repeated, this could translate into hundreds of thousands of dollars.

With rapidly changing social behavior patterns, companies have to design work schedules that accommodate employees' needs, while minimizing the cost of fringe benefits. Reengineering efforts constantly create upheaval in organizational behavior, thereby complicating goal setting and strategic planning without a focus. Many companies claim to have a mission, but most have developed a mission statement without a thorough process. They lack a focused approach to untangle the web of complexity from an economic, cultural, environmental, social, and political standpoint. Simply put, most companies are pursuing goals that are irrelevant, untimely, and too diversified, without being mission driven.

Managers must *minimize* the maximum diversity in conflicting concepts by "simultaneous thinking" through the "power of the people." It is impossible to optimize ever-increasing business variables without relying on people as the most appreciable asset.

Continued Emphasis on Labor Productivity and Labor Costs

The problems with the labor productivity concept were pointed out in detail in Chapter 1. Traditional management's emphasis on labor productivity has much to do with our present economic and social status. This strong statement requires some explanation. Many outsourcing decisions are based only on the labor productivity measure, which can lead to layoffs. For example, one company that made most of the critical components for an item in the United States found out that its labor productivity for these components was poor compared to companies in Taiwan and South Korea. Several workers were laid off, and the components were procured from overseas. The layoffs turned into permanent job displacements because of lack of a retraining program. The social setup in the families of the workers who were laid off was disrupted drastically, including foreclosures on homes, depression, and physical and mental illness. Some families were even broken up as a result of the layoffs. Ironically, such companies have only a very small percentage of their costs in labor. They ignore the potential to improve productivity in other areas using the same employees. Management has had a narrow view of productivity. Because of the wrong emphasis, many managers have achieved improved labor productivity at the expense of quality. A gradual erosion of quality that resulted in foreign companies resulted in U.S. markets for consumer electronics, appliances, automobiles, and many other products being dominated by foreign companies. Customers slowly switched to high-quality imports, more plants shut down, and more people became displaced—wandering and floundering. In some cases, even entire families have become homeless.

Emphasis only on direct labor productivity can certainly produce large quantities with minimum setup. However, this in turn would result in high inventories, in direct contrast to the successful Japanese concept of Just-in-Time (JIT).

A study[16] by Andersen Consulting revealed that "while only 10–15% of product cost is labor, a typical manufacturer spends over 75% of its time trying to reduce it."

Ineffective Incentive Programs

Companies have used both individual and group incentive programs, but almost one-third of such programs are ineffective, as shown by a survey by Sibson & Company.

Sibson & Company Survey[17] (1990)

- 50% of the 644 companies surveyed offer variable-pay programs to salaried and hourly employees by executive ranks. Six percent more are planning such programs within one year.
- A third of companies with these programs rate their incentives as ineffective or in need of improvement.
  Possible reason—Some companies implement incentive programs without considering goals or conditions, solely because the competition does it.
- According to Charles Cumming of Sibson & Company, "Incentive programs can cause more harm than good if the wrong type of plan is installed."

Present managerial concepts, including TQM, have not incorporated effective incentive systems to consistently motivate employees through financial and non-financial rewards. As a result, management concepts such as management by objectives (MBO) and TQM have not maximized human creativity and ingenuity.

Managerial Ineffectiveness

Dr. Deming used to say that 80% of problems in companies are due to management. While it may be difficult for management to admit it, this statement is indeed true in most organizations. A study by Peter Sassone, an economist at Georgia Tech, revealed an interesting fact: mid-level managers spend only 27% of their time in real managerial activities, while 73% of their time goes into nonproductive activities.

Sassone Study[18]

Basis—1,563 employees in 77 offices, representing 4 Fortune 500 companies, were surveyed in 17 separate studies from 1985 to 1990 in manufacturing, consumer products, financial services, and commercial banking. Hourly logs were used.

Results—Mid-level managers (184) spent only 27% of their time managing—attending to management-level responsibilities such as staff supervision and decision making. Most of their work week went into support tasks and non-productive activities.

A 1980 study by Theodore Barry and Associates revealed shocking statistics. In a typical 8-hour day, 30% of the time (2.4 hours) was wasted, and all the reasons for this were centered around ineffective supervision. This study has been validated with my students from various types of companies during the last 15 years; the results confirm the claims of the Barry study not only in the United States, but also in several other countries where I have conducted seminars on total productivity management. Actually, it is interesting to note that the assertions of the Barry study are conservative in most situations.

Theodore Barry and Associates Study (1980)[19]
(Based on 50+ Reviews)

Typical 8-hour day
- 4.4 hours (55%) productive time
- 1.2 hours (15%) unavoidable delays
- 2.4 hours (30%) wasted time

Reasons for Productivity Loss

• Poor planning and scheduling of work	= 35%
• Unclear and untimely instructions to employees	= 25%
• Inability to adjust staff size and duties, peak and valley workload periods	= 15%
• Poor coordination of material flow, unavailability of needed tools, excess travel time, lax supervision of workers' starting and quitting times	= 25%
	100%

From these two studies, it is fair to say that presently known management philosophies, for the most part, have built-in redundancies for wasteful effort and communications which are inadequate, untimely, and even irrelevant.

2.4 CHALLENGES AS OPPORTUNITIES

Companies (as well as individuals) fall into one of two categories—reactive or proactive—that is, those that react to circumstances when they occur and those that cannot wait until circumstances occur but anticipate them ahead of time and take the necessary actions. Today, enterprises are facing virtually chaotic conditions, but, as Tom Peters points out in *Thriving on Chaos,* many companies have been able to turn chaos into success and challenges into opportunities.

Track star Wilma Rudolph was stricken with scarlet fever at age four. She lost the use of her left leg and had to learn to walk again, but she went on to win three gold medals in the 1960 Olympics. The point is, in spite of extremely challenging times—economically, politically, and socially—we have the greatest opportunities to excel individually and as corporations.

Bayer Japan Ltd., formed in 1911, not only took on the challenge of entering the Japanese market but decided to become a leader and make its name prominent in Japan's highly competitive pharmaceutical market. Instead of complaining about the often allegedly "closed" Japanese market, Theodore Heinrichon, president of the company, points to the following statements as reflecting his company's strategy: "Be patient, spend a lot of money, expect good returns not quick ones, build your personnel and have continuity. Short term, quick, cheap, and fast are not adjectives which are going to be successful in Japan. Bonsai does not become beautiful in a few years."[20] Present managerial philosophies do not have a built-in strategic component to convert challenges into opportunities.

Transnational Strategic Alliances

Proactive organizations have converted their economic challenges into great opportunities. For example, Ford and Mazda have cooperative ventures and strategic alliances which resulted in the Ford Probe, which uses a Mazda 626 chassis and engine. The 1991 Mazda Navajo is a version of Ford's Explorer utility vehicle. In fact, this was the first time a U.S.-based manufacturer built a vehicle for a Japanese company.

Figure 2.4 shows how transnational alliances have evolved. During the 1970s and 1980s, many U.S. companies created their designs in the United States, had many or most of their products manufactured in Japan, and shipped them back to the United States for sale. Beginning in the late 1980s, many Japanese companies, such as Matsushita, Sony, and Sharp, started doing the same with Southeast Asian companies. This phenomenon will continue to intensify as the world becomes smaller as a result of the Information Superhighway.

In 1989, T.F. Gross correctly predicted the future of strategic alliances when he said:

> The 21st Century is shaping up to be a time when global business competition—and paradoxically, collaboration, in the form of strategic alliances—will grow more strongly than ever.[21]

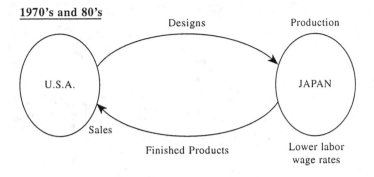

1970's and 80's

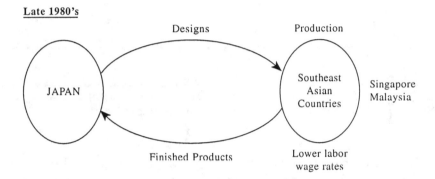

Late 1980's

1990's

    Examples of Japanese Co's doing this:

- MATSUSHITA
- SANYO
- SHARP

FIGURE 2.4   The evolution to transnational strategic alliances.

2.5 BRIDGING TECHNOLOGY DISCONTINUITIES

A growing phenomenon today is technology discontinuities. A technology discontinuity occurs when one technology replaces another (Figure 2.5).

In his 1986 book, *Innovation: The Attacker's Advantage,* Dr. Foster argues forcefully for the need to manage such discontinuities. Unfortunately, even the

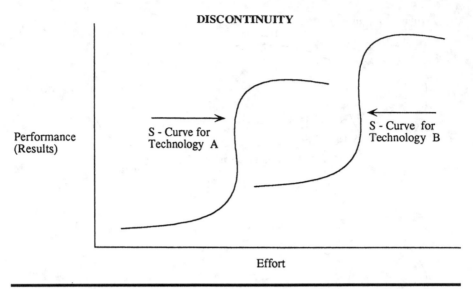

FIGURE 2.5   Technology discontinuities when technologies change. (Source: Foster, Richard, *Innovation: The Attacker's Advantage,* Summit Books, New York, 1986, p. 102.)

latest management philosophies such as TQM, reengineering, and deengineering miss out on this important issue. Later on in this book, we shall see how the total productivity management concept can be applied to manage technology discontinuities using a quantitative model.

2.6 SOCIAL CHANGES

Dr. Nam Suh[22] of MIT, speaking at the Institute of the Industrial Engineers Conference in 1985, declared:

> Many of our firms have not kept pace with the changing environment of the world and have not been able to cope with the challenging social value system here at home.

Social values in the United States have changed to the point where citizens are increasingly assertive, so much so that the lawyers are quite busy these days. In fact, as President George Bush said at the 1992 Republican Convention:

> America has 5 percent of the population of the world, but has 70 percent of the lawyers in the world. Our legal system is costing us

$300 billion a year. We must sue each other less and care for each other more.

The World Future Society forecasts that:

"Electronic immigrants" could become a hot international trade issue by the late 1990s. These new service workers who telecommute "across borders via computers will perform a variety of services electronically and compete against workers in affluent countries."[23]

This can clearly have social implications in the form of lost jobs.

Social changes in the workplace have increased dramatically during the last ten years. Today, you rarely find a company that does not talk about people solving problems in teams and people participating in various ways, such as quality circles, employee participation groups, labor management committees, etc. Employee empowerment has become a common practice in many corporations, even if the concept has not been institutionalized. Self-directed teams are another example of the recognition that today's employees are of a different breed. They cannot be motivated in an autocratic environment, and they cannot simply be given orders to be executed. Rather, they prefer environments where they are free to make the best decisions for their work situation in terms of product quality customer responsiveness. Companies like 3M, Harley-Davidson, IBM, Motorola, and Federal Express are excellent examples of this new phenomenon in the American workplace. Management approaches such as Theory X are fast disappearing. Other social changes rapidly taking place in the United States, Europe, and Japan center around work force diversity from a cultural, economic, and ethnic standpoint. Traditional management approaches, including MBO, are not capable of effectively gaining employee support to achieve the most fundamental goals of an enterprise—highest customer satisfaction at the lowest cost and highest profit margin possible.

2.7 THE FAMILY UNIT—AN ENDANGERED SPECIES

According to the National Center of Health Statistics and the Bureau of the Census, the divorce rate in the United States has increased dramatically from 4.1 per 1,000 married females in 1900 to 21 per 1,000 in 1988. The divorce rate in the United States is higher than in almost any other country. Experts have suggested a number of reasons, which include the following: (1) divorce is more socially acceptable than ever before, (2) many people expect more of marriage than earlier generations did and thus are likely to be more easily disappointed, (3) more high-paying jobs are open to women and wives therefore are less dependent economically on their husbands than they used to be, and (4) changes in divorce laws have made divorce easier to obtain. The family unit as we knew it in a traditional sense is rapidly disappearing. Single-parent families are as common as two-parent families. People in their late thirties and early forties are increasingly fed up with material achievement at the expense of harmony in the family unit. They are tired of the "rat race" and are starting home businesses in order to spend more time with their families. Many companies are encouraging their employees to work out of their homes, particularly in real estate and insurance. Today, it is possible to get work on a home computer and transport files electronically to your employer. Perhaps this approach would reduce the rate of disintegration of the family unit and help rebuild the nucleus of society, namely the family. People who are happy at home make happy and productive employees at work. Even though employees are often expected to separate personal life from professional performance, in reality, this is easier said than done. It is impossible to expect an employee on the verge of a divorce to give his or her best at work. It is equally difficult for an employee who has been laid off to keep his or her family happy. Managerial concepts such as TQM initially proclaimed that employees were an important part of providing the best possible quality and service to customers. Yet, many companies with TQM programs have laid off thousands of employees, virtually causing an emotional collapse for the wage earner of the family. Most recently, the concept of reengineering has been applied as a so-called "powerful" managerial philosophy—only to get rid of employees by the hundreds and thousands. Ten years ago, at least 15 major U.S. companies had a record of no layoffs. Today, the number is less than a handful. Until we learn to take responsibility for rebuilding the family unit and restoring the sanctity of relationships within that unit, we will continue to be unable to address the root causes of many of the problems in today's society, such as increased crime rate, teenage violence, and irresponsible parental behavior—just to name a few. All these problems are resulting in unnecessary and ever-increasing social costs which impact every taxpayer. Unfortunately, we are good at addressing the symptoms rather than causes of our social problems. Present management concepts, including TQM and reengineering, are totally insensitive to the preservation and promotion of the family unit as a complementary action to improve an enterprise's economic competitiveness.

2.8 TECHNOLOGY—THE UNCONTROLLABLE MONSTER

The unspoken but commonly expected norm of the day is "How much quicker," whether waiting in line at a bank or shopping for groceries. Our lives seem to be centered around:

- One hour to develop film
- Thirty minutes to delivery a pizza
- Ten seconds to communicate with any country in the world via fax
- Instant communication, whether in a car or on a plane
- On-line, 24-hour electronic communication with millions of people, companies, and services via the Internet

According to a professor at New Mexico University, technology has leaped forward so dramatically that we have seen considerably more technological advances in our lifetime than any other generation. In fact, he says that your age represents what you have seen as the percentage of all the technologies since the beginning of recorded history. Product development life cycles are dramatically decreasing because of the exponential growth in microprocessor speed. For example, the product development cycle for personal computers has decreased from 3 years to less than 18 months. It was about 18 years ago that the personal computer was introduced, with random access memory (RAM) of just 64 K. Today, most PCs have 4 megabytes (MB) (4000 K) RAM. Table 2.4 compares the memory capacity of the Macintosh computer in 1984 (when it was introduced) and 1995, just 11 years later.

Floppy diskette storage capability was 800 K in 1984. Today, optical disk storage is as much as 128 MB (a 15,900% increase). By the time we get used to one product, another is already on the market, making what we acquired just a few months ago obsolete. Further complicating matters is the fact that we cannot trade in personal computers, for the most part, in order to update obsolete technology at an incremental cost. Instead, we are forced to discard the old technology because the cost of upgrading is greater than the replacement cost.

The uncontrollable nature of today's technological developments can be compared to rolling a huge stone down a cliff, with no way to steer it to the right (where there is an ocean) or to the left (where there is a mountain). The only option is to race down the hill faster than the rate of descent of the stone. Today,

TABLE 2.4   The Enormous Increase in Computer Memory Capacity

	1984 Macintosh	*1995 Power Macintosh*	*% Increase*
RAM, installed	128 kB	16 MB = 16,000 kB	12,400
Maximum expandability to	512 kB	512 MB = 512,000 kB	99,900
Hard drive capacity, installed	20 MB	2 GB = 2,000 MB	9,900

corporations are confused about how to manage technologies, which are evolving and evaporating so rapidly. Yet, if companies do not learn the art and science of managing product technologies, process technologies, information technologies, and managerial technologies, they will quickly become uncompetitive and lose market share. Many universities, including MIT, IIT, Stanford, Northwestern, Case Western Reserve, and the University of Miami (just to a name a few), have a formal master's degree program in Management of Technology to educate a new breed of managers who will be equipped with the knowledge and skills to manage technologies with both a strategic and tactical thrust. The University of Miami has been organizing conferences on the management of technologies since 1988, under Dr. Tarek Khalil's leadership. Portland State University in Oregon and the Ecole Polytechnic of Canada have also been organizing conferences on this subject to grapple with the basic issues of managing technologies. It seems as though technology is no longer our servant, but rather has become our master in many ways.

Traditional concepts of management have had very little relevance to understanding the impact of technology on productivity, quality, and profitability. In fact, only a few companies have learned to integrate technology strategies with business plans. We need a management concept that addresses the unique nature of today's technology revolution.

2.9 ECOLOGICAL IMBALANCE

According to a recent study, the ozone layer has become thinner over Canada and Russia.[24] As reported in *National Geographic World* magazine, scientists estimate that 45 different species of plants and animals become extinct each day. The main reason is human disruption of the environment.

For the most part, we do not think systemically. We have a propensity to create an ecological imbalance. We know that "prevention is better than cure," yet we do not apply this wise adage because, by nature, we are "suboptimizers." A study[24] by the U.S. Centers for Disease Control revealed that two million people per year get infections, at a cost of $4.5 billion in the United States annually, with 77,000 related deaths. Yet, one-third of these infections can be prevented, thereby reducing the cost by simply following procedures for cleanliness. Not applying this adage in companies results in billions of dollars of ecological damage which could have been prevented by spending a proportionately small amount of revenues on environmental control.

Present models of management decision making are utterly inadequate, and possibly inappropriate, to relate ecological imbalance to the dramatically increased cost of designing, developing, and delivering products and services. We need a management tool that explicitly factors in environmental and ecological efforts in order to offer an ecologically friendly product or service.

2.10 THE "ONE-WORLD SYNDROME"

In 1943, Wendell Willkie prophesied a unified world economy, but it still is not here. Although we may be many years away from a truly globally integrated economy, the pace at which information technology is increasing, in both depth and breadth, leads us to a reasonable hypothesis that a one-world currency, a one-world government, and a one-world economy may not be utopian in the early part of the 21st century. Grant Jeffrey is one of several people exploding the secrecy surrounding stunning developments leading us toward a one-world government.[25] Today, for example, a change in economic conditions or even a perception thereof in one country can dramatically affect the economy in another country 10,000 miles away. In 1987, we witnessed the impact of the drop in the Dow Jones Index on the Tokyo Nikkei Index. The Persian Gulf War in 1991 was just about fought "on-line" on our TV sets. Today, the power of information technology and the media is so enormous that no major event—or even a minor one—can escape the attention of the "electronic eye."

　　Technology changes have been known to mankind from the very beginning of recorded history, but the *rate* of change is what makes this generation an unusual one in that, for the first time, instead of us driving the technology, technology is driving us. Perhaps we have already entered what can be called a period of "technology turmoil." Clearly, every enterprise is caught up in this whirlpool of technology transformation. A company either must learn how to manage this technology or will be thrashed by it. On the flip side of this burdensome approach to managing technology, companies can look at opportunities to offer their products and services not only to just a few hundred of thousand or million people, but rather to literally billions of people! For example, Coca-Cola saw an opportunity in China, with a population of more than a billion, and capitalized on it to increase its global market share dramatically, long before China was granted favorable nation status by President Clinton in May 1994. MIT Professor Paul Krugman predicts that "come the millennium, everything will be tradable. We'll put on our virtual-reality helmets and be able to supply anything to—or buy anything from—anybody in the world"[26] Cyrus Freidheim of Booz Allen thinks the competing interests of nationalism and globalism will bring forth what he calls the Trillion Dollar Enterprise—a world-girdling organization that would operate more like a political federation than a corporation. Because of its huge size, no industry could field more than a few of these organizations.[27]

Many progressive companies such as 3M pay much attention to the ISO 9000 standards in order to sell their products worldwide. The ISO 9000 series of standards, established by the International Organization for Standardization, is moving toward creating a uniform standard for trading products globally. Proactive companies stay ahead of the game by following the ISO 9000 registration procedures and by marketing their products throughout the world. More than 100 countries participate in ISO.[28]

The performance measurement systems known in the literature are inadequate and often irrelevant to provide an objective picture of transnational alliances and companies that are truly global. Of course, companies must also assess their risks carefully before going global—particularly in politically unstable economics. In fact, "political and economic risk analysis is a growing field because more businesses are growing into the international marketplace,"[29] and a number of companies are offering services in this area.

The "one-world" concept has accelerated the need to have world-class service—whether an organization is a mega business corporation or even a multinational church. While the definition of world-class service itself is changing constantly because of the information revolution, we can still identify useful criteria for ensuring success as a world-class service enterprise. A list of 12 such criteria is provided in Table 2.5.

To determine the extent to which an enterprise is a global competitor, a simple test can be used to determine the *global quotient* (GQ) (Table 2.6). An

TABLE 2.5   Criteria for World-Class Service

1. *Customer-focused* products/services
2. Quality levels *better* than the *best* in the world
3. Rapidly *innovated* products/services
4. Continuous *adaptability*
5. Mega *speed* of *responsiveness*
6. Professional service with *personal touch*
7. *"Delighted"* employees
8. *"Enchanted"* customers
9. Customer-based *and* employee-based *reengineering* in customer service
10. Customer-focused *boundaryless* partnerships
11. *"Universal"* products
12. *"Portable"* products

Source: Sumanth, D.J., *Customer Service Management (CSM): A Necessary Approach for Survival into the 21st Century,* 1996, p. 23. ©1996, D.J. Sumanth.

enterprise can continuously strive to improve its GQ by offering world-class products/services as assessed by the criteria in Table 2.5.

TABLE 2.6   Test for Global Quotient (GQ)

Note: Maximum points for each question = 100

1. What proportion of your total sales (revenues) come from countries other than where your company is headquartered?
2. What is your market share globally?
3. What percentage of the time have you been an industry leader globally in the last five years?
4. What proportion of your employees are located globally?
5. What portion of your board of directors are from outside the country in which your enterprise in headquartered?
6. Is your enterprise considered global in all major industrial countries?
7. What proportion of your executives manage global operations?
8. What percentage of your global operations are completely autonomous in terms of decision making with respect to:
   - Technology investments
   - Employment policies
   - Product pricing
   - Alliances, etc.
9. What proportion of your facilities are interconnected globally through information networks?
10. What proportion of your facilities are ISO 9000 and/or ISO 14000 certified?
11. What proportion of your employees are trained in global culture?
12. What proportion of your facilities enable customers to change their order specification operations electronically?

Scoring

Point Range	GQ	Point Range	GQ
0–120	10%	601–720	60%
121–240	20	721–840	70
241–360	30	841–960	80
361–480	40	961–1,080	90
481–600	50	1,081–1,200	100

Source: Sumanth, D.J., *Customer Service Management (CSM): A Necessary Approach for Survival into the 21st Century,* 1996, p. 19. ©1996, D.J. Sumanth.

2.11 SUMMARY

Traditional management concepts such as MBO, zero defects, TQM, and reengineering have served companies' needs well to some but not to their full extent. They tend to emphasize one-dimensional competitiveness to the exclusion of other factors and ignore the critical human dimension. They also tend to look for short-term gains rather than long-term profits. Most importantly, they tend to be suboptimal, not systemic. For example, companies that have used TQM for three to four years are still groping in the dark for a way to relate their TQM efforts to total productivity and to profits. Many companies are searching for an alternative approach to address their dilemma after trying out TQM or reengineering. Companies that feverishly jumped on the bandwagon of reengineering have discovered that it is an extremely painful process, particularly for employees who are displaced after many years of loyal service. Whereas TQM stresses teamwork and people, reengineering focuses on eliminating redundant business processes and restructuring the company, even if it means getting rid of employees by the thousands. The TPmgt philosophy, concept, methodology, and principles presented in this book will not only achieve all the noble objectives of MBO, TQM, and reengineering, but will also achieve the more fundamental yet most important objective—to improve human welfare emotionally, physically, economically, and even spiritually in a uniform and long-lasting manner. This systems approach to total productivity is in line with contemporary thinkers like Barry Oshry,[30] whose recent work highlights the fact that the breakdown in organizations results from our blindness to the human systems of which we are all a part. Beginning in next chapter, our focus moves toward revealing the essence of this approach.

QUESTIONS TO PONDER

2.1 High-speed global communication, information technology, and "electronic immigrants" were discussed in this chapter. What other revolutions are shaping the social culture of corporations?

2.2 Corporate objectives of U.S. and Japanese companies were significantly different until at least the early 1990s. What changes do you see now? Why?

2.3 For three selected products, analyze objectively the trends in product life cycle. What challenges do these trends pose to the business strategies of the respective industries?

2.4 In your particular enterprise, how have information technologies affected the productivity and quality of products and/or services?

2.5 Table 2.3 lists some conflicting objectives faced by companies today. Think of some examples where each of these objectives has been visibly and substantially noticed.

2.6 Is the emphasis on labor productivity still prevalent? If so, why? If not, why not?

2.7 What is the extent of your organization's role in forming transnational strategic alliances? Among the examples you identify, it would be useful to analyze lessons learned from such alliances—both positive and negative. Do the analysis, and provide some practical recommendations for management.

2.8 Does your company/organization still place a great deal of emphasis on labor productivity? If so, identify some specific areas where this is happening and what problems you are facing as a result.

2.9 "Incentive programs can cause more harm than good if the wrong type of plan is installed, according to Charles Cumming of Sibson & Company in a survey done by his company in 1990. Conduct an analysis in your company/organization to see if this statement is true. If so, what actions would you take to undo the damage?

2.10 The Sassone study of 1990 revealed a rather surprising situation—mid-level managers spent only 27% of their time managing. Conduct a study to determine to what extent mid-level managers actually spend time managing. What lessons can be learned from this study?

2.11 The Barry study is another interesting indictment of the ineffective and inefficient utilization of supervisors and managers. The study showed that an average of 30% of the time in a day is wasted. Can you validate this study in your organization? Comment on the findings, and prescribe a strategy to reduce this unproductive time.

2.12 Conduct a benchmarking study of companies doing business successfully in Japan. Identify the common obstacles, opportunities, and successes experienced by these companies. You might gain more insight by dividing the sample into manufacturing and service organizations. Within each of these broad sectors, perhaps your study could be narrowed in focus to several particular product categories.

2.13 Repeat the above exercise for Japanese companies doing business in the United States. What contrasts can you discern from these two exercises?

2.14 Conduct an analysis of transnational strategic alliances in (a) the auto industry, (b) the electronics/computer industry, (c) banking/financial services, and (d) retail. What differences and similarities exist in these four industry groups with respect to (1) ease of starting such an alliance, (2) perpetuating it, and (3) the cultural and political factors that must be overcome for success?

2.15 For each of the major technologies you have had during the last ten years, analyze the "technology discontinuities" that impacted the organization's ability to compete nationally and/or internationally.

2.16 Many social changes are sweeping across our world at a rapid pace. Identify some such social changes that are affecting your business now— whether positively or negatively. What other changes do you foresee on the horizon?

2.17 How do you think the breakdown in the traditional family concept is affecting businesses today? Substantiate your analysis with facts and figures. What special actions, if any, are needed to mitigate circumstances created by this situation?

2.18 Benchmark yourself against companies/organizations that are taking formal measures to create environmentally responsible products and/or services. What challenges have these enterprises faced during the transition to such products/services? Discuss the benefits of such experience from a balanced perspective.

2.19 To what extent is the "one-world syndrome" a reality today? Within the context of your organization's business, what global trends in social, cultural, and informational areas have impacted your business significantly? Also, identify any major new developments shaping the "New World Order."

REFERENCES AND NOTES

1. For more information, contact The Berkana Institute at 3857 North 300 West, Provo, UT 84604 (phone: 801-377-2996, fax: 801-377-2998).
2. See "America's Little Dragons, *U.S. News & World Report,* p. 19, July 30, 1990.
3. These figures were provided by Michael Evans, president of Washington-based Evans Economics, in his speech to 500 Latin American bankers at the Annual Congress of the Latin American Banking Federation (FELABAN). See *International Business Chronicle,* p. 13, Dec. 9–22, 1991.
4. Business News, *The Miami Herald,* Sec. C, Jan. 6, 1990.
5. *International Business Chronicle,* Vol. 1, No. 1, p. 5, Jan. 8, 1990.
6. See the Buick advertisement in *U.S. News & World Report,* p. 63, July 1990.
7. Flaherty, M. Therese, *Global Operations Management,* McGraw-Hill, New York, 1996.
8. See *Wall Street Journal,* p. A12, Oct. 12, 1989.
9. Cardenas, D., Letizia, C., Morton, G., and Trueba, L., Principles of Productivity Improvement at Saturn, Class Project, April 9, 1994, p. 44.
10. Seal, G.M., "1990's—Years of Promise, Years of Peril for U.S. Manufacturing," *Industrial Engineering,* Vol. 22, No. 1, pp. 18–21, Jan. 1990.

11. For more information, see Hemenway, Caroline G., "10 Things You Should Know About ISO 14000," *Quality-Digest,* pp. 49–51, Oct. 1995.
12. This famous NBC Special was reported by Lloyd Dobyns and aired June 24, 1980. Dr. Deming's recognition in the United States was dormant until then. After this broadcast, he received major attention until his final days in 1993. Videotape copies are available from Films, Inc., Wilmette, Illinois, and transcripts are available from NBC News.
13. Reported in *Manufacturing Competitiveness Frontiers,* 1990. Original data from the *American Machinist.*
14. Korten, David D., *When Corporations Rule the World,* Berrett-Koehler, San Francisco, 1995.
15. See *Perspectives '92,* published by the American Productivity and Quality Center, Houston, Texas. The original data for this statement came from the Organization for Economic Cooperation and Development (OECD).
16. See Sutton, J.R., "America in Search of a Competitive Advantage in World Class Manufacturing," *Industrial Engineering,* Vol. 22, No. 5, p. 14, May 1990.
17. See *The Wall Street Journal,* p. 1, Nov. 6, 1990.
18. *Industrial Engineering,* p. 10, Nov. 1990.
19. *Industrial Engineering,* p. 14, Nov. 1980.
20. Morgan, James C. and Morgan, J.J., *Cracking the Japanese Market: Strategies for Success in the New Global Economy,* The Free Press, New York, 1991, p. 105.
21. Gross, T.F., "American Firms Blaze the Hottest Frontier," *Management Review,* Vol. 78, No. 9, pp. 24–29, Sept. 1989.
22. Suh, Nam P., "Prerequisites of Industrial Leadership of the World," Luncheon Speech at the Fall IIE Conference, Chicago, 1985.
23. "Social and Technological Forecasts for the Next 25 Years" by World Future Society. For more information, contact the society at 7910 Woodmont Avenue, Suite 450, Bethesda, MD 20814 (phone: 301-656-8274, fax: 301-951-0394).
24. Reported on the NBC Evening News, Nov. 14, 1992.
25. Jeffrey, Grant R., *Final Warning: Economic Collapse and the Coming World Government,* 1995.
26. "Global—Or Just Globalony?" *Fortune,* p. 98, June 27, 1994.
27. Ibid., p. 100.
28. Dedhia, Navin S., "The Basics of ISO 9000," *Quality Digest,* pp. 52–54, Oct. 1995.
29. Busey, Jane, "Going Global? Assess the Risk," *The Miami Herald,* p. 17, April 18, 1994.
30. Oshry, Barry, *Seeing Systems: Unlocking the Mystery of Organizational Life,* Berrett-Koehler, San Francisco, 1995.

3

THE BASIC CONCEPT AND MANAGEMENT PHILOSOPHY OF TPmgt

In Chapter 2, we established the basis for justifying the need for a management theory more relevant to present times. Now, we embark on a journey to introduce the basic concept and management philosophy of Total Productivity Management (TPmgt™).

3.1 THE TOTAL PRODUCTIVITY PERSPECTIVE

The backbone behind TPmgt is the total productivity perspective which, in turn, is based on the *productivity cycle* (Figure 3.1) introduced in 1979.

The productivity cycle denotes a continuous process, linking together four phases:

- Measurement (M)
- Evaluation (E)
- Planning (P)
- Improvement (I)

The productivity cycle may seem like a two-dimensional concept, but in reality, it is three dimensional in that it includes time. I call this the *productivity spiral* (Figure 3.2).

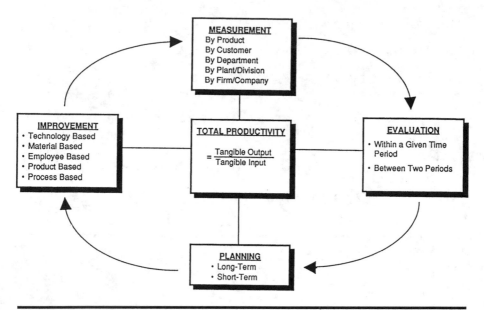

FIGURE 3.1 The total productivity perspective through the "productivity cycle." (©1979, D.J. Sumanth.)

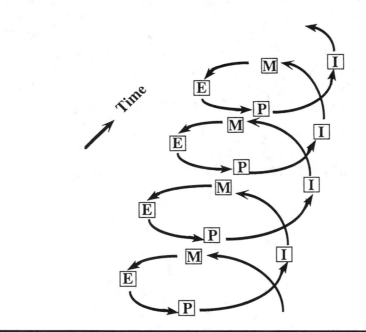

FIGURE 3.2 The "productivity spiral." (©1979, 1984, 1987, D.J. Sumanth.)

The Measurement Phase

The first phase of the productivity cycle is *measurement*. A company must initiate productivity measurement at some point. Without measurement, improvement lacks a focus, a systematic and analytical approach.

In the total productivity perspective, all improvements are driven by a total-productivity-based measurement system. A taxonomy of productivity measurement methodologies (Table 3.1) confirms the fact that, unfortunately, most measurement systems are oriented toward partial productivity. Among the total-productivity-based measurement systems, Sumanth's Total Productivity Model is applicable at all seven levels shown in Table 3.1—from corporate to task. Therefore, this model is presented next.

Sumanth's Total Productivity Model

The Total Productivity Model (TPM©) was developed by the author in 1979. The model defines a total productivity measure (Figure 3.3) which includes all the output and input factors. The formulas and notations for the model are provided in Appendix B. For additional information on the theory associated with this model, refer to the author's earlier works.[1,2]

The TPM is based on tangible output and tangible input elements. "Tangible" in this context means directly measurable or quantifiable. These tangible output and input elements are shown in Figures 3.4 and 3.5.

Although intangible elements such as quality, goodwill, concern for the environment, etc. are not explicit in this model, the TPM reflects the impact of such intangibles rather directly. For example, if the total productivity level goes down in a particular time period, it could be because of (a) poor quality of raw materials or purchased parts which increased the human and material inputs, or (b) reduced output as a result of directing effort to rework component parts, or both (a) and (b).

The TPM takes both a total systems view as well as a subsystems view. It is both diagnostic and prescriptive in nature.

The Operational Unit Concept

One of many unique features of the TPM is its ability to provide total and partial productivity indices at not only the aggregate firm level, but also at the most micro level of operation desired. For example, in an automotive company, productivity indices might be desired at the *product* level (such as for each type of automobile), *plant* level, *division* level, and at the *corporate* level. In this case,

TABLE 3.1 A Taxonomy of Productivity Measurement Methodologies at Different Levels of the Organization

	Level 1: Corporation	*Level 2: Division*	*Level 3: Plant*
Total Productivity	• TPM • Kendrick-Creamer model • Craig-Harris model • Hines' model • APC's model • MFPMM	• TPM • MFPMM	• TPM • MFPMM
Total Factor Productivity	• Kendrick-Creamer model • Taylor-Davis model	—	—

Partial Productivity	• Craig-Harris model
	• Performance measures
	• DEA
		• Performance measures
		  −Objective matrix
		  −OFA
		  −NGT
		• API
		• MOPI
		• DEA
			• Performance measures
			  −APC's approach
			  −Objective matrix
			  −OFA
			  −NGT
			• MOPI
			• NP/PMM
			• API

the *operational units* are product, plant, division, and corporation. Similarly, in a bank that has several branches, the operational units could be checking transactions, savings transactions, local branches, regional branches, and the corporation. In a local municipality, the operational units could be the fire department, police department, parks and recreation, water and sewer department, public works, etc. In a fast-food business, the operational units might be sandwiches, soft drinks, franchise stores, company-owned stores, and the corporation. In a hospital, the operational units could be related to type of patient service, for example, inpatient services, outpatient services, or Diagnosis-Related Groups.

TABLE 3.1   A Taxonomy of Productivity Measurement Methodologies at Different Levels of the Organization (continued)

Level 4: *Department*	*Level 5:* *Work Center*	*Level 6:* *Machine*	*Level 7:* *Task*
• TPM • MFPMM	• TPM	• TPM	• TPM
—	—	—	—
• Performance measures −APC's approach −Objective matrix −OFA −NGT • MOPI • NP/PMM • API • FACT	• Performance measures −Objective matrix −OFA −NGT • MOPI • API • FACT • NP/PMM	• Performance measures −OFA −NGT • Work measurement −Stopwatch time study −M-T-M −Work sampling −MOST	• Performance measures −OFA −NGT • Multiple linear regression analysis • Work measurement −Stopwatch time study −Work sampling −M-T-M −MOST • FACT

$$\text{Total Productivity (TP)} = \frac{\text{Total Tangible Output}}{\text{Total Tangible Input}}$$

$$= \frac{O_1 + O_2 + O_3 + O_4 + O_5}{H + M + FC + WC + E + X}$$

FIGURE 3.3 Dr. Sumanth's "Total Productivity Model" (TPM©). (©1980, D.J. Sumanth.)

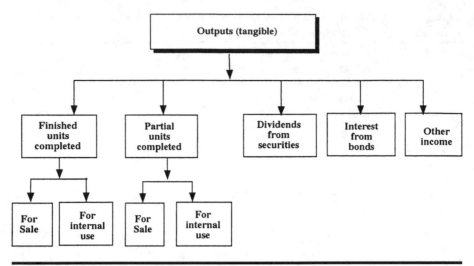

FIGURE 3.4 *Output* elements considered in the TPM. (©1979, D.J. Sumanth.)

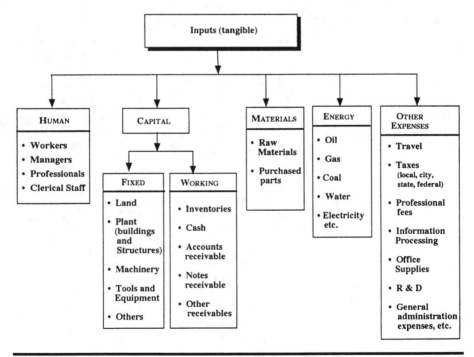

FIGURE 3.5 *Input* elements considered in the TPM. (©1979, D.J. Sumanth.)

In fact, the TPM can be applied in every type of organization where there are people or where machines, equipment, materials, and energy are used. The operational unit concept applies equally to a multinational, multibillion-dollar firm and a one-person consulting firm.

Unique Features of the TPM

Micro-Macro Feature—The TPM is a systematic approach to measure and monitor the total productivity and the partial productivities of the operational units of a firm, as well as of the firm itself. This is a distinct advantage over those total-productivity-based systems that produce indices only at an aggregate or macro level—usually at the company/firm level. Because the TPM is both aggregate and detailed in nature, it is both *diagnostic,* in that it shows the trends in productivity, and *prescriptive,* in that it can pinpoint the specific input resources that are not being utilized effectively and efficiently.

Universality—The TPM is universally adaptable to any type of economic entity—hospitals, banks, insurance companies, manufacturing or retail firms, fast-food businesses, consulting firms, architectural firms, construction contractors, hotels, motels, cities or municipalities, state or federal governments, educational institutions, advertising agencies, publishing companies, transportation companies, utilities, religious institutions, or at home—in fact, anywhere there are resources. The operational unit concept of the TPM makes this universality of application possible.

Software Availability—Computer software has been developed for the TPM on mainframe, mini-, and microcomputers, more specifically for the following hardware:

- Univac 1100/82 (mainframe computer)
- PRIME 400 (minicomputer)
- IBM PC or compatibles (microcomputer)

A user's manual with documentation is available for these systems. (For information on price and support, contact Dr. Sumanth via e-mail (dsumanth @eng.miami.edu or prody peopl@miami.aol.com) or fax (305-252-2707).

Integration into Productivity Management—The TPM enables an enterprise to set up a productivity measurement system that forms the basis for formal evaluation, planning, and improvement of total productivity. Management of total productivity is made possible with the installation of the TPM.

Implementation Time—Implementing the TPM in a company/organization is a relatively easy task if the people in charge of implementation attend a one-day seminar on the subject. Implementation time will vary with the magnitude and scope of the productivity measurement effort, management's desire to institute a productivity system as part of its management philosophy, the level of training received, and the level of commitment. Field implementations have varied from two months to five months. The availability of the software makes inputting the data extremely easy, with minimal education and training.

Linkage to Profitability—The TPM has a unique linkage to profitability. The *break-even point concept of total productivity* (Figure 3.6) indicates that there is a region of profit above the break-even point and a region of loss below it. Management can use the TPM to monitor not only total productivity changes, but also profit changes. For example, a "what if" analysis helps to determine expected profit levels for a range of target values of total productivity (Figure 3.7). Thus, the TPM is a very practical tool for productivity management in general and productivity measurement in particular.

Three Winning Strategies—When total productivity is increased, the total cost per unit decreases. If we assume that selling price per unit of a product or service

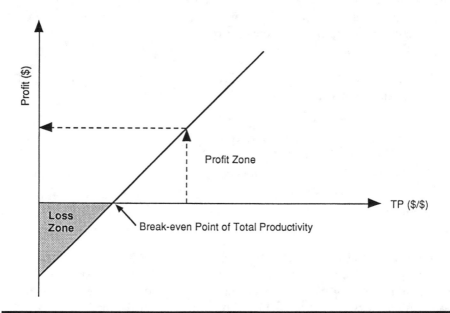

FIGURE 3.6   The "TP–profit linkage." (©1979, 1990, D.J. Sumanth.)

Target Total Productivity Value	Expected Profit or Net Income At the Present Resource Level	Increase From Previous Resource Period
1.10	$260.8 Million	+45.0%
1.20	319.8	+77.8%
1.30		
1.40		
1.50		

FIGURE 3.7   "What if" analysis. (©1990, D.J. Sumanth.)

is total cost per unit + profit margin per unit, a simple example (Figure 3.8) shows that three winning strategies are possible.

Strategy for Using the TPM

The proven strategy for using the TPM as a measurement tool is to follow the *Level 1 to Level 4 analysis.*

Level 1 Analysis—Observe the graphical trends in the total productivity value against the break-even point for the firm as a whole. Even if the firm-level total productivity values for certain time periods exceed the corresponding break-even points, go to Level 2. Analyze graphically the trends for the partial productivity indices for the firm.

Level 2 Analysis— Observe the graphical trends for the total productivity value against the break-even point for each one of the *operational units*. For those operational units for which the total productivity value falls below the break-even point, go to Level 3.

Level 3 Analysis—Analyze the trends in the partial productivity indices for all operational units for which the total productivity value is less than the break-even point. Usually, one or more of the partial productivities will decline.

Level 4 Analysis—Analyze in detail the input resources that correspond to the partial productivities using an industrial engineering approach. This strategy uses the management-by-exception principle, which in itself is "total productive." The many case studies presented in Chapter 5 will give you an excellent understanding of how to apply the *Level 1 to Level 4 analysis.*

Price = Cost + Profit Margin

$$\frac{\text{Total Productivity} \uparrow}{\text{Cost} \downarrow}$$

Example:

Before Productivity Improvement

Price   = 5.0 + 2.0

           = $7/unit

After Productivity Improvement

Price   = 4.0 + 2.0   } **More Market Share**

           = $6/unit

or Price = 4.0 + 3.0   } **More Profit/Unit**

            = $7/unit

            = 4.0 + 2.5   } **3rd Favorable Strategy**

            =$6.5/unit

FIGURE 3.8   The three winning strategies with improvement of total productivity.

Numerical Example for the TPM

To demonstrate the computations in the TPM, let's examine a firm with three operational units over two time periods: period 0 (base period) and period 1.

The sample calculations for operational unit 1 are given in Table 3.2. The calculation for the weighted average cost of capital is determined by the following rule of thumb:

$$\text{Weighted Average Cost of Capital} = (\text{PLR} + 2\%)$$

where PLR is the prime lending rate for the base period. This value, which is readily available in the *Wall Street Journal,* is needed to compute the working capital input.

Table 3.3 shows the summary of computed values for all three operational units. Table 3.4 summarizes the total and partial productivity values and indices for the three operational units. Table 3.5 does the same for the firm as a whole.

Total Productivity and Break-Even Point Profiles

Figure 3.9 shows the total productivity profiles for the three operational units and for the firm. *Trends* must be noted rather than emphasizing absolute values for individual time periods. Although this figure shows that total productivity improved for the firm and for each of the operational units, the true profitability condition is only discerned by analyzing the break-even point of total productivity. This is done through Figure 3.10, which shows that for operational unit 1, the total productivity value is below the break-even point in both period 0 and period 1, indicating that it is operating in the loss region.

Partial Productivity Profiles

To analyze the causes for operational unit 1 being in the loss region, an analysis of the partial productivities is done (see Figure 3.11). The partial productivity profiles indicate that the human, material, and energy productivities declined in period 1 when compared to the base period. This should trigger an action plan on the part of productivity engineers and managers to further analyze the causes for inefficient utilization of human, material, and energy resources.

For convenience, a management summary (Figure 3.12) is prepared, which indicates that operational unit 1 (product 1) needs major improvement.

Sumanth's Comprehensive Total Productivity Model

After nearly eight years of research, the TPM was expanded to the Comprehensive Total Productivity Model (CTPM©) in 1987. This model was presented at the Second International Conference on Productivity Research in 1989. The model is shown in deliberately simplified form in Figure 3.13. The *intangible factor index* is calculated by considering all *user-definable* intangible factors. Some examples of such factors considered in the CTPM are shown in Table 3.6.

Numerical Example

Table 3.7 summarizes the data and computations for applying the CTPM. The indices for *partial productivities, total* productivity, and *comprehensive total* productivity are shown in graphical form in Figure 3.14. From this example, we see that even though total productivity declined, comprehensive total productivity increased. This is a typical situation when a company emphasizes quality during a particular time period, while in another time period it may have devoted greater attention to tangible items such as finished units of output, human input, fixed capital input, energy input, etc.

TABLE 3.2 Sample Calculations for Operational Unit 1

	Period 0 (Base Period)	Period 1
Human Input		
Workers	150 man-hours × $4/man-hour = $600	160 man-hours × $4/man-hour = $640
Clerical staff	30 man-hours × $5 + 50 man-hours × $6.5 = $475	35 man-hours × $5 + 60 man-hours × $6.5 = $565
Professionals	25 × 10 + 40 × 14 = $810	30 × 10 + 45 × 14 = $930
Managers	10 × 14 + 20 × 18 = $500	12 × 14 + 25 × 18 = $618
Total Human Input	**$2,385**	**$2,753**
Material Input		
Raw material 1	2 tons × $50/ton = $100	2.5 tons × $50/ton = $125
Raw material 2	1,000 gal × $1/gal = $1,000	1,100 gal × $1/gal = $1,100
Raw material 3	1,500 lb × $1.5/lb = $2,250	2,000 lb × $1.5/lb = $3,000
Purchased part 1	1,200 units × $0.5/unit = $600	1,220 units × $0.5/unit = $610
Purchased part 2	2,200 units × $0.25/unit = $550	2,300 units × $0.25/unit = $575
Total Material Input	**$4,500**	**$5,410**
Fixed Capital Input		
Land	$1,000	1,000/1.15 = $870
Buildings and structures	$3,000	3,500/1.20 = $2,917
Machinery	$4,000	4,600/1.10 = 4,182
Tools and equipment	$1,200	1,500/1.17 = $1,282
R&D	$500	500/1.14 = $438
Total Fixed Capital Input	**$9,700**	**$9,689**

Working Capital Input

Inventory	$3,000 \times 0.073 = \$219$	$4,000 \times 0.073/1.20 = \$243$
Cash	$10,000 \times 0.073 = \$730$	$11,000 \times 0.073/1.25 = \$642$
Accounts receivable	$2,000 \times 0.073 = \$146$	$1,500 \times 0.073/1.15 = \$95$
Notes receivable	$1,000 \times 0.073 = \$73$	$1,300 \times 0.073/1.10 = \$87$
Total Working Capital	**$1,168**	**$1,067**

Energy Input

Oil	$500 \text{ gal} \times \$0.60/\text{gal} = \$300$	$550 \text{ gal} \times \$0.60/\text{gal} = \$330$
Gas	$1,000 \text{ cft} \times \$0.30/\text{cft} = \$300$	$1,300 \text{ cft} \times \$0.30/\text{cft} = \$390$
Coal		
Electricity	$2,000 \text{ kWh} \times \$0.15/\text{kWh} = \$300$	$2,300 \text{ kWh} \times \$0.15/\text{kWh} = \$345$
Water	$1,000 \text{ gal} \times \$0.1/\text{gal} = \$100$	$1,100 \text{ gal} \times \$0.1/\text{gal} = \$110$
Total Energy Input	**$1,000**	**$1,175**

Other Expense Input

Travel	$500	$300/1.14 = \$263$
Taxes	$400	$420/1.02 = \$412$
Professional fees	$1,200	$1,000/1.05 = \$952$
Marketing	$2,000	$2,300/1.25 = \$1,840$
Information processing	$600	$1,000/1.05 = \$952$
Office supplies	$200	$250/1.10 = \$227$
Total Other Expense Input	**$4,900**	**$4,646**

Total Input	**$23,653**	**$24,740**

TABLE 3.3 Total Productivity Indexes for the Firm's Operational Units

	Units	Unit 1		Unit 2		Unit 3	
		Period 0	Period 1	Period 0	Period 1	Period 0	Period 1
Output							
Value of finished units completed	$	12,000	13,200	39,000	45,500	90,000	108,000
Value of partial finished units completed	$	3,000	2,880	3,900	7,800	9,450	13,860
Dividends from securities	$	3,000	3,636	2,500	4,018	3,200	4,348
Interest from bonds	$	1,000	1,091	2,100	1,786	2,700	2,522
Other income	$						
Total Output	**$**	**19,000**	**20,807**	**47,500**	**59,104**	**105,350**	**128,730**
Input							
Human							
Workers	$	600	640	1,600	1,750	438	500
Clerical staff	$	475	565	1,235	1,598	1,545	1,950
Professionals	$	810	930	2,240	2,550	2,220	2,580
Managers	$	500	618	1,367	1,559	1,250	1,472
Total	**$**	**2,385**	**2,753**	**6,442**	**7,457**	**5,453**	**6,502**
Material							
Raw material	$	3,350	4,225	300	375	9,100	11,300
Purchased parts	$	1,150	1,185	3,450	3,725	1,600	1,800
Total	**$**	**4,500**	**5,410**	**3,750**	**4,100**	**10,700**	**13,100**

Capital							
Fixed capital	$	9,700	9,689	26,600	27,024	25,300	25,056
Working capital	$	1,168	1,067	2,325	2,446	2,294	1,821
Total	**$**	**10,868**	**10,756**	**28,925**	**29,470**	**27,594**	**26,877**
Energy							
Oil	$	300	330	0	0	720	900
Gas	$	300	390	840	1,200	0	0
Coal	$	0	0	2,000	2,400	0	0
Electricity	$	300	345	750	900	900	1,050
Water	$	100	110	200	230	330	400
Total	**$**	**1,000**	**1,175**	**3,790**	**4,730**	**1,950**	**2,350**
Other Expense							
Travel	$	500	263	1,500	455	2,000	870
Taxes	$	400	412	1,000	1,143	1,200	1,339
Professional fees	$	1,200	952	0	0	1,000	0
Marketing	$	2,000	1,840	1,000	1,026	1,300	1,818
Information processing	$	600	952	2,000	2,091	1,900	1,963
Office supplies	$	200	227	500	631	600	714
Total	**$**	**4,900**	**4,646**	**6,000**	**5,346**	**8,000**	**6,704**
Total Input	**$**	**23,653**	**24,740**	**48,907**	**51,103**	**53,697**	**55,533**
Total productivity	$	0.803	0.841	0.971	1.157	1.962	2.318
Total productivity index	$	1.000	1.047	1.000	1.191	1.000	1.181

Note: Values shown under period 1 are in base period terms.

TABLE 3.4 Total and Partial Productivities for Individual *Operational Units*

	Operational Unit 1		Operational Unit 2		Operational Unit 3	
	Period 0	Period 1	Period 0	Period 1	Period 0	Period 1
Total productivity	0.803	0.841	0.971	1.157	1.962	2.318
Total productivity index	1.000	1.047	1.000	1.191	1.000	1.181
Total productivity (break-even point)	0.951	0.957	0.952	0.952	0.957	0.967
Human productivity	7.966	7.558	7.373	7.926	19.320	19.799
Human productivity index	1.000	0.949	1.000	1.075	1.000	1.025
Material productivity	4.222	3.846	12.667	14.416	9.846	9.827
Material productivity index	1.000	0.911	1.000	1.138	1.000	0.998
Capital productivity	1.748	1.934	1.642	2.006	3.818	4.790
Capital productivity index	1.000	1.106	1.000	1.222	1.000	1.255
Energy productivity	19.000	17.708	12.533	12.496	54.026	54.779
Energy productivity index	1.000	0.932	1.000	0.997	1.000	1.014
Other expense productivity	3.878	4.478	7.917	11.058	13.169	19.202
Other expense productivity index	1.000	1.155	1.000	1.396	1.000	1.458

Note: All values other than indices are expressed as constant dollars of output per constant dollar of input with respect to period 0.

TABLE 3.5 Total and Partial Productivities for the *Firm* as a Whole

		Period 0	*Period 1*
Total productivity	Value	1.361	1.588
	Index	1.000	1.167
Partial Productivities			
Human productivity	Value	12.034	12.485
	Index	1.000	1.037
Material productivity	Value	9.069	9.228
	Index	1.000	1.018
Capital productivity	Value	2.550	3.109
	Index	1.000	1.219
Energy productivity	Value	25.497	25.275
	Index	1.000	0.991
Other expense productivity	Value	9.093	12.496
	Index	1.000	1.374

Note: All values other than indices are expressed as constant dollars of output per constant dollar of input with respect to period 0.

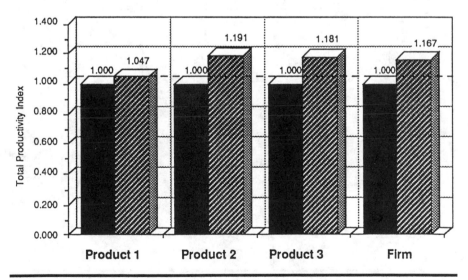

FIGURE 3.9 Total productivity index for the three products or operational units. Black bar = period 0, shaded bar = period 1, dotted line = break-even points.

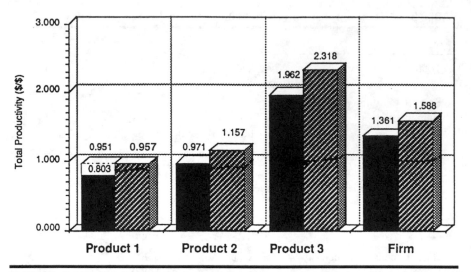

FIGURE 3.10 Total productivity and break-even points of the three products or operational units. Black bar = period 0, shaded bar = period 1, dotted line = break-even points.

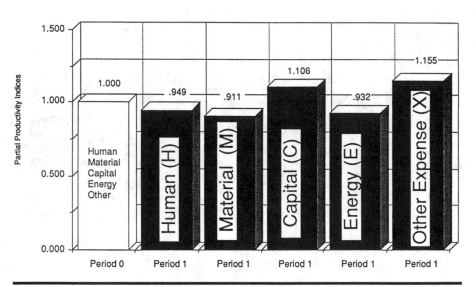

FIGURE 3.11 Partial productivities for product 1. (©1979, 1990, D.J. Sumanth.)

	% Change in Partial Productivities				
	Human	Material	Capital	Energy	Other
Product 1	-5.1%	-8.9	+10.6	-6.8	-15.5
Product 2	+7.5	+13.2	+22.2	-0.3	+39.6
Product 3	+2.5	-0.2	+25.5	+1.4	+45.0
Firm	**+2.5**	**-0.2**	**+25.5**	**+1.4**	**+45.0**

	Total Productivity			
	Value	B.E.P	Index	Status
Product 1	0.841	0.957	1.047	Action!!!
Product 2	1.157	0.952	1.191	O.K
Product 3	2.318	0.967	1.181	O.K
Firm	**1.588**	**0.959**	**1.167**	**O.K**

FIGURE 3.12   Management summary: period 1. (©1979, 1990, D.J. Sumanth.)

The Power of the CTPM

The TPM is a major advancement in productivity measurement concepts for most companies. Since the CTPM has even greater advantages than the TPM, clearly, the CTPM is the most sophisticated, comprehensive, and practical model available for organizations of any type or size.

Applications of the CTPM

The CTPM has been applied in both manufacturing and service organizations. For example, a manufacturer of electrical products applied the CTPM in the late 1980s. The model has also been used by a major civil engineering consulting firm based in Orlando, Florida. There are many other examples of the application of the CTPM in the United States and other countries worldwide.

An enterprise can start with the TPM first, mature with it as a productivity measurement system for a year or two, and then advance to the CTPM. The other approach is to start with the CTPM from the beginning. Both approaches work well. Fortunately, because the CTPM has been designed to extend the TPM, it is relatively easy to go from the TPM to the CTPM. The only extra

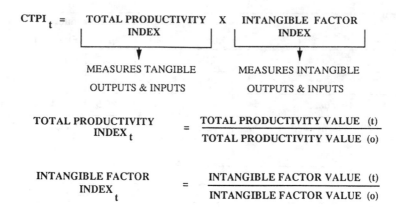

$$CTPI_t = \underbrace{TOTAL\ PRODUCTIVITY\ INDEX}_{\substack{MEASURES\ TANGIBLE \\ OUTPUTS\ \&\ INPUTS}} \times \underbrace{INTANGIBLE\ FACTOR\ INDEX}_{\substack{MEASURES\ INTANGIBLE \\ OUTPUTS\ \&\ INPUTS}}$$

$$TOTAL\ PRODUCTIVITY\ INDEX_t = \frac{TOTAL\ PRODUCTIVITY\ VALUE\ (t)}{TOTAL\ PRODUCTIVITY\ VALUE\ (o)}$$

$$INTANGIBLE\ FACTOR\ INDEX_t = \frac{INTANGIBLE\ FACTOR\ VALUE\ (t)}{INTANGIBLE\ FACTOR\ VALUE\ (o)}$$

t = TIME PERIOD OF MEASUREMENT
o = BASE PERIOD

INTANGIBLES = GOODWILL GENERATED, LEVEL OF
CUSTOMER SATISFACTION, RELIABILITY
QUALITY OF SERVICE, ETC.

$$TOTAL\ PRODUCTIVITY\ VALUE = \frac{TANGIBLE\ OUTPUTS}{TANGIBLE\ INPUTS}$$

INTANGIBLE FACTOR VALUE: CALCULATED WEIGHTED
AVERAGE FROM CUSTOMER SURVEYS

FIGURE 3.13   Dr. Sumanth's "Comprehensive Total Productivity Model" (CTPM©). (©1987, D.J. Sumanth.)

TABLE 3.6   Some Examples of Intangible Factors Considered in the CTPM

1. **Customer-related factors**
   - Product quality
   - Product reliability
   - Service quality
   - Price competitiveness
   - Product/service loyalty
   - Customer responsiveness
   - Customer loyalty
2. **Market-related factors**
   - Market standing/niche
   - Company/organization image
   - Market saturation
3. **Society-related factors**
   - Community attitude
   - Pollution
   - Environmental consciousness
4. **Process-related factors**
   - Process timeliness
   - Process time
   - Process effectiveness
   - Process efficiency

TABLE 3.6   Some Examples of Intangible Factors Considered in the CTPM (continued)

5. **Employee-related factors**	6. **Vendor-related factors**
• Job satisfaction or employee morale	• Payment satisfaction
	• Vendor timeliness
• Salary or wage raises	• Vendor quality
• Productivity gainsharing	• Vendor loyalty
• Job security	7. **Owner-related factors**
• Employee loyalty	• Stockholder/owner's financial benefit
• Employee turnover	• Stockholder loyalty

Note: Each company/enterprise can define its own intangible factors instead of or in addition to those used here, depending upon its particular needs.

Updated/adapted from the Comprehensive Total Productivity Model (CTPM©), Version 1.0, developed by Dr. David J. Sumanth. ©1987, 1996, D.J. Sumanth.

TABLE 3.7   Typical Format of Management Summary Using the CTPM

	Units	*Constant $ Value in Time Period*		
		t = 0 (base)	*t = 1*	*t = 2*
Tangible Outputs				
Finished units completed	$	39,000	45,000	49,015
Partial units completed	$	3,900	7,800	7,910
Dividends from securities	$	2,500	4,018	3,710
Interest from bonds	$	2,100	1,786	1,695
Other income	$	0	0	0
Total Tangible Output	**$**	**47,500**	**58,604**	**62,330**
Tangible Inputs				
1. Human Input				
Workers	$	1,460	1,460	1,460
Clerical staff	$	1,250	1,250	1,250
Managers	$	3,400	3,100	3,100
Professionals	$	2,740	2,600	2,600
Total Human Input	$	8,850	8,410	8,410
2. Materials Input				
Raw materials	$	11,793	10,858	10,611
Purchased parts	$	4,922	9,764	10,540
Total Material Input	$	16,715	20,622	21,151

TABLE 3.7   Typical Format of Management Summary Using the CTPM (continued)

	Units	*Constant $ Value in Time Period*		
		t = 0 (base)	*t = 1*	*t = 2*
3. *Capital Input*				
Fixed capital	$	6,150	10,670	12,275
Working capital	$	4,900	7,777	7,904
Total Capital Input	$	11,050	18,447	20,179
4. *Energy Input*				
Total Energy Input	$	3,210	4,815	4,975
5. *Other Expense Input*				
Total Other Expense Input	$	5,875	8,810	9,615
Total Tangible Input	$	**45,700**	**61,104**	**64,330**
Total productivity (value)	$/$	1.039	0.959	0.969
Total productivity index		1.000	0.923	0.933
Break-even point of total productivity	$/$	0.893	0.872	0.877
Intangible factor index		1.000	1.173	1.230
Comprehensive Total Productivity Index		1.000	1.179	1.239
Partial Productivities				
Human productivity	$/$	5.367	6.968	7.411
Index		1.000	1.309	1.381
Material productivity	$/$	2.842	2.866	2.947
Index		1.000	1.008	1.037
Capital productivity	$/$	4.299	3.204	3.089
Index		1.000	0.745	0.718
Energy productivity	$/$	14.798	12.275	12.529
Index		1.000	0.830	0.847
Other expense productivity	$/$	8.085	6.709	6.483
Index		1.000	0.830	0.802

Source: David J. Sumanth, The Comprehensive Total Productivity Model (CTPM©), Version 1.0, 1987, pp. 27–28. ©1987, 1996, D.J. Sumanth.

effort needed with the CTPM is the time spent to reach consensus on the selection of the intangible factors for a particular situation. This is usually a one-time effort for a given operational unit.

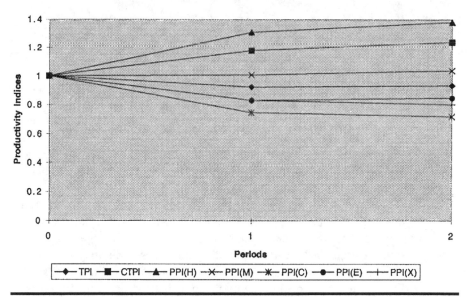

FIGURE 3.14   Profiles of *partial*, *total*, and *comprehensive total productivity* indices.

Major advantages of the CTPM over other productivity measurement systems include the following:

1. The CTPM is truly comprehensive in that it includes both tangible and intangible output and input factors.
2. It combines the best features of the TPM, which includes all the measurable output and input factors, with quality measurement approaches that capture factors which affect internal and external customers directly or indirectly.
3. For measurement of the intangibles, the CTPM captures factors related to many more aspects of an enterprise than quality and customer satisfaction measurements currently do.
4. The CTPM shows how the profitability of an organization is being affected by both operational and administrative functions. As a matter of fact, it shows directly the impact of decisions made in developing certain strategies in the past and the present. Thus, the CTPM can be used as a major strategic planning tool as well.
5. The CTPM pinpoints the sources for improvement as a management-by-exception tool. In some time periods, extra managerial attention may have to be directed toward certain tactical decisions. The CTPM helps in this process. Thus, it is a powerful tactical tool.

6. In decisions about managing technologies, particularly expensive ones, the CTPM can be applied to minimize technology discontinuities, thereby facilitating a smooth transition from one type to another type of technology.
7. *Profit targeting* can be done routinely by using the CTPM because its TPM component provides a means of linking profit to total productivity.
8. Because of its ability to reflect the impact of strategies and decisions by all managers at all levels, the CTPM can be a valuable team-building tool. Trade-offs between different strategic emphases can be simulated, so that intelligent decisions can be more of a routine than an exception.
9. Input from total quality management, reengineering, benchmarking, and other concepts can be assessed through the CTPM. Also, the impact of future concepts on the profitability of the organization can be projected for long-term planning purposes. This may be particularly helpful for multinational companies whose business plans often have to include special economic, political, and cultural factors in international operations.
10. Allocation of resources and budget preparations are more easily done with the CTPM by considering the need to enhance certain activities while scaling down others.

Many other unique features of the CTPM are being discovered as applications of this powerful model are expanded.

The Evaluation Phase

Productivity *evaluation*[3] is the second phase of the productivity cycle. It links the measurement and planning phases together. Productivity evaluation is a comparison of productivity in general and total productivity in particular. All concepts discussed in this section are applicable to any type of productivity measure, including partial productivities. There are two basic types of productivity evaluation: type I and type II.

Type I Evaluation

In type I evaluation, the actual levels of total productivity are compared *between* two time periods. For example, if total productivity (TP) is $/$ 1.250 in January and \$/\$ 1.375 in February, then the percent variation in TP between the two months is given by:

$$\left(\frac{1.375}{1.250} - 1 \right) \times 100\% = 0.10 \times 100\% = 10.0\%$$

Referring to Figure 3.15, the percent variation in TP between two periods, t −1 and t, is given by:

$$\mathrm{PVTP}_t = \left(\frac{\mathrm{TP}_t}{\mathrm{TP}_{t-1}} - 1 \right) \times 100\%$$

where TP_t and TP_{t-1} are the actual values of total productivity for periods t and t-1, respectively, and t = 0 (base), 1, 2, 3, ..., etc.

- ## Between 2 Periods:

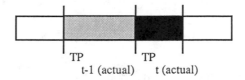

TP   TP
t-1 (actual)   t (actual)

- ## Within a Given Period:

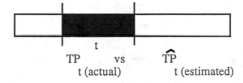

t
TP   vs $\widehat{\mathrm{TP}}$
t (actual)   t (estimated)

2 Methods:
- Using Forecasting Models
  (e.g. single-exponential smoothing)
- Using managerial judgement

FIGURE 3.15   Productivity evaluation. (©1993, D.J. Sumanth.)

This type of productivity evaluation is common and consistent with sales comparisons. Most companies regularly compare their sales or revenues between weeks, months, quarters, or years. The same should be done for productivity.

The type I evaluation helps an enterprise achieve two basic objectives:

1. Determine the extent to which today's measured TP level is different from a similar measurement a month, quarter, half-year, or year ago
2. Determine the trend in variation in TP in order to set realistic targets of TP for future time periods

Type II Evaluation

Type II evaluation is a comparison of productivity in general and total productivity in particular *within* a particular time period.

Let's return to the example used in the type I evaluation. Suppose the company forecasted (or estimated or budgeted) its TP level to be 1.410 for February. Since actual TP for February was 1.375, the percent variation in TP for February is given by:

$$\left(\frac{1.375}{1.410} - 1 \right) \times 100\% = (0.975 - 1) \times 100\% = -2.5\%$$

This indicates that even though TP in February was 10% greater than it was in January, it still fell short of the targeted value by 2.5%.

Referring again to Figure 3.15, the formula for percent variation in the type II evaluation is given by:

$$PVTP_t = \left(\frac{TP_t}{TP'_{t-1}} - 1 \right) \times 100\%$$

where TP_t and TP'_t are the actual and estimated values of TP for any given period t.

Two methods[4] which can be used for the type II evaluation are the single exponential smoothing (SES) model and the productivity evaluation tree (PET) model. These and other models are powerful analytical tools for comparing the actual versus expected achievement of TP in a company. The SES is a forecasting-type model. The PET uses managerial judgment in determining estimated TP. Although both models are practical, the PET tends to appeal more to management since managers are directly involved in its usage.

The type II evaluation enables the following important objectives to be achieved:

1. Determine the gap between actual and expected productivity
2. Help in the process of productivity planning, through a more realistic estimation of future productivity levels
3. Enable management to investigate the reasons for achieving, or falling short of, expectations for TP

The Planning Phase

Productivity *planning,* the third phase of the productivity cycle, is concerned with the establishment of *targets* for productivity in general and TP in particular. For example, in the preceding example, the company had a target of 1.410 for February; this target was set in the planning phase of the productivity cycle.

The TP target for a particular time period has to be set at least one time period before the current one. For instance, the target for February must be set at least by January. Of course, the target can be set much earlier, say, in December or November of the previous year.

My formal definition of productivity planning, slightly modified from my earlier work, is as follows:

> Productivity planning is concerned with the setting-up of target levels of total productivity or comprehensive total productivity so that such targets can be used as benchmarks for comparison in the *"evaluation"* stage of the productivity cycle, and for mapping strategies to improve productivity in the *"improvement"* phase of the productivity cycle.

Formal productivity planning helps an enterprise to compete more intelligently and wisely in the ever-increasing competitive market. Such planning helps to gather vast amounts of information, filter it, and then apply it to set targets, which are necessary to (a) be a market leader and sustain that position, (b) regain market share lost, and (c) manage the decline when truly warranted.

Productivity *planning* and *planning for productivity improvement* are not the same. The former is concerned with the establishment of productivity targets in general and TP targets in particular. On the other hand, the latter is implicit in the improvement phase of the productivity cycle. We will learn more about this in the discussion of the improvement phase in the next subsection.

The Total Productivity Curve

Total productivity for any particular product resembles the product life cycle. After a product is initiated (either in a manufacturing firm or a service enterprise), TP grows dramatically after a brief *initiation* period. Then, the TP level reaches a *saturation* point, where it may hardly change, except for random fluctuations. Finally, the decline begins, and the TP level deteriorates in a natural way. This phenomenon is captured through the *total productivity curve* (Figure 3.16). A similar curve exists for comprehensive total productivity (CTP).

The big question is: *Can the total productivity of a firm be increased forever?* Notice use of the word *firm*, not product. The answer is yes, for a firm that manufactures more than one product or offers more than one service and introduces new products without discontinuities.

Consider a *non-TPmgt company* (Figure 3.16a) which starts out with its first product, P_1. The company introduces its second product, P_2, at time D and then its third product, P_3, at time J. For product P_1, TP increases from point A, levels off at point B, and then declines down to point C, at which time TP for product P_2 begins at zero, goes up to G, and drops down to H when the third product, P_3, is initiated. When, P_1 is discontinued at a TP level of C, it takes a period of time from D to F to catch up to the previous level with P_2, and when P_2 is discontinued, it takes a period of time from J to L merely to attain the previous level, and so on. Clearly, during the periods of gaps (discontinuities), the TP level drops to zero and momentum is lost during the periods of discontinuities. Thus, even though product P_2 has peaked at a level higher than P_1 (point G is higher than point B), and product P_3 has peaked at a level higher than P_2 (point M is higher than point G), the net effect of the discontinuities is that the total

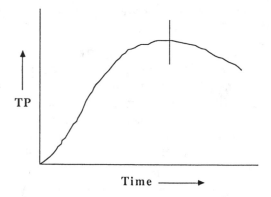

FIGURE 3.16   The total productivity curve. (©1989, D.J. Sumanth.)

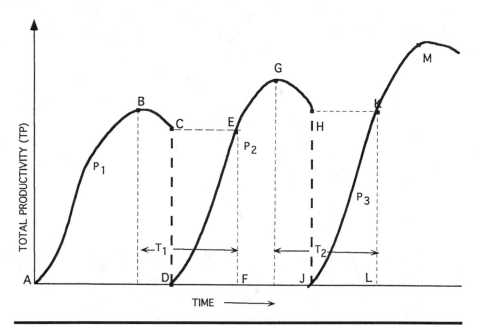

FIGURE 3.16a   A "non-TPmgt company" which has *not* introduced its three products at the right time, thereby causing discontinuities and a sawtooth total productivity curve for the firm.

productivity for the firm (TPF) follows the path A-B-C-D-E-G-H-J-K-M. Since TP directly affects profits, the financial implications for this company are enormous—and unfortunately negative. The company's profits will decline for long periods of time (periods T_1 and T_2).

Now let's consider a *TPmgt company* which introduces products in such a way that there are no discontinuities, as shown in Figure 3.16b. This company introduces products P_2 and P_3 long before the saturation points are reached at B and E, respectively. The net effect of this situation is that the TPF *never* drops to zero. As a matter of fact, the firm has a composite total productivity curve, represented by A-H-I-J-K, corresponding to products P_1 and P_2. Using this curve, the company can predict and set targets for TPF. Thus, total productivity planning enables an enterprise to do strategic planning in a non-traditional way—by superimposing the expected total productivity curves for anticipated products or services. "What if" scenarios can be played out with an existing product mix, a totally new product mix, or a hybrid product mix (a combination of the old and new product mixes).

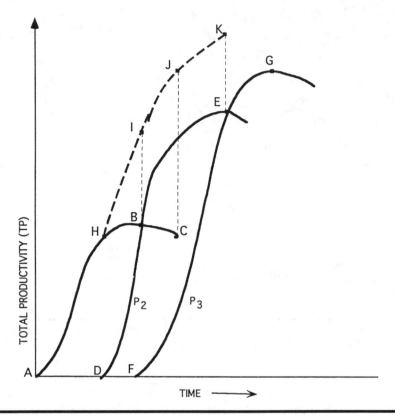

FIGURE 3.16b   A "TPmgt company" which introduced its three products at the right time, thereby *always* increasing total productivity of the firm.

A mature "TPmgt company" will aim at maximizing its TPF; this will automatically maximize its profits. The reverse may not always be true, because profits can be maximized merely by jacking up the selling price, particularly when there is hardly any competition. Most companies that resort to the strategy of increasing prices will quickly find that they are opening up opportunities for their competitors to enter the market and slowly chip away at their lead. We are all too familiar with what happened to the U.S. auto companies in the early 1970s, Xerox in the early 1980s, and many others in the 1990s when their pricing strategies were not tied into their TP trends. It took nearly 20 years for the American auto companies to regain most of their lost market from the Japanese and the Europeans and for Xerox to fully regain its market leadership from the Japanese. A TPmgt company would be wise to compete with total productivity as its primary strategic variable.

There are two types of productivity planning:

- Short-term productivity planning (SPP)
- Long-term productivity planning (LPP)

SPP is for time periods of one year or less, and LPP is for time periods longer than one year, generally three to five years.

Strategic planning in most U.S. enterprises has a three- to five-year connotation. However, there are some exceptions, such as AT&T, which plans ahead for 10 to 25 years. Many large Japanese companies plan ahead for as much as a 50- to 100-year period! Such companies can easily do their total-productivity-based planning for up to ten years. Since profit planning and total productivity planning are related concepts, a company can adopt the same planning horizon it uses for profits for total productivity planning as well.

SPP planning is possible through at least five different models:

- Weighted partial productivity model (WPP)
- Productivity evaluation tree (PET) model
- Linear trend model
- Comparative productivity evaluation model
- Seasonal variation model

LPP is feasible through at least two practical models:

- Total productivity maximization model
- Total productivity profit model

All these models are quantitative but are relatively simple to apply in companies. (They are detailed in Chapters 11 and 12 of my earlier work.)[5]

The Improvement Phase

The fourth phase of the productivity cycle is productivity *improvement*. Productivity improvement here is implied improvement of TP and/or CTP.

There are about 70 different techniques available for improving TP and/or CTP. These techniques, updated from my previous work,[6] are shown in Table 3.8 under five basic categories, which cover techniques based on industrial engineering, systems control, operations research, computer engineering management, psychology, and other behavioral sciences and many other disciplines.

A distinction is made here between techniques and tools. Techniques are much broader in applicability than tools. Techniques may actually include tools. For example, the methods engineering technique uses process flowcharts, Pareto analysis, and other such tools now commonly used in total quality management.

TABLE 3.8   List of Total Productivity Improvement Techniques

Technology-Based Techniques
 1. Computer-aided design
 2. Computer-aided manufacturing (CAM)
 3. Integrated CAM
 4. Robotics
 5. Laser technology
 6. Energy technology
 7. Group technology
 8. Computer graphics
 9. Emulation
10. Maintenance management
11. Rebuilding old machinery
12. Energy conservation technology
13. Digitizing technology
14. Telecommuting
15. Bioengineering
16. Object-oriented programming
17. Fiber optics
18. Computer-aided software engineering
19. RISC technology
20. Simultaneous/concurrent engineering
21. Desktop video conferencing

Material-Based Techniques
22. Inventory control
23. Materials requirement planning (MRP)
24. Just-in-time (JIT) inventory
25. Materials management
26. Quality control
27. Material handling systems
28. Material reuse and recycling

Employee-Based Techniques
29. Financial incentives (individual)
30 Financial incentives (group)
31. Fringe benefits
32. Employee promotions
33. Job enrichment
34. Job enlargement
35. Job rotation

36. Worker participation
37. Skill enhancement
38. Management by objectives (MBO)
39. Learning curve
40. Communications
41. Working condition improvement
42. Training
43. Education
44. Role perception
45. Supervision quality
46. Recognition
47. Punishment
48. Quality circles
49. Zero defects
50. Time management
51. Flextime
52. Compressed work week
53. Harmonization
54. Work at home

Product-Based Techniques
55. Value engineering
56. Product diversification
57. Product simplification
58. Research and development
59. Product reliability improvement
60. Emulation (benchmarking)
61. Advertising and promotions

Process- or Task-Based Technologies
62. Methods engineering
63. Work measurement
64. Job design
65. Job evaluation
66. Job safety design
67. Human factors (ergonomics)
68. Production scheduling
69. Computer-aided data processing
70. Reengineering

The productivity improvement phase involves a two-step process:

1. *Selection* of an appropriate set of productivity improvement techniques from the list in Table 3.8
2. Developing an *implementation plan* to install the selected productivity improvement techniques

Step 1: Selection of Appropriate Techniques

From the vast number of techniques available, a company has to select a manageable few, so that collectively they would help achieve or exceed the target of TP established in the planning phase. Clearly, the applicable set of techniques varies with type of business, size of the company, and many other factors. For example, in a fast-food restaurant, the productivity cycle is rotated or iterated on a monthly basis. Where productivity measurement is done at a monthly frequency, the applicable techniques may be limited to a small number (e.g., training, quality control, flextime, energy conservation technology, inventory control, advertising and promotion, etc.). On the other hand, if the monthly iteration of the productivity cycle applies to a high-tech electronic parts manufacturer, the applicable set of techniques may be a vast majority of those listed in Table 3.8. In a toy manufacturing business, product concepts change dramatically, because the most popular children's movies often determine the products; once the craze wears off, the products are phased out. In such situations, it would be difficult to use monthly iteration of the productivity cycle for certain products; therefore, selecting a set of productivity improvement techniques for such products is not only meaningless, but also impractical.

In selecting a set of appropriate techniques, three basic approaches are suggested:

1. **Common-sense judgment**—Intuitive sense, often backed up by experience
2. **Quantitative model(s) or methodologies**—Simple to sophisticated mathematically oriented strategies
3. **Semi-quantitative methods**—Combining the best of the above two approaches

A quantitative methodology[7] belonging to the second approach above is beyond the scope of this book but might be of interest to many. Its basic strategy is to first select a set of preliminary candidate techniques from the master list in Table 3.8 by applying multiple regression and then maximize the TPF by applying a mathematical programming technique known as integer programming. This methodology takes into consideration constraints such as:

- Maximum budgets/funds for implementing the techniques
- Minimum time to pay back the investment of money in the techniques
- Maximum time allowed for implementing the techniques

Of course, the best way to begin productivity improvement is to start out with the common-sense approach, then progress to a combination of common sense and some form of quantitative modeling, and finally move to the somewhat sophisticated (but powerful) quantitative methodologies.

Step 2: Implementation Plan for Total Productivity Improvement

In this step, as shown in Figures 3.17 and 3.18, there are five basic strategies to improve productivity:

Strategy 1:   Increase output for the same input level
Strategy 2:   Increase output and also decrease input
Strategy 3:   For the same output level, decrease the input
Strategy 4:   Increase the output at a faster rate than the input
Strategy 5:   Decrease the input at a faster rate than the output

Strategies 3 and 5 are *reactive*, particularly 5, but strategies 1, 2, and 4 are *proactive*. Enterprises with poor leadership and management adopt strategy 5 as a last resort to survive. Much of the downsizing we see is attributed to these two reactive strategies. Companies with good top leadership and excellent management practice the proactive strategies. The organization that follows strategy 4 is ideal, if the momentum can be maintained. When a company is in the initiation portion of the total productivity curve, there is so much to be done that it usually goes on a hiring binge; as people are added, naturally, they require office space, furniture, etc., and soon the fixed capital input climbs.

Figure 3.17 also shows five strategies for productivity decline in an enterprise. Companies that confuse the term *production* with *productivity* (unfortunately, almost 80% do, according to my surveys) are easily fooled by scenario #2, where output is increasing, even though input is increasing more rapidly.

Every enterprise must recognize where it is on the total productivity curve, for a given time period. Then, based on whether it is in the initiation/growth, saturation, or decline portion of the curve, the company should select a strategy for productivity improvement, saturation, or decline.

The implementation step of the *improvement* phase of the productivity cycle should also include an implementation action plan, with people responsible for the implementation, a budget, and a time schedule in Gantt chart form or in the format of other project scheduling tools such as a CPM and PERT.[8]

Productivity Decline Possibilities

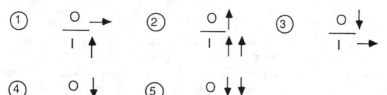

Productivity Improvement Possibilities

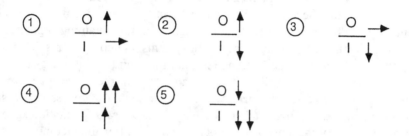

FIGURE 3.17 Possibilities for productivity improvement and decline.

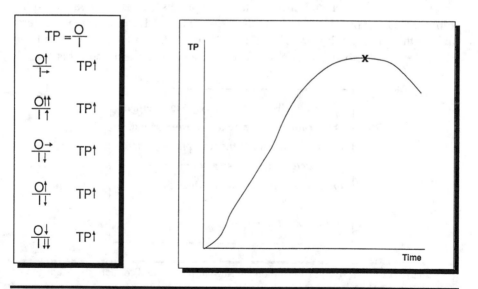

FIGURE 3.18 Options for total productivity improvement. (©1983, D.J. Sumanth.)

3.2 TPmgt: THE DEFINITION

I *formally* defined "Total Productivity Management" in 1981 (Figure 3.19). The acronym, TPmgt™ (also a trademark of this author), has a special significance. It denotes emphasis on the management (*mgt*) of total productivity (*TP*) in this definition. In fact, to borrow Abraham Lincoln's words from his Gettysburg Address, TPmgt is truly the management *of* total productivity, *by* total productivity, *for* total productivity.

The six words in bold italic type must be noted in this definition. First, TPmgt is *formal.* It has a theoretical basis, subjected to 17 years of testing, validation, and practical implementation in hundreds of companies and organizations worldwide. Second, TPmgt is a *philosophy* of management; it is a different way of designing, developing, managing, and maintaining organizations as systems, with highly interconnected subsystems and components. This management paradigm is a type of techno-human thinking that integrates technical and behavioral sciences. Third, TPmgt is anchored in the power of the previously described *productivity cycle,* which is a continuous process to measure, evaluate, plan, and improve total productivity. This *process* orientation keeps an enterprise from falling into a one-shot mentality and enables commitment to continuous renewal of organizational systems and subsystems. Long before the popularization of Shewhart/Deming's PDCA cycle beginning in the mid-1980s, I was lecturing all over the world about the importance of continuous total productivity improvement through the four phases (measure, evaluate, plan, improve) of the productivity cycle. Some years ago, I wrote a book centered around this productivity cycle.[9] Fourth, TPmgt is driven by the heart and soul of the TPM, described in condensed form in the previous section of this chapter.

> "Sumanth's Total Productivity Management
> is a *formal* management *philosophy* and
> *process* that follows the four phases of the
> "*Productivity Cycle*," so as to increase
> *total productivity*, and to reduce the total
> unit costs of products or services at the
> *highest quality* possible."

FIGURE 3.19 The formal definition of Sumanth's Total Productivity Management (TPmgt™). (©1981, 1984, D.J. Sumanth.)

As already pointed out, the main thrust of the TPM is on the *total productivity* measure and its break-even point—a concept that relates directly to profit. This unique model helps enterprises to understand the impact of virtually any organizational variable on total productivity and on the bottom line. It is like the blood pressure and heart rate of a living being. From these two vital signs, many other related variables can be investigated, diagnosed, and monitored for the best possible system performance. The fifth and sixth key words in the definition of TPmgt focus on the desired outcome of any system, namely *highest quality*.

The lessons learned from the tumultuous corporate challenges of the 1980s are simple:

1. Quality is not a luxury; it is an absolute necessity. It is a necessary condition, not a sufficient one.
2. Without global quality in products and services, a company's future is doomed and its days numbered.
3. Aspirations of people around the world are rising rapidly with the revolution in information technology, including the Internet. Those companies that do not have a continuous commitment to quality will have to "throw in the towel."

The definition of TPmgt recognizes and promotes an aggressive posture toward continuous total quality improvement which translates into perpetual total productivity enhancements. Simply stated, quality, which is one of the three major strategic variables, is emphasized in a deliberate manner in the TPmgt concept and philosophy.

3.3 TPmgt: THE CONCEPT AND THE PHILOSOPHY

The basic elements of the definition of TPmgt offered in the previous section are now incorporated into the practical concept of TPmgt (Figure 3.20).

Let's start from the left of this figure, with the *Inputs* block. All the input resources—human, material, fixed capital, working capital, energy, and all other types—are considered in this concept, unlike the 100-year-old traditional labor productivity thinking that focuses only on the labor input. These input resources go through a *transformation* process to become *outputs*. These outputs include completely finished products/services, partially completed products/services, and any other outputs. The *costs* of input resources used, when subtracted from the value of outputs generated, result in *profits* or *losses,* as the case may be. The TPM, explained in Section 3.1, is a diagnostic performance measurement system

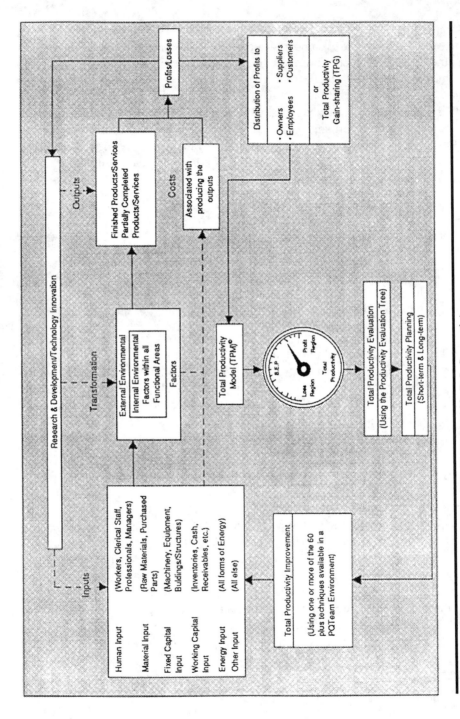

FIGURE 3.20 The concept of TPmgt™. (©1984, 1989, D.J. Sumanth.)

and works as a gauge to monitor the profitability of any organizational system or subsystem. When the total productivity level exceeds the break-even point of total productivity, the system under consideration is in the *profit region*. When the total productivity level is below the break-even point, it signals trouble, as the company is in the *loss region*. The information from the TPM is processed through the *total productivity evaluation* phase of the productivity cycle. In this phase, actual levels of total productivity are compared against forecasted levels and against levels in previous time period(s). The PET helps to show that there are 22 possible ways of changing the total productivity level. Next, the *total productivity planning* phase helps to determine short-term and long-term targets. Short-term usually means one year or less, and long-term implies more than one year, typically three to five years or more. The planning horizons for long-term planning vary among companies and countries. In the United States, five to ten years is very long-term thinking, for the most part. Some companies, such as AT&T, have an exceptional 25-year planning horizon. In Japan, some companies, such as Nippon, have as much as 50- to 100-year long-term plans. Ideally, a company should integrate total productivity planning into its strategic planning process. The *total productivity improvement* phase involves the planning, selection, and implementation of one or more of the nearly 70 available productivity improvement techniques, to achieve the targets of TP set in the planning phase. The mathematics and theory of the productivity evaluation, planning, and improvement methodologies are detailed in this author's book.[10] The TPmgt concept recognizes *research and development/technology innovation* as critical to constantly improving the inputs, transformation processes, and outputs. One of the important features of TPmgt thinking is *total productivity gainsharing*, which basically says that an enterprise should strive to share the gains in total productivity with all the stakeholders—owners (stockholders), employees, suppliers (vendors), customers, and society.

3.4 TPmgt: THE THREE-LEGGED STOOL ANALOGY

The concept of TPmgt, discussed in the previous section, gives a comprehensive picture of the systematic flow of key processes. In this section, the concept is depicted in a simple schematic form.

As shown in Figure 3.21, the TPmgt concept has the customer in the key position. TPmgt is analogous to a three-legged stool. The three legs—*quality, total productivity, and technology/innovation*—are all the same height and all located equidistant from each other. This implies equal emphasis on all three variables rather than just one or two, as is often the case. Also, each variable

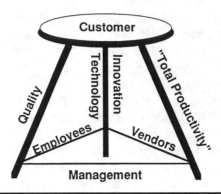

FIGURE 3.21   Three-legged stool analogy for TPmgt. (©1988–1990, D.J. Sumanth.)

must be pursued at the same time, just as all three legs of the stool are necessary to support the weight of the person sitting on the stool.

Next, notice the three braces connecting the three legs—*management, employees, and suppliers (vendors)*. If these braces are absent, the load on the stool will eventually begin to spread the legs out and ultimately even shear them off from the seat. There must be equal commitment and participation from each of these three groups to meet and exceed the customers' expectations on a continuous basis. In fact, "customer delight," as practiced by a number of companies, becomes necessary when the competition is rough and tough. If one of the braces is broken and/or missing, the uneven distribution of the load on the three legs will cause a problem. Well-managed companies have learned that the traditionally ignored suppliers are just as important a part of successful customer orientation as management and the employees. Ford Motor Company's "Taurus Project" in the early 1980s involved these three groups so successfully that the Taurus became the best-selling American car and the best-selling import in Japan the year it was introduced. The car continues to receive rave reviews.

The underlying concept of involving management, employees, vendors, and customers from the concept phase to the design, production, and launching stage is known as *simultaneous engineering* or *concurrent engineering*. Today, this concurrent thinking is widespread in most auto companies and in many other types of enterprises. The underlying principle is simple but profound. If you involve all the affected groups of people from the very beginning, you will offer products and services that customers need or want; you will reduce, and possibly eliminate, the irrelevant features in products and services that really do not add any substantial value as perceived by the customers, thereby reducing product costs and improving turnaround time and responsiveness; and you will also reduce the number of categories and quantities of spare parts, thereby reducing inventory costs, distribution costs, and warranty costs. No matter how you look at it, this is a win–win situation for everybody.

Figure 3.21 also brings up another important aspect of TPmgt—*integration*. We tend to use the term integration somewhat loosely, because we do not seem to understand the system concept very well. A system is a set of interrelated components or subsystems. When a component or one part of a system is affected negatively in performance, the other parts or even the entire system may be adversely affected. Often, it is a seemingly unimportant part of a system that may cause the entire system to crash. For example, a worn-out tire may mean the driver loses control of the car and crashes, just as a faulty hydraulic valve in an airplane may mean an emergency landing. The point is that total productivity management recognizes and reinforces the fact that everyone directly and indirectly involved in producing customer delight must be made to feel an important contributor to the goal of providing the highest quality product/service at the lowest total unit cost possible. Sporadic emphasis on one of the strategic variables, such as quality, total productivity, or technology/innovation, will not work, because it represents the lack of a true systems understanding; it may produce quick results but can create serious problems later. Instead, *consistent, conscious*, and *conscientious* management strategies that recognize the value of systemic synergy will pay rich dividends in the short term as well as the long term.

In short, from a systemic standpoint, anything that seems to be a quick-fix and instant gratifier is very likely going to be the most simple-minded strategy. Companies spend millions and even billions of dollars trying to patch up here and there, only to find a major economic disaster in their financial picture; then they resort to the all-too-familiar downsizing or so-called rightsizing, with major negative consequences in terms of morale, motivation, productivity, quality, and all the other important indicators of performance. All organizations are complex, techno-human systems. Unfortunately, because most matters which deal with people are not easily modeled theoretically, organizations cannot be treated as isolated islands. Although systems thinking is somewhat more difficult, because understanding various aspects of a system takes more knowledge and patience, it does prove that "prevention is better than a cure," which can save companies large sums of scarce capital and other valuable resources. The bottom line is that TPmgt thinking is holistic; therefore, it has a higher probability of success. Because it integrates technical and human dimensions systematically, it has the power of *both* people and technology. Simply stated, the foregoing discussion can be summarized as follows:

TPmgt builds a successful system of People + Technologies.

3.5 TPmgt: THE CONCEPTUAL FRAMEWORK

Over the years, I have often represented the TPmgt concept in various forms to explain a somewhat complex, intertwined set of mathematical formulas in a simple conceptual framework (Figure 3.22), which distills this complexity into a simple form. There are six major subconcepts to the TPmgt concept, as can be seen from this framework:

1. The productivity cycle
2. Quality–total productivity linkage
3. Profitability–total productivity linkage
4. Interfunctional team emphasis
5. The 12 principles of TPmgt
6. Education and training

The Productivity Cycle—As pointed out in Section 3.1, the main emphasis of the productivity cycle is that productivity in general and total productivity in particular must be (a) measured, (b) evaluated, (c) planned for, and (d) improved continuously, without complacency. The TPM, as explained in Section 3.1, is a

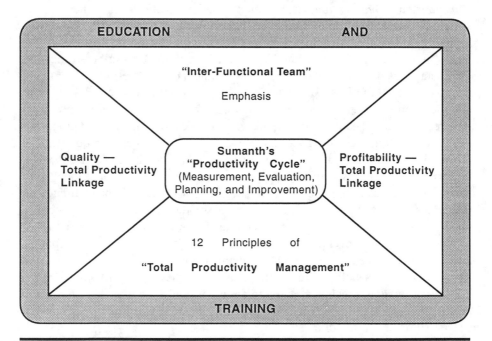

FIGURE 3.22   The conceptual framework for TPmgt. (©1988, D.J. Sumanth.)

measurement system that provides a common platform for understanding these four phases. *That which must be improved must be measured; that which is rewarded will be improved.* This basic principle applies to organizations as well as our daily lives. As employees or students, we are *measured,* or evaluated, so that we can improve our performance. We are bombarded daily with carefully *measured* "doses" of programming on television. When we go to the grocery store, we buy *measured* amounts of everything from milk to detergent. When we drive on the highway, someone is *measuring* our speed with a radar gun. If we think about it carefully, we realize that right from the time we are born (and actually even before that), we are *measured*, monitored, and improved upon.

The same is true for organizations. From the time an organization is conceived to provide a product/service, some measurement begins. The most common indicators are sales quantities and revenues—regularly measured and monitored closely on a monthly basis, frequently on a weekly basis, and sometimes even on a daily basis. Sales revenues are an integral part of everything from daily tactical planning to strategic planning. Yet, how often does a company measure and monitor total productivity with the same regularity, intensity, and focus? Ironically, as pointed out previously, improving sales revenues does not necessarily imply enhanced total productivity, let alone improved profitability. The point is to measure the *right* things first and set up a reward mechanism to improve the measure(s). We have already shown that total productivity is a *right* measure, because its improvement implies increased profits; therefore, it makes business sense to apply the total productivity focus in all four phases of the productivity cycle.

Quality–Total Productivity Linkage—Quality and total productivity are directly related. Notwithstanding the complexity of the definition of quality, which is an open-ended concept, the following axiom is true: When quality improves, total productivity definitely improves in the long run and may improve in the short run as well. A detailed discussion of this relationship is presented in Section 6.8.

Profitability–Total Productivity Linkage—As illustrated in Figure 3.6, one of the most significant relationships established in the TPM is that an enterprise's profit is directly related to total productivity. The concept of the break-even point of total productivity is derived from this relationship.[11] In fact, the TPM is the only total productivity-based measurement system that incorporates this break-even point concept. Sections 6.13 and 8.9 further amplify the significance of linking profit to total productivity.

Interfunctional Team Emphasis—The fourth important concept of TPmgt is its interfunctional nature. This concept has been designed as a cross-functional, barrier-diminishing approach from the first step through the last step of implementation (described in detail in Chapter 4).

TPmgt philosophy is heavily anchored in the principle of system simplification. Every system, which is comprised of a set of innerconnected and interrelated elements, can indeed be simplified by eliminating redundant elements. The most effective way to do this is to look at all the functional areas of an organization (not just manufacturing or operations, as is usually the case), with the understanding that each functional area is related to at least one other and the realization that elimination of redundancies begins by bringing together the people from all contributing functional areas. Interfunctionality and its emphasis in TPmgt are discussed at length in Chapters 6 and 8.

The 12 Principles of TPmgt—The fifth major concept of TPmgt is the application of a set of 12 principles. Each of these principles enables an enterprise to focus on its competitiveness, from the operational unit level to the firm level. The principles are applicable to all types of entities, although some have more direct relevance than others based on type, size, and time period. Chapter 9 is devoted to the presentation and discussion of these principles.

Education and Training—The sixth important concept of TPmgt is education and training. The premise behind this emphasis is the notion that all enterprises and their constituents (internal and external) must be educated and trained consistently throughout their lives. Because corporations are like living organisms, they need constant care and attention. In the organizational vernacular, this translates into the unending duty of top leadership and top management to create, monitor, and sustain a learning environment on a perpetual basis, so that new knowledge, new proficiencies, and new wisdom will promote the flexibility, adaptability, and dynamism that would propel a company to continuously explore new frontiers. This concept reverberates throughout the pages of this book, particularly since TPmgt believes in "people-building" and the power of people for progress and prosperity.

3.6   TPmgt: THE INTEGRATION MINDSET OF THREE COMPETITIVENESS DIMENSIONS

Wise organizations in general and business enterprises in particular tend to adopt *concurrent thinking* as opposed to *serial thinking*. They correctly recognize that competitiveness comes from a simultaneous and joint thrust on more than one strategic variable.

TPmgt involves a three-dimensional emphasis (Figure 3.23) on *quality*, *total productivity*, and *technology*, where these three dimensions are considered the three *strategic variables*. This thrust is continuously innovated, resulting in an *integrated business strategy* by the conscious application of three powerfully emerging sciences:

- Total Productivity Management (TPmgt)
- Total Quality Management (TQM)
- Management of Technology (MOT)

This integrated business strategy results in improved:

- Customer responsiveness and satisfaction
- Profitability
- Market share
- Satisfaction of everyone directly and indirectly related to the enterprise
- Employee welfare
- Environmental balance
- Vendor loyalty
- Enterprise dynamics (i.e., the ability to be resilient for adaptability)

The *dominant* strategic variable in TPmgt is total productivity, in TQM is quality, and in MOT is technology. Of these three "sciences," MOT is probably the least focused; it is quite broad in scope, ranging from a national technology policy to task-level technology adaptation. All three are so multidimensional that, after a certain point, their commonalities may dwarf their differences. It may seem difficult to narrow down the special focus of each of these independently evolving sciences, but close examination reveals that:

- TQM considers *quality* as the most important strategic dimension an organization should concentrate on, with the premise that when quality is improved, productivity automatically improves. Of course, quality is a difficult entity to define, and there are, therefore, many variations of TQM in definition, interpretation, and application and, hence, varied levels of success and failure. Also, productivity in the TQM context is mostly the partial productivity measure, which is totally suboptimal.
- TPmgt focuses centrally on *total productivity*, which is defined in a definite manner within the context of the TPM. The premise here is that when total productivity becomes the main target of an enterprise, quality and technology are automatically considered in both a direct and indirect manner. For example, the TPM considers the impact of quality and technology on the five output factors and the six input factors in the definition of total productivity, since

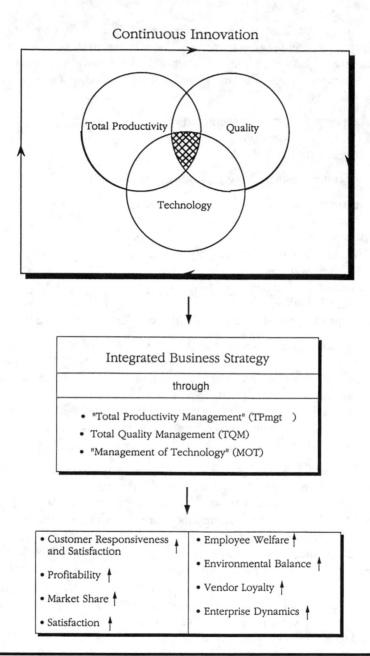

FIGURE 3.23   TPmgt: the integration mindset of three competitiveness dimensions.

$$TP = \frac{O_1 + O_2 + O_3 + O_4 + O_5}{H + M + FC + WC + E + X}$$

For every action taken and every decision made, the question asked here is: What is the impact on total productivity? If the answer is positive, then that action or decision has been "total productive." If not, it has only been "partial productive."

- MOT focuses primarily on *technology*—also a term which is understood in a very broad sense. The premise in MOT is that technology has become an overriding variable in everything a business or enterprise does, and not looking at technology as a major strategic variable would be suboptimal.

Thus, although TPmgt, TQM, and MOT are developing in parallel, with international conferences separately organized under these three broad categories to legitimize them, there is now a greater convergence of the basic ideas from these three sciences than ever before. That is why the integration of these three foci is considered important in TPmgt, as depicted in Figure 3.23.

QUESTIONS TO PONDER

3.1 Discuss the importance of the productivity cycle in the total productivity perspective as it applies to your company/organization.

3.2 Validate the seven unique features of the TPM in your enterprise. What lessons can be learned from this validation?

3.3 Discuss the significance of the concept of the break-even point of total productivity. How can this concept change the conventional profit orientation?

3.4 What are some of the significant features of the CTPM as opposed to the TPM?

3.5 How are the *evaluation* and *planning* phases of the productivity cycle linked together conceptually and analytically?

3.6 Discuss the relevance and importance of the total productivity curve in enterprises in general and yours in particular.

3.7 Analyze the definition of total productivity management carefully. Provide your commentary.

3.8 Discuss the following statement: "TPmgt builds a successful system of People + Technologies."

3.9 Add to the list of productivity improvement techniques in Table 3.8, based on your own research. Provide a brief description of such additional techniques, and indicate specific companies in which they are being applied.

REFERENCES AND NOTES

1. Sumanth, D.J., *Productivity Measurement Models for Manufacturing Companies,* published Ph.D. dissertation, University Microfilms International, Ann Arbor, MI, 1979.
2. Sumanth, D.J., *Productivity Engineering and Management,* McGraw-Hill, New York, 1984, 1985, 1990, 1994, Chapter 8.
3. Ibid., 1994 edition.
4. Ibid., pp. 243–251. In addition to the SES model, there are other models such as Double Exponential Smoothing (DES) and Winters' Smoothing model, discussed in Chapter 11.
5. Ibid., Chapters 11 and 12, pp. 260–299.
6. Ibid., pp. 318–476, for a detailed listing and explanation of 54 of the nearly 70 techniques.
7. Ibid., pp. 320–329.
8. CPM = Critical Path Method and PERT = Program Evaluation and Review Technique. These are well-established project scheduling tools to determine the critical path in terms of implementation time, cost, etc.
9. Sumanth, D.J., *Productivity Engineering and Management,* McGraw-Hill, New York, 1984, Chapters 8–19. See also the later versions of this book from McGraw-Hill; International Student Edition, Singapore (1985); Tata McGraw-Hill edition, New Delhi (1990); Spanish edition, Mexico City (1990); and Custom Series edition, New York (1994).
10. Sumanth, D.J., *Productivity Engineering and Management,* McGraw-Hill, New York, 1984, Chapters 9–18.
11. Ibid., pp. 179–190.

4

THE SYSTEMATIC 10-STEP PROCESS© FOR TPmgt

The basic concepts of Total Productivity Management (TPmgt™) are brought together in a systematic, step-by-step procedure (Figure 4.1) to implement TPmgt with the greatest success possible. Beginning in 1981, the implementation methodology for TPmgt has undergone repeated careful observation, "perfecting" it along the way—changing the sequence and timing of the steps, learning what worked well and what did not, and refining the process for the highest probability of success, with the fewest side effects. The implementation process is like a good recipe. The type, quantity, and quality of ingredients are important, but even more important is the sequence in which they are added.

The methodology has been tested worldwide during the last 15 years. It can work in any type of enterprise anywhere in the world, if the steps are followed the way they are explained here. The present form of the implementation methodology has evolved through many different stages into two versions—Basic TPmgt and Comprehensive TPmgt. These are explained next.

4.1 IMPLEMENTATION OF THE BASIC TPmgt

The *Basic TPmgt* involves ten steps for successful application in an enterprise. These steps are as follows:

1. Mission statement development
2. Total Productivity Model (TPM©) and/or Comprehensive Total Productivity Model (CTPM©) analysis
3. Management goals development

111

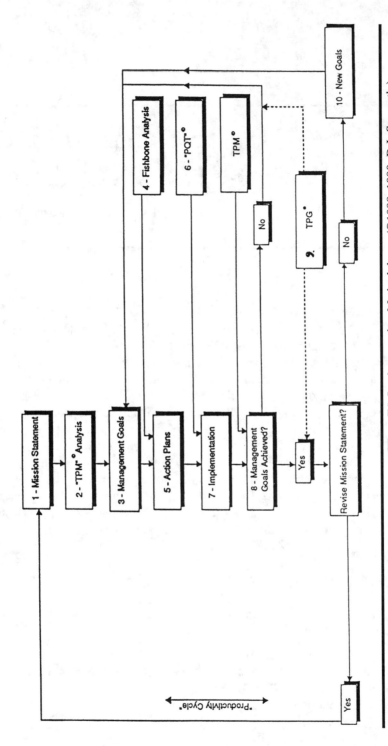

FIGURE 4.1 The Total Productivity Management (TPmgt™) Implementation Methodology. (©1988–1990, D.J. Sumanth.)

4. Fishbone analysis
5. Action plans development
6. Productivity Quality Team (PQT) training
7. Implementation of action plans
8. Assessing the extent to which the management goals are achieved
9. Total productivity gainsharing (TPG)
10. New goals development

4.2 IMPLEMENTATION OF THE COMPREHENSIVE TPmgt

The *Comprehensive TPmgt* involves two pre-TPmgt steps in addition to the ten steps of the *Basic TPmgt*. These two pre-TPmgt steps are:

1. Customer Satisfaction Survey (CSS©)
2. General Organizational Analysis (GOA©)

Each of these steps will be discussed briefly a little later.

Both versions of TPmgt are equally successful. The choice depends on many factors, including the following:

- Size of the company
- Extent of geographical dispersion within and outside the country where the company is headquartered
- Budget for implementation that top management is willing to invest

The comprehensive version naturally involves a larger budget than the basic version, but the additional information gathered in the pre-TPmgt steps of the comprehensive version will pay for themselves in 1 to 1.5 years in most cases.

The unique features of TPmgt and the benefits of its implementation are discussed at length in Chapters 6 and 8, respectively. We shall now briefly discuss each of the implementation steps.

The Customer Satisfaction Survey

The CSS is a scientifically defined and administered survey of a random sample of *external* customers. This computerized survey instrument captures valuable information from external customers. The results of this analysis are represented in graphical form in 12 different sections, for easy understanding by top management.

The General Organizational Analysis

The GOA is a survey instrument to capture valuable opinions of the *internal* customers—the employees. Representative samples of employees are interviewed in this step, and the results from the GOA questionnaire are summarized in terms of the *proactiveness index*. This index, which can have a minimum value of 0 and a maximum value of 100, essentially represents the extent to which a company is proactive in its management style. For example, in a major financial corporation made up of seven different companies, one had a proactiveness index of about 65% and another about 82%. The first one clearly was faltering in its ability to provide well-planned leadership. The company with the 82% index, on the other hand, was always looking ahead, aggressively benchmarking itself against its domestic and international competition.

4.3 STEP 1: MISSION STATEMENT

An enterprise without a mission statement is like a building without a well-planned, well-designed, and well-constructed foundation. Most companies have so little success with new ideas and concepts because they do not have a central guiding philosophy, captured through a vision and/or mission. Ten years ago, maybe 5 to 10% of organizations had mission statements. Today, more than 50 to 60% do. The total quality management (TQM) philosophy of management has to be credited for this kind of a response. Yet, many companies do not really know the correct ingredients of a mission and a vision. Even when they do, the process by which they develop their vision and mission is far from right. Many companies have combined vision, mission, and values into one set of statements, with the result that even top management and the select few individuals who claim to have articulated them cannot even state them, let alone remember them.

It is important to distinguish between vision, mission, and values in the context of an organization or a person. A *vision* represents a very long-term-oriented "calling." A *mission* represents a short- to medium-term statement of purpose. A mission, stretched over a relatively long period of time, becomes a vision. For example, as AT&T is achieving its mission with much passion and zeal, it is moving closer toward its ultimate vision of being a company "universal" in nature—in providing communications products and services.

There are many factors to be considered before the mission statement is actually drafted, refined, and adopted. Some of these critical factors are listed in Table 4.1.

A correctly developed mission statement usually has the following characteristics:

TABLE 4.1 Mission Statement: Factors to Be Considered

1. Major strengths (good points)
2. Major weaknesses (bad points)
3. Environmental factors (economic, political, social, and cultural)
4. Competition
5. Quality of service
6. Suppliers/vendors
7. Customer characteristics
8. Research and development (for future growth)
9. Market characteristics
10. Spin-off products: possibilities and challenges
11. Opportunities for global markets

1. It articulates the guiding philosophy of the enterprise with a central focus.
2. It is concisely worded—short and sweet!
3. It comes very naturally to *everyone* in the organization; they "live" by it on a daily basis.
4. It is so easy to memorize that everyone can recite it.
5. It is developed thoughtfully, carefully, and through active involvement of representatives of all constituents at all levels of the enterprise. A mission statement drafted by a small group of people at the board level and "rubber-stamped" by vice presidents at the next level is often ineffective, because it lacks the "ownership" of the process for developing the mission.
6. It does not have to be revised every year, but it does not remain unchanged forever either. A properly developed mission statement lasts about five years or more.
7. It is visually posted in all areas of customer interaction so that customers can hold the company accountable for public pronouncement of its mission. For example, Wendy's mission statement is prominently displayed in its restaurants:

> *We will create a unique environment where our focus on guest satisfaction leads our company and is unchallenged throughout the service industry.*

Indeed, Wendy's guest satisfaction is outstanding. By the time you place your order and pay the cashier, your food is ready to be picked up! Clearly, Wendy's mission statement tells us what the main thrust of its business is—a guest satisfaction level that is not just the best in its industry, the fast-food business, but throughout the service industry.

The mission statement says what the main focus of the organization *is,* or *is expected to be,* as perceived by internal and external customers. It answers two fundamental questions:

- Who are we as a business entity?
- How do we want to be known by all our stakeholders (employees, owners/ stockholders, customers/clients/constituents, suppliers, and community)?

Citibank's mission is:

> *to be the best and only place for target customers and businesses to manage all of their money anytime, anywhere, any way they want.*

This mission statement of the largest bank in the United States (and more than 100 years old) has three key elements—*anytime, anywhere,* and *any way.* These words have major implications for the company's commitment to serve its customers any time of the day, anywhere in the world, in any way possible. The bank has designed and developed technologies of its own to live up to its mission statement. Two years ago, while conducting a reengineering study at two of Citibank's branches, I discovered that with just one Citigold card, a customer can do his or her banking 24 hours a day, anywhere in the world, in one of 14 different languages. Not only that, the customer can do all of his or her business transactions related to checking and savings accounts, investment accounts, mortgage accounts, etc. with this one card. There is an industrial engineering touch you can feel everywhere—from the sophisticated automated teller machines to the queueing systems and "personal bankers" inside the branches. Citigold customers can even call their personal Citigold officer, make an appointment, and take care of their business at their convenience. The bank blends the best of personalized service (characteristic of a small bank) and superior versatility (characteristic of a megabank).

The significance of the mission statement in implementing TPmgt is perhaps better understood when we compare traditional thinking (Figure 4.2) with nontraditional thinking (Figure 4.3) while implementing a new concept. Unfortunately, most enterprises fall into the traditional mode of Figure 4.2, wherein a new concept C is serially superimposed on top of a previous concept B, which previously replaced an older concept A. If the company did a poor job of implementing concept A, credibility is lost to implement any subsequent concepts such as B or C. Once employee trust is lost, it is extremely difficult to regain it no matter how hard top management tries to enforce and institutionalize new concepts.

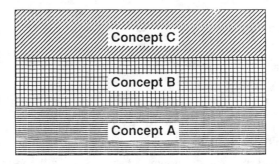

FIGURE 4.2   Traditional thinking. (©1989, D.J. Sumanth.)

For example, one company tried to implement quality circles (QCs) but did a poor job of it in an atmosphere of layoffs. Morale dipped so low that the employees did not believe top management when they announced the implementation of TQM six months later. The TQM concept was resisted, but top management was in a state of denial, wanting to believe that it was working well when in fact it was not. A year later, management decided to implement the reengineering concept. You can easily guess the outcome. This company's major problem was lack of a guiding philosophy and a focus as to what its purpose is and what it wants to be. Simply put, the company lacked a clear mission. Top management personnel showed a "knee-jerk" reaction every time they heard or

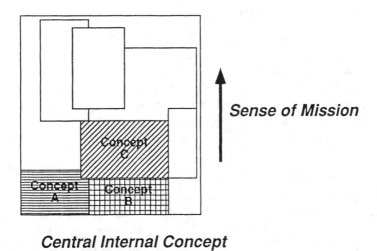

FIGURE 4.3   Non-traditional thinking. (©1989, D.J. Sumanth.)

read about a new concept that their competitors were applying. Usually, when companies reach this stage, they show signs of intellectual panic. They are willing to try anything out of desperation. They are like little children—not knowing which toys to play with. They "play" with one concept for a while, think it's not fashionable anymore or get bored, and want to try another one which seems to be the "in thing." QCs, TQM, and reengineering are not bad concepts. In fact, each is a powerful tool, but a company must first have a "central internal concept," or a core philosophy with a mission. Then, a new concept can fit in relevantly within the company's overall framework to accomplish its vision and mission, as shown in Figure 4.3. This non-traditional thinking can prevent many problems companies face today. Firms that lack a core philosophy lack a focus; concepts and techniques become a panacea rather than useful tools to accomplish the vision and mission.

Developing a mission statement is an important step in consolidating the foundation for implementing TPmgt. The next step is the TPM and/or CTPM analysis.

4.4 STEP 2: TPM AND/OR CTPM ANALYSIS

This is another crucial step in the TPmgt implementation. It provides a quantitative basis before developing management goals in Step 3. Depending upon the situation, the TPM analysis and/or CTPM analysis is conducted using the TPM and CTPM described in Chapter 3. The results of the TPM analysis will provide the company with the trends in:

- Total productivity
- Break-even point of total productivity
- Human productivity
- Materials productivity
- Fixed capital productivity
- Working capital productivity
- Energy productivity
- Other expense productivity

If the CTPM analysis is also done, then additional information in terms of the intangible factor index is also provided. Since the intangible factor index is a composite of all user-definable qualitative factors, such as product quality, process timeliness, customer responsiveness, market share penetration, community attitude toward the company, enterprise goodwill, etc., the CTPM will provide substantial information as to the strengths, weaknesses, opportunities, and trends in all critical areas of the business from the viewpoints of both internal and external customers—in short, all the stakeholders.

With this quantitative analysis completed, the next step is to set management goals.

4.5 STEP 3: MANAGEMENT GOALS

Based on the TPM and/or CTPM analysis, the TPmgt Team, comprised of representatives from each functional area, is brought together for a one-day meeting. In this meeting, the facilitator—preferably the chairman of the board, CEO, president, or executive director—reinforces to the group the vision and mission of the company and then shares the results of the TPM and/or CTPM analysis with everyone present. An honest discussion takes place in the context of the results of the GOA and CSS as well.

Next, the facilitator lists four criteria for a goal to qualify as a management goal. Every management goal must:

1. Achieve the mission statement
2. Be very specific, without ambiguity
3. Be time based
4. Be verifiable

Then, through brainstorming, the management goals are listed on a flip chart. The period of time for the goals to be achieved varies from one to three years.

In one machine tool manufacturing company, the TPmgt Team established its goals based on the TPM analysis. The first three of these goals were as follows:

1. Increase human productivity (PP_h) by 7% per year from January 1, 1992 to December 31, 1994
2. Increase other expense productivity (PP_x) by 3.5% per year from January 1, 1992 to December 31, 1994
3. Reduce inventories by 5% in calendar year 1992 and 7% in calendar year 1993, in order to increase working capital productivity (PP_{wc})

This approach to setting up management goals differs from the traditional approach. In the traditional strategic planning process, for the most part, goals are established based on budgets, information from annual reports, and quite a bit of subjectivity. The goals are often oriented toward adding human resources or reducing head count, facilities expansion, acquiring new technology, mergers, acquisitions, leveraged buyouts, quality deployment, etc.

The TPmgt approach provides a frame of reference in which goals are oriented toward achieving the mission and vision of the organization. By making the goals very specific and verifiable, people in all functional areas of the company are intrinsically motivated to achieve them. The Barry study discussed in Chapter 2 pointed out that most productivity loss is due to lack of timely goals. People perform better when they are involved in the goal-setting process and when they have something to achieve that is clearly linked to their organization's mission. Also, this type of goal setting enables the heads of various functional areas to focus their attention on the relevant goals rather than their own goals in the name of "management by objectives." The latter creates "empire building" and "fat" in the system. Later on, trimming this excess will invariably result in layoffs and the associated social costs to people's lives. Prevention is better than a cure in organizations as well as individuals' lives. With TPmgt thinking, companies can prevent layoffs rather than create opportunities for them through conventional management thinking.

The TPmgt approach to setting management goals is a deliberate strategy to create a *natural focus* in the entire organization toward its vision and mission. Further, progress toward these goals will be evaluated in the next cycle of TPmgt, and more meaningful reward mechanisms can be established for the effective accomplishment of the management goals.

4.6 STEP 4: FISHBONE ANALYSIS

Fishbone analysis, also called the Ishikawa diagram (named after Dr. Kauro Ishikawa of Japan), is a well-established tool to analyze the causes for a problem. This tool is applied for a different purpose in the TPmgt implementation. The TPmgt Team does a fishbone analysis for each of the management goals established in Step 3. The idea is that if a company carefully analyzes all the tasks, processes, and techniques needed to accomplish each management goal, it will be better equipped to allocate resources (which are becoming scarcer every day) to goals that would attain its mission, instead of squandering them on goals that are irrelevant.

Continuing with the machine tool company cited in Step 3, a fishbone analysis was done for the first management goal, as shown in Figure 4.4. This analysis shows, at a glance, various things to be done in the areas of manpower, methods, finances, machines, and materials. Where appropriate, more areas can be added to the diagram. The diagram is usually more detailed than shown in Figure 4.4, but the figure still illustrates the idea.

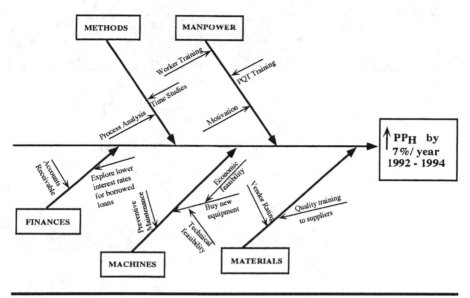

FIGURE 4.4   Fishbone analysis for the first management goal.

4.7 STEP 5: ACTION PLANS

In this step, an action plan is developed for each management goal. The action plan includes details of tasks, starting and ending dates, and people responsible for each task. Continuing with the example of the machine tool company, Figure 4.5 shows a portion of the action plan for the first management goal—increase human productivity by 7% per year from 1992 to 1994.

An action plan is another way to create a carefully thought out plan of action to achieve a management goal. It is also an excellent tool to assign people to tasks which, when accomplished, will achieve an important management goal, which, in turn, will help achieve the organization's mission and vision. Clearly, there is a deliberate linkage in all that is accomplished in the step-by-step implementation process for TPmgt. If the management goal to be attained is a fairly tough one, it is recommended that task force teams be assigned as needed.

An action plan helps to identify the bottlenecks. A Gantt chart can be used to represent the action plan or the network approach can be taken, using the critical path method (CPM) or the program evaluation and review technique (PERT). The CPM is deterministic, whereas PERT is probabilistic. With the network approach, the critical path in the network can be determined using well-established methods.

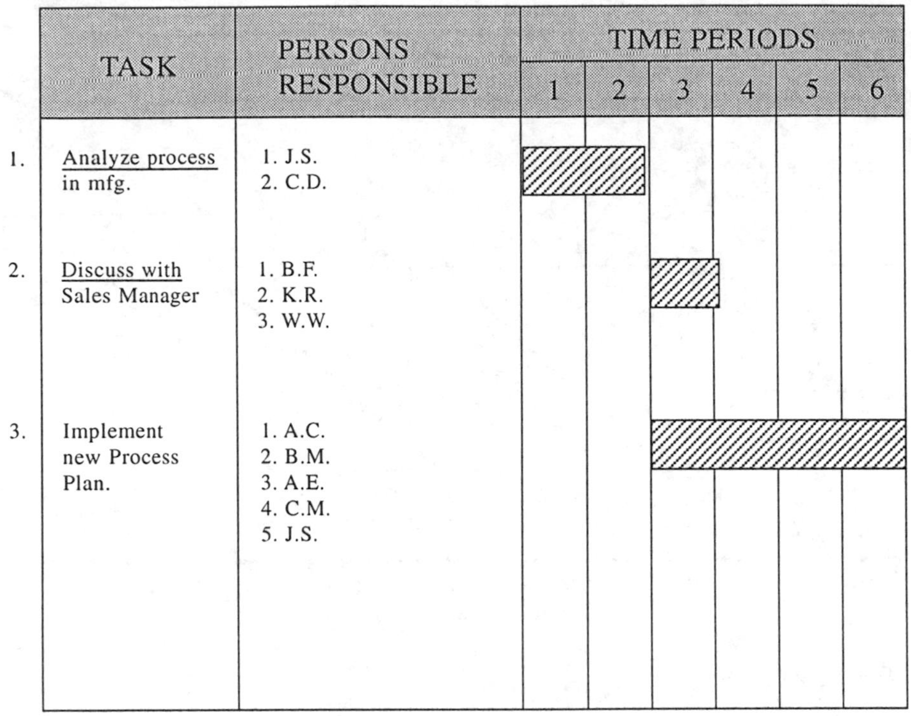

TASK	PERSONS RESPONSIBLE	TIME PERIODS					
		1	2	3	4	5	6
1. Analyze process in mfg.	1. J.S. 2. C.D.	▨					
2. Discuss with Sales Manager	1. B.F. 2. K.R. 3. W.W.			▨			
3. Implement new Process Plan.	1. A.C. 2. B.M. 3. A.E. 4. C.M. 5. J.S.			▨▨▨▨▨▨▨			

FIGURE 4.5   Action plan for goal #1.

4.8 STEP 6: PRODUCTIVITY QUALITY TEAM TRAINING

In this step, Productivity Quality Team (PQT) training is provided to *all* the employees so that they have the necessary tools to accomplish the tasks in the action plans in an effective and efficient manner. The least expensive way to offer this training is to use the train-the-trainer approach. The first group to be trained is the TPmgt Team. This training is done in a three-day format—sometimes including weekends, depending on the employees' and trainers' schedules. Each TPmgt Team member who undergoes this training then goes on to train 20 others. This is a practical approach and provides stunning results. When employees train other employees, they understand the TPmgt process very naturally; therefore, they tend to believe in it and help implement it more wholeheartedly.

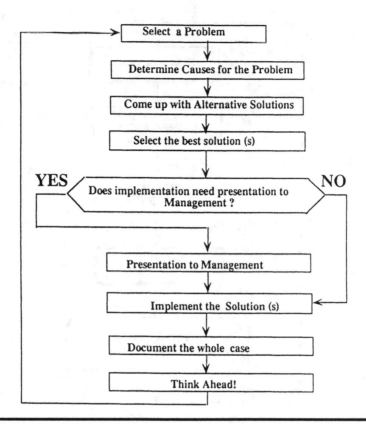

FIGURE 4.6   The PQT approach—the step-by-step process.

Further, they feel important when they take on a coaching role. They also appreciate the "people problems" much better. The residual effect of the PQT training is visible even after many years.

The PQT training primarily focuses on problem solving, although many facets of this training include supervision aspects such as planning, organizing, motivating, delegating, communicating, and controlling. By teaching the problem-solving approach (Figure 4.6), each employee becomes a problem solver rather than a problem creator.

By equipping employees with the tools and techniques to solve problems systematically, companies can prevent spending massive amounts of money on fixing things which did not have to become problems and situations which were not perceived as problems but caused more damage than anyone cares to admit.

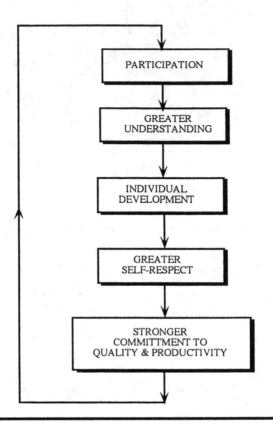

FIGURE 4.7   Synergistic effect of PQTs.

The synergistic effect of PQTs (Figure 4.7) is enormous, particularly on the people side. Often, this aspect is more difficult to deal with than technical matters.

The many benefits of PQTs (Figure 4.8) more than justify the relatively small amount of money invested in the training. I have been doing this training since 1981, beginning with the American Bankers Insurance Group, one of the most successful insurance firms in the country, headquartered in Miami. (We will talk more about this company in Chapter 5.) Of all the segments of the TPmgt process, the PQT training has had a more long-lasting, visible effect on people, profits, and products. After nearly 15 years, American Bankers Insurance Group still acknowledges the positive effects of the PQT training given to its employees in 1981, as does every company where I conducted this training.

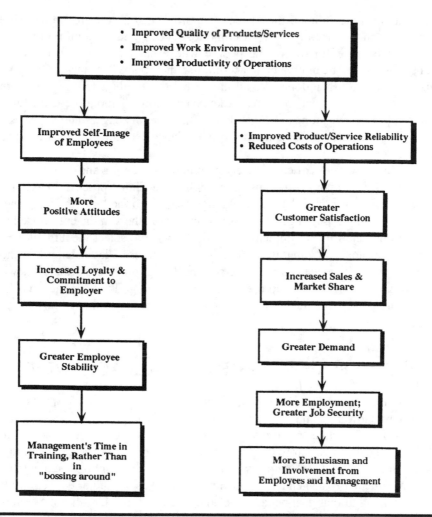

FIGURE 4.8 Benefits of PQTs.

4.9 STEP 7: IMPLEMENTATION OF ACTION PLANS

A major part of the TPmgt Team's effort is, of course, devoted to the implementation. Implementation becomes more systematic with detailed action plans, developed in Step 6. Needless to say, action plans are constantly revised as the tasks progress. If the action plans are pursued with regular feedback and communication of deviations, they become more realistic and are implemented effectively and efficiently. If not, people lose focus, and the action plans may be perceived as extra work. The people whose names appear on the action plans must indeed be motivated to accomplish their respective tasks. Of course, this is easier said than done. We all know that those things that get measured and/or rewarded get done, but those tasks that are noticed, monitored, and talked about in progress meetings also get done. Therefore, managers and supervisors should approach the implementation with a balance between appraisal/feedback and control.

The first few weeks of close supervision in implementing and monitoring the action plans are important, because this is when the TPmgt process "makes it or breaks it." The responsibility of the TPmgt Team is to facilitate the implementation. The team must not get into a situation where others in the enterprise look solely to the team for all implementation. It is wise to select the TPmgt Team members in such a way that they are in a position to provide leadership in their respective functional areas for all facets of the TPmgt process. Further, it is wise to have a backup for each representative on the TPmgt Team. If these backup people are good communicators and delegators, the implementation becomes easier.

4.10 STEP 8: MANAGEMENT GOALS ACHIEVED?

On a monthly, quarterly, six-month, and yearly basis, the TPmgt Team assesses the progress toward achieving each of the management goals set in Step 3. This follow-up is important to provide positive reinforcement to those who accomplish their goals on or before the target dates and to offer assistance, encouragement, and additional motivation when achievement falls short of expectation.

If a particular management goal is not achieved as expected, the action plan corresponding to that goal needs to be analyzed carefully. Usually one or more of the people assigned to the tasks will have had something to do with such an outcome. It could be that one or more of the tasks were not realistically identified and executed. Maybe the business environment internally or externally has changed so dramatically that certain tasks have become redundant. Whatever the reason, it is important for the TPmgt Team to do some brainstorming before deciding that the goal cannot be accomplished and must be dropped.

At least once a year, it is a good practice to ask: "Should we revise the mission statement?" If there is a need to revise it, the original process for developing a mission statement can be followed, as outlined in Step 1. If the nature of the business has changed significantly in terms of the market itself; political, economic, and social conditions; products; or any number of other factors, this should signal the need to revise the mission statement. The mission statement for Florida Power and Light Company, which won the prestigious Deming Prize for Quality, was not revised for almost 11 years.

4.11 STEP 9: TOTAL PRODUCTIVITY GAINSHARING

Total productivity gainsharing (TPG) is basically a gainsharing approach based on total productivity and comprehensive total productivity. More specifically, this step provides for a tangible, monetary incentive to achieve the maximum possible potential of TPmgt thinking. Many reasons can be offered for including TPG in TPmgt, but three are significant:

1. **Most new concepts fail because of a lack of sustainable motivation.** Intangible motivational techniques of positive reinforcement, like "one-minute praise" and "pats on the back," usually work, up to a point, but after the "Hawthorne Effect" wears off, the level of motivation drops. Intangible motivation is only a necessary condition, not a sufficient one, to sustain positive motivation. Monetary incentives must supplement non-financial motivation techniques.

2. **It is fair, just, and equitable to share prosperity with those responsible for it.** Gainsharing is a positive factor in making any new concept work. The absence of it could be due to greed. Unfortunately, all too often, we see top management getting richer and lower management and the workers getting poorer.

3. **The rate of new hiring can be reduced dramatically, saving millions of dollars in employee wages, salaries, and benefits.** If, in spite of good management practices, some abnormal business conditions are encountered, a company does not have to lay off employees, but rather can utilize, albeit partially, the existing loyal work force. Employees who have shared a "piece of the pie" through TPG will rise to the occasion and will even make sacrifices to keep the company afloat.

TPG works as follows:

1. For the past 12 months, determine the average rate of change of total productivity in the firm. If this rate is zero or negative, no bonus is offered. If the rate of change is positive, that is, if total productivity of the firm has improved at rate r, then decide on 50% of this increase (0.5r) as the TPG bonus rate. For example, if the total productivity of the firm has had an average growth rate of 10% in the last 12 months, then 50% of this is $0.50 \times 10\% = 5\%$ as the TPG bonus rate. The remaining 50% is shared with other stakeholders in the form of dividends, price discounts, etc.

2. Give each employee in the company an annual TPG bonus, based on the TPG bonus rate. The TPG bonus for an employee = (TPG bonus rate × annual salary without benefits). In this example, if an employee grossed $40,000, his or her annual TPG bonus would be 5% × 40,000 = $2,000. A simple, straightforward total-productivity-based bonus like this is easy to explain and to administer.

The big question is: Can TPmgt work without TPG? The answer is yes, but the company that tries to avoid TPG in the TPmgt process does not truly understand the core value of human welfare in this whole concept. A better question for companies to ask is: When is the right time to install the TPG system while going through the TPmgt process? The best time to introduce TPG may not be in the very first year of operating with the TPmgt philosophy. It is usually about 15 months after the first iteration of the TPmgt process until the results are truly felt. Therefore, the best time to plan and introduce TPG is in the second year of implementation.

4.12 STEP 10: NEW GOALS

Three fundamental approaches can be taken to set new management goals. The first is to set new goals only when all previous ones have been attained. Of course, this approach will work in an ideal situation when all the goals are accomplished on or before their target dates. The second approach is to set goals only annually. This sounds straightforward, but in reality, business conditions change, and it may be too late to set new goals if done only annually. It is obvious that a third approach may be the more practical one, namely, adding new management goals as business conditions change or on a quarterly basis, whichever happens first.

As in Step 3, the management goals should be developed only after the TPM and/or CTPM analysis is done. Recall that this analysis helps to identify only those goals that have a maximum impact on the mission and the vision of the organization.

4.13 IMPORTANT NOTE ON THE TPmgt IMPLEMENTATION

In Section 7.2, I elaborate and point out the importance of managing the "RTC factor," the phenomenon of resistance to change. As with any change, implementing the TPmgt process brings about change, but a positive one for the most part. It would be appropriate to recall that this systematic, step-by-step process for TPmgt is like a recipe. If the steps are short-circuited or done halfheartedly, the full impact of the concept will not be realized. Like a recipe that is perfected after cooking repeatedly, the TPmgt process has to be iterated two or three times before it becomes a natural rhythm. TPmgt is also like genuine leather—the more it is used, the softer it becomes. As an enterprise goes through all the steps in the implementation process, the application becomes easier to maneuver, and the rough edges are smoothed out.

As with any other concept, such as TQM or reengineering, top management must be patient and let the process take its full course, usually 12 to 18 months. Compared to TQM, this cycle is much shorter. However, if management provides only lip service and the entire responsibility for implementation is delegated to the TPmgt Team, results will not be what they should be—visible and verifiable improvements in customer responsiveness, employee morale, total productivity, quality, and profitability.

QUESTIONS TO PONDER

4.1 If your enterprise has a mission statement, analyze it carefully against the requisites of a good mission statement. What observations and recommendations would you make based on this analysis?

4.2 If you do not have a vision statement and/or mission statement, outline a plan to develop one, including a schedule, people to be involved, etc.

4.3 If you do have a mission statement, benchmark it against some of the best in your industry, as well as outside your industry.

4.4 Do a comparative analysis of mission statements of some of the well-known American and Japanese competitors.

4.5 After answering Question 4.4, determine if any correlations exist between the profoundness of the mission statement of an enterprise and its financial success.

4.6 What process is currently used in your organization to develop management goals? Examine the deficiencies, if any, in the manner of defining and developing these management goals. Develop a strategy for rectification.

4.7 If you have financial incentive(s) of some sort, document their basic emphases, their effectiveness to date, and areas of opportunity for improving their effectiveness further. To what extent are these financial incentive systems based on productivity of functional areas as opposed to total productivity of individual product lines or total productivity of the firm?

4.8 Examine systematically the challenges or obstacles faced by your enterprise in implementing a major management concept or a critical technology. List and analyze each of these obstacles with an unbiased, probing mind. As a result of this exercise, what should your company avoid in future implementations?

4.9 From your personal knowledge of your company/organization, assess what it would take to implement TPmgt successfully. Would you implement the Basic TPmgt or the Comprehensive TPmgt? Justify your selection. Prepare a brief proposal to your top management to implement the TPmgt version you have selected.

5

CASE STUDIES: SELECTED APPLICATIONS

The Total Productivity Management (TPmgt™) philosophy, concept, and/or methodology has been applied in more than 300 companies/organizations around the world since 1979. Only a few cases will be covered in this chapter, due to space limitations.

Many components or elements of the TPmgt concept—in particular the Customer Satisfaction Survey (CSS©), the General Organizational Analysis (GOA©), the Productivity Quality Team (PQT©) process, the Total Productivity Model (TPM©), mission statement, goals, and action plans—have been demonstrated to be applicable to various types of companies/organizations, including

- Airlines
- Auto dealerships
- Bakeries
- Banks
- Chemical manufacturing
- Communications company (telephone utility)
- Computer/peripherals manufacturing
- Construction
- Consulting
- Dance academy
- Deep-sea fishing

- Defense contractors
- Dry cleaning
- Electrical components manufacturing
- Electrical utilities
- Electronics manufacturing
- Electronics retail store
- Engineering/architectural firm
- Flower warehousing and distribution
- Gas station
- Government agencies
- Grocery store
- Healthcare
- Heat treatment facility

- Heavy equipment manufacturing
- Household
- Insurance
- Machine tool manufacturing
- Medical devices manufacturing
- Medical products manufacturing
- Mining
- Newsprint equipment manufacturing
- Printing
- Rental car agencies
- Restaurants/fast-food business
- Retail stores
- Schools

- Seafood distribution
- Shoe manufacturing
- Space systems
- Steel manufacturing
- Television/electronics manufacturing
- Tire manufacturing
- Tourism office
- Transportation
- University
- Welding equipment manufacturing

This representative sample covers nearly every possible industry in the economy. The 21 cases presented in this chapter can be grouped into three arbitrarily broad categories:

- Service (Cases 5.1 to 5.13)
- Manufacturing (Cases 5.14 to 5.19)
- Other (Cases 5.20 and 5.21)

The reader should get a fairly good cross-section of insights on TPmgt by going through these 21 cases.

5.1 BANKING

Background—This study deals with how the TPM is applied to a medium-sized bank with approximately 700 employees in Latin America. The analysis was performed for a five-year time period from 1987 to 1991. The total productivity of the firm and the individual partial productivities for each input factor were computed to give a thorough insight into the financial status and health of the corporation. Having been established for nearly 110 years, the company has enjoyed a long-standing tradition of offering quality financial services to its clients, thus making the TPM analysis an effective measure for furthering the company's image, as well as helping to increase the company's profitability and competitiveness in the market.

Implementation—In performing the TPM analysis, the firm itself was considered as the operational unit under observation. Consequently, the partial productivity indices measure the individual inputs in relation to the entire organization.

The input factors considered consisted of human, fixed capital, working capital, and other expense. Material input was not analyzed due to its significant level in the total input.

Results—Results are shown in Figures 5.1 and 5.2 and Table 5.1.

Analysis—The TPM four-level analysis yielded some very interesting and revealing observations about the productivity levels of the company. A description of the findings pertaining to each level of analysis is summarized below.

Level 1—This first level of observation dealt with comparing the total productivity of the firm to its break-even point over the five-year time span (Figure 5.1). A fairly strong upward projection for the total productivity of the firm occurred from 1987 until 1990, in spite of a dangerous downward slope in 1989, during which it nearly fell below the break-even point. However, in 1990, a sharp downward trend developed, leading into the final time period, although the total productivity of the firm still managed to remain above the break-even point. The break-even point showed a similar trend, rising linearly until 1990 and then beginning its decline at a slope parallel to the total productivity of the firm.

Level 2—Since the only operational unit was the firm itself, the results for Level 2 are the same as Level 1, as Level 2 analysis is concerned with charting the operational units against their respective break-even points. We then proceeded to Level 3 for further investigation.

Level 3—First, the other expenses input was analyzed, noting that over the five-year span it comprised, on average, 66% of the total input, which made it a major consideration for further inquiry. Although there were sporadic increases in this input's productivity, the gains were rather meager, considering the great percentage this input consumed, and only averaged a 10% increase over the time period.

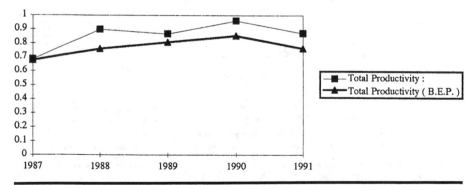

FIGURE 5.1 Total productivity versus break-even point of the bank.

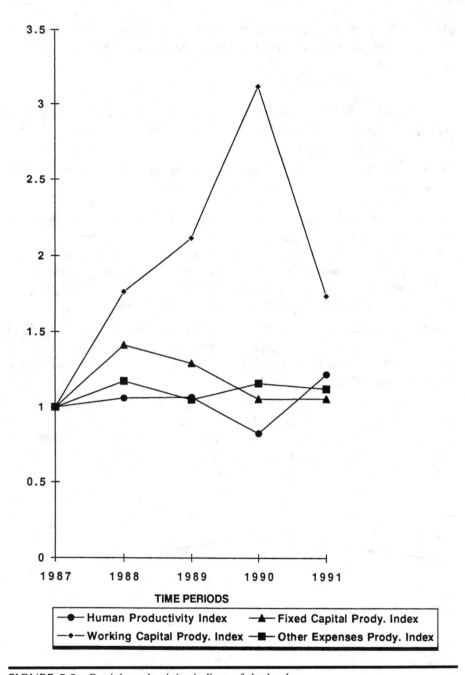

FIGURE 5.2   Partial productivity indices of the bank.

TABLE 5.1   Percentage Changes in Total Productivity of the Bank
and Its Inputs

	% (base = 1987)			
	1988	*1989*	*1990*	*1991*
Total productivity	31.20	26.5	40.4	27.2
Human productivity	6.0	6.7	−17.4	21.8
Fixed capital productivity	41.2	29.1	5.5	5.6
Working capital productivity	76.5	111.9	212.2	73.8
Other expense productivity	17.1	5.0	15.8	12.1

However, as of 1991, there was a 12.1% improvement, which shows possible growth and better management of this resource. Since other expenses did account for nearly two-thirds of the total input resources, this leveling off in the other expense productivity needed to be reversed quickly, so as to enhance the productivity and profitability of the firm as soon as possible.

The next input considered was human input, traditionally an overused and narrow-minded measure of productivity in the firm (i.e., labor productivity measures). Our observations showed that human input comprised roughly 8% of the total input resources, thereby not making it a very serious consideration quantitatively but nonetheless important because of the many intangible factors that are associated with human effort (job satisfaction, employee morale, etc.). We observed slight increases in human productivity from the base period 1987 until 1989. In 1990, the company experienced a nearly 17% drop in productivity associated with this input, only to bounce back up in 1991 by approximately 22%. These rapid fluctuations in productivity levels, and the effect that they inherently have on the entire company, indicated the need for further investigation and the application of possible improvement techniques.

The fixed capital input yielded results calling for some actions to be taken. From 1987 to 1989, this bank showed strong, steady increases in its fixed capital productivity, peaking at a 41% improvement in 1988. Yet, in the following periods, the company showed a serious downward slide in productivity values regarding this input. Productivity values hovered around the 1.0 vicinity, with meager 5% improvements with respect to the base period in 1990 and 1991. How is it that just two years later, productivity levels dropped off so dramatically that improvement was sliced by nearly 35% in this short period of time? This question caused us to investigate this input in a more in-depth fashion, so that the root cause of the problem could be addressed and corrected. Although this input comprised only about 3% of the entire inputs, the fact that such drastic reductions in productivity occurred warrants some further investigation.

The final input considered was working capital, which appeared to be in the best shape out of all the inputs in terms of productivity growth. It was also the second largest input resource used, accounting for nearly 23% of the total inputs. Working capital productivity increased dramatically until 1990, experiencing a 212% increase during this time. However, from 1990 to 1991, this marked improvement was slashed to 74%, signaling a tremendous drop-off in the manner in which working capital was handled and used during this time period. In spite of this recent turn of events, the company was still very productive in managing this particular resource.

In observing and analyzing each of the inputs, our attention was drawn primarily to the fixed capital, citing the meager 5% increases in productivity over the last two periods as evidence for the implementation of improvement methods. Also, since this input was so small (3%), a slight tweaking or adjustment might have been enough to improve profitability, with investment of little effort or time spent. Similarly, the other expenses input merited consideration for further in-depth analysis because of the large percentage it encompassed in the entire input resource picture. Using highly sophisticated industrial engineering techniques, the following recommendations were made as part of the Level 4 analysis. Based upon these recommendations, major improvements took place, resulting in greater and more long-lasting profits for the firm.

Level 4—

1. The interest expense must be analyzed in detail and goals set up to reduce the rate of growth in this expense.
2. The "other" category under other expenses must also be broken down for further analysis and rationalization. All avoidable expenses must indeed be avoided.
3. Accounts receivable should be cut down by devising means to reduce the collectible period, such as offering incentives for early payment, etc. All unnecessary inventories of stationery and supplies could be reduced through prudence.
4. Investments in computers and information systems must be evaluated carefully in terms of their long-term impact on the total productivity of the company.
5. Sufficient training and continuing education must be provided to all employees at all levels.
6. The top executives should set a personal example of leadership in managing all types of expenses, but they must also seek aggressive means to increase revenues with existing human resources.

7. Total-productivity-based gainsharing should be implemented to reward the company's employees and management.
8. Additional management goals should be added to the ones recently developed, based on the CSS, GOA, and this TPM analysis.

Benefits—This analysis rewarded the company with a long-term outlook on the future of the firm and established ideas for improving the company's profitability. Also, flaws were uncovered in the mismanagement of input resources, which had a tremendous effect on the company's financial condition.

Summary—In performing the TPM analysis on this medium-sized bank in Latin America, we were able to critically analyze some of the problems and difficulties the organization was encountering and thereby provide feasible, pragmatic recommendations and solutions. Several of these suggestions were implemented and have translated into greater profitability for the firm over the past four years. Clearly, this case enhances the viability of TPmgt and demonstrates the flexibility it offers in improving productivity and profit levels within any organization, regardless of sector.

Questions to Ponder—

5.1.1 Why should a TPM analysis be performed, in spite of the fact that the company's productivity levels are above their respective break-even points?

5.1.2 What suggestions might be made to management to reduce the high percentage of the other expenses input?

5.1.3 Discuss some of the possible reasons or causes for the declines in productivity growth with respect to working capital and fixed capital inputs.

5.1.4 Perform a comparative study using five to ten other banks, and evaluate the respective productivity levels using the Level 1 to 4 TPM analysis. Discuss your results and observations.

5.2 CONSULTING

Background—In this case,[1] a total-productivity-based measurement system was applied in an engineering consulting firm at the subregional operating level. The duration selected was an approximately 3.5-year period prior to the acquisition of a complementary engineering service firm. This acquisition resulted in a major reorganization and readjustment of the operation's employees, worker classifications, and expenses. The idea was that productivity measurements resulting from this study could further provide a basis for strategy development to improve the total productivity of the aggregate firm.

The employees of this firm were primarily knowledge workers—engineers and other technical professionals.

Application—The Sumanth-Nag Model©[2] was applied to evaluate white-collar/knowledge worker productivity, using information concerning human input, adjusted billings, and staff size, to determine the total productivity for the firm at the subregional level. These data were provided for each accounting period for fiscal years 1986 to 1989.

For knowledge work, the costs associated with human input are generally assumed to far exceed the non-labor input costs such as materials, capital, energy, and other expense costs. Human input used in this evaluation represented actual salaries expended during each fiscal period.

Information on capital input (fixed and working), material, energy, and other expense inputs was not routinely recorded at the subregional level. Lacking the operational data at this level, a composite value for material, capital (fixed and working), energy, and other expense costs was estimated at 25% of the human input expended each period. This was considered a reasonable firm-wide estimate.

Detailed information on the tangible outputs, such as number of reports produced per period, number of drawings, or other similar measurable outputs, was not recorded at any corporate level within the firm. However, one measure of output available for each period on a subregional basis was adjusted income. This available, composite, subregional value represents actual labor hours compensated but not billed at the subregional level. It was therefore considered a reasonable and measurable indicator of the firm's output at the subregional level.

Results—The results of the total productivity measurement study indicated a positive increasing trend in total productivity over the period of evaluation. The total productivity index also indicated a general increasing trend over time when compared to respective base periods. Base periods coincided with changes in the personnel roster and personnel classifications mix. These results were supported by reported increases in profitability over this same time period.

Recommendations to Management—While results of the model were positive and generally agreed with the subregional trends in profits, these trends were general and limited by the available data and aforementioned assumptions. The data needed further refinement in terms of economic labor adjustment indices, detailed data for non-labor input factors, personnel roster changes, and associated cost and classification impacts. These factors were expected to modify the apparent magnitude of the observed trends, and a positive increasing total productivity was expected to result.

The model provided a measure of total productivity not available to or utilized by the firm up to this point in time. This model did, however, require accurate data and reasonable assumptions in order to provide meaningful results for productivity evaluation, planning, and improvement. Some tangible components of the output measure needed further evaluation and consideration. Output, in this application, reflected a high intangible component when compared to typical blue-collar output.

Questions to Ponder—

5.2.1 What are some of the challenges in measuring total productivity in an engineering consulting firm?

5.2.2 What factors would be primarily responsible for success in applying the TPmgt philosophy to an engineering consulting firm?

5.2.3 Answer Question 5.2.2 in the context of any type of consulting firm.

5.2.4 Study three or four consulting firms and see what you can learn in terms of the presence of the basic elements of the TPmgt concept.

5.3 CONSTRUCTION

Background—This study applied the TPM in a unique way to measure productivity during the structural phase of the construction of a tower comprised of a 33-story high-rise building, a seven-level parking garage, and an adjoining plaza. The time period covered in this study, the months of June, July, and August 1985, was chosen based on the fact that both the parking garage and the high-rise building were under construction during these months. This choice was important to maintain consistency in the type of activities going on during the periods of analysis.

Implementation—The study developed measurements and analysis of the following:

1. Total productivity
2. Human productivity
3. Material productivity
4. Capital productivity
5. Energy productivity
6. Subcontractor productivity
7. Other expense productivity

The only major deviation in applying the TPM was in defining the subcontractor input as a separate input, because it was a major one in terms of dollar expense.

In the construction industry, there are various types of construction, depending upon the nature of the project; therefore, methods and emphases vary. For instance, in a heavy construction project such as the building of a highway, a large fixed capital input is necessary because of the use of costly earth-moving equipment. On the other hand, a nuclear power plant requires extensive planning and high levels of quality control. For a building construction project such as the case in point, emphasis is placed on materials and labor. The need for proper planning is a major factor in combining these two large inputs.

The main building, called the "tower," had approximately 750,000 square feet of rented space, of which 10,000 square feet was initially designated as retail service space and the remainder as office space. For convenience and safety, 15 high-speed elevators and 2 service elevators were included. An adjacent seven-level parking garage was built to accommodate 1,300 cars.

The entire cost of the tower was estimated at $101 million. This cost included the initial feasibility and planning expenses, land purchase price, design costs, developer's costs (specialized consultants during the construction phase, including a threshold inspector), and the actual construction cost.

In this productivity measurement project, we were concerned with the general contractor's construction cost (the general contractor was responsible for the construction of the tower and the garage). To simplify the construction phase, it was separated into two parts:

1. Structural
2. Finishes

The structural part consisted of all concrete, reinforcement and structural steel. This included the foundation, floors, columns, etc. The "finishes" part covered all architectural work which makes the structure esthetically pleasing and functional. Chronologically, the structural phase is first, followed by the finishes phase. Of course, realistically, there is an overlap between these two phases.

In this particular case study, only the structural phase was analyzed. This restriction was necessary to use the pertinent available data. In addition, an operational unit was readily identified, and objectivity was easier with data availability for several monthly periods for the structural phase.

Results—Results are shown in Table 5.2 and Figures 5.3 and 5.4.

Analysis—The trend analysis part of the TPM was, by far, the most important, because it was at this point that the productivity figures were interpreted so that appropriate management action plans could be initiated.

The management summary indicated that the partial productivities of human, material, energy, and other expenses showed *significant* downward trends, but the capital and subcontractor partial productivities showed a slightly decreasing upward trend. While total productivity showed an increasing trend, four partial

TABLE 5.2 Total and Partial Productivity Indices of the Construction Firm

	June	*July*	*August*
Total productivity at break-even	0.98	0.97	0.96
Total productivity	1.07	1.74	2.00
Total productivity index	1.00	1.63	1.87
Human input productivity	29.60	48.62	44.43
Human input productivity index	1.00	1.64	1.50
Material input productivity	4.76	8.62	6.95
Material input productivity index	1.00	1.81	1.46
Capital input productivity	46.06	51.06	52.76
Capital input productivity index	1.00	1.11	1.14
Energy input productivity	178.39	272.83	177.95
Energy input productivity index	1.00	1.53	1.00
Subcontractor input productivity	1.51	2.42	3.25
Subcontractor input productivity index	1.00	1.60	2.15
Other expense input productivity	373.90	837.13	665.64
Other expense input productivity index	1.00	2.24	1.78

productivities decreased to differing degrees and two increased from July to August.

The four input categories—human, material, energy, and other expense—accounted for 25 to 35% of the total input, depending upon the time period. However, these were the categories that indicated significant declines in productivity, which prodded management to investigate them further.

Human Productivity—

- Suggested changes in the scope of work (changing from the mild-steel design to a post-tension design) offered to the owner of the tower resulted in considerable savings. As a result of these changes, the general contractor inherited additional work activities not formerly identified in the subcontractors' scope of work.
- The labor force was carried over from the previous periods (June and July) to avoid layoffs, despite the fact that the actual work required a lower level of operation by the general contractor.

Material Productivity—

- The purchase of materials increased for reasons stated in the first item above. Most of the materials, as well as human input, were consumed in July, due to the floor level to which the construction had progressed.

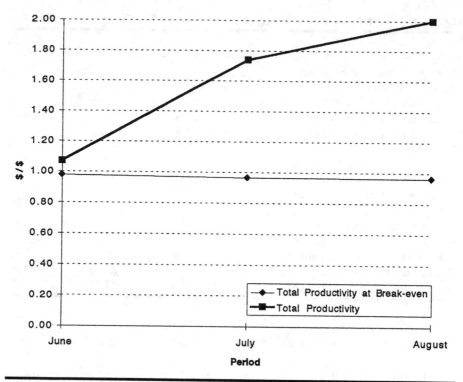

FIGURE 5.3 Total productivity versus break-even point of total productivity for the construction firm.

Energy Productivity —

- The energy cost was reallocated internally, but since energy only represents 1% of the total input, its overall impact on total productivity was insignificant.

Note—Toward the later phase of the project, energy was a more significant cost item, because of the need to protect the architectural finishes that run the air-conditioning units in order to prevent buildup of mildew.

Other Expenses Productivity —

- Travel expenses were incurred in the month of June by various outside consultants throughout the United States.
- Capital productivity showed a positive trend in both periods but showed a slowdown in productivity gains in August. This was due to the added expenses incurred (for example, the temporary hoist, which was mandatory as the higher floor levels were constructed).

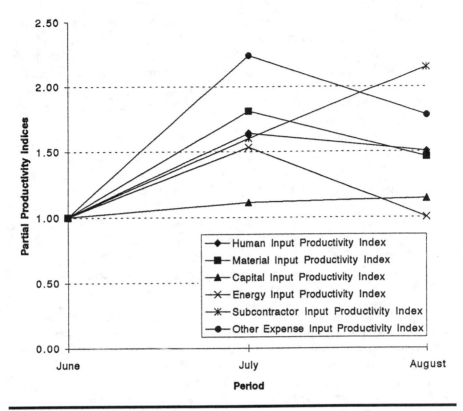

FIGURE 5.4 The partial productivity profiles for the construction firm.

- The subcontractor input represented the most significant input cost (i.e., 60 to 70%), and it also showed a slowdown in productivity gains in August; this was due to the completion of the major concrete garage slab pours.

Benefits—Implementation of this study resulted in a strategy to save significant dollars, by scheduling some of the construction workers so as to minimize idle time. The application of the TPM to the Lincoln Tower construction project produced many benefits, the most important of which were the following:

1. It was shown that the TPM was a viable means of tracking productivity for a building construction project, and valuable productivity information was generated.
2. The actual application of the TPM showed that some modifications were necessary due to the nature of the building construction industry. One modification was emphasis on the partial productivity of other expense (subcontractor) productivity due to the large amount of subcontracted

work. It is important to note that in these subcontract costs, stored material expense and large mobilization costs were included in the first monthly payments. This could have distorted the productivity data. Also, all the available data had to be readily reallocated into the six partial productivity measures. This task would have been very time consuming if done manually, but with the help of the automated spread sheet, the task was simplified considerably.

3. The graphical analysis achieved a concise yet accurate representation of the total and partial productivity values and their indices. Being able to recognize productivity trends at a glance, without having to review a lengthy report, was a definite advantage to the management team.

4. An analysis of the trends in order to recognize possible problem areas was probably the most important and beneficial aspect of this study. The TPM analysis showed a downward trend in both labor and material productivities. Having identified the problem areas, management was able to focus on these areas to make corrections, thereby saving a considerable amount of money.

Summary—This case reinforces the fact that the TPM is flexible enough to be applied to any business situation. For example, the subcontractor input was added to the model for a practical reason—subcontractors do not disclose their total expenses to general contractors, unless a subcontractor is a subsidiary of a general contractor. This study also demonstrated the feasibility of applying the TPM to redesign work schedules for optimum utilization of the work force and hence savings for the company.

Questions to Ponder—

5.3.1   Losses in human and material productivity resulted, in part, from changes in design. Explain how this happened and how it might be accounted for in the TPM.

5.3.2   Each productivity loss or slowdown is well explained. Which of them might have been corrected by management and might have had a significant impact on the output?

5.3.3   Does the second reason identified in the section on human productivity show an inability to adjust to fluctuations in demand, resulting in reduced productivity, or does it show company loyalty to employees who could increase productivity in the future? Explain your stance.

5.3.4   Discuss the need for including the subcontractor as an individual input.

5.3.5   What are the reasons for measuring output as square footage? Are there any other alternative ways to represent the output in a construction project of this type?

5.3.6 Describe the "structural" and "finishing" phases of building construction. Which one of these do you think has a greater effect on the total productivity of the firm?

5.3.7 How does the break-even analysis of total productivity help the general contractor to be profitable?

5.3.8 What are some of the unique factors in the construction business that become barriers to total productivity improvement? Study two or three successful construction companies and identify a list of characteristics that contribute to their success. Discuss how TPmgt can help to enhance their success.

5.4 DRY CLEANING

Background—After considering various options, one of my graduate students acquired a dry-cleaning company in 1985 (see Section 8.7 for further details on this case study). After the purchase of the dry-cleaning business, a thorough market research study followed to ascertain the demographics and customer preferences. As a result, the company was named Le Cleniere, Inc. to carve out a niche—the dry cleaning of silk.

The business was operated by five individuals (excluding the president). Each had a specialized function in the company. A brief description of the duties and responsibilities of each of these individuals is given below:

President
- All budgeting, advertising, and personnel
- Directly involved in purchasing (equipment, supplies, etc.)
- All customer-related activities

Manager
- Supervise all work distribution
- Assume all the responsibilities of the president in his absence
- Inventory control

Clerks (2)
- Ticketing
- Flow of garments from customers to the dry-cleaning facilities and vice versa
- Collect fee for service
- Sort and distribute work orders

Presser (1)
- Garment inspection
- Press clothing

Spotter (1)
- Garment inspection
- Operate dry-cleaning machines

Implementation—The TPM was applied to the company at the product level as well as the firm level. There were three products:

- Operational Unit 1—Shirts
- Operational Unit 2—Suits
- Operational Unit 3—Dresses

The concern from an operational standpoint was to maintain a high production level at the lowest cost and provide the best customer satisfaction possible, in order to realize the maximum possible profits. The TPM offered a unique mechanism to monitor resource utilization by pinpointing the areas needing action. It was applied from April 1985 to December 1986.

Results—The total and partial productivity profiles were generated for the firm as a whole, as well as for each of the three operational units. These results were tabulated and also depicted in graphical form.

Analysis—From the graphical depiction of the results, it was observed that the total productivity trends were very similar for all the operational units because their inputs had to be allocated according to their contribution to sales. Thus, the proportion of input and output remained almost identical, which made the total productivity trends identical.

All three operational units showed an abnormal inflection in the total productivity measure during the initial period. The main reason for this was that a small change in the input–output categories during the start-up phase of production represents a big change in the total productivity measure but is not really related to real increased utilization of resources. Hence, this change was viewed as abnormal and inconsequential, particularly because the business was not in operation for three months prior to the acquisition.

Due to seasonality factors in the cleaning business, sales were typically low in the summer months and more acute in July and August. This contributed greatly to the big fluctuations in the parameters.

The partial productivity profiles for each of the operational units pinpointed the areas that required extra attention from month to month and explained the reasons for lower or higher productivity. Finding out what caused a decline or an increase in productivity helped the company to minimize losses and boost profits on a consistent basis.

Benefits—Implementation of the TPM resulted in such rapid and consistent benefits that the value of the business increased by a significant factor—so much so that a lucrative offer to sell the business resulted in a substantial ownership change. Because of the overwhelmingly positive profit experience with the business and the goodwill created, the company's trade name—Le Cleniere—was not sold, with the intention of eventually starting a chain of dry-cleaning stores.

This case was the first time the TPM was applied in both selecting and running a business profitably. In today's competitive environment, this approach offers a better alternative to acquiring and managing enterprises than merely financial ratios and partial productivity measures.

Summary—The TPM approach was applied to the acquisition of a dry-cleaning company from among three alternatives. After the acquisition, the TPM was consistently applied, with much success, for each of the three operational units. The net worth of the company increased substantially in just under two years. This case demonstrates that the TPM is a viable tool not only in selecting a business for acquisition, but also in operating a small business profitably on a daily basis.

Questions to Ponder—

5.4.1 What are two most significant features of this case study with respect to application of the TPM?

5.4.2 Do an in-depth study of two recent acquisitions—one a success and one a failure—in terms of sustained profitability. Analyze the reasons for the success and the failure. Would the TPM approach have benefited both of these acquisitions? If yes, why? If not, why not?

5.4.3 Conduct a benchmarking study of dry-cleaning companies (nationally and/or internationally). List and discuss some of the major findings of your study.

5.4.4 Draw up an action plan to implement some of the major findings/recommendations from Question 5.4.3.

5.5 EDUCATION

Background—Education is the backbone of a country. "A good system of education is bound to its community, by unique ties of pride and service. It is based squarely on the wants and needs of the community it serves and is operated for social reasons and social gains. It grows and develops for the sake of the community, rather than for any inner purpose of its own. It can be measured by the quantity and extent of its achievement in these social terms.

Since the school is a complex organization, efforts to characterize schools by use of quantitative data are never complete. The factors selected for inclusion in this study are among those considered to be most indicative of the total school environment and of great concern to the educational community."[3]

Why productivity management in an educational environment?—"Many people define competitiveness in terms of satisfactory growth in the standard of living. Competitive advantage once focused on the availability of raw materials, labor, transportation, and sources of capital. Then, with the explosion of scientific knowledge and its application to the benefit of mankind, advanced technology became a new dimension of competitive advantage. But the conditions in the world today are rapidly changing. In today's global economy, globalization of production erased most of the traditional bases of industrial competitive advantage. The increasingly rapid globalization of technology is also nullifying technology's competitive edge of one country over another. Competitive advantage will increasingly depend on the human talent and skill to manage technology and technological enterprises."[4]

Education plays a major role in the competitive advantage of not only a company, but the entire nation. A 1990 survey of competitiveness in the United States found that 70% of those surveyed felt that improving general education was the way to improve the nation's competitiveness. Even more compelling is that three of the top four criteria for improving competitiveness all dealt with improving some educational factor.[5]

The Dade County school system is one of the largest public school systems in the country, with a very progressive outlook. Many innovations take place in this school system which has adopted Florida's educational goals, including Blueprint 2000.

During the 1992–93 school year, each school in Dade County developed a School Improvement Plan (SIP) to be implemented during the 1993–94 school year. Each school's plan reflected priorities for improvement which were cooperatively identified by the principal, parents, teachers, students, and representatives from the community served by the school. This important effort to help all students perform at their very best is called Blueprint 2000. It is Florida's system for school improvement and education accountability.[5]

According to Blueprint 2000, there are seven goals which all school districts in Florida are striving to reach;

Goal 1	Readiness to start school	Communities and schools collaborate to prepare children and families for children's success in school.
Goal 2	Graduation rate and readiness for post-secondary education and employment	Students graduate and are prepared to enter the work force and post-secondary institutions.

Goal 3	Student performance	Students successfully compete at the highest levels nationally and internationally and are prepared to make well-reasoned, thoughtful, and healthy lifelong decisions.
Goal 4	Learning environment	School boards provide a learning environment conducive to teaching and learning.
Goal 5	School safety and environment	Communities provide an environment that is drug free and protects students' health, safety, and civil rights.
Goal 6	Teachers and staff	The schools, districts, and state ensure professional teachers and staff.
Goal 7	Adult literacy	Adult Floridians are literate, have the knowledge and skills needed to compete in a global economy, and exercise the rights and responsibilities of citizenship.

Relevance of the TPmgt Principles to an Educational Institution—To better attain these goals, Juan Albelo, a teacher at ABC Senior High School (fictitious name for an actual school in Dade County), who also happened to take the author's 15-week productivity course in 1995, felt enthusiastic about applying the 12 principles of TPmgt at this high school.

Application—What follows is a discussion of the relevance of the TPmgt principles to ABC Senior High. The tone of discussion indicates how a principle is already being applied or how it can be applied. (All the principles [in italic type] are discussed in detail in Chapter 9.)

Customer Orientation Principle[6]—The global marketing subprinciple under this main principles says:

> *Design and manufacture products for global markets.*

Goal 3 in Blueprint 2000 states that Florida students need to successfully compete at the highest levels nationally and internationally. ABC Senior High's curriculum is specifically structured so that the graduating student is able to compete in the global arena. This school practices the leading competitor subprinciple:

> *Be the leading competitor for as many product/services as possible.*

If we take the classes themselves to be the service in question, then this high school is a leading-edge organization. It has classes that are not offered anywhere else and also has pilot programs that are not offered in other schools.

As part of global marketing, this school can practice the international outlook principle, which says:

> *Keep an international perspective in management activities related to planning, research and development, marketing, operations/production, and technology transfer.*

The way this principle was proposed to be implemented in a school setting is for someone to keep track of the educational advancements in other countries and then try to implement them.

People Orientation Principle—This principle centers around developing harmony, which is a subprinciple:

> *Seek harmony in human relations at all levels of management, from the top executive to the production/operations-level employee.*

This simply means setting goals and gaining commitment to these goals from the staff, students, and administration. At ABC Senior High, everyone strives to accomplish all the goals together. But there are some instances, especially involving students and teachers, where the goals are ignored, and the harmony does not exist. For example, the teachers union is consistently at odds with the administration. This causes friction between both parties, and a communication dilemma develops.

Learning Curve Principle—

> *Wherever possible, plan productivity levels and product costs on a learning curve.*

If a goal is set and a teacher pressures the student for immediate results, the student will expedite the process without allowing for the proper time to learn and understand the goal. This, in turn, will jeopardize long-term productivity. At ABC Senior High, teachers are supposed to set goals for their classes at the outset of the semester. Each student is supposed to attain these goals at his or her own speed. Even though this is dictated by the school, and special students (i.e., advanced, learning disabled, handicapped, etc.) are placed in classes with other students like them, many teachers still do not allow for the learning curve of individual students. To make their jobs easier, most teachers go at a set pace. This set pace of teaching jeopardizes the advanced students in the class by slowing them down. By the same token, it also jeopardizes the slower students by "losing" them altogether. This is definitely an area in need of improvement at ABC Senior High.

Emulation Principle—

Take the best of at least three competitors' technologies in product design, development, and production.

Although not yet implemented, two ideas borrowed from the Japanese and the Europeans are in the works. First, the idea of year-round school at ABC Senior High is being discussed. This idea comes directly from the Japanese educational system. The second idea is a dual-track school system—one for those students who want to go on to college and one for those students who plan to work after graduation. This idea is taken from the German school system. A student who chooses to go to college follows a college-prep curriculum. A student who chooses the work experience track must pass a fairly difficult entrance exam. Both of these ideas are being tested to see if they should be implemented at the school.

Miniaturization Principle—

Attempt miniaturization whenever possible by using microprocessor-based technology in products and processes.

At ABC Senior High, microprocessor-based technology is used throughout the school. The school has all records, data, and relevant statistics for both students and staff on a computer. This facilitates the process of printing report cards, obtaining a student's class schedule, scheduling classes, researching a student's school history, running the payroll for the staff, and many other functions that were previously done by hand. Also, microprocessors are used in the classroom. Computer education is a must for all graduating seniors. Even the school's alarm system is computerized. One major advantage of computers has been in the grading of tests. With this ability, teachers can spend more time teaching and planning instead of grading papers. More material can now be covered in class. It basically has freed up the teachers to do more things with the students.

Cooperative Research Principle—

Work closely with universities and generic research establishments to bring in ideas for productivity improvement.

This principle is already in place at ABC Senior High. The school works closely with Florida International University (FIU) by allowing the university to set up curricula, by establishing dual high school/university enrollments for ABC's students, and by addressing the needs of the university itself. In the future, an engineering program that will work hand in hand with the School of Engineering at FIU will be established at ABC Senior High. Other programs of this nature will soon follow. In return, FIU sends a great number of its student teachers to this high school for their internships.

Product Mix Planning Principle—

> *Develop a product mix that consistently shows the largest gains in total productivity and market share.*

In the manufacturing world, this basically means not putting all your eggs in one basket. But in an educational setting, if you treat the students as products, then you need a diversity of students to improve productivity. Although this high school is predominantly Hispanic, a good portion of the student population is made up of whites, blacks, Asians, Indians, and others. This serves two purposes: it exposes students to other people and customs, and it allows students to better understand what a global economy entails through their interactions with other students.

Another view of product mix in the educational environment is to consider the classes themselves as the product. Then, a diversity in classes will give you a good product mix.

Secrecy Principle—

> *Productivity improvement strategies that are novel when compared to the competitors must be kept secret.*

This principle is not needed in the educational environment—at least at the school level. The last thing needed is to keep a teaching method or an educational advancement a secret. (On the other hand, in higher educational institutions such as universities, many research labs practice this principle.)

Mutual Benefit Principle—A subprinciple under this principle is productivity gainsharing:

> *Always share the gains in productivity improvements with everyone directly or indirectly responsible for them, particularly employees and customers.*

One of ABC Senior High's best attributes is its attendance policy. The school has shared its technique with the district, and shortly it will be policy for all Dade County public schools. Also, this school rewards its students and staff for perfect attendance as a way of distributing or sharing the gains the school has experienced.

Consistency Principle—

> *Productivity improvement must be an ongoing day-to-day process and not a one-time program or project.*

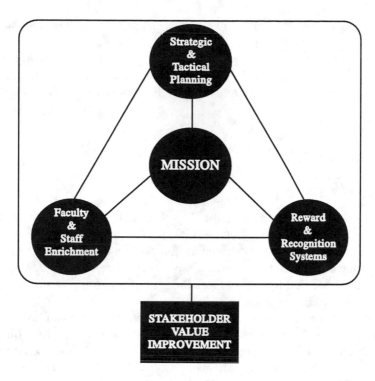

FIGURE 5.5   Conceptual framework for TPmgt in an educational institution.

Although ABC Senior High is still too young to be able to analyze the impact of productivity at the school, it is reasonable to believe that it will continue the productivity process, because it is a model school of the future. The teachers plan to implement the above principles as an ongoing process.

Closing Suggestion—Perhaps every school and university might want to consider a TPmgt process along the lines of the conceptual idea proposed in Figure 5.5.

Questions to Ponder—

5.5.1   Which of these principles (read Chapter 9 also) are being applied in your enterprise and to what extent?

5.5.2 Compare the application of these principles in a middle school, a primary school, and a preschool.

5.5.3 How can these and other principles in Chapter 9 be applied to a university? Identify specific departments and colleges where the principles can help improve the comprehensive total productivity of the unit and the university.

5.6 HEALTHCARE

Case Study #1

Background—Healthcare costs in the United States have been on the rise for the last decade and have reached intolerable levels. The government's Medicare system has been criticized because hospitals and doctors function without effective measures for cost justification and efficiency. As a result, the U.S. Congress introduced the Medical Reimbursement Program (Diagnostic Related Groupings or DRGs) to control healthcare costs.

For hospitals to cut costs, they must first identify where and how they are incurring costs. Effective cost containment should be accounted for through a reliable productivity measurement method. Such a method should keep track of all input factors, but particularly human productivity, since 60 to 70% of costs in the healthcare industry are personnel related.

This case study involved the application of the TPM to a major children's cardiac hospital in Florida. The TPM, as we know, takes into consideration all the input factors and their partial productivities so as to allow the evaluation of utilization of individual resources, as well as the combined effect of partial productivities.

Implementation—There are at least six measurements of work performance of an organizational system, of which productivity is one. Other indicators are effectiveness, efficiency, profitability, quality, and quality of work life. The methodology used to measure and evaluate productivity is not in itself sufficient to guarantee successful results in cost containment, unless it is integrated into a strategically planned productivity management process that is continuously maintained and developed. Under this process, the responsibility for productivity improvements is delegated to each individual manager, supervisor, and employee. This makes the productivity management process an interdisciplinary, interfunctional management activity. This is particularly true of the healthcare industry, wherein service to a client is rendered through a series of interventions by several highly skilled professionals.

Productivity management is a continuous process with a built-in information feedback mechanism; it is not a one-time project. In the healthcare industry, the objective of such a process is to reduce the cost of providing healthcare services without compromising the quality of patient care and the economic viability of the hospital in question. The TPM provides us with an effective means to carry out the TPmgt process.

Traditionally, industry has relied on partial productivity measures to evaluate work performance and resource utilization using the most commonly known labor productivity ratio. In contrast, the TPM takes into consideration all input factors so as to allow the evaluation of individual resource utilization, as well as the combined effect of the partial productivities, to come up with the total productivity value for the hospital. Because of the unavailability of complete data, the TPM was applied to the extent that the data allowed.

The DRGs were chosen as operational units (units of service) because they are the entities upon which reimbursement for services rendered is based. Also, by doing so, the productivity management process remains compatible with what may be an alternative means to healthcare reimbursement in the future.

Results—Results are shown in Tables 5.3 and 5.4 and Figures 5.6 to 5.8.

Analysis—Total productivity for the hospital and partial productivities for the nursing input factor, along with the respective indices for Medicare patients, were computed. The results obtained were evidence of the effectiveness of the TPM in analyzing the total productivity of the hospital as a whole, total productivities for each operational unit, and the corresponding partial productivities for various input factors.

Benefits—Information from the TPM analysis, when *fully* applied, is invaluable to physicians, nurse executives, and hospital administrators. It permits better

TABLE 5.3   Percent Change in Total Productivity for Each DRG

DRG	May–Jun	Jun–Jul	Jul–Aug	Aug–Sep	Sep–Oct
182	105	−81	105	16	8
183	−76	133	−55	3	136
200			98	49	4
205			60	−72	244
207		32	60	−42	−55
294	−10	145	−55	30	
395	176	−16	1	−64	−28
397	−67	−30	43		
403	−77			−62	384
462	−22	−26	−7	47	12

TABLE 5.4 Total Productivity per DRG ($/$)

DRG	TP/TPI Index	May	Jun	Jul	Aug	Sep	Oct
182	TP	1.06	2.17	0.42	0.86	1.00	1.08
	TPI	1.00	2.05	0.40	0.81	0.94	1.02
183	TP	3.46	0.82	1.91	0.86	0.89	2.10
	TPI	1.00	0.24	0.55	0.25	0.26	0.61
200	TP	5.74	0.00	3.51	3.35	4.99	5.17
	TPI	1.00	0.00	0.61	0.58	0.87	0.90
205	TP	0.00	0.00	0.45	0.89	0.25	0.86
	TPI	0.00	0.00	1.00	1.98	0.56	1.91
207	TP	0.00	0.76	1.00	1.60	0.93	0.42
	TPI	0.00	1.00	1.32	2.11	1.22	0.55
294	TP	1.05	0.95	2.33	1.04	1.35	0.00
	TPI	1.00	0.90	2.22	0.99	1.29	0.00
395	TP	1.34	3.70	3.12	3.16	1.15	0.83
	TPI	1.00	2.76	2.33	2.36	0.86	0.62
397	TP	1.80	0.60	0.42	0.60	0.00	0.77
	TPI	1.00	0.33	0.23	0.33	0.00	0.43
403	TP	2.43	0.56	0.00	1.45	0.55	2.66
	TPI	1.00	0.23	0.00	0.60	0.23	1.09
462	TP	1.41	1.10	0.81	0.75	1.10	1.23
	TPI	1.00	0.78	0.57	0.53	0.78	0.87

management of the hospital by allowing them to control various resources and hence their costs—particularly in nursing care, housekeeping, and outpatient and inpatient care.

Summary—This case demonstrates the feasibility of applying the TPM to a hospital as a major step toward the implementation of TPmgt. One of the challenges faced is extracting data from various sources in the hospital. This challenge is overcome to a great extent by educating all the important "players" in the hospital about the need to work as a team to reduce resistance to accepting new measurement systems. Further, the financial accounting system in a hospital can incorporate a "TPM module" to make the data extraction relatively routine and easy.

Case Study #2

Background—This case deals with a hospital that is a full-service medical center. It provides quality healthcare and a complete range of services for inpatients and

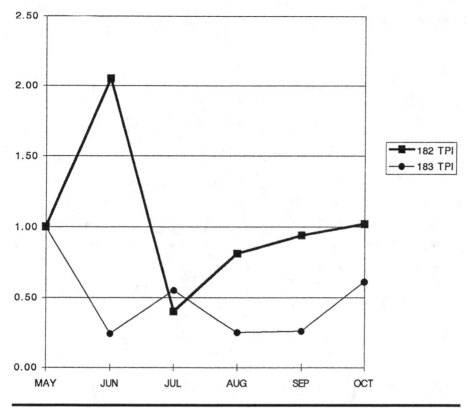

FIGURE 5.6 Total productivity for DRG No. 182 and 183.

outpatients. The hospital opened in 1950 and has since grown from a little community hospital to a fully accredited healthcare center. In 1991, the medical center employed more than 1,200 healthcare professionals, with more than 800 competent physicians who practice nearly 30 different medical specialties. The center has just recently expanded and renovated its Emergency Department and Psychiatric Center, in addition to opening a new Radiation and Oncology Center and Hospice Center. The hospital's expenses were distributed as follows: salaries and wages (49%); supplies, services, and utilities (30%); capital costs (7%); charity and indigent care (8%); and new technology and equipment (6%).

Implementation—Financial statements for the hospital were obtained for a five-year period from 1987 to 1991. From this information, two operational units were selected for the study—inpatients and outpatients. All output and input elements were gathered for each of the operational units. The base period

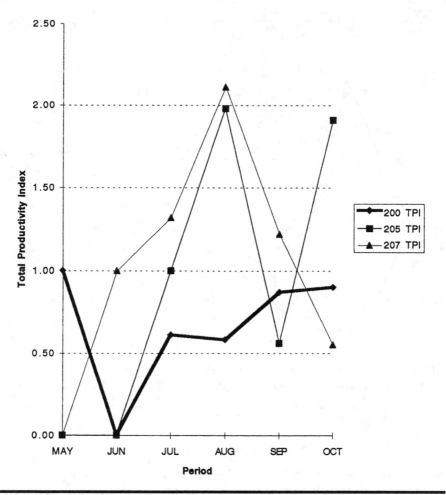

FIGURE 5.7   Total productivity index for DRG No. 200, 205, and 207.

selected was 1987, and the need for deflators arose because the outputs and inputs were not given in uniform physical terms. The deflator information was obtained from Bureau of Labor Statistics publications, in particular the Monthly Labor Review and the Survey of Current Business. Consumer price indices, producer price indices, and wage rates were used as deflators in the productivity computations.

Results and Analysis—Tables 5.5 and 5.6 show the results of the study in the hospital for inpatients and outpatients, respectively.

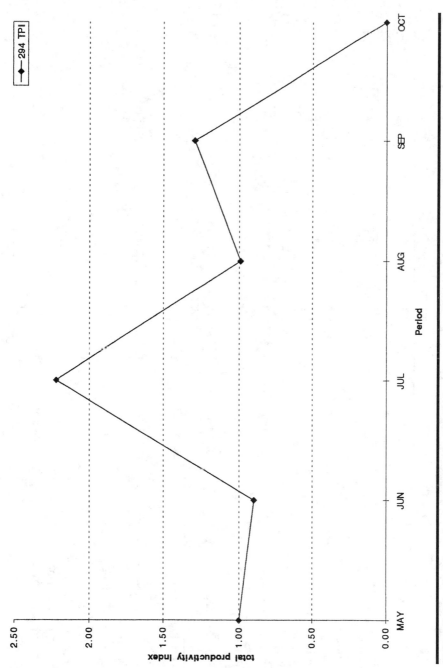

FIGURE 5.8 Total productivity index for DRG No. 294.

TABLE 5.5 Data for Inpatients

			Time Period		
Monetary unit	1987 (base period) Dollars	1988 Dollars	1989 Dollars	1990 Dollars	1991 Dollars
Output elements					
Patient income (O_1)	64,901,974	71,182,145	70,732,781	81,458,835	72,582,035
Other income (O_2)	2,672,525	2,540,078	3,013,930	3,516,719	2,457,613
Total output[a]	67,574,499	73,722,223	73,746,711	84,975,555	75,039,648
Deflator	1.000	1.093	1.220	1.352	1.454
Total tangible output[a]	67,574,499	67,449,426	60,448,124	62,851,742	51,609,112
Input elements					
1. Human					
Total human input[a]	28,658,620	30,230,270	31,957,881	36,418,061	34,327,681
Deflator	1.000	0.700	0.734	0.768	0.788
Total human input[a]	28,658,620	43,186,100	43,539,347	47,419,350	43,563,047
2. Materials					
Total materials expenses (supplies)[a]	10,045,367	12,103,426	12,780,620	13,350,891	12,776,713
Deflator	1.000	1.012	1.037	1.054	1.065
Total materials input[a]	10,045,367	11,959,907	12,324,610	12,666,879	11,996,913
3. Fixed capital					
Depreciation on property, plant, and equipment					
Total fixed capital expense[a]	40,084,882	35,255,652	33,488,202	32,757,410	35,800,482
Deflator	1.000	0.961	0.917	0.870	0.841
Total fixed capital input[a]	40,084,882	36,686,423	36,519,305	37,652,196	42,568,944

4. Working capital

Current asset items					
Cash, accts. rec., etc.	17,719,242	14,705,557	16,321,418	22,938,812	25,467,802
Amounts due—third parties	0	2,240,251	2,308,676	759,828	5,407,688
Inventories	1,166,462	1,542,791	1,369,014	1,680,771	1,759,965
Prepaid expenses	305,984	1,400,254	1,369,149	913,127	1,813,795
Investments—short term	0	0	0	0	0
Other receivables	1,492,861	0	0	0	806,900
Total current assets[b]	20,684,548	19,888,853	21,368,257	26,292,538	35,256,150
Total working capital[a]	413,691	397,777	427,365	525,851	705,123
Deflator	1.000	0.961	0.917	0.870	0.841
Total working capital input[a]	413,691	413,920	466,047	604,426	838,434

5. Energy

Total energy expenses[a] (gas, electric, water)	1,535,468	1,644,015	1,591,925	1,620,719	1,436,557
Deflator	1.000	1.016	1.047	1.075	1.099
Total energy input[a]	1,535,468	1,618,921	1,520,464	1,508,348	1,307,149

6. Other expenses

Interest	2,368,843	3,051,507	2,679,766	2,331,415	2,105,735
Consultant fees	880,049	730,587	713,000	886,618	598,108
Other departmental expenses	7,938,267	8,720,579	8,742,768	9,479,572	8,526,879
Other gen. & admin. expenses	4,537,127	5,357,583	3,364,511	3,921,268	3,467,313
Fringe benefits	6,697,900	6,877,960	6,426,354	7,715,245	7,574,219
Amortization	89,483	263,639	84,024	399,811	45,433
Malpractice	0	0	1,104,932	1,338,191	1,112,316

[a] In constant monetary terms with respect to the base period.
[b] Prime lending rate.

TABLE 5.5 Data for Inpatients (continued)

	1987 (base period)	1988	1989	1990	1991
			Time Period		
Total other expenses[a]	22,511,669	25,001,854	23,115,353	26,072,119	23,430,004
Deflator	1.000	1.046	1.097	1.158	1.203
Total Other Expenses Input[a]	22,511,669	23,902,346	21,071,425	22,514,784	19,476,312
Total tangible input	103,249,697	117,767,618	115,441,197	122,365,983	119,750,800
Total productivity	0.654	0.573	0.524	0.514	0.431
Total productivity index	1.000	0.875	0.800	0.785	0.752
Total productivity (break-even point)	0.996	0.996	0.996	0.995	0.993
7. Partial Productivities					
Human productivity	2.358	1.562	1.388	1.325	1.185
Human productivity index	1.000	0.662	0.589	0.562	0.502
Material productivity	6.727	5.640	4.905	4.962	4.302
Material productivity index	1.000	0.838	0.729	0.738	0.639
Fixed capital productivity	1.686	1.839	1.655	1.669	1.212
Fixed capital productivity index	1.000	1.091	0.982	0.990	0.719
Working capital productivity	163.345	162.953	129.704	103.986	61.554
Working capital productivity index	1.000	0.998	0.794	0.637	0.377
Energy productivity	44.009	41.663	39.756	41.669	39.482
Energy productivity index	1.000	0.947	0.903	0.947	0.897
Other expenses productivity	3.002	2.822	2.869	2.792	2.650
Other expenses productivity index	1.000	0.940	0.956	0.930	0.883

[a] In constant monetary terms with respect to the base period.

TABLE 5.6 Data for Outpatients

	1987 (base period)	1988	1989	1990	1991
			Time Period		
Monetary unit	Dollars	Dollars	Dollars	Dollars	Dollars
Output elements					
Patient income (O$_1$)	8,960,870	10,369,365	12,174,199	17,562,835	17,371,397
Other income (O$_2$)	368,928	369,852	517,250	758,408	588,134
Total output[a]	9,329,798	10,739,217	12,691,449	18,321,242	17,959,531
Deflator	1.000	1.093	1.220	1.352	1.454
Total tangible output[a]	9,329,798	9,825,450	10,402,827	13,551,215	12,351,809
Input elements					
1. Human					
Total human input[a]	3,956,175	4,401,727	5,498,613	7,853,834	8,214,990
Deflator	1.000	0.700	0.734	0.768	0.788
Total human input[a]	3,956,175	6,288,181	7,491,299	10,226,347	10,425,114
2. Materials					
Total materials expenses[a]	1,386,711	1,762,339	2,199,010	2,879,222	3,057,607
Deflator	1.000	1.012	1.037	1.054	1.065
Total materials input[a]	1,386,711	1,741,441	2,120,549	2,731,710	2,870,993
3. Fixed capital					
Depreciation expense					
Amortization					
Rent					
Maintenance and repairs					

[a] In constant monetary terms with respect to the base period.

TABLE 5.6 Data for Outpatients (continued)

			Time Period		
	1987 (base period)	1988	1989	1990	1991
Total fixed capital expense[a]	5,533,511	5,133,456	6,566,183	7,064,387	9,284,188
Deflator	1.000	0.961	0.917	0.870	0.841
Total fixed capital input[a]	5,533,511	5,341,785	7,160,505	8,119,985	11,039,462
4. Working capital					
Current asset items					
Cash, accts. rec., etc.	1,873,226	2,138,948	2,807,716	3,800,512	6,094,724
Amounts due—third parties		326,195	397,227	126,681	1,294,119
Inventories	161,024	224,641	235,550	312,842	421,179
Prepaid expenses	42,239	203,886	235,573	255,438	434,061
Investments—short term					193,100
Total current assets[b]	2,076,490	2,893,670	3,676,066	4,495,473	8,437,183
Total working capital[a]	41,530	57,873	73,521	89,909	168,744
Deflator	1.000	0.961	0.917	0.870	0.841
Total working capital input[a]	41,530	60,222	80,176	103,344	200,646
5. Energy					
Total energy expenses[a] (gas, electricity, and water)	211,963	239,379	273,904	331,005	343,784
Deflator	1.000	1.016	1.047	1.075	1.099
Total energy input[a]	211,963	235,726	261,608	308,055	312,815
6. Other expenses					
Interest	327,007	444,319	461,075	502,788	503,926

Consultant fees	121,486	106,378	122,678	191,206	143,134
Other departmental expenses	1,095,837	1,269,774	1,504,264	2,044,342	2,040,576
Other gen. & admin. expenses	626,327	780,100	578,891	845,651	829,766
Fringe benefits	924,610	1,001,476	1,105,706	1,663,852	1,812,593
Amortization	12,353	38,388	14,457	15,262	10,872
Malpractice			190,112	288,591	266,190
Total other expenses[a]	3,107,620	3,640,435	3,977,185	5,551,693	5,607,056
Deflator	1.000	1.046	1.097	1.158	1.203
Total Other Expenses Input[a]	**3,107,620**	**3,480,339**	**3,625,510**	**4,794,208**	**4,660,895**
Total tangible input	14,237,510	17,147,695	20,739,647	26,283,648	29,509,925
Total productivity	0.655	0.573	0.502	0.516	0.419
Total productivity index	1.000	0.874	0.765	0.787	0.730
Total productivity (break-even point)	0.997	0.996	0.996	0.996	0.993
7. Partial Productivities					
Human productivity	2.358	1.563	1.389	1.325	1.185
Human productivity index	1.000	0.663	0.589	0.562	0.502
Material productivity	6.728	5.642	4.906	4.961	4.302
Material productivity index	1.000	0.839	0.729	0.737	0.639
Fixed capital productivity	1.686	1.839	1.453	1.669	1.119
Fixed capital productivity index	1.000	1.091	0.862	0.990	0.664
Working capital productivity	224.653	163.154	129.750	131.127	61.560
Working capital productivity index	1.000	0.726	0.578	0.584	0.274
Energy productivity	44.016	41.682	39.765	43.990	39.486
Energy productivity index	1.000	0.947	0.903	0.999	0.897
Other expenses productivity	3.002	2.823	2.869	2.827	2.650
Other expenses productivity index	1.000	0.940	0.956	0.941	0.883

[a] In constant monetary terms with respect to the base period.
[b] Prime lending rate.

Level 1 Analysis—Figure 5.9 shows that the hospital as a whole is not very "total productive" and hence not very profitable. The total productivity value is well below the break-even point and is also showing a steady downward trend.

Level 2 Analysis—By analyzing the total productivity profiles for inpatients (Figure 5.10) and outpatients (Figure 5.11), we see that both of these operational units are doing poorly, with virtually similar trends.

Year	1987	1988	1989	1990	1991
Total Productivity	0.678	0.568	0.537	0.530	0.446
Break-even Point	0.983	0.980	0.973	0.971	0.958

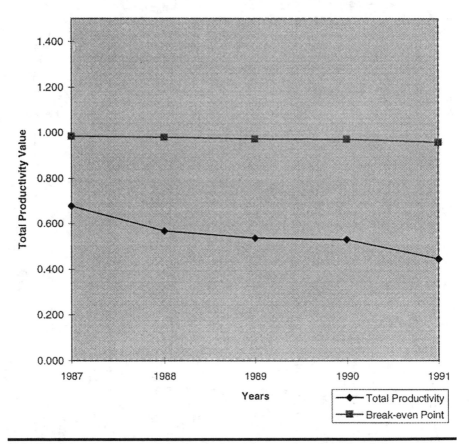

FIGURE 5.9 Total productivity versus break-even point of the hospital.

Year	1987	1988	1989	1990	1991
Total Productivity	0.654	0.573	0.524	0.514	0.431
Break-even Point	0.996	0.996	0.996	0.995	0.993

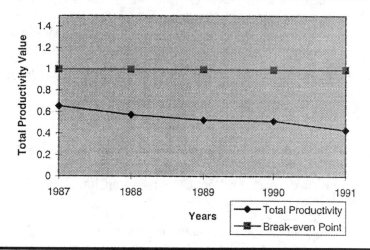

FIGURE 5.10 Total productivity versus break-even point for inpatients.

Year	1987	1988	1989	1990	1991
Total Productivity	0.655	0.573	0.502	0.516	0.419
Break-even Point	0.997	0.996	0.996	0.996	0.993

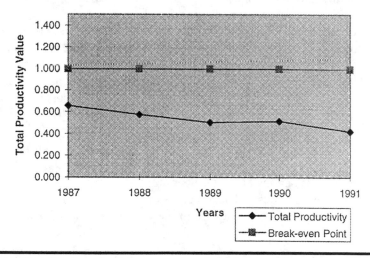

FIGURE 5.11 Total productivity versus break-even point for outpatients.

Level 3 Analysis—In considering operational unit 1 (inpatients), Figure 5.12 clearly indicates that the main contributors to this operational unit's decline were the drops in human productivity, materials productivity, and working capital productivity. There were also declines in all the other partial productivities. Obviously, management had to be concerned about this situation from a total productivity standpoint. The partial productivity profiles for outpatients are shown in Figure 5.13. Both illustrations are self-explanatory.

Benefits—The management of the hospital now has a full-time industrial engineering function—an increasingly common feature in hospitals that are trying to increase their competitiveness. It has become a matter of necessity for management to revisit traditional approaches to managing healthcare facilities.

Summary—This study demonstrated the feasibility of applying the TPM to a U.S. hospital. It also pointed out that both inpatient care and outpatient care were equally unproductive from a total productivity standpoint.

Questions to Ponder—

5.6.1   Explain the importance of controlling healthcare costs in that industry in general and in children's hospitals in particular.

5.6.2   Analyze some of the models for productivity measurement available for the healthcare industry in general and hospitals in particular.

5.6.3   What insights do you think you can gather from the TPM analysis that conventional management information systems fail to offer?

5.6.4   In the first case study, what happens to the TPF and PPF (human) during the six months of operation? Do you think this was due to productivity improvements or economies of scale?

5.6.5   Compare and contrast the human productivity for nurses/therapists with that for aides, and comment on these trends for the two groups.

5.6.6   Should the human productivity of aides be greater than that for nurses/therapists because the latter perform more sophisticated functions?

5.6.7   Before implementing TPmgt on a full scale, what must be in place for maximum success?

5.6.8   Why is TPmgt necessary in hospitals today?

5.6.9   Study at least three hospitals in your area from the total productivity standpoint. Contrast their positive and negative aspects. What are your recommendations based on your study?

5.6.10   Outline strategies and action plans to improve the total productivity of inpatient and outpatient care in the hospital of the second study.

Year	1987	1988	1989	1990	1991
PPI_H	1.000	0.6624	0.589	0.5621	0.502
PPI_M	1.000	0.8384	0.729	0.7376	0.639
PPI_{FC}	1.000	1.0906	0.982	0.9902	0.719
PPI_{WC}	1.000	0.9976	0.794	0.6366	0.377
PPI_E	1.000	0.9467	0.903	0.9468	0.897
PPI_{OE}	1.000	0.9401	0.956	0.93	0.883

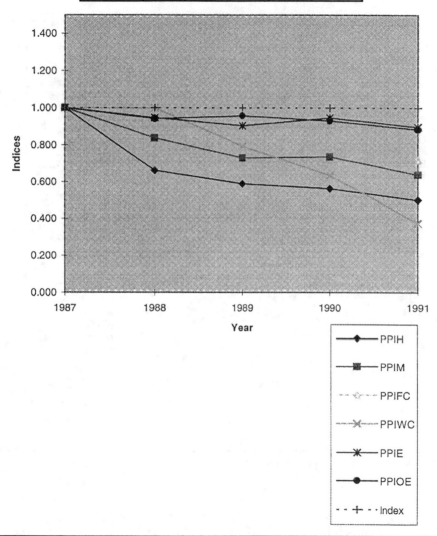

FIGURE 5.12   Partial productivity indices for inpatients.

Year	1987	1988	1989	1990	1991
PPI_H	1.000	0.6626	0.589	0.5619	0.502
PPI_M	1.000	0.8386	0.729	0.7373	0.639
PPI_{FC}	1.000	1.0909	0.862	0.9898	0.664
PPI_{WC}	1.000	0.7262	0.578	0.5837	0.274
PPI_E	1.000	0.947	0.903	0.9994	0.897
PPI_{OE}	1.000	0.9403	0.956	0.9415	0.883

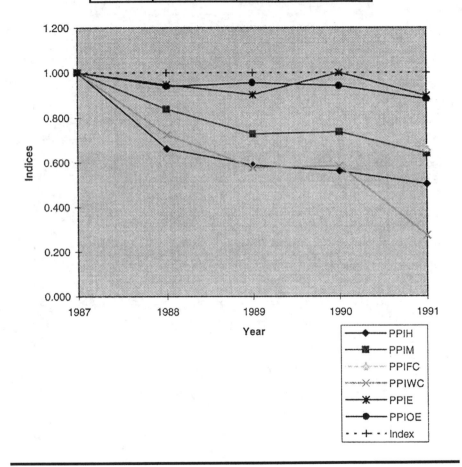

FIGURE 5.13   Partial productivity indices for outpatients.

5.7 INSURANCE

Case Study #1

Background—This case study deals with a medium-sized insurance company based in Latin America. The company is headed by a director who has had this position for nearly 15 years. He is assisted ably by a general manager. This company's progressive and enthusiastic management initiated and oversaw the entire TPmgt process and was an active participant in this task.

Implementation—Both of the pre-TPmgt steps—the external customer analysis through the CSS and the internal customer analysis through the GOA—were done for the company. In addition, the step-by-step implementation process for TPmgt was undertaken with the complete involvement of all the top management, middle management, and a large proportion of the lower management. Step #1 (mission statement development) was done first. In this step, all the managers and supervisors at all levels of the company were involved collectively to develop a mission statement. Step #2 (TPM analysis) was undertaken with the company's historical data. We will discuss the TPM analysis in detail later. The next steps—management goals (Step #3), fishbone analysis (Step #4), and action plans (Step #5)—were done with participation from managers and supervisors. PQT training (Step #6) was done for all the employees through the "Train the Trainer" concept; that is, all managers and supervisors were trained first, and then each of them trained about 20 people, each of whom trained 15 to 20 others.

The company did not implement total productivity gainsharing (TPG) in the first year because of the transition from a traditional to the TPmgt philosophy.

The TPM was applied at the firm level of the organization; that is, no individual operational units were considered. Partial productivities were computed for four of the seven inputs—human, fixed capital, working capital, and other expenses. The materials and energy inputs were not analyzed because they represented negligible values when compared to the remaining four input factors, but some attention was given to these two inputs in the final analysis and recommendation stage of the process. The analysis was performed for the time period 1988 to 1991.

Results—The TPM analysis consisted of four levels of investigation. The team began by charting the firm's total productivity against its break-even point. Figure 5.14 illustrates this idea graphically. Also, the individual input productivity indices were measured against the base period (Figure 5.15), and percentage changes in the respective input productivities were calculated (Table 5.7).

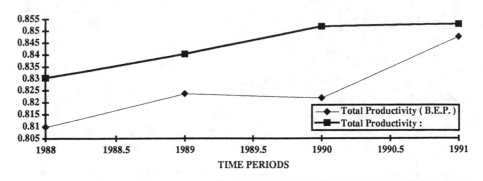

FIGURE 5.14   Total productivity versus break-even point of the insurance company.

Analysis—We begin our discussion by commenting on the observations and results of our Level 1 to 4 analysis.

Level 1: Total Productivity of the Firm versus Total Productivity Break-Even Point—At first glance, we noticed a fairly strong rise in the total productivity of the firm from 1988 until 1990, at which time the rising slope of the curve began to flatten out, running nearly parallel to the x-axis from 1990 to 1991. During this same time period, the break-even point began to rise linearly, coming very close to surpassing the total productivity of the firm. This disturbing trend prodded us to perform a more detailed analysis on the input factors and how they were managed.

Level 2: Total Productivities of Operational Units versus Total Productivity Break-Even Points for Operational Units—Because we were considering the firm as a whole as the operational unit, this level of analysis is the same as Level 1 in this case. We then proceeded to Level 3 analysis.

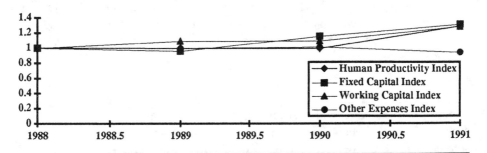

FIGURE 5.15   Partial productivity indices of the insurance company.

TABLE 5.7   Percentage Changes in Total Productivity of the Insurance Company and Each Input

	% (Base = 1988)		
	1989	*1990*	*1991*
Total productivity	1.2	2.6	2.7
Human productivity	−1.1	−1.0	28.0
Fixed capital productivity	−4.2	15.6	31.0
Working capital productivity	9.1	9.5	28.1
Other expenses productivity	−0.3	1.3	−6.0

Level 3: Partial Productivity Analysis—Here, we took a closer look at each input factor and analyzed the productivity levels corresponding to them over the four-year period. We began by analyzing the other expenses input, noting that it comprised nearly 70% of all the input resources during this time span. Productivity levels during the first three years were found to be acceptable, roughly 20% above their respective index values. However, in 1991, while the 20% margin remained the same, the total productivity value dropped by almost 10% and the percentage change in other expenses productivity dropped by 6%. Because of the major role that other expenses play in the makeup of the organization, even a slight drop like this contributed a great deal to the decline in overall productivity of the firm, thereby making it a candidate for further investigation and improvement.

The next input considered was human input. Extremely high productivity values were observed during the four years, as compared to the human productivity indices. Although human input accounts for only about 11% of the total inputs, the high levels of productivity among the employees, as evidenced by the 28% increase in productivity in 1991 after a 1% drop in 1990, signals that the company seems to be moving in a favorable direction for this input resource.

Fixed capital showed a trend similar to human input. Productivity values increase by nearly 16% in 1990 and 31% in 1991. However, this input only comprises eight-tenths of 1% of the total input. If this input were magnified, the high productivity values could be substantiated further, and profits could be increased dramatically.

Working capital input made up the remaining 17% of the total inputs. Here again, we did not observe any real problems in the productivity values, which actually increased each period, while at the same time keeping the indices near 1.000. Although there was a nearly slight increase in the index value in 1991, the corresponding productivity value increased by nearly 28%.

Level 4: Industrial Engineering Analysis and Recommendations—After investigating all the input factors, and taking into account the overall financial health of the firm, we were able to come up with some positive feasible solutions to the problems presented, particularly the drop in productivity for the other expenses input. The following are a few recommendations made to management to improve the firm's total productivity and profitability:

1. An aggressive *strategic planning* process is necessary for the company to be able to increase its total productivity and profitability on a consistent basis at high levels.
2. Loans receivable and premiums receivable are extremely high among the working capital input items. Definite strategies are needed to reduce these amounts substantially.
3. Human resource development, training, and continuing education are essential to helping the company become aggressively "total productive."
4. All items under the other expenses category should be analyzed, rationalized, and controlled very systematically and consistently. A Pareto analysis may be undertaken and a cause-and-effect analysis done to reduce this category.
5. For a company this size, in terms of revenues, there has to be a very meticulously planned organizational system, supported by an incentive to reduce waste and improve the system continuously.

Benefits—Several benefits were realized by implementing the TPmgt methodology. For the first time in its history, the company now has a clearly defined and practiced vision through a mission statement which was developed through careful analysis and the participation of all the employees. Management and employees were able to understand the areas of concern and how to take effective action to correct them. Also, the firm was able to increase its public image, its customer satisfaction, and its profit levels. The company's employees have developed a policy manual for administration, gone through the PQT training (led by their supervisors and the general manager), and morale has improved.

Summary—This insurance company in Latin America represents an example of applying the TPmgt methodology very meticulously. The TPM was used to ascertain significant quantitative values of productivity and to evaluate these values in terms of how they affected the firm's profitability. From our investigation, we concluded that the other expenses input was a major source of concern, considering the large volume of the input resources it represents and the fact that its productivity levels dropped during the last year observed, something the other inputs did not encounter. On the contrary, human, fixed capital, and working capital seemed to be in favorable situations, and further improvements could only help those inputs. From our preliminary analysis of the firm, we knew that the firm's total productivity needed to be improved substantially so that the company did not experience losses in profits. The company took many practical steps to improve the total productivity picture, and the efforts are paying off now.

Case Study #2

Background—In this case study, the logic of the TPM was applied to a U.S. insurance company that has been in existence for over 50 years. The major products of this company included credit property, unemployment, accident and health, homeowners, physical damage, livestock, and individual and group life policies. These products were marketed through financial institutions, retail trade establishments, automobile and manufactured housing dealers and manufacturers, and agency representatives. Furthermore, the insurance company distributed its products and services in and through markets that were not traditionally served by other insurance companies. Deflators were used to eliminate fluctuations due to price changes and inflation, which allowed the true changes in productivity to be seen. The company also developed a mission statement: "to sell innovative insurance products through affiliated organizations." The leadership position attributed to the company was a reflection of its service and its appreciation of customers and clients. Finally, high service standards were promoted continually through internal campaigns, classes, and one-on-one counseling. Today, this company's leadership position in the financial market can be attributed in large part to the manner in which customers and clients are treated and served.

Implementation—The company was evaluated only at the firm level, without trying to break down its multiple and complex processes into individual operational units. Both total productivity and partial productivity measures were calculated for the years 1986–90. By analyzing these results, management was able to identify areas where further investigation and improvement were needed. The financial data for this analysis were obtained from a 1990 annual report and from 1986–90 10K reports. We chose 1986 as the base period because this was the earliest year for which the data could be compared to later years.

Also included as a part of the investigation was a break-even point analysis. This value represents the minimum level toward which a company should strive to generate profit. This productivity "profit" should not be confused with conventional profit. Although the two can be shown to be equal when the deflators are unity, they are not always equal in a dollar-to-dollar sense. There is, however, a distinct linear relationship between the two.

Results and Analysis—Results and analysis are shown in Table 5.8. Upon observation, we noticed that the firm showed a general downward trend in its total productivity values over the five years investigated. The lowest total productivity level of the firm occurred in 1987, when total productivity fell by 10.2% from the base period. This decline was due in large part to a 9.9% drop in human productivity and an 11.6% decrease in other expense productivity when compared to the base period.

In 1988, a 1.7% decrease in the other expense total productivity was noted, and a 10.3% decrease in human productivity was also observed. This contributed to the 7% gain in total productivity from 1987 to 1988 (although it was a 3.9% drop compared to 1986, the base). However, total productivity values slipped again in 1989, dropping 2% from the previous year and nearly 5.6% from the base period of 1986. Human and capital productivities also decreased, with fixed capital input taking a huge 33.3% drop in its partial productivity.

The final two years showed an upward trend in total productivity, with the total productivity of the firm increasing by 4% in 1990—considerably above the break-even point of 0.939. But human productivity once again decreased in 1990, by 7.8%, although there were noticeable improvements in fixed capital and working capital productivities.

The results of the TPM at the aggregate level indicate a strong need to take a closer look at the operations of the firm. Although the company as a whole has showed financial gains, the productivity levels are low and the break-even points were barely being met in three of the five years.

When looking at the partial productivity measures of the firm as a whole, it was difficult to pinpoint detailed areas of needed improvement, although it was clear that capital productivity was low. The low level may be due to a group of products or services, a particular product or service, or even an entire subsidiary. In order to draw a conclusion, the TPM must be implemented at the operational unit level. This should be determined by management, depending on how detailed it wants the analysis to be.

Benefits—In this study, the TPM was implemented for the firm as a whole. The next step would be to implement the TPM at the operational unit level (e.g., for the different product lines or for underwriting and claims).

The company had PQT training and also ran a pilot TPM at the firm level. The company initiated some form of a financial incentive system but not exactly TPG.

Summary—The TPM recognizes all input factors and provides total productivity information at both the aggregate and operational unit level. This case

TABLE 5.8 TPM Results for the Insurance Firm

	Time Period				
	1986 (base period)	*1987*	*1988*	*1989*	*1990*
Monetary unit	Dollars	Dollars	Dollars	Dollars	Dollars
Output elements					
Finished units (O_1)					
Partial units (O_2)					
Dividends from securities (O_3)					
Interest from bonds (O_4)					
Other income (O_5)	9,400	7,300	8,600	10,700	11,400
Net premiums earned	519,300	613,600	629,300	584,200	661,800
Net investment income	78,300	71,000	65,000	63,300	72,300
Gain on sale of subsidiary			28,200		
Total output[a]	607,000	691,900	731,100	658,200	745,500
Deflator	1.000	1.044	1.090	1.140	1.211
Total tangible output[a]	607,000	662,739	670,734	577,368	615,607
Input elements					
1. Human					
Total human input[a]	189,000	235,300	251,600	214,300	263,900
Deflator	1.000	1,036	1.081	1.115	1.153
Total human input[a]	189,000	227,124	232,747	192,197	228,881
2. Materials					
Total materials expense[a]					
Deflator	1.000	1.000	1.000	1.000	1.000
Total materials input[a]					
3. Fixed capital					
Depreciation expense	3,952	4,974	5,570	5,635	5,724
Amortization					
Rent					
Maintenance and repairs					
Total fixed capital expense[a]	3,952	4,974	5,570	5,635	5,724
Deflator	1.000	1.000	1.000	1.000	1.000
Total fixed capital input[a]	3,952	4,974	5,570	5,635	5,724

[a] In constant monetary terms with respect to the base period.

TABLE 5.8   TPM Results for the Insurance Firm (continued)

			Time Period		
	1986 (base period)	*1987*	*1988*	*1989*	*1990*
4. *Working capital*					
Current asset items					
Cash	12,500	12,900	13,600	12,300	27,700
Deferred policy acquisition costs	194,000	207,600	171,800	169,800	171,600
Other assets	152,100	179,100	147,900	182,800	193,500
Total current assets	358,600	399,600	333,300	364,900	392,800
Prime lending rate + 2%	10.330	10.210	11.320	12.870	12.010
Total working capital[a]	37,043	40,799	37,730	46,963	47,175
Deflator	1.000	1.021	1.046	1.101	1.155
Total working capital input[a]	37,043	39,960	36,070	42,655	40,844
5. *Energy*					
Total energy expenses[a]					
Deflator	1.000	1.000	1.000	1.000	1.000
Total energy input[a]					
6. *Other expenses*					
Interest	15,100	12,600	12,300	11,500	13,700
Benefits, claims, losses, and settlement	246,800	277,700	284,900	269,100	282,800
Taxes and contributions	5,700	4,400	20,000	5,200	15,700
Credit bond losses and expenses	19,300	77,200	19,500	9,000	12,600
Operating expenses less depreciation	96,700	112,100	114,400	121,100	126,800
Total other expenses[a]	383,600	484,000	451,100	415,900	451,600
Deflator	1.000	1.021	1.046	1.101	1.155
Total Other Expense Input[a]	383,600	474,045	431,262	377,748	390,996
Total tangible input	613,595	746,103	705,650	618,234	666,445
Total productivity	0.989	0.888	0.951	0.934	0.924
Total productivity index	1.000	0.898	0.961	0.944	1.040
Total productivity (break-even)	0.940	0.946	0.949	0.931	0.939

[a] In constant monetary terms with respect to the base period.

TABLE 5.8   TPM Results for the Insurance Firm (continued)

	Time Period				
	1986 (base period)	*1987*	*1988*	*1989*	*1990*
7. Partial Productivities					
Human productivity	3.212	2.918	2.882	3.004	2.690
Human productivity index	1.000	0.909	0.897	0.935	0.922
Fixed capital productivity	153.593	133.241	120.419	102.461	107.548
Fixed capital prod. index	1.000	0.867	0.784	0.667	0.807
Working capital productivity	16.386	16.585	18.595	13.536	15.072
Working capital prod. index	1.000	1.012	1.135	0.826	0.909
Other expenses productivity	1.582	1.398	1.555	1.528	1.574
Other expenses prod. index	1.000	0.884	0.983	1.093	1.012

study measured productivity in a U.S.-based insurance company for the years 1986–90. The company was evaluated as a whole, and graphs and charts representing productivity levels, changes in productivity, and numerical indices were provided for easier understanding. Due to the unavailability of essential data, the company was not broken down into operational units. However, based upon the implications of the previous analysis, management was strongly encouraged to pursue further investigations at a more in-depth level. The company has had stable management at all levels, particularly the top level, since 1981. The chairman of the company has consistently provided dynamic leadership, with innovation as the company's hallmark.

Questions to Ponder—

5.7.1   What external forces can contribute to lower productivity levels in an insurance-type organization?

5.7.2   Is the distribution of inputs in the first case normal for this type of company? Why or why not? Give supporting evidence for your argument.

5.7.3   Benchmark the company in the first case with several other insurance groups by performing a TPM analysis on each. Explain your observations and the similarities and differences that you encounter.

5.7.4   What is management's role in improving productivity levels in the firm, based upon your knowledge of productivity?

5.7.5   Why was 1986 chosen as a base period in the second case study?

5.7.6 In what year was the total productivity of the firm in the second case study smaller than its respective break-even point?

5.7.7 Compare the human productivities of the firm in the second case study with three or four others in your area. Are the values similar or different? Give evidence for your argument.

5.7.8 What reasons would you give for the low productivity levels of the other expense input in 1987 for the firm in the second case study?

5.7.9 How could the company in the second case study benefit by implementing the TPM on an operational unit level? Cite other real companies as evidence.

5.8 PRINTING

Background—This case is about a printing company started by a graduate student* and her husband in the 1980s. She applied the TPM as part of a course work in productivity measurement and evaluation. The company's two major products—bond paper items (product 1) and no-carbon items (product 2)—accounted for most of its revenues.

Implementation—The TPM was applied within the first six months of the start-up of the company. Therefore, this is a somewhat unique situation, like the dry-cleaning case study (Section 5.4). Data collection was relatively easy for two reasons: (1) one of the owners (the graduate student) had access to all the financial and operational information and (2) the company, having just started, did not have too many products to keep track of for data collection.

Results and Analysis—A summary of the values and indices for total productivity and partial productivities is given in Table 5.9. Based on this information, the percentage changes were computed for each of the partial productivities and total productivity, corresponding to products 1 and 2 and the firm in Table 5.10.

Table 5.9 indicates an increase in total productivity for both products 1 and 2 and for the "balance of products." The growth is enormous across the board. This is not uncommon for a company in the initiation phase of its life cycle. Because of this infancy, the partial productivities have wide fluctuations, although they are positive for the most part (see Tables 5.9 and 5.10).

If we analyze the proportion of inputs in the total (Table 5.11), we notice that human input represents about 40% for product 1 and 36% for product 2, capital input is less for product 2 (approximately 25%) compared to product 1 (31%),

---

* I gratefully acknowledge this student's contribution to the application of the TPM in her family-owned company.

TABLE 5.9　Partial and Total Productivity Values and Indices for the Printing Firm's Products

		Product 1				Product 2				Balance of Products		
		$t=0$	$t=1$	$t=2$	$t=3$	$t=0$	$t=1$	$t=2$	$t=3$	$t=0$	$t=1$	$t=2$	$t=3$
Total Productivity													
Value		0.369	0.974	1.072	1.461	0.518	0.904	0.845	1.180	0.859	1.319	1.166	1.713
Index		1.000	2.636	2.902	3.956	1.000	1.747	1.632	2.279	1.660	2.549	2.253	3.310
Partial Productivities													
Human:	Value	0.822	2.347	2.815	3.907	1.319	2.432	2.166	3.991	2.181	3.520	3.258	5.293
	Index	1.000	2.857	3.425	4.755	1.000	1.844	1.642	3.026	1.000	1.614	1.494	2.427
Material:	Value	3.934	5.514	4.833	5.920	2.482	3.531	2.848	2.808	4.263	5.217	4.219	5.067
	Index	1.000	1.402	1.229	1.505	1.000	1.423	1.148	1.131	1.000	1.224	0.990	1.189
Capital:	Value	1.155	3.401	3.456	4.914	1.852	3.466	3.453	5.371	3.032	5.058	3.964	6.556
	Index	1.000	2.944	2.991	4.253	1.000	1.872	1.865	2.901	1.000	1.668	1.307	2.162
Energy:	Value	10.977	37.108	44.310	79.513	17.593	37.817	44.271	65.717	28.810	55.180	99.104	80.219
	Index	1.000	3.380	4.036	7.243	1.000	2.150	2.516	3.735	1.000	1.915	3.440	2.784
Other:	Value	3.582	10.143	16.999	23.070	5.740	10.336	16.984	25.217	9.400	15.082	19.499	30.782
	Index	1.000	2.832	4.746	6.441	1.000	1.801	2.959	4.393	1.000	1.605	2.074	3.275

TABLE 5.10   Management Summary of Productivity Trends

Type of Productivity	Firm			Product 1			Product 2		
	t = 1	*t = 2*	*t = 3*	*t = 1*	*t = 2*	*t = 3*	*t = 1*	*t = 2*	*t = 3*
Human	93.9	−1.3	66.0	185.7	19.9	38.8	84.4	−10.9	84.3
Material	15.8	12.8	−24.0	40.5	−13.1	23.5	42.5	−19.4	−1.5
Capital	94.6	−10.8	62.5	187.4	1.4	42.6	89.8	−0.6	56.1
Energy	136.0	26.5	37.7	248.5	19.9	78.8	121.6	17.5	47.9
Other	92.9	46.9	53.4	184.8	67.1	34.7	81.1	63.9	47.3
Total productivity	83.1	−4.8	46.8	163.4	10.0	36.8	74.1	−6.5	40.7

energy input is about the same for both products (about 2.5%), and other expense input is a bit less for product 2 (about 7%) compared to product 1 (8%). The most significant difference between the two products is the material input, which is about 18% for product 1 and about 29% for product 2. This is to be

TABLE 5.11   Proportion of Inputs in the Total Output

	Time Period (%)				
	0	*1*	*2*	*3*	*Average*
Product 1					
Human input	45.18	41.66	38.21	37.67	40.68
Capital input	32.13	29.44	31.94	30.64	31.04
Material input	8.94	16.76	21.20	23.49	17.60
Energy input	3.38	2.56	2.34	1.79	2.52
Other input	10.37	9.58	6.31	6.41	8.16
Total	100.00	100.00	100.00	100.00	100.00
Product 2					
Human input	39.43	37.23	39.05	29.70	36.35
Capital input	28.09	26.75	25.14	22.57	25.64
Material input	20.46	24.99	28.99	41.26	28.93
Energy input	2.96	2.32	1.85	1.75	2.22
Other input	9.06	8.71	4.97	4.72	6.86
Total	100.00	100.00	100.00	100.00	100.00

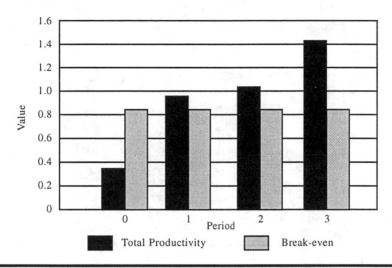

FIGURE 5.16 Total productivity versus break-even point for product 1 (bond paper items).

expected, since no-carbon items (product 2) are relatively more expensive than bond paper items (product 1).

Figure 5.16 clearly shows that the total productivity level for product 1 exceeded the break-even point level beginning in period 1. The trend shows the gap between these two values widening significantly in period 3, indicating a favorable profit-making posture. On the other hand, the first three periods for product 2 (0, 1, 2) were not very favorable situations, but, like product 1, the situation changes to very favorable in period 3 (Figure 5.17).

The company became more conscious of these productivity trends as time went on from period 0. The favorable situation for both products was a result of measures taken by top management to be careful with all resources—particularly human, capital, and material, which together accounted for almost 90% of the total.

Figure 5.18 shows the dramatic growth in human productivity for both products, particularly product 1. This was because top management was consciously careful in not hiring people too fast. They wanted the learning curve effect to stabilize first.

Material productivity for this firm showed a declining trend from period 2 to period 3, primarily because of the declining trend for product 2, whose material input accounts for nearly 29% of its total input (Figure 5.19).

For both products, capital productivity increased dramatically from period 0

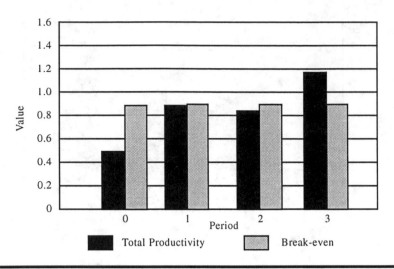

FIGURE 5.17   Total productivity versus break-even point for product 2 (no-carbon items).

to 1 and from period 2 to 3. The overall trend was a positive, steady one (Figure 5.20).

The energy productivity and other productivity profiles also indicate steady, upward growth (Figures 5.21 and 5.22). This is not surprising, as the output was increasing at a significantly faster rate than the energy and other expense inputs.

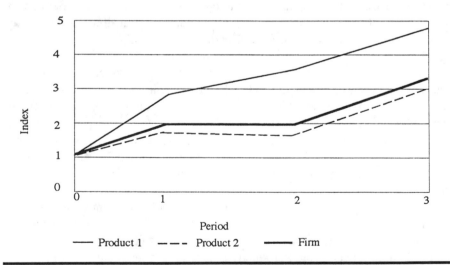

FIGURE 5.18   Human productivity indexes for product 1, product 2, and the firm.

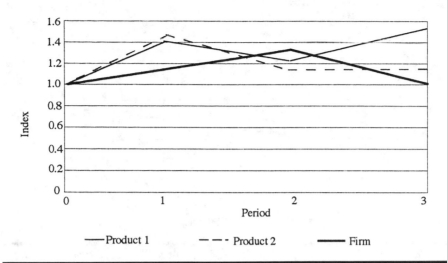

FIGURE 5.19 Material productivity indexes for product 1, product 2, and the firm.

Benefits—The owners of the company truly appreciated the opportunity to apply the TPM analysis to their company from its infancy. Fortunately, because of solid training in the concepts of TPmgt, top management realized savings in material costs by managing the materials through an inventory control system, by being careful not to hire people too quickly, and also by being careful to introduce techniques which were relevant rather than for the sake of using "superior" technologies.

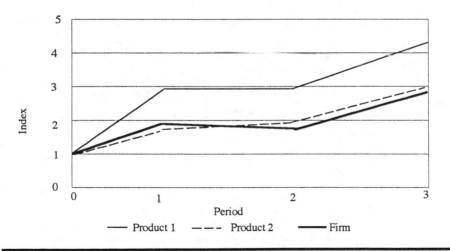

FIGURE 5.20 Capital productivity indexes for product 1, product 2, and the firm.

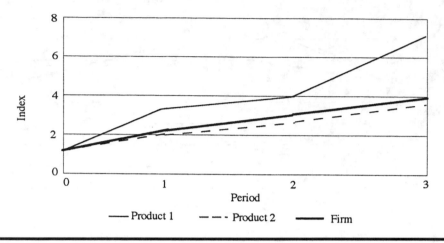

FIGURE 5.21   Energy productivity indexes for product 1, product 2, and the firm.

Summary—This case study pertained to a printing company wherein the brain of TPmgt—the TPM—was applied. Results of this study helped the owners of the company to take measures to manage very carefully the human, material, and capital resources. This helped the firm to be profitable very quickly, unlike many small firms which struggle to make money in the first year of operation.

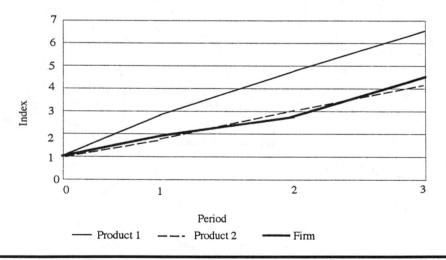

FIGURE 5.22   Other productivity indexes for product 1, product 2, and the firm.

Questions to Ponder—

5.8.1 What are the most important input factors in a printing company? Why?

5.8.2 Study three small printing companies in your area, and apply the lessons learned from them to the company discussed in this case study.

5.8.3 Do a "total productivity benchmarking" study of the top 50 printing companies in your country. How does the company discussed in this case study compare against the average total productivity value of these 50 companies?

5.9 RESTAURANT

TPmgt has been adopted in at least three different restaurants with varying product characteristics. For purposes of illustration, however, just one restaurant is discussed here.

Background—The company studied is a restaurant owned by a major multi-national food chain. The regional head office is located in the southern part of the United States and the main head office is on the West Coast. At the time of this study, the restaurant operated two shifts per day. Each shift had one manager, one shift manager, and two to three workers, depending on sales during the shift. The income statements for 1987–88 were studied, covering a 20-month period.

Implementation—The raw materials for the restaurant were supplied by the parent company (the restaurant is part of a chain) two to three times weekly, from requisitions prepared by the manager. The raw materials are converted into cooked food, ready to be served per the menu.

The output values were taken directly from the sales at the register, less sales tax and "over-rings." The income statement received by the restaurant on a monthly basis contained the actual profit (or loss) figures and the planned revenues and costs.

The outputs and inputs were not allocated by individual products on the menu because the analysis would have become too cumbersome, and the real essence of the TPM's message would have been lost in the complexity of the analysis—at least in this first attempt to apply the TPmgt concept in this restaurant. Therefore, all raw material resources were considered as material input and all sales as consolidated output. The other inputs considered included human, capital, energy, and other. Working capital was considered to be petty cash and the cash over/short, which the restaurant (unit) manager was authorized to use as necessary. The necessary deflators were used to deflate all the output and input values to constant dollars for the base period (January 1987).

Results and Analysis—Detailed record synthesis was done first. Computations were made for 20 months, beginning January 1987. The summary of results is shown in Table 5.12.

The restaurant's total productivity fluctuated widely, although it was well above the break-even point. Table 5.12 also shows how the profit levels increased significantly when total productivity values were above 1.00. Also, it can be noted that the profits change significantly in a relatively narrow bandwidth of total productivity values. This emphasizes that the restaurant business is very much affected by its total productivity levels and trends.

Figures 5.23 and 5.24 show a consolidated picture of all the productivity

TABLE 5.12   Summary of Productivity Indices, Break-Even Point, and Productivity-Oriented Profit for the 20-Month Period for the Restaurant

Period	Total Productivity	TP Index	Profit[a]	Partial Productivity Indices				
				Human	Material	Capital	Energy	Other
0	1.32	1.00	8,824	1.00	1.00	1.00	1.00	1.00
1	1.29	0.97	8,468	1.00	0.99	1.05	1.11	0.87
2	1.31	0.99	10,051	1.01	0.98	1.16	1.26	0.90
3	1.34	1.01	10,824	1.09	1.03	1.21	1.00	0.84
4	1.37	1.04	10,857	1.05	1.02	1.12	1.02	1.02
5	1.21	0.91	6,816	1.09	0.95	1.11	0.87	0.65
6	1.17	0.88	5,834	1.08	0.85	1.15	1.51	0.62
7	1.34	1.01	10,463	1.17	0.88	1.21	1.26	0.93
8	1.27	0.96	9,320	1.12	0.83	1.24	1.18	0.90
9	1.25	0.95	8,627	1.09	0.87	1.21	0.73	0.88
10	1.22	0.92	7,054	1.09	0.94	1.09	0.71	0.71
11	1.06	0.81	2,882	1.07	0.90	1.22	0.99	0.46
12	1.36	1.03	11,272	1.01	0.88	1.09	1.19	1.49
13	1.1	0.83	4,595	1.02	0.91	1.24	0.95	0.53
14	1.31	0.99	11,837	1.01	0.90	1.06	0.89	1.16
15	1.24	0.93	9,176	1.00	0.89	1.20	0.82	0.90
16	1.4	1.06	14,419	1.05	1.04	1.23	1.16	1.05
17	1.4	1.06	13,597	1.01	1.14	1.18	1.35	0.95
18	1.19	0.90	7,811	1.01	1.03	1.16	0.90	0.63
19	1.28	0.97	10,174	1.06	1.03	1.11	0.89	0.79
20	1.27	0.96	10,224	1.06	0.95	1.18	0.88	0.84

[a] Productivity-oriented profit.

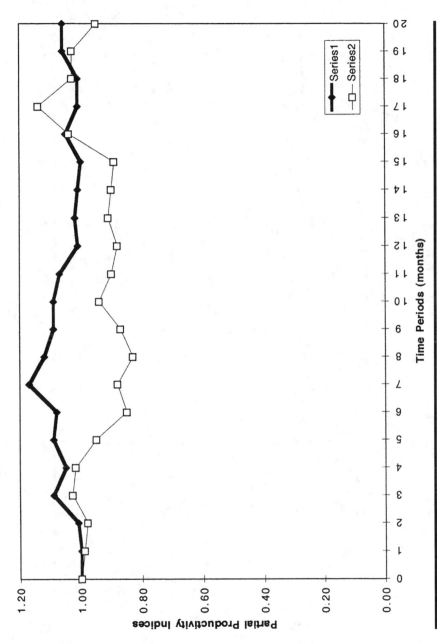

FIGURE 5.23 Partial productivity indices: human (series 1) and material (series 2) inputs.

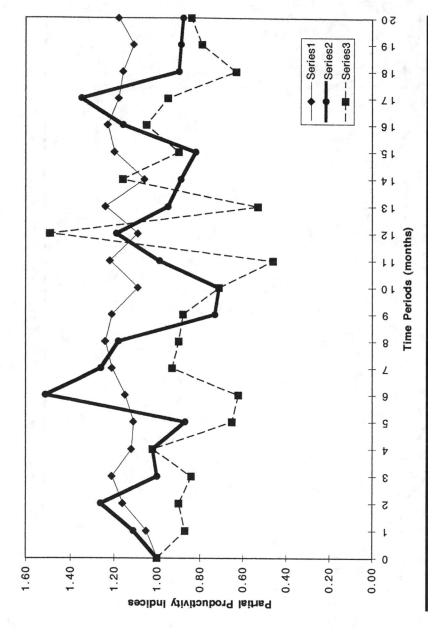

FIGURE 5.24   Partial productivity indices: capital (series 1), energy (series 2), and other expense (series 3) inputs.

indices. Notice the wide fluctuations in the other expense productivity. This indicates that the restaurant was not making a conscious effort to control expenses in this category. The manager was concentrating more on the human and material inputs, largely because they accounted for most of the total input.

Benefits—This study indicated the potential of applying the TPM to a restaurant unit of a major multinational company. The analysis also demonstrated the close relationship between profit and total productivity over a 20-month period. Any restaurant can do the "profit targeting" based on a regression model, linking the productivity-oriented profit and the total productivity level. Alternatively, using total productivity as a random variable, it is possible to develop a computer simulation so that various profit scenarios can be simulated.

Summary—It is safe to conclude from this study that the TPM can be implemented in any type of restaurant—fast-food with eat-in, drive-through, a combination or the two, or strictly eat-in. Because of space limitations, other types of restaurants are not covered in this section, but their experience reinforces the same fundamental fact—the TPM is a powerful tool to manage any restaurant and provides insights that traditional management does not offer.

Questions to Ponder—

5.9.1 Which of the input resources in a restaurant are relatively more difficult to control? Why?

5.9.2 What are the traditional measures of performance most fast-food restaurants use? Prepare a critique of these measures.

5.9.3 What insights are added by the TPM analysis in a restaurant, as gleaned from this case study?

5.9.4 Develop a regression model, linking productivity-oriented profit to total productivity. Play the "what if" game with this model, and develop a methodology to integrate this model into strategic planning and business plans.

5.9.5 Conduct a total productivity benchmarking study of the fast-food restaurant business. Discuss the lessons learned.

5.9.6 Repeat the preceding question for restaurants in general. Compare the average total productivity in both these cases. Comment on the similarities and differences.

5.10 RETAILING

Background—This case deals with a major retail company, headquartered in the United States. The scope of the study covers four years (1990 to 1993) for all operations nationwide. The company does not operate overseas, except for factories in Asia. In this project, human, fixed, and working capital; material, energy, and other expense; and the total productivity of the company were assessed after measurement. Data for intangible factors were not available at the time of the study; therefore, the Comprehensive Total Productivity Model could not be applied.

The objective of the study was not only to analyze the ratios of the TPM, but also to validate the claims of a well-known management writer that this company is a leader in productivity in its industry. This company provides the best product handling and delivery to its outlets and retailers in the clothing business, and it has been managed so well that it has been singled out by many authors.

The company purchases, develops, and sells women's apparel. It also creates, develops, and manufactures bath and personal care items and sells men's and children's apparel as well. In 1992, the company employed 100,700 workers, and recorded sales were $6,944,296,000. The company has five major subsidiaries, whose merchandise is commonly seen in U.S. malls.

Implementation—The data were obtained from a university library's Disclosure database and were then transformed into constant dollars.

Results and Analysis—According to company records, sales during the fourth quarter of 1992 increased 18% (to $2.428 billion) and net income was a record 10% of sales. This can be further confirmed by the total productivity trend. Indeed, there is a big gap between total productivity and the break-even point of total productivity for 1991 and 1990 (Figure 5.25).

However, the gross income of the company was flat when compared to 1991. There have been increases in human, other expense, and working capital productivities (Figure 5.26). The following is a list of the most important aspects of the study:

- The average store size increased 7% in 1991, and sales per average store increased 5%. Human productivity, however, was the lowest in the four-year period, but has been increasing gradually. The company considers its sales productivity in terms of a ratio of sales per average selling square foot.

- The company had announced its intention to add approximately 2.5 million selling square feet in 1993, representing an 11% increase over 1992. This increase represented approximately 350 new stores and 290 remodeled ones.

- The consistent increase in human productivity could be due to retirement benefits made available to all associates who completed 1,000 hours of

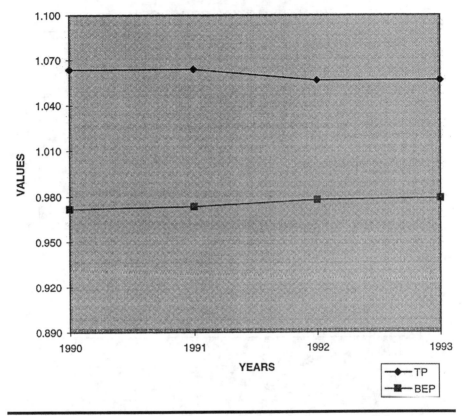

YEARS	TP	BEP
1990	1.064	0.972
1991	1.064	0.974
1992	1.056	0.978
1993	1.057	0.979

FIGURE 5.25 Total productivity versus break-even point of the retail firm.

service with the company during certain 12-month periods and reached the age of 21. Company contributions to this plan increased from $14.6 to $16.3 to $20.1 million from 1990 to 1992.

- The working capital input also had an upward trend over the last few years. The company spent $428.8 million in 1990, $523.1 million in 1991, and $429.5 million in 1992 for remodeling, expanding existing stores, completion of a fulfillment center and office, and the acquisition of some office facilities. These purchases were said to be more profitable

YEARS	PPI_H	PPI_{WC}
1990	1.000	1
1991	0.995	1.064287
1992	1.007	1.246953
1993	1.021	1.31266

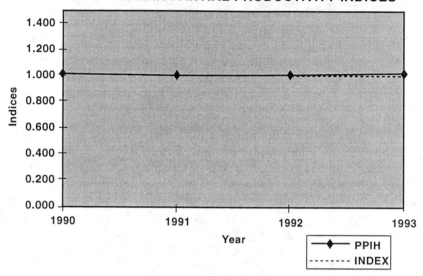

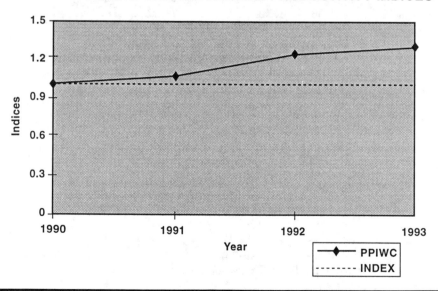

FIGURE 5.26   Partial productivity indices of the retail firm.

YEARS	PPI$_{M\&E}$	PPI$_{OE}$
1990	1	1
1991	0.998707	1.006183
1992	0.972366	1.168569
1993	0.965554	1.211261

MATERIAL AND ENERGY PARTIAL PRODUCTIVITY INDICES

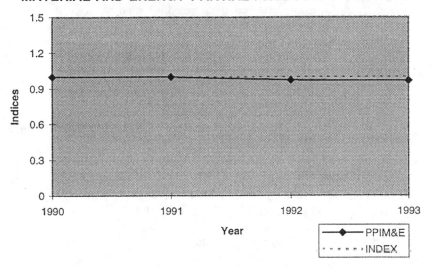

OTHER EXPENSES PARTIAL PRODUCTIVITY INDICES

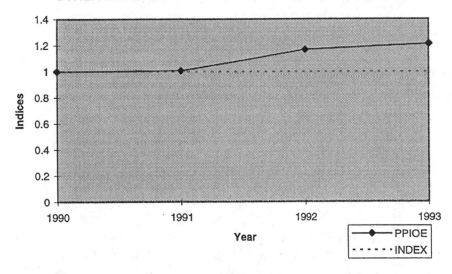

FIGURE 5.26   Partial productivity indices of the retail firm (continued).

to the company than their opportunity cost. The increase could be seen in the working capital productivity.

- Operating income as a percentage of sales was 11.4%, 11.6%, and 13.3% for fiscal years 1993, 1992, and 1990. It increased, as did working capital productivity. The company's explanation was that there were high costs of buying and occupancy.
- Energy productivity showed a decreasing trend. A possible explanation for this is that the costs of materials and energy had risen steadily in the last four years, while the tangible outputs also rose, but at a lower rate.
- Other expense productivity went up, due to purchasing buildings, stores, and warehouses and even remodeling. The company recognized that the foreign component of pretax income rose principally from overseas sourcing operations. The figures were $58.7 million in 1990, $44.7 million in 1991, and $72.9 million in 1992.
- Human, working capital, and other expense productivities increased, and material and energy partial productivities decreased. However, the most important one—total productivity—increased slightly from 1990 to 1992, but stayed around the same from 1992 to 1993.

In general, the company was performing well—acquiring more assets, buying and indexing companies which became more profitable after acquisition, and hiring more people. There seemed to be slow but secure growth, and the right steps were being taken toward success. One of the company's strategies to increase sales was through catalog sales, which increased every year, as did the number of catalogs mailed.

Summary—This case demonstrates the power of the TPM to help a major company, considered one of the leaders in quality, customer responsiveness, and total productivity.

Questions to Ponder—

5.10.1 What two input factors make up the biggest part of the firm's total input?

5.10.2 What percentage of total inputs does each of these factors represent?

5.10.3 What strategies are used by this company to increase total sales?

5.10.4 Why does working capital show an increasing trend from 1990 to 1993?

5.10.5 Study three major retail firms similar to the one presented in this case. What lessons and general principles can be learned from this study?

5.11 TOURISM

Background—This case study* deals with a major regional tourism office in the United States. The TPM was applied, and recommendations were made in the hope of improving total productivity at the firm (office) level, as well as at the operational unit level. The office was observed during fiscal years 1987 and 1988, for the equivalent of four quarters. The study focused on how trips to the Virgin Islands were marketed to prospective clients and how productive the methods of operation actually were. Output was measured in terms of three operational units—(1) sales calls, (2) trade shows, and (3) other promotions, which were the three main promotional activities of the tourism office. Partial productivities were calculated for each of the five inputs—human, material, capital (fixed and working), energy, and other expense. Several unique observations were made, and the following summary details the methodology and process whereby feasible, creative solutions and recommendations were made to improve the office's overall competitiveness.

This project accomplished its stated purpose of measuring the total productivity of a regional tourism office, a non-profit governmental entity, in a manner that reflects a direct relationship between output and inputs. The process involved collecting, organizing, and applying on a quarterly basis office data to the TPM. The three operational units analyzed were sales calls, trade shows, and other promotions, the three primary marketing tools the office used to promote the Virgin Islands within the southeast region.

Implementation—As stated above, the study was conducted over a two-year period, with the TPM focusing on the operation of selling trips to the Virgin Islands. The first step in our analysis was to look at the productivity values of each operational unit and to determine which component of the firm's output would benefit the most from productivity improvements. Based upon our extracted data, we were able to calculate the total productivity for each unit and measure this value against the respective break-even point. By analyzing each operational unit and knowing that the total output is merely the sum of the individual operating unit, we get a clear picture of how each product or, more precisely, method of marketing is performing and are equipped to make the necessary changes where needed.

---

* I wish to thank Ms. Elizabeth Stanley, who did this study under my supervision. Her project was titled "Tourism in the United States, Virgin Islands: A Productivity Measurement Study," Master's Project, August 1994. This case has been extracted from her study, with much gratitude.

Results and Analysis—Beginning with the operational unit sales calls, it was found that they constituted only about 2% of all output for the entire period of observation. On the other hand, trade shows and other promotions made up nearly 33 and 65% of the total output, respectively. However, the cost of each of these promotional services varied in an opposite fashion. Sales calls cost $12.80, trade shows $3.14, and other promotions, the greatest source of output in the company, only $2.66 per activity. Thus, we can argue that if even minor improvements could be made in the way other promotions were handled, this would have a tremendous impact on the total productivity and hence the profitability of the office, since the costs are already very low for this marketing strategy.

The total productivity values for the tourism office (firm) and for each of the promotional activities (operational units) are shown in Table 5.13 (for 1986–87) and Table 5.14 (for 1987–88). In general, total productivity trends for each promotional activity demonstrated an inverse relationship. In other words, positive productivity changes between periods in one activity were generally counteracted by negative productivity changes in another activity. In addition, the magnitude of these changes was mostly due to consistent positive or negative trends in each of the partial productivity values.

A good starting point is an evaluation of productivity trends and their impact on total and partial productivity values for each promotional activity. Productivity values oscillated widely between time periods. The results of sales calls best exemplify this trend. Productivity values for sales calls skyrocketed between the first and second quarters in both 1987 and 1988. This change is attributed to significant increases in sales calls output and partial productivities. Sales calls output jumped more than 130-fold between quarters 1 and 2 in 1986–87 and 1987–88. Moreover, partial productivity indices for sales calls indicated tremendous increases in every input factor during the same time period.

Total and partial productivity values for the office and each promotional activity were evaluated between successive time periods during fiscal years

TABLE 5.13   Summary of Total Productivity Values for the Office and Each Promotional Activity, 1986–87

Activity	Quarter 1	Quarter 2	Quarter 3	Quarter 4
Office	0.2252	0.2598	0.5388	0.1369
Sales calls	0.0019	0.2191	0.1056	0.0749
Trade shows	0.1426	0.0794	0.9101	0.0570
Other promotions	0.5169	0.5234	0.5943	0.2991

TABLE 5.14 Summary of Total Productivity Values for the Office and Each Promotional Activity, 1987–88

Activity	Quarter 1	Quarter 2	Quarter 3	Quarter 4
Office	0.5861	1.0534	0.3935	0.2004
Sales calls	0.0021	0.2377	0.0607	0.0062
Trade shows	1.3656	2.3322	0.7610	0.1648
Other promotions	0.3532	0.5862	0.3498	0.4188

1987 and 1988. It is on the basis of these evaluations that two important questions were answered.

The first question concerned effectiveness, or the degree to which division standards for promotional activities were being achieved. Productivity values for the office and each promotional activity indicated that the division requirements for some of the promotional activities were achievable, but only at the expense of other promotional activities.

Trade show contacts surpassed division-imposed standards during the first and second quarters of 1988. By the end of the second quarter of 1988, halfway through the year, the office completed more than 80% of the total trade show contacts for the fiscal year.

However, this accomplishment came at a great expense to sales call activity and, to a lesser extent, other promotions, such as familiarization trips. Sales calls were essentially zero during the first quarter of each fiscal year. Moreover, the wide oscillation in productivity values for sales calls suggested the absence of a proper plan of action for that activity.

The dramatic highs in one promotional activity and corresponding lows in another activity suggested that while division objectives may be achievable, one reason they were not met is that there were not enough physical bodies to "mind the store," target 70% of all trade show attendees at various trade shows, and still initiate 200 sales calls per month to travel agents in eight states!

An evaluation of promotional activity values revealed one discernible office condition that played a vital role in the prioritizing of promotional activity achievements—irregular receipt of appropriated funds.

An examination of office financial records revealed a history of unusual reimbursements. Reimbursements to office personnel for apparent office expenses was the norm. The personal income of office employees regularly supplemented the office budget to pay for promotional expenses during periods of limited office funds.

Second, a history of prepaying non-promotion-related office bills several months in advance existed. This appeared to be a likely consequence of unpredictable funding. As soon as funds were received, survival office needs, such as rent, postage, telephone, and other similar expenses, were met first, before promotion activities. These conditions were likened to management by crisis rather than management by objectives.

This study made it clear that the office engaged in more promotional activities when it had a larger budget. Tables 5.13 and 5.14 indicate that office productivity was much higher in fiscal year 1988 than in 1987. Office expenditures of $193,713.44 for fiscal year 1988 exceeded the previous year's expenditures by more than 55%.

Recommendations and Benefits—Three recommendations were made in reference to the first question. First, it is imperative that the office regularly receive appropriation funds when scheduled—on the first day of October, January, April, and July. This is a necessary first step in making promotional activities genuine office priorities. Second, the office's budget must be increased.

Third, the manpower must be increased. A different organizational structure was recommended for the regional office. This structure would expand the office's present sales staff from one sales representative to six: one each for Atlanta, Orlando/Tampa, Miami, Dallas, Houston, and the states of Alabama and Louisiana. For clearly cost-minimization reasons, sales representatives should live in their respective marketing regions, working basically out of their homes and reporting to the regional office.

Four administrative assistants will assist the representatives in sales maintenance as follows: one each for Georgia, Florida, and Texas and another for Alabama and Louisiana. A minimum of two office clerks will be needed for clerical duties and assistance in sales maintenance, as necessary. This is clearly the most effective way of gaining maximum promotional results with minimum cost.

As to the second question—whether the office can do a better job of using its resources efficiently—there was room for improvement. A few recommendations were made for creating a more cost-effective office data collection system:

1. Consistency of sales call reporting
2. Differentiation between trade show and other promotions reporting
3. Consistent Object Code usage
4. Maintain current, complete, and accurate files

The third and fourth recommendations are worth emphasizing, because they concern reporting on the distribution of government funds. In the preparation of office records, computerization of the entire division into a giant computer network, where the central and all offshore offices are linked into one system, would mean that the regional office could communicate very inexpensively with the central or another regional office without lifting the telephone or sending a fax.

Questions to Ponder—

5.11.1 What are some of the critical factors contributing to erratic fluctuations in total productivity of a tourism office?

5.11.2 What are the most common operational units in a regional tourism office? Which ones contribute the most to revenues?

5.11.3 Study three tourism offices, possibly in other countries. What can you learn from this comparative study in terms of productivity management in general and total productivity in particular?

5.12 TRANSPORTATION

Transit productivity is becoming an important matter as the rate of growth in transit funding declines and revenues through additional taxes become an unpopular political strategy.

Background[7]—This case represents the first application of the TPM in the transit industry. This project was done through the sponsorship of the Urban Mass Transit Authority of the U.S. Department of Transportation.

Traditionally, transit managers have relied on labor productivity measures, expressed as:

- Vehicle miles per operator, or
- Vehicle revenue hours per operator

As articulated several times before, one of the serious dangers of relying exclusively on such partial productivity measures is the risk of ignoring other important input resources. For example, in transit systems, energy input (fuel) is one of the most dominant input factors, accounting for as much as 60% of the total operating expense. Therefore, the traditional emphasis tends to steer management away from careful control of critical resources such as fuel, maintenance technologies, and the like, while focusing disproportionately more attention on labor, which accounts for a relatively small proportion of input.

The transit operation where the study was conducted and the TPM applied is located in the state of Florida, with 45 operational units (county cost centers). Three operational units—paratransit, transit (buses), and emergency medical services (EMS)—accounted for 75% of the transit operation's revenues. Therefore, these three were selected for the study/implementation.

The study was undertaken at an interesting time. Prior to June 1985, the county transit system was run as a public operation. During 1985–86, a private company was given the responsibility for equipment maintenance, facilities, and management functions as a privatization experiment.

Transit Division—The physical plant of the transit division consisted of municipal buses, which served ten fixed routes county-wide.

Paratransit Division—The physical plant of the paratransit division consisted of 20 special-purpose buses. They were equipped with special equipment to transport the physically and mentally handicapped, the elderly, and the disabled.

Emergency Medical Services—The physical plant of EMS consisted of 12 modular full-service ambulances and 6 auxiliary rescue vehicles. The ambulances carried most of the medical equipment needed for life-support and sustainment. The rescue vehicles included devices for rescue operations.

Implementation—The operational version of the TPM was applied to the selected transit and ambulance operations. The two seasonal base period quantities (t = 0) for all three operational units were established by seasonal adjustments of the average of all months over the previous two fiscal years (1983–84 and 1984–85). All input and output values starting with July 1985 (t = 1) were compared to the average monthly input costs as a private sector business, and the output for the last two years was compared as public sector operational units. The difficulty in data collection came from the fact that the county transit system—a public entity—controlled the output mileage, energy, and fixed capital inputs, while the private company controlled the human, material, working capital, and other expense inputs as they pertained to servicing of vehicles. After a somewhat difficult but comprehensive data collection and allocation of resources, the TPM was applied to the first three months after privatization.

Results—Table 5.15 summarizes the total productivity values and the corresponding break-even point values for each of the three operational units and for the "firm" overall. Table 5.16 summarizes the partial productivity indices for operational unit 1.

Analysis—Figure 5.27 shows that the transition system as a whole was losing money—a fact confirmed by the firm's accountants; the total productivity level is below the break-even point for all the periods. Analysis of Figures 5.28 to 5.30 indicates the following points:

Operational Unit 1—
1. This unit was not profitable at this time; the total productivity values consistently stayed below the break-even point values for all the time periods.

TABLE 5.15   Summary of Total Productivity Values and Corresponding Break-Even Points of Total Productivity in $/$

	Period (monthly)				
	0	1	2	3	Remarks
One					
TP_1	0.457	0.533	0.537	0.519	Unprofitable operation
TP_1 (BEP)	0.963	0.992	0.881	0.978	
Two					
TP_2	1.061	1.213	1.14	1.105	Profitable operation
TP_2 (BEP)	0.955	0.976	0.995	0.988	
Three					
TP_3	0.997	0.898	1.037	1.098	Profitable operation
TP_3 (BEP)	0.971	0.965	0.972	0.978	
Transit operation (overall)					
TPF	0.774	0.832	0.854	0.851	Unprofitable operation
TPF (BEP)	0.963	0.979	0.939	0.982	overall

    2.   Operational productivity was very low in the base period.
    3.   Initial productivity was very low in the base period, and significant increases were needed to make the unit profitable.

Operational Unit 2 —
    1.   This was a very profitable operation.
    2.   Values during the third period tended to indicate a slight slowdown, possibly reaching a plateau.
    3.   Performance was strong and stable.

TABLE 5.16   Partial Productivity Indices with Respect to Various Input Factors for Operational Unit 1

		Period (monthly)		
Input Factor		1	2	3
Energy	1.000	1.014	1.133	0.983
Human	1.000	1.406	1.778	1.32
Material	1.000	1.117	1.27	1.151
Working capital	1.000	5.109	0.363	2.065
Fixed capital	1.000	1.000	1.000	1.000
Other expense	1.000	1.004	1.107	1.107

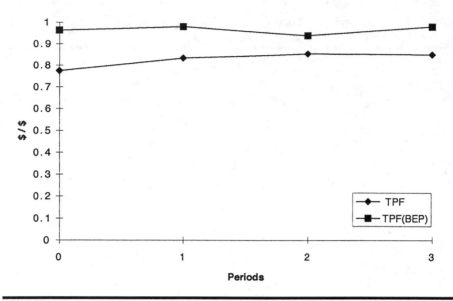

FIGURE 5.27   Total productivity and break-even point for the firm (transit operation as a whole).

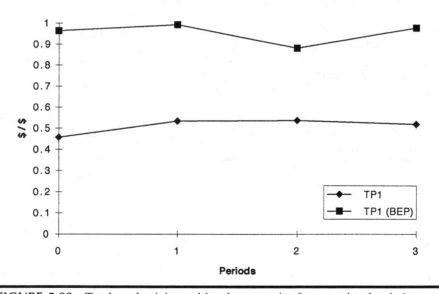

FIGURE 5.28   Total productivity and break-even point for operational unit 1.

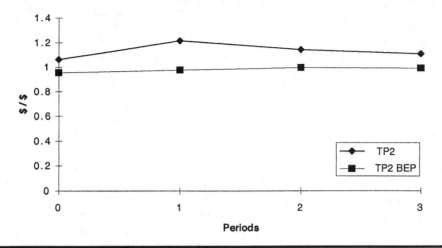

FIGURE 5.29   Total productivity and break-even point for operational unit 2.

Operational Unit 3—

1. This unit was a slow starter, but showed profitable operation.
2. All indicators showed a trend toward further and a rapid rate of improvement.
3. This unit has good growth potential.

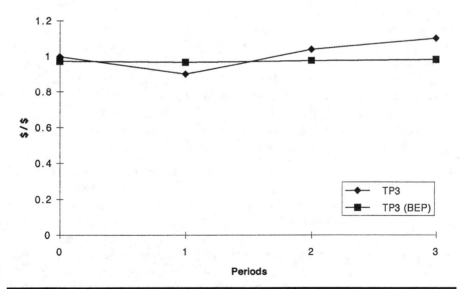

FIGURE 5.30   Total productivity and break-even point for operational unit 3.

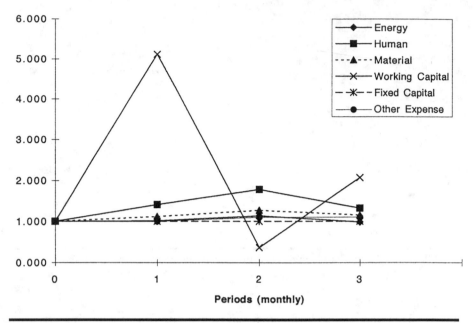

FIGURE 5.31   Profiles of productivity for operational unit 1.

Since operational unit 1 was the main problem, its partial productivities were analyzed from Figure 5.31, which clearly shows that energy productivity, after an initial increase, dropped significantly, as did the trend for human productivity. Material productivity increased steadily up to period 2, but dropped in period 3. Working capital productivity showed wide fluctuations, indicating a lack of formal control by management. Fixed capital productivity remained virtually the same, because no additional facilities, technologies, or machines were added during the three months after the base period. Other expense productivity showed reasonable improvement on a steady basis, because this was relatively easier to control through managerial actions.

Benefits—The results of the productivity measurement contributed to a framework for more accurate budgeting and profit sharing among public operations and private contractors. Through the use of the TPM, the performance of both public and private entities can be quantified and documented to promote public and private sector partnerships in equitable productivity gainsharing. The benefits of this approach to evaluating current and future productivity profit-sharing opportunities among private contractors and similar public agencies is significant. The technique can contribute to more efficient contracting, administration, and price negotiations for the public sector and cost reductions in bid preparation, more accurate bid preparation, and greater profitability for the private sector.

Summary—This study involved a private company that was given a public contract to maintain the physical plant of a large metropolitan county. To reduce the scope of the TPM implementation, only three operational units were studied: mass transit, paratransit, and EMS. The difficulty in analysis stemmed from the fact that a public administrator controlled output mileage, energy, and fixed capital inputs, while the private company controlled human, material, working capital, and other expense inputs as they pertained to servicing of vehicles. After difficult, but versatile, data collection and allocation of resources, the study analyzed the first three months after privatization, relying heavily on the total productivity break-even analysis. These results showed the effects of the learning curve and the drastic need for increased productivity in some areas. The studies demonstrated the versatility and usefulness of the TPM in measuring the productivity of a public/private transit operation.

Also, the concept of productivity-oriented profit as measured by the TPM provides clear mathematical definition to the difficult issues of rate adjustment, target budgets, and bid prices.

Questions to Ponder—

5.12.1   Discuss productivity measurement in the public sector as a central issue in private contracting and privatization in areas of public regulation and administration.

5.12.2   As part of the Level 4 analysis for this case, what specific industrial engineering approaches or other techniques would you recommend to significantly change the total productivity situation positively for operational unit 1?

5.12.3   Visit a local transit agency and conduct a similar study. Compare the results with those of the case study presented here. Comment on the results.

5.12.4   What are five major challenges faced by transit managers today? Discuss them briefly and develop some insights into the commonalities of issues.

5.12.5   Does privatization work profitably in the transit industry? Give examples of successfully operating privatized transit operations.

5.12.6   Develop a complete plan to implement the TPmgt process in a transit operation that has ground, rail, and ferryboat modes of transportation. Make suitable assumptions, recognizing the uniqueness of these three modes of operation.

5.13 UTILITIES

Every city in the world probably has an electric and water utility. Application of the TPmgt philosophy in an electric and water utility was demonstrated over a period of nearly two years in the mid to late 1980s.

Background—This small utility (employing about 250 engineers, technicians, and staff) produces and distributes electricity and water to an entire island in the Dutch Antilles. This utility is about 70 years old.

The island, being a popular tourist spot, was registering on average about 10 to 12% growth in demand for electricity at the time of the implementation.

Implementation—A request to implement TPmgt came from the technical director of the utility, who had been a graduate student in my two productivity courses.

Pre-TPmgt Phase—Before the mission statement step, I gave a one-hour presentation on TPmgt to management, the union leaders, and the union stewards. Following my evaluation through a "readiness survey," management and I agreed that there appeared to be sufficient reason to implement the TPmgt philosophy.

Mission Statement—In a one-day retreat, I facilitated a group of about 35 management and union people to develop their company's mission statement—for the first time in its history! All 12 factors (as pointed out in the TPmgt implementation methodology in Chapter 4) were taken into consideration *before* the mission statement was developed. The union president could not believe the way we involved him right from day one. The mission statement, ratified by the company's employees, was the starting point for a change in management thinking. The mission statement adopted is shown in Figure 5.32. The buy-in was easy, because all the union stewards were involved in carving out the mission statement from the very beginning.

PQT Training—I then trained about 30 managers and supervisors, including the "management team" (that's how the company characterized its top management) in the PQT training. Then, some of them were asked to train a group of 15 to 20 people. Almost all the employees in the company were trained by this "train-the-trainer" approach. Most of them, for the first time, received training in QC tools, industrial engineering tools, and techniques of planning, organizing, motivating, delegating, controlling, and communicating. Many engineers and older supervisors had been previously trained in Holland. Nevertheless, this was an interesting departure from their usual understanding of management principles, particularly those related to productivity, quality, and technology.

---

1. To produce and distribute reliable and continuous electricity and water supply and service, in an effective and efficient manner at least cost to the community.

2. To create, foster, and secure healthy working conditions for all employees.

3. To stimulate, develop and utilize employees' potential to the fullest, for the common good of all.

FIGURE 5.32   The mission statement of the electric and water utility.

Management Goals and Action Plans—The key group of managers, supervisors, and union stewards was brought together to develop the management goals and action plans, as suggested in Chapter 4.

Results and Benefits—As the implementation of the action plans began, I saw some exciting results. For example, a supervisor who had been with the company for 16 years came forward to suggest a way to cut down the accounts receivables rather dramatically. He said he was hesitant to suggest his idea all those years for fear of rejection by management. He and I spent about half a day turning his idea into a proposal with a cost–benefit analysis. The idea was accepted by the director and the general manager within a week! The result was a recurring savings of about $230,000 per year from an idea to improve the bill collection process through a new policy, enabled by a software change in the billing module.

The human dimension truly began to mature in the managerial decision-making process. One of the constant challenges the company faced was the rising demand for electricity and water. The power plant and water plant always seemed to be expanding with new engines and water treatment facilities. The typical "blame routines" surfaced here and there all the time. Nevertheless, the utility managed to bring in "appropriate" technologies. For example, the engineers decided to purchase and install Finnish diesel engine technologies to increase power generation capacity, rather than continue the 60-year tradition of using Dutch diesel engine technologies. This bold step paid off in dramatically reducing the total cost per kilowatt-hour (Figure 5.33).

Company management and the union leadership worked together closely, for the first time in a long time!

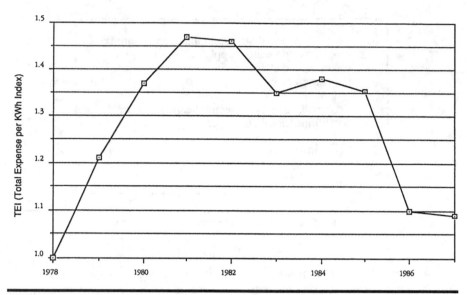

FIGURE 5.33   Total expenses per kilowatt-hour produced.

Questions to Ponder—

5.13.1   Are electric and water utilities unique in terms of the readiness factors to implement TPmgt? Give reasons to support your answer(s).

5.13.2   Conduct a study of an electric and/or water utility in your area, using the "total productivity perspective." Identify the deficiencies from this perspective. Develop a list of recommendations, and present them to the management of that utility.

5.13.3   From the study in the preceding question, develop a strategy to tailor TPmgt to address the unique conditions prevailing in the utility. Discuss the strategy with the top management.

5.13.4   Do a benchmarking study of electricity and/or water utilities in your state and/or country. Document the insights learned. Share them with those who could benefit most from the study.

5.14 CHEMICALS

Background—This chemical company is one of the largest in the world. It manufactures and sells chemicals and performance products including chlorinated solvents and latex coatings, thermoplastics and thermoses, styrofoam products, agricultural products such as herbicides, pharmaceuticals, consumer products such as freezer bags, ethylene and propylene, and cogencrates power and steam. Its 240 subsidiaries all over the world produce a wide range of products that can be classified as follows: basic chemicals, basic plastics, hydrocarbon and energy, and consumer products.

Implementation—Since the company under consideration is a very large corporation, with hundreds of subsidiaries and thousands of products, every product has it own value of total productivity, and the total productivity of the company is calculated as the weighted sum of these individual total productivities. Naturally, the ups and downs of the individual products tend to cancel each other, so that the total productivity of the firm follows a much smoother pattern than the individual total productivities. Therefore, the product portfolios are divided into product segments that exhibit similar production or marketing considerations. This way, the effects of the major factors on a product segment do not disappear in a large mix of products.

Results and Analysis—The results and analysis presented below pertain to the four fundamental product segments.

Basic Chemicals—The 1980s began with only a moderate productivity increase for basic chemicals for several reasons. First, there was a global overcapacity in this segment. Second, due to the overvalued dollar, the pricing climate remained unfavorable, thus strengthening imports into the United States. Third, the company incurred some heavy initial costs for these increments while opening new plants. However, in the second half of the 1980s, this segment had an outstanding performance. Supply and demand in this segment were in balance globally. Also, the prices maintained an upward momentum, and energy costs were relatively flat during this period. All these factors contributed to a record level of total productivity (Figure 5.34). Nonetheless, this favorable climate did not continue into the 1990s. Sales and earnings dropped sharply due to declines in both volume and price; thus, total output declined. This situation was complicated by some non-recurring charges due to the shutdown of some facilities and higher energy costs.

Basic Plastics—During the early 1980s, the conditions under which this segment operated were fairly good. Most products had a substantial growth in demand. However, the company decreased prices in anticipation of the start-up of new capacity in gas-rich countries. These factors caused a moderate increase in total productivity. In the late 1980s, favorable economic conditions allowed the company higher sales, and thus higher total output, for almost all products. As this segment was very much dependent on economic cycles, its productivity performance decreased in the early 1990s (Figure 5.35). However, this segment

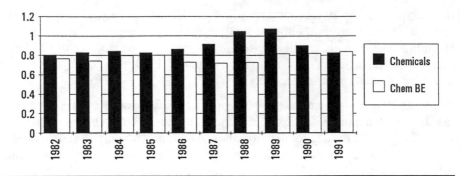

FIGURE 5.34   Total productivity levels of the basic chemicals segment.

was expected to recover slowly as the key sectors, like automotive, construction, and consumer durables, started to recover.

Hydrocarbons and Energy—This segment experienced slow growth in the early 1980s, although the total output for this segment increased significantly. However, major products incurred losses in this period, since the cost of newly modernized production processes offset the increase in sales. During the mid and late 1980s, the company had a moderate increase in sales and income and thus total output. Also, energy markets were fairly stable, especially crude oil prices. In addition, production continued at or near full capacity. All of these factors brought about a moderate increase in total productivity (Figure 5.36). However, during the early 1990s, this segment experienced drops in total productivity. First, high inventory-carrying costs contributed to an increase in total

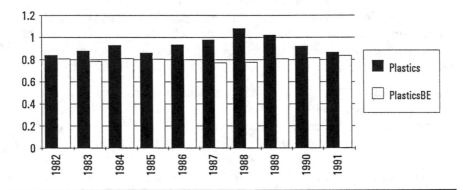

FIGURE 5.35   Total productivity levels of the basic plastics segment.

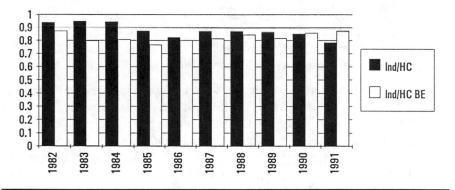

FIGURE 5.36   Total productivity levels of the hydrocarbon and energy segment.

input. Second, prices declined, and third, overcapacity further complicated the situation.

Consumer Products — In this segment, sales and earnings rose in the early 1980s. However, total productivity did not increase in proportion, due to some unfavorable economic conditions. In the late 1980s, sales rose more consistently. At the same time, prices were going up. Thus, some raw material cost increases were passed on to customers. In 1989, the company entered joint ventures, made acquisitions, and launched new products. All these efforts increased the total input, but the total output increased later due to the time lag between the start of the productivity improvement efforts and their results. When the benefits were realized later in the early 1990s, sales reached record levels, with total productivity also improving significantly (Figure 5.37). The main reasons for this improvement were strategic acquisition and internal growth.

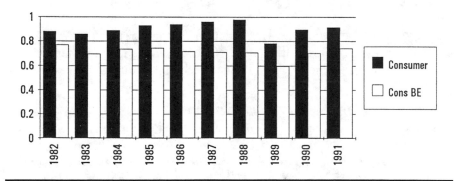

FIGURE 5.37   Total productivity levels of the consumer products segment.

As a result of this study, major factors affecting the total productivity levels of the company were identified as corporate strategies—in this case, diversification, economic conditions and business cycles, effects of product life cycles, environmental considerations, and research and development.

Summary—This case was concerned with the total productivity of a major chemical company from 1982 to 1991. It is one of the largest corporations in the U.S. chemical industry. This empirical study is based on observation of the total productivity levels of the selected company and correlation of observed trends with relevant events in order to identify the major factors affecting total productivity levels. Since the company under consideration is mostly an industrial company, the Operational Total Productivity Model, a version of the TPM, was considered appropriate for analysis. A number of useful insights were gleaned from this case.

Questions to Ponder—

5.14.1   Why did the basic chemicals segment of the company experience an unfavorable climate during the 1990s?

5.14.2   What factors caused a moderate increase in the total productivity of the basic plastics segment during the early 1980s?

5.14.3   What segment experienced major declines in total productivity during the early 1990s?

5.14.4   Why did the consumer products segment experience an increase in total input during 1989?

5.14.5   Study other major chemical companies and contrast their total productivity trends with this one. What can be learned as general truths from this study?

5.15   COMPUTER PERIPHERALS

Background—The electronics systems manufacturing organization in this case consisted of five functional areas, each of which reports to the systems manufacturing manager. These areas are defined according to functional responsibility, as follows.

Electronic Card Production Facility—This function was responsible for the procurement of parts, scheduling parts and coordinating production work flow, and actual manufacturing of the card assemblies used in the product. The function was made up of production employees as well as all the support groups needed to produce the cards. The support groups included manufacturing engineering, quality assurance, planning, procurement, and production control organizations.

System Production—The system production function was responsible for final production of units which were shipped to the parent organization's marketing group. Its responsibilities included procurement of parts, scheduling production of final assemblies, and processing customer orders. In addition, the function had responsibility for planning the inventory levels of parts for the entire production operation, both those purchased and those used in the card assembly production.

System Technical Services—The technical services function was responsible for manufacturing engineering and quality assurance support needed for the system production. This function was also responsible for introduction of new products into the systems manufacturing plant. This new product administration responsibility included the interface between product planning, development engineering, and various other groups involved with the release of new products.

Distribution and Plant Systems—This function was responsible for two major work areas within the systems manufacturing unit. The first was material distribution, including responsibility for moving parts from initial receipt to various warehouse storage areas, storing and controlling parts while in the warehouse, and moving them to various major assembly areas. This function was also responsible for shipment of the final system to the parent organization's marketing group. The second responsibility, plant systems, included all information-processing support for the various manufacturing operations. This did not include support for systems and software associated with other areas, such as product development or support of the general site. The plant systems group was responsible for various distributed processing systems that control such tasks as parts shipping, manufacturing logistics control, and quality data collection, among others.

Planning—The planning function was the smallest of the five. Its tasks included the coordination of all other areas of planning input and tracking the various control measurements for the entire systems manufacturing unit. This function was also responsible for coordination of any new product sizings to assure that all plant resource requirements were identified.

Implementation—The project was limited to analysis of those aspects under total control of the systems manufacturing unit. This included procurement, stocking, and distribution of components and subassemblies; scheduling of internal production; and assembly and testing of circuit cards and the final product itself. Excluded were the marketing and sales functions and collection of revenue from the customer, since these were taken care of by systems manufacturing's parent organization. Therefore, evaluation of systems manufacturing with respect to the total productivity break-even point was not attempted. The TPM was applied to the organization for the ten-month period from January 1985 through October 1985.

The general methodology used was the application of the TPM to the systems manufacturing operational unit. This effort was guided by the systematic steps in implementing the TPM.

The operational unit chosen for this study was a medium-priced computer, because of its versatility and the complex configurations that this versatility required. The product was offered in discrete modules that performed various functions. These modules could be assembled into several configurations based on the customers' needs. The product had a well-established base that was continually improved through the introduction of new models or the addition of new or upgraded features. The upgrades could be installed in existing customer systems through an upgrade ordering system which was supplied by the systems manufacturing operation. This allowed the customer to have the most current hardware and to include new functions as needs changed.

The system was used in a wide variety of applications in both industrial and business settings. The applications, as diversified as the customer set, included energy control systems, industrial manufacturing controls, and networking systems—just to name a few.

The product was sold to a wide range of customers, from small business operations with single-system orders to customers with large accounts and large volume orders. All systems were customized to a unique set of customer requirements and integrated into systems as they were manufactured.

The central order-processing system identified when the units would be available, based on the order, manufacturing, and shipment lead times. Once a specific order was placed and the various items to be integrated into the system identified, the order was sent to the systems manufacturing location. The process of accepting the order and subsequent manufacturing of the units was then initiated.

The TPM required the allocation of the input and output elements according to the individual products being manufactured. In the case of systems manufacturing, many different models of computers were produced, but there were many similarities among them. The assembly and test procedures in the plant were standardized for all of the many different models manufactured; each individual system was customized, using generic modules and assembly techniques. Because of this, the financial control used a uniform cost allocation system to perform its regular auditing and reporting functions. Each individual model within the product line is allocated a share of all costs based on that model's relative volume. Therefore, for the purpose of applying the TPM to this particular organization, it was determined that the various models produced by systems manufacturing would be considered one product. This meant that no allocation of inputs and outputs was required.

Results—A graphical profile of total and partial productivities was developed using the personal-computer-based program as was used above for data synthesis and computations. A partial productivity graph was developed for each of the input factors as well as the total productivity of the operational unit. Graphical representations were done for the partial and total productivity indices, in bar graph format, and for line graph comparisons of various groupings of related indices. These graphs proved very helpful in presenting findings to the functional groups and to systems manufacturing management.

Analysis—The analysis of trends in partial and total productivities was accomplished in three phases. First, the tabular (Table 5.17) and graphical (Figures 5.38 and 5.39) data were reviewed by the project team to ensure that the data were complete and error-free. This internal review also served as an opportunity for the project team to note the areas of concern. Concerns identified were resolved prior to reviewing the results with any other individuals.

Second, the data were reviewed with the key managers from those functional areas that had contributed data to the study. This review served to familiarize them with the results and implications of the study and also allowed them an opportunity to comment on any areas of particular interest to them. These managers were very interested in the results of the study and how they might indicate

TABLE 5.17 Total and Partial Productivity Indices for the Computer Peripherals Company

	Jan	*Feb*	*Mar*	*Apr*	*May*	*Jun*	*Jul*	*Aug*	*Sep*	*Oct*
Partial productivity index										
Human input	1.000	1.209	1.270	1.210	1.188	1.187	0.902	1.031	1.047	0.974
Material input	1.000	0.810	0.735	0.779	0.798	0.738	0.711	0.969	0.996	1.012
Capital input	1.000	1.156	1.168	1.035	1.058	0.993	0.730	0.795	0.840	0.793
Other input	1.000	1.201	1.278	1.165	1.184	1.221	0.903	0.984	0.987	0.942
Total productivity index	1.000	1.116	1.114	1.008	1.031	0.967	0.729	0.809	0.852	0.809

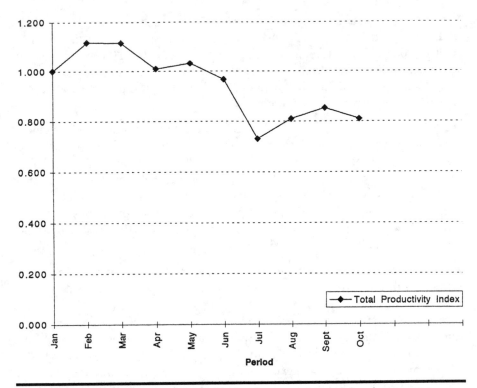

FIGURE 5.38   Total productivity index for the computer peripherals company.

progress toward their goals in the year to date. It was also pointed out to the managers that the TPM could serve as a basis for setting their organizational goals in the future.

The final review of the productivity trends was conducted with upper management from the key functional areas of electronic card production, system production, and planning. This review was intended to be an interim checkpoint for these managers, since it was proposed at the outset that the team was to meet with upper management from these areas upon completion of the project.

Human Productivity—The human productivity index showed a trend that followed the output curve very closely. This apparently was caused by the fact that the two major areas of input in this category (salaried workers and salaried professionals) had not changed significantly during the periods, while output was changing dramatically. The human productivity index for hourly paid professionals did show significant gains during the last several measurement peri-

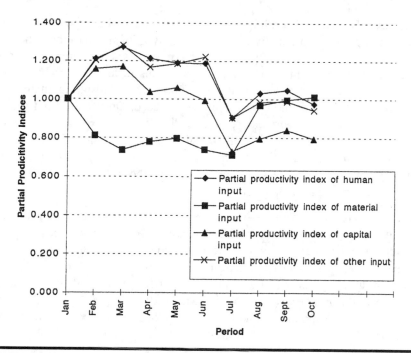

FIGURE 5.39 Partial productivity profiles for the computer peripherals company with respect to human, capital, material, and other expense input factors.

ods due to decreases in input. The opposite was true for the partial productivity measure for the hourly paid workers, which showed high levels of inefficiency throughout most of the measurement periods.

Material Productivity—Overall, material productivity showed a very interesting phenomenon. The index showed a steady decline through the first seven measurement periods and then showed a dramatic improvement for the final periods. This was apparently caused by the way purchases of materials from source #1 were planned. These purchases were planned at the beginning of the year, based on a then-current forecast for total productivity demand. Through the year, as demand fell short of the forecast, the appropriate action would have been to curtail purchases of materials from all sources. However, contracts that were in place between systems manufacturing and source #1 contained a clause that froze the level of purchases for several periods. For this reason, material productivity declined until the orders could be reset to lower levels to more accurately reflect the lower demand for the product.

Capital Productivity—Working capital input represented a major input. Therefore, working capital productivity was extremely critical. The index showed a stable or improved trend through the first six periods, but a dramatic drop in productivity was evident in the final periods. This, again, relates back to the problems with the controls on material inputs and the resulting increases in material inventory until the inputs could be reduced. During the final four periods, a slight improvement was seen, and this could be expected to continue because this measurement will follow the trend of the material productivity index, lagging by several periods. The occupancy and depreciation productivity measurements followed the same basic trend as the output, since they had a small degree of variance and output had a large variance.

Other Expense Productivity—This category of partial productivity included many diverse types of expense inputs. It was apparent, when looking at the individual indices, that certain items received considerable attention throughout the year, and their respective partial productivities improved. For example, the partial productivity for travel and professional fees improved during the last several periods primarily due to management attention. However, the partial productivities corresponding to stationery, telephone, and education did not show any improvements, but rather followed the output trend.

Total Productivity—The total productivity index followed the trend of the capital partial productivity (Figures 5.38 and 5.39) most closely. This is due to the fact that capital input accounts for a large part of the total input. The total productivity index followed the output level of the product very closely. That is, the total productivity index showed a decline when output was below the base period level, and the index showed improvement when output was above the base period level. The dramatic decline in total productivity in the seven periods was offset by a slight improving trend since that time. This trend was expected to continue as material inputs are reduced and other expenses are managed downward.

Benefits—Many aspects of TPmgt—in particular, the TPM—were consciously looked at in this case study. Application of the TPM demonstrated that practical insights which otherwise might be missed were gained from an observation of trends in the partial productivities.

The management of the company received presentations from the study team. A communication channel was established to understand the TPM and the philosophy of management associated with it.

Summary—This case dealt with the application of the TPM to a high-tech computer systems manufacturer. It analyzed total and partial productivities. Based on the analysis, a number of practical approaches were reviewed to improve the total productivity situation. Working capital input is a major, dominant input factor, and it pretty much dictates the trend in total productivity.

Questions to Ponder—

5.15.1 Discuss the importance of applying the TPmgt philosophy and methodology in the computer industry in light of some of the unique factors facing it today.

5.15.2 What was the major assumption made in this study in order to apply the TPM?

5.15.3 What is the effect of customized products on measuring productivity?

5.15.4 Conduct a benchmarking study of computer companies with respect to total productivity.

5.15.5 What can you learn from the study results in the previous question?

5.15.6 With whom were productivity trends reviewed and why?

5.15.7 Explain the influence and relationship of the material and working capital productivities.

5.15.8 How could the other expense productivity be increased? Explain and defend the historical basis for this answer.

5.15.9 Are TPG and PQT (see Chapter 3 for details)—two of the important elements of TPmgt—relevant for this company? Defend your arguments against the backdrop of assumptions you might make.

5.16 ELECTRONICS

Background—This case involves a major electronics firm in India. It manufactures three basic product lines and has several thousand employees geographically dispersed in nine different parts of the country. Its product lines are:

Electronics equipment
- Digital communication equipment
- Naval equipment
- Finance equipment
- Space electronics
- Digital microwave systems

Electron tubes
- Broadcasting and TV equipment

Semiconductors
- PC boards

In July 1989, about 30 top-level executives, representing all the major product lines and most functional areas, attended my two-day seminar on TPmgt. The following discussion represents the outcome of this training.

Implementation, Results, and Analysis—The TPmgt implementation methodology was applied as follows:

Step 1: Mission Statement—The company has a well-developed mission statement. Management did not consider revising it at this time.

Step 2: TPM Analysis—Using past data from five fiscal years (1983 to 1988), the managers developed the total productivity and partial productivity profiles for the firm as a whole as an initial start to the TPmgt process (Figures 5.40 and 5.41). Clearly the situation is not very good.

Step 3: Management Goals—These were developed by four groups of managers after they reached consensus. The goals were as follows:

1. Improve total productivity by 15% per year over the next five years, from 1.075 (present) to 2.16 (1993–94)
2. Improve profit before taxes from the present level of 7.8% (of sales) to 20% by 1990–94
3. Reduce inventory level from the present ten months of turnover to four months of turnover

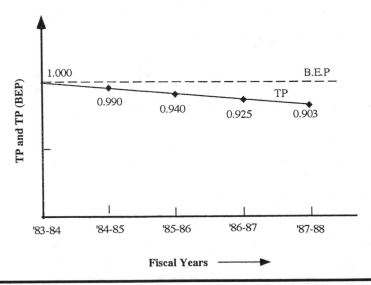

FIGURE 5.40 Total productivity versus break-even point of total productivity for the electronics firm.

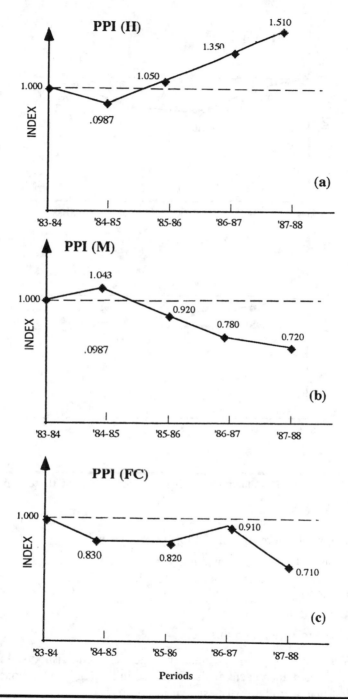

FIGURE 5.41   Partial productivity profiles in index form for the electronics firm.

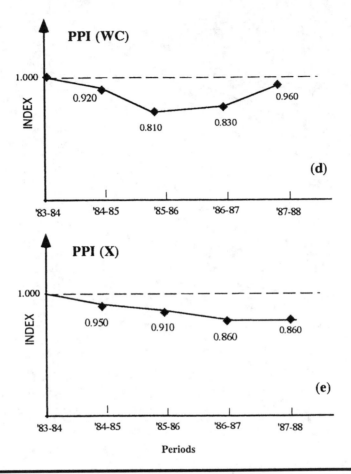

FIGURE 5.41   Partial productivity profiles in index form for the electronics firm (continued).

All these goals were formulated to:

1. Achieve the mission statement
2. Be very specific and practically feasible
3. Be time based
4. Be verifiable

Much deliberation went into this step.

Step 4: Fishbone Analysis—A team of managers created a fishbone diagram for each of the three management goals developed in Step 3. The fishbone diagram for the first management goal is shown in Figure 5.42.

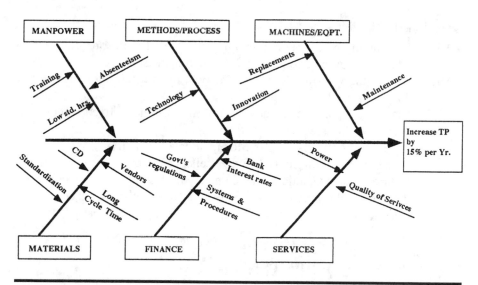

FIGURE 5.42 Fishbone analysis before developing the action plan for the electronics firm.

Step 5: Action Plans—An action plan was developed for each of the management goals. The plans included a listing of tasks necessary, starting and ending dates, and persons responsible.

Step 6: PQT Training—About 30 of the managers were trained in the basics of the PQT. In turn, they would train the people under them on the organizational ladder.

Step 7: Implementation—An implementation plan was formulated by management so that it would first be approved by the people affected by the plan.

Benefits—The company's application of the TPmgt methodology following the seminar helped it to view the management of *all* of its resources with equal emphasis and scrutiny. For example, the company's working capital productivity was enhanced by renegotiating the interest rates for its long-term and short-term loans. The company was also able to assess its production processes and the technologies therein with greater systemic thinking.

Summary—This case showed that TPmgt is feasible in a major electronics firm that produces a wide variety of products, ranging from civil to defense applications. The TPG component cannot be assessed yet in terms of its effectiveness, as the company has many unions and ratification by these groups is time consuming.

Questions to Ponder—

5.16.1 Is there any uniqueness in applying the TPmgt philosophy and methodology in an electronics firm? State your reasons.

5.16.2 Why is the working capital productivity in an electronics firm an important factor?

5.16.3 Discuss the possible reasons for a drastic decline in fixed capital productivity in this case.

5.16.4 Repeat the previous question for materials productivity.

5.16.5 Do a benchmarking study of five excellent electronics firms that manufacture products similar to the company in this case. What recommendations would you offer to the top management of these companies based on your study?

5.17 HEAVY EQUIPMENT

Background—This study deals with the valve-manufacturing division of the high-pressure boiler plant unit of a major heavy equipment manufacturer (fictitious name HEM) in India.

The objective of the study was to establish total productivity values and bring the concept of total productivity to the company. The project dealt with a newly established section of the valve division. The study showed the effect of tangible inputs in addition to labor, which has been traditionally measured in the company.

Experts observe that the demand for electrical power quadruples every decade. In 1989, when the study was done, the energy requirement for India was expected to be around 18,000 megawatts (MW) from 1990 to 1995. To meet this expected demand, HEM expanded its manufacturing facilities to supply 3,500 MW annually. The need for high-capacity valves with higher pressure and temperature ratings was significant in order to cater to the needs of high-capacity boilers. To manufacture the valves, the company decided on a collaboration with TOA Company (Japan); however, there had been no study on the effective utilization of resources. Production managers monitored progress based on standard hours; that is, they only monitored labor productivity.

HEM's annual sales for the year 1988–89 were $1.6 billion. It had a work force of 65,000 people, with six major manufacturing units in different parts of the country.

The study was concerned with the high-pressure boiler plant unit in India. It manufactures high-pressure boilers and valves, and the study was limited to high-pressure gate valves, as these contributed over 70% of the sales revenues of high-pressure valves. This unit had 15,000 employees and annual sales of $480 million. It had annual installed capacity of 33,500 MW. The valve division manufactured 54,000 valves annually. Of these, 45,000 were of small size, and these contributed about 30% of sales. Of the remaining 70% of sales, high-pressure gate valves contributed 60%. These valves were used in utility boilers and process industries. More than 60% of its output catered to the boiler division and the rest to outside sales. The valve division had 500 employees and sales of $36 million; 70% of the components for the valves were bought from outside as standard items. The study concerned the remaining 30%, which were manufactured in the shop. This 30% constituted about 80% of the value of the valve. The components manufactured were the body, bonnet, stem, wedge, and seat rings.

Implementation—HEM manufactured six different types of valves. For this study, only the high-pressure gate valves of sizes 8″ to 14″ nominal bore and pressure ratings of 1500 and 2500 class as per ANSI were selected. The high-pressure gate valves were chosen as the operational unit for the TPM.

The valves division of HEM has had technical collaboration with:

- TOA Company (Japan) for high-pressure gate valves and globe valves
- Dresser Company (United States) for safety and safety relief valves
- Sulzer Company (Sweden) for high-pressure and low-pressure bypass valves

The following assumptions were made in applying the TPM:

1. The percent contribution to sales by each type of valve is equal; therefore, gate valves were taken as one operational unit.
2. A depreciation rate of 10% was assumed for fixed capital. Depreciation charges for period 0 were assumed to be the same as for subsequent years. Hence, no deflators were used.
3. The OTPM version of the TPM was used. Thus, the O_3, O_4, and O_5 components of the output were ignored.

Results and Analysis—

Level 1 Analysis: Operational Unit (Gate Valve)—Figure 5.43 shows the total productivity and break-even point profiles for the gate valve operational unit. We see that in periods 0 and 1, the total productivity value is below the break-even point value, indicating a loss for the operational unit.

Between periods 3 to 5 and 7 to 8, there is a drop in the value of total productivity, indicating that the product is in danger of creating a financial loss. However, this is averted by an increase in total productivity after periods 5 and 8.

Figure 5.44 shows the total productivity index versus time periods. It indicates that the total productivity index has a cyclical pattern every year, and the

Value	0	1	2	3	4	5	6	7	8	9
TP	0.882	0.942	1.026	1.095	1.011	0.991	1.032	1.182	1.07	1.119
Break even point	0.974	0.973	0.971	0.969	0.971	0.971	0.969	0.966	0.972	0.97

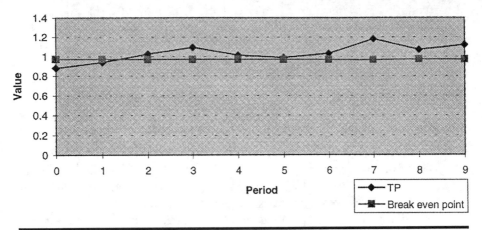

FIGURE 5.43   Gate valve total productivity versus break-even point.

index is going up every year. There is a drop in the total productivity index in the first quarter of each year. The total and partial productivities should be analyzed further in Level 3 analysis.

Value	0	1	2	3	4	5	6	7	8	9
TP	0.882	0.942	1.026	1.095	1.011	0.991	1.032	1.182	1.07	1.119
TP Index	1.000	1.048	1.142	1.19	1.15	1.11	1.22	1.25	1.21	1.45

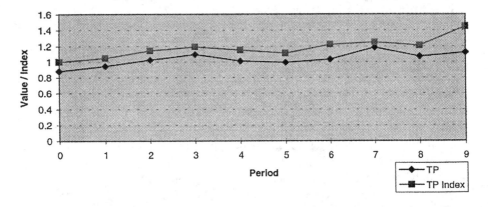

FIGURE 5.44   Gate value total productivity and total productivity index.

Level 3 Analysis—Figure 5.45 shows both the total and partial productivities versus time periods. We see that the total productivity profile is amidst the partial productivity graphs, confirming the theory that the total productivity is a weighted sum of partial productivities.

Productivity Input	0	1	2	3	4	5	6	7	8	9
TP Index	1.000	1.048	1.142	1.19	1.15	1.11	1.22	1.25	1.21	1.45
HP Index	1.000	1.1	1.255	1.394	1.223	1.226	1.367	1.497	1.268	1.386
MP Index	1.000	0.994	0.988	0.960	1.000	0.994	0.988	0.960	1.000	0.994
CP Index	1.000	1.200	1.593	2.044	1.506	1.574	2.035	2.615	1.837	2.273
EP Index	1.000	0.996	1.010	0.961	0.984	0.980	1.040	0.940	1.030	1.020
XP Index	1.000	0.866	0.916	0.847	0.996	0.731	0.938	0.872	0.983	0.968

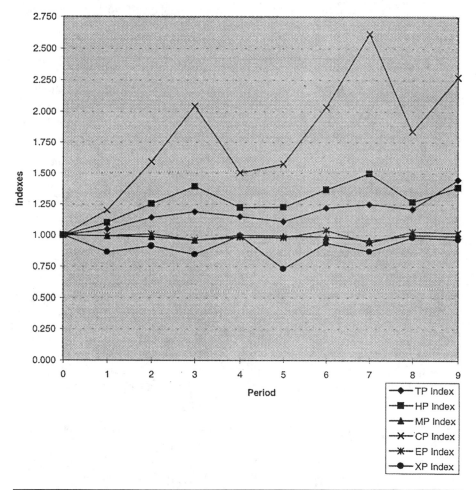

FIGURE 5.45   Total productivity index and partial productivity index versus time period.

Human Productivity—There was an overall increase in human productivity each year, corresponding to the same period last year. However, in periods 4 and 8, which were the first quarters of the production years, there was a drop in the human productivity index. There were two main reasons for this:

1. During this period, there was a 30% loss of available man-hours due to vacations.
2. There was a 25 to 30% loss of available man-hours due to idle time. The main reasons for this were:
   - Improper flow of material
   - Supervisors also on vacation
   - Machine tools taken for annual maintenance and workers reallocated to other machines
   - Development jobs loaded on a few machines
   - More setup time due to job changes

Material Productivity—Material productivity dropped after the first quarter. The rate of fall was the highest in the last quarter of the year because the quantity of material handled was also highest, and there was pressure to increase output, which resulted in small but costly non-conformances and rejections.

Capital Productivity—This followed a trend similar to human productivity. There were drops in periods 4 and 8 for the following reasons:

1. Lack of full-capacity utilization of machinery due to use of temporary operators.
2. The machinery underwent yearly preventive maintenance; therefore, machines were unavailable for production.

It was also observed that the capital productivity increased between periods 4 and 5 because of the installation of a new vertical boring machine and a set of welding machines.

Energy Productivity—This showed a big drop in period 5 and also a cyclical decline in the last quarter of each year. This was due to the above-mentioned horizontal boring machines and welding machines. The regular dip in the last quarter was because departments which normally work a single shift operated on a two-shift basis to meet annual production commitments.

Other Expense Productivity—The other expense input was directly proportional to the contribution of high-pressure gate valves to total sales. Other expenses also included machine installation in period 5. This productivity underwent a cyclical pattern, and there was a sharp drop in period 5 because of new machine installation. Also, the drop in the last quarter was because of significant travel expenses by administration to collect outstanding accounts receivables.

The observations from the TPM analysis can be summarized as follows:

1. Total productivity of the valves division is getting better each year, partly because of the learning curve phenomenon.
2. Total productivity took a dip regularly in the first quarter; the main contributors to this were human and capital productivities.
3. Although human and capital productivities tended to pick up after a drop in the first quarter, material and other expense productivities continued to follow a downward path through the year.

The percent contributions to total input were as follows:

- Human, 3.5%
- Material, 61.5%
- Capital, 20.9%
- Energy, 3.3%
- Other expenses, 10.8%

Recommendations to the Company—The following recommendations were offered to the company by the senior engineer who conducted this study:

1. Create productivity engineering groups
2. Plan the preventive maintenance of machines much better
3. Prevent absenteeism of labor to a greater extent
4. Have full-fledged, frequent training for operators
5. Reduce setup turnovers

Questions to Ponder—

5.17.1 What two input factors were responsible for the regular drop in total productivity in the first quarter?
5.17.2 What percentage of total inputs does each of these factors represent?
5.17.3 How could the human input requirements have been decreased?
5.17.4 In what periods is total productivity greater than its respective break-even point? Why?
5.17.5 Conduct a study of two other heavy equipment manufacturers in your country. What lessons from this study can you apply to the one you just read?

5.18 MACHINE TOOLS

Background—This study involves one of the largest machine tool manufacturers in the Far East. It employs several thousand people and exports many of its products to Europe and other countries in the Far East. Some of the company's top and upper middle management attended my seminar on TPmgt on May 16, 1989.

Implementation—The executives developed an implementation plan based on the TPmgt steps taught in the seminar. Company data for five fiscal years (1983–84 to 1987–88) were gathered, synthesized, and applied.

Results—The company primarily concentrated on the TPM analysis. The results of data collection and computations through the TPM were summarized as shown in Table 5.18. From this information, the profiles for total productivity (Figure 5.46) and partial productivities (Figure 5.47) were plotted graphically. It must be noted that the energy input was captured as part of the other expense input in this case. Ideally, it should have been separated from the other expense input, because it is a fair amount of the total.

TABLE 5.18   Data and Computed Values for the Machine Tool Manufacturer

	83–84	84–85	85–86	86–87	87–88
Total output	3,115	3,698	3,960	4,380	4,735
Human input (H)	686	777	904	968	1,107
Material input (M)	1,550	1,713	1,885	2,200	2,360
Fixed capital input (FC)	148	168	207	193	199
Working capital input (WC)	159	221	286	340	360
Other expenses input (X)	247	584	592	621	706
Total input	2,790	3,463	3,874	4,322	4,732
TPF	1.116	1.067	1.022	1.013	1.001
TPIF	1.000	0.956	0.9	1.102	0.897
TPF(BEP)	0.943	0.936	0.926	0.921	0.924
PPF(H)	4.541	4.759	4.381	4.525	4.277
PPIF(H)	1.000	1.048	0.965	0.996	0.942
PPF(M)	2.010	2.159	2.101	1.991	2.006
PPIF(M)	1.000	1.074	1.045	0.991	0.998
PPF(FC)	21.048	22.012	19.130	22.694	23.794
PPIF(FC)	1.000	1.046	0.909	1.078	0.885
PPF(WC)	19.591	16.733	13.846	12.882	13.153
PPIF(WC)	1.000	0.854	0.707	0.658	0.671
PPF(X)	12.611	6.332	6.689	7.053	6.707
PPIF(X)	1.000	0.502	0.530	0.559	0.532

Note: All numbers other than TPF, TPIF, and TPF(BEP) are in millions of monetary unit.

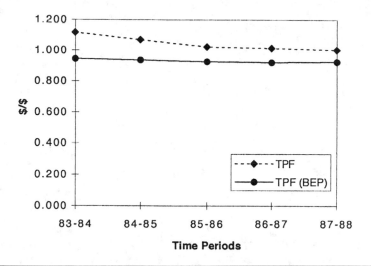

FIGURE 5.46   Total productivity profile for the machine tool manufacturer.

Analysis—Figure 5.46 shows that the company is profitable because its total productivity is above the break-even point; however, the downward trend in total productivity of the firm is dramatic and needs major improvement.

Figure 5.47 shows at a glance that human productivity and working capital productivity have been going down steadily and in some periods dramatically. Human and working capital inputs have not been utilized effectively and efficiently, and these are the major contributors to the firm's decline in total productivity since 1983.

Austere measures taken by the company in 1984–85 helped to stop the major decline in other expense productivity.

Material productivity gained positive momentum after a steady decline from 1984 to 1987. Its erratic behavior indicated to management that the company's materials management lacked consistent leadership and that it was always reacting to unfavorable situations rather than being planned to face them.

A strong capital justification process in the company has enabled it to consistently improve fixed capital productivity from fiscal year 1985–86 onward.

Benefits—As a result of the TPM analysis, the company's management developed a number of management goals. One of them was to:

* Improve return on investment from 8% to 25% by 1990–91 through the following measures:

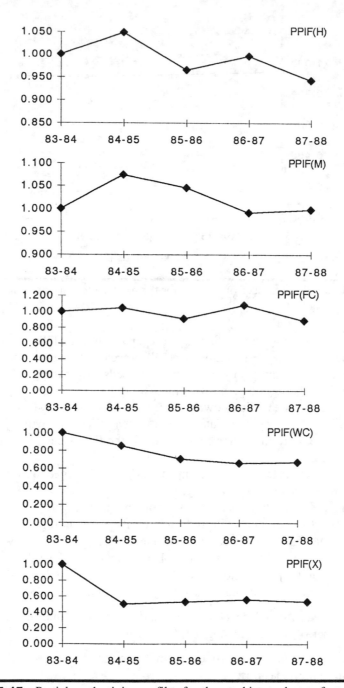

FIGURE 5.47 Partial productivity profiles for the machine tool manufacturer.

○ Better working capital management
○ Improved productivity across all product lines
○ Improved technologies in processes
○ Overall cost reduction throughout the company
○ New product development (CNC, etc.)
○ Human resources development through total quality control, PQT, etc.
○ Improved capacity utilization
○ Training and communication at all levels
○ Strategic planning to avoid unfavorable situations

To meet the first submanagement goal of better working capital management, the company was very specific in declaring that it wanted to increase the PPF(wc) from the present 13–14 to 20.0 in fiscal year 1990–91. Management then created a fishbone analysis (Figure 5.48).

Management recognized, as never before, that improving working capital productivity was as important as improving human productivity. The fishbone analysis helped the management team to develop a practically feasible action plan to achieve its management goals for fiscal year 1990–91.

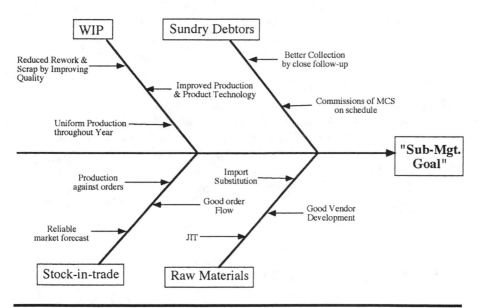

FIGURE 5.48 Fishbone analysis for the submanagement goal of increasing PPF(wc) from 13–14 to 20 in 1990–91.

Summary—TPmgt has been proven to be a feasible process in a major machine tool manufacturer which exports its large- and medium-size machine tools to Europe, the Far East, and other regions of the world.

The company's process technologies, worth hundreds of millions of dollars, are being managed well because of a specific policy and deployment of that policy. However, the company has not been as effective in managing its hundreds of millions of dollars worth of working capital, particularly finished and unfinished inventories, cash, and accounts receivable.

The top management of the company took the first step in the right direction by going through the TPmgt seminar, understanding its philosophy, and initiating the TPmgt process with true commitment.

Questions to Ponder—

5.18.1   Why was working capital productivity in the machine tool company declining so steadily? What could have been done to prevent this trend?

5.18.2   Study a major machine tool manufacturer in the United States or any Western country. Compare the findings of your TPM analysis with that of the Far Eastern company discussed in this case study.

5.18.3   Carefully analyze the human productivity profile in this case study. How would you go about reversing this unfavorable downward trend? Specify strategies that are practically feasible.

5.18.4   Machine tool manufacturers of the size covered in this case are often bogged down with huge inventories of unfinished machine tools. Also, they are highly capital intensive, with some machines costing as much as a million dollars apiece. Develop a materials management strategy that can address this issue.

5.18.5   In a mega-company of this type and size, with several thousand employees scattered over ten geographical areas, how do you manage product delivery and distribution, particularly when some of the subsystems of a machine tool are made in more than one geographical location?

5.18.6   Develop a full-fledged TPmgt implementation plan for your own company, if it is a large manufacturing organization with geographical and cultural diversity.

5.19 MEDICAL DEVICES

Background—XYZ Corporation was founded in the 1950s and became a major international manufacturer of cardiovascular devices. The company developed a number of specialized, sophisticated products and devices under contract with university and government laboratories. Although designed primarily for research purposes, the products enhanced the company's reputation in the field of bio-medical instrumentation.

The first cardiac pacemaker was successfully implanted in a human in 1962. In 1965, sales for the first time exceeded the million-dollar mark. In that same year, the company broadened its implantable and external pacemaker line in terms of application and sophistication with the introduction of three new prod-ucts. Also, the Atomic Energy Commission licensed the company to embark on a nuclear-powered cardiac pacemaker program, and entry into the neurosurgical field began with the introduction of the Hakim valve.

In 1967, the company established a foreign division. By 1969, sales reached $6.8 million, with approximately 500 workers employed. That year also marked the company's entry into the rapidly growing field of artificial kidneys and related accessories for hemodialysis, as well as the introduction of another new pacemaker.

In 1973, the company introduced a revolutionary device that incorporated a system of programmable pacing. For the first time, a physician could adjust, without surgery, the operating parameters of an implanted pacemaker and moni-tor changes in the patient's cardiac requirements.

In 1977, the corporation introduced a programmable pacemaker powered by long-life lithium batteries, and in 1978, the company introduced a thinner, smaller, and lighter non-programmable lithium-powered pacemaker. By the end of 1979, sales exceeded $92 million and employees numbered 2,500. From then on, the company's products and services kept serving a variety of medical specialties and satisfying a variety of human needs.

Implementation—The purpose of this study was to implement and apply the TPM to measure the total productivity for each of the main products manufac-tured by the corporation, as well as the firm as a whole for the years 1976 through 1981. The main products were grouped into three types:

1. Pacing systems
2. Angiographic devices
3. Other products

The output and input for each group of products were calculated according to the percentage of contribution to the total output and input of the firm for the periods studied.

In order to derive the values of the output and input for each of the products, the relative contribution of each product to total production was considered appropriate and reasonable.

TABLE 5.19   Partial Productivity Indices, Total Productivity, Total Productivity Index, and Break-Even Point of Total Productivity for the Firm

	1976	1977	1978	1979	1980	1981
PPIF(H)	1.000	1.035	1.972	1.470	1.478	1.413
PPIF(C)	1.000	2.466	2.352	3.279	1.327	0.995
PPIF(M)	1.000	1.091	4.133	3.197	2.537	2.322
PPIF(E)	1.000	1.261	2.279	2.669	3.536	3.764
PPIF(X)	1.000	1.113	0.910	0.799	0.902	0.948
TPF	0.846	1.008	1.118	1.012	1.028	0.917
TPIF	1.000	1.191	1.404	1.196	1.215	1.084
TPF(BEP)	0.865	0.926	0.931	0.969	0.932	0.970

Results—Results are presented in Tables 5.19 and 5.20 and Figures 5.49 to 5.52.

Analysis—

Level 1 Analysis—The total productivity of the firm as a whole shows the trend in the company's financial position. It reflected losses for 1976 and 1981 and an increase in total productivity for the year 1978, during which the company enjoyed a profitable position (Figure 5.49).

Level 2 Analysis—The analysis of total productivity with respect to each of the three products indicated that the pacing systems were the most productive for the company for almost all periods of the study.

The break-even analysis of total productivity for each product indicated that in most of the years the total productivity levels for angiographic devices and other

TABLE 5.20   Partial Productivity Indices, Total Productivity, Total Productivity Index, and Break-Even Point of Total Productivity for the Pacing Systems

	1976	1977	1978	1979	1980	1981
PPI(H)	1.000	1.150	2.537	1.522	1.604	1.375
PPI(C)	1.000	1.746	1.649	2.600	1.239	0.738
PPI(M)	1.000	1.119	4.173	3.310	2.750	2.616
PPI(E)	1.000	1.462	2.301	2.764	3.836	3.897
PPI(X)	1.000	1.067	0.918	0.827	0.995	0.984
TP	1.030	1.243	1.510	1.465	1.357	1.135
TPI	1.000	1.207	1.467	1.422	1.317	1.102
TP(BEP)	0.865	0.826	0.923	0.928	0.972	0.964

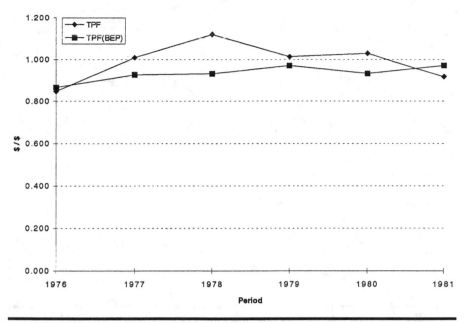

FIGURE 5.49 Total productivity versus break-even point of total productivity for the firm.

products were all below the break-even point of total productivity, reflecting a loss situation. On the other hand, total productivity for the pacing systems (Figure 5.51) was always above the break-even point—a highly desirable situation—indicating that the pacing systems were in a profitable position.

Level 3 Analysis—From the analysis of the partial productivity graphs (Figures 5.50 and 5.52), some important highlights were observed. In 1977, other expense productivity was higher than in any other year. In 1978, human and material productivities were higher than in any other year. In 1979, capital productivity played a greater role than in the other years. In 1981, energy productivity reached its peak level. The biggest observed total productivity level for the firm was 1.188 in 1978. It was also observed that the pacing systems were the most profitable for all the years studied. The other two groups of products (angiographic devices and other products) showed a loss in almost all the years.

The study team encountered some difficulties in trying to obtain data, but these difficulties were not unmanageable.

Benefits—This case shed light on a number of issues confronting the company at the time of the study. The company's top management was mostly made up

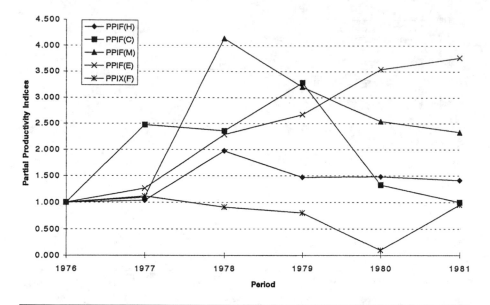

FIGURE 5.50 Partial productivity profiles for the firm with respect to human, capital, material, energy, and other expense input factors.

of scientists and engineers who, largely because of their backgrounds, did not pay much attention to financial and other non-technical matters. From the TPM analysis, they were able to see some of the problems that needed to be addressed in the non-technical realm. Some actions were initiated in the angiographic products division and the other products division. Unfortunately, in some situations, the company waited too long, and the economic damage was already inflicted.

Summary—Medical device manufacturing is a high-tech and high-risk operation. For example, if a pacemaker corrodes in operation as an implant, the damage to a patient can be significant. There are not many such manufacturers in the country. It is a highly specialized field. This case demonstrated that the TPmgt concept is applicable even in such settings.

Questions to Ponder—

5.19.1   Discuss some of the advances made in research and development by XYZ Corporation. Where are the costs of this research included in the TPM?

5.19.2   What would have been some possible effects of using Pareto's law and not including the "other" product line in productivity calculations?

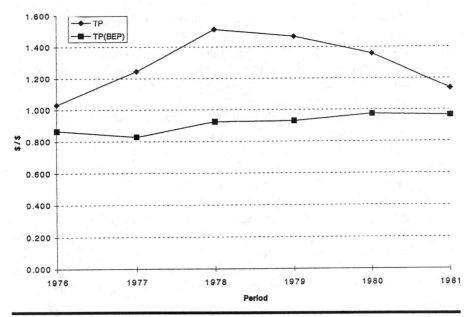

FIGURE 5.51 Total productivity versus break-even point of total productivity for the pacing systems.

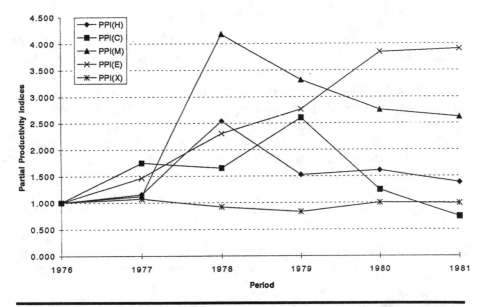

FIGURE 5.52 The partial productivity profiles for the pacing systems, with respect to human, capital, material, energy, and other expense input factors.

5.19.3 Do some research on a company that manufactures angiographic devices. Based on this research, what can you recommend that XYZ Corporation do for the same product?

5.19.4 Study another similar company, perhaps in the same industry. What can you suggest to XYZ Corporation based on the total productivity profiles of this company?

5.19.5 What are the recent trends in the human, capital, and material productivity indices for the firm? In view of this, should partial productivities be examined at the firm level and/or the product level?

5.19.6 What, if any, complications were involved in the productivity measurement process of this international company?

5.19.7 Conduct a Level 4 analysis of the TPM by applying some of the well-established industrial engineering tools. What techniques would you recommend to improve the total productivity levels for the angiographic devices and other products?

5.19.8 Based on the Level 1 through Level 3 analysis, would you suggest that any product lines be phased out? If so, why? If not, why not?

5.20 SEAFOOD PROCESSING, WHOLESALE, AND DISTRIBUTION*

Background—This case pertains to a company that is vertically integrated. The company has a seafood processing operation in a Central American country. The plant packages the seafood and sends it to its affiliate in South Florida. The affiliate then distributes the product(s) (fish, shrimp, and lobster). The distributing company in South Florida employed ten people in 1988 and had annual sales in the range of $15 to $20 million. It imported containers, transported by water from Central and South America, and then sold to wholesalers and distributors throughout the United States. The company also traded other products and brokered other seafood, but shrimp was the primary source of income for the company. The nature of the business was such that it was not easy to trace a trend in sales because the trades and broker deals were sporadic. The plant itself had a few hundred employees, including the sea-vessel crews and fishermen.

Implementation—A group of about 25, representing major functional areas of the plant and the distribution company in South Florida, were brought together

---

* I wish to acknowledge the president of this company, Richard D., and the owner of the group, Robert D., for their contribution to this case in terms of information.

> *"We, (company name) want to be an **innovative and successful leader**
> in our products, through a **commitment** to the goals of **harmony,**
> **excellence, quality, productivity**, and open **communication**, so that
> we can satisfy our investors, employees, and customers at **all** times,
> thereby providing **stability, unity, and job opportunities** in our
> country."*

FIGURE 5.53   Mission statement developed by 25 representatives of the seafood company.

in 1988 for a full week at a hotel in Miami. The group included about four union representatives. I conducted a five-day training session for them in TPmgt. It took major persuasion on the part of Robert, the owner of the company, to convince the union leadership to join the training; the union was suspicious of top management's intentions in light of past strikes at the company. Nevertheless, the union representatives joined the training.

Mission Statement—During the training, I facilitated the group to develop the corporation's mission statement (Step 1 of the TPmgt process; see Chapter 4). It read as shown in Figure 5.53. This group also developed management goals (Step 2) during this important exercise.

Management Goals and Action Plans—The big group was divided into small groups of about six. The input from all the team members in each group was condensed. The management goals developed by each group were presented on flip charts, and then, with facilitation, these goals were condensed into a single list. As part of the initial training, action plans were drawn up only for selected management goals that were considered most critical by the group.

PQT Training—All 25 participants were then trained in the PQT process. The training dramatically changed the attitudes of the trainees—particularly the union representatives. One moving experience during this training occurred when, for the first time, both the union representatives and top management admitted how much they had misunderstood each other all these years, which were wrought with worker unrest, dissatisfaction, and lack of mutual respect and trust. The verbal admissions were followed by warm and teary hugs between union representatives and top management personnel.

What was also amazing to top management was the abilities, skills, and knowledge displayed by the so-called uneducated worker representatives. They not only participated in the training process with vigor and energy, but also presented their recommendations like professionals, including using overhead transparencies. Their analysis and results included the application of Pareto analysis, Ishikawa diagrams, process flowcharts, flow diagrams, etc.

Another moving experience during this training came when one of the participants—an expectant mother in not-so-good health—volunteered to do simultaneous translation in the training sessions so that the company could save a substantial sum of money. On the last day of the training, Robert D., the owner, was so moved that he not only acknowledged this lady's devotion but also announced an unexpected two-day paid vacation for her!

After the Initial Training—When the seminar attendees (most of whom were from the processing plant in Central America) returned home, they imparted the PQT training to most of the several hundred employees there.

In keeping with the mission statement, no one was laid off when productivity shot up dramatically in the six months following the initial training in Miami. The mission statement the representatives came up with emphasized providing job opportunities, not taking them away. How would they deal with the situation? If management laid off anyone, the union leadership would have been quick to reply: "See, we told you when you went to Miami for that training that management was up to something. We can't trust them." Robert D., the owner and chairman of the board, challenged the employees to find a way to prevent any layoffs. To the dismay of even the union leaders, the employees came up with a new product idea. Fish gills, which normally were scrapped in the processing plant, would be used to produce fish meal. The idea was so good that the chairman let the employees design and build a facility for the new product. Not only did they not have to go through painful layoffs, but they actually created additional jobs, thereby fulfilling the intent and content of the mission statement.

Productivity Committee and the TPM—The distribution company in South Florida created a Productivity Committee, comprising everyone except the CEO. They met twice a week for 30 minutes prior to the beginning of the work day. The members of the committee brainstormed to arrive at the best strategy for implementing the TPM. They agreed that the accounting department would change its reporting format so that personal computers could be used for the TPM computations.

After analyzing the sales figures, the committee decided that shrimp, fish, and lobster would all count toward one operational unit, because shrimp represented 97% of total sales.

The shrimp business is a commodity business, where month-to-month behavior does not show predictable trends; prices change on a weekly basis depending on several factors which have no particular pattern. In addition, the company, prior to the TPmgt training, had changed direction and policies so many times that it would be hard to compare one period to another when the input and output factors were different. The Productivity Committee decided to start with January 1989 as the base period for the TPM computations.

Benefits—Three visible benefits were noticed as a result of the TPmgt implementation up to this point:

- *Improved Communication*—Communication between employees and all levels of management improved because of the teamwork while implementing the TPM. Everyone got a chance to express his or her opinions, and decisions were made based on what the group thought was best. Communication barriers were broken down in a very short period of time.

- *Improved Motivation*—Because of the participation of the personnel and the consequent improvement in communication at all levels, top management saw a definite improvement in employee motivation. There was a growing sense of group and a family feeling among everyone. In asking employees how they felt before and after the TPmgt implementation, the general response was that they felt closer to management and "felt a big improvement in morale and motivation."

- *Improved Knowledge of the Business*—There are several variable and hidden expenses that tend to be overlooked in this type of business (e.g., delivery costs, recurring storage expense, returns, deductions, etc.). By working through the TPM, the company's top management, in particular, Richard, the president, "got a better grasp of the impact of these expenses." As a matter of fact, the TPM implementation helped management and the employees change their ways of operating their company. For instance, the company opted for selling container loads for cash instead of distributing the product and selling it on 30-day terms. This resulted in savings on delivery expenses, accounts receivable costs, inventory costs, bank interest, and other expenses. The savings projected under this scenario amounted to approximately $80,000 per month, which resulted in a profit increase of about $20,000 per month.

Summary—This case demonstrated the power of TPmgt in a seafood processing plant with several hundred employees in Central America and in its affiliate, a wholesale and distribution seafood company with headquarters in the United States. The study also showed that layoffs are not only preventable but can actually be turned into company expansion when there is a commitment to employee welfare in the mission statement, which sets the tone for the guiding philosophy of any company. The employees, who otherwise would have been laid off, created a new product and helped design and build a new facility to create additional employment for themselves and for others in their community. That's *true* management in the "people-building" style!

Questions to Ponder—

5.20.1   Is the seafood wholesale and distribution business unique in many ways compared to other businesses? Substantiate your answers with objectivity.

5.20.2   What are two most significant lessons any corporation can learn from this study?

5.20.3   Conduct a study of at least three seafood businesses. Contrast their experiences with the company studied in this case.

5.20.4   Design a TPG plan for a company operating with a strong union. In designing this plan, consider all relevant factors derived from empirical experience and from literature-based research.

5.20.5   What was the significance of the mission statement and the TPM in this company?

5.20.6   How did the PQT training help the company in developing better communication and motivation?

5.21 SPACE SYSTEMS

Background—This space systems company was awarded the Payload Ground Operation Contract (PGOC) by NASA in 1986. As a result, the company is a major payload processor for the Space Shuttle. The company performs or supports all phases of payload processing from the time a payload is scheduled to fly through launch, landing, and cargo deintegration.

The Launch Operations Support Contract (LOSC), another service contract held by the division, is also responsible for receiving, processing, and integrating Department of Defense payloads with that of Expendable Launch Vehicles (ELVs). The company began processing ELVs in 1982 at facilities located across the river from Kennedy Space Center at the Cape Canaveral Air Force Station in Florida.

These contracts employed some 2,200 people and represented a multibillion-dollar operation encompassing both direct and indirect manpower. The contracts had received an extension to the year 2001. The organization that supports the variety of services performed has ten major directorates, each with uniquely defined tasks and responsibilities.

Implementation—In order to determine the total and partial productivities for the firm as well as the two units that comprise the firm, an 11-point analysis plan was established:

1. Meet with the financial manager, explain the overall objective, and determine which documentation contains the data required.
2. Select a set of sales, profits, and cost analysis from historical data on the PGOC operational unit.
3. Allocate outputs to operational units based on contribution to sales. Allocate inputs based on actual or proportion of total sales.
4. Evaluate the existing data collection system to ensure that the output and input data for TPM can be obtained.
5. Select a base period for referencing productivity values and calculations.
6. Obtain deflator indices for each category of input.
7. Review data collected and sanitize the output and input values in the TPM for maintaining confidentiality of sensitive information.
8. Compute productivities for each input and output element.
9. Chart indices for total and partial productivities for each operational unit.
10. Develop management summary of trends and analysis for the division level, and record operational productivity increases and decreases.
11. Develop an action plan to implement the productivity cycle.

Results—Figure 5.54 shows the Level 1 analysis of the TPM for the company as a whole, and Figure 5.55 shows the Level 2 and Level 3 analysis for the first operational unit, PGOC.

Period	1988	1989	1990	1991	MAR. 92	
TPF ($/$)	0.987	0.988	1	0.985	0.992	
BEP	0.956	0.954	0.954	0.954	0.955	

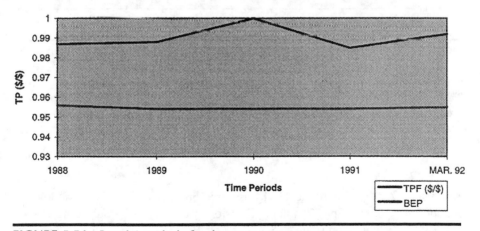

FIGURE 5.54   Level 1 analysis for the space systems company.

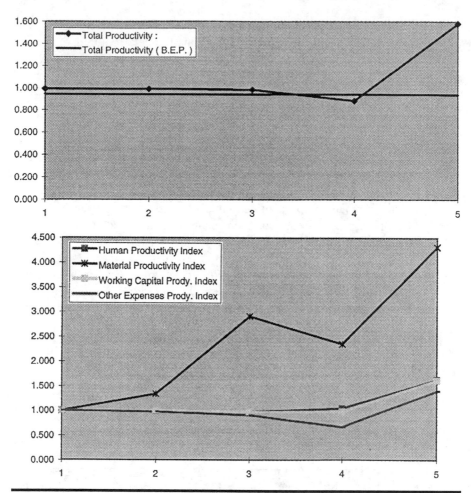

FIGURE 5.55   Top: Level 2 analysis for operational unit 2 (LOSC). LOSC demonstrated steady total productivity above the break-even point from 1988 through 1990. It fell below in 1991 due to recompete of the contract and other expenses consuming earnings. There was a net loss for that year. Bottom: Level 3 analysis. Unit 2 had significant productivity gains in material input during March of 1992, possibly attributed to cycle time of cost accrual. Human productivity increased due to transfer of people off the contract because of shrinking value of the LOSC.

Analysis—Application of the TPM was based on 1988 as the base period. Total productivity for the Space Systems Division was derived by summing PGOC and LOSC, which represented 98% of sales. Both units actually started up in

1987, but that year could not be used due to the phaseout of old contracts and the transition of the cost accounting. In other words, 1987 presented a skewed financial picture with some elements unknown due to the classified nature of the LOSC. Additionally, the content of the contracts changed in scope. PGOC and LOSC are government service contracts awarded as cost plus fee. These contracts must be operated and maintained within government cost guidelines.

Total productivity for the firm is most affected by increased award fees and incentives from the government, increasing other income through core technology spin-offs, and reduced unallowed costs in the contracts. Since price is set by negotiation of cost of the service and sales by adding an award fee, the firm must manage cost very well or else total productivity will drop off quickly.

Input Side—Total cost of the PGOC (operational unit 1) and LOSC (operational unit 2) is derived by adding a "fee" to the total price of operations. Thus, total costs equal actual sales, or actual sales minus earnings equals total cost.

The TPM analysis was initiated as follows. The human input element consists of labor tracked as general engineering, production support, assembly, quality assurance, and other miscellaneous direct costs. Capital is defined in terms of working capital (represents six weeks of total salary for the firm). Fixed capital is provided by $2 million a year in government-furnished equipment; not provided are plant and utilities, which are provided by NASA–Kennedy Space Center and the U.S. Air Force. Material elements include purchased parts, inventory, carrying costs, insurance, direct shipped spares, major subcontracts, operations and maintenance, and outside service subcontracts. Other expenses include taxes, new business funds, unallowed costs, utilities for off-center facilities, travel, and other miscellaneous costs. The energy element becomes part of other costs due to its lack of identity and full description as cost data. To illustrate, data collection of costs for one off-site facility began in 1990. The company's work force was intermixed in facilities where energy costs were paid by the government.

Output Side—The output side of the total productivity equation includes actual sales plus other income. Other income was allocated to the operational units based on their contribution as a percentage of total sales per year. Sales and income elements do not include other miscellaneous sales because they amount to less than 2% of sales and earnings. The actual sales and earnings data are excluded from this case based on the sensitive nature of the data and management direction.

Benefits—In utilizing the operational unit concept of the TPM, it was possible to identify the input and output values from which the total productivity measurements of the firm were derived.

   As actual company data were utilized in the development of partial and total productivities, it is important to note that the overall goal of this study was to identify for senior-level management the base indices that show company trends for the first 5 years of a 15-year contract. Management recognized the need for a comprehensive and formal productivity measurement function after this preliminary study.

Summary—This documentation is based upon the actual findings and subsequent analysis of data resulting from the investigation of the effects of productivity on profitability at a space systems company. The data were formulated from earnings statements and financial data for the PGOC and LOSC. These two contracts represented 98% of the total company's earnings.

Questions to Ponder—

5.21.1   What does this case point out with regard to the implementation of the TPM in a space systems company?

5.21.2   Study similar companies in France, the United Kingdom, or other countries with space programs. What can you learn from such comparative studies?

5.21.2   Are government-controlled contracts generally "total productive"? Explain your answer(s).

REFERENCES AND NOTES

1. My personal gratitude to Gary M. Nemeth, who conducted this study under my supervision and applied the Sumanth-Nag Model©, an extension of the TPM.
2. Sumanth, D.J. and Nag, D., *White-Collar and Knowledge Worker Productivity Management,* Working Monograph, 1989.
3. Juan C. Albelo, Analysis of Productivity at (ABC) Sr. High School, IEN 660 Final Project, April 29, 1995, p. 2. His contribution to this case is acknowledged with much gratitude.
4. Ibid., p. 3; District & School Profiles 1993–94 Report: Management and Accountability, Dade County Public Schools, Miami, 1995.
5. 1994 Florida Department of Education School Report.
6. All the principles of TPmgt stated here in this section are detailed in Chapter 9.
7. For a more detailed discussion of this case, see Sumanth, D.J. and Adya, B., "Practical Implementation of Total Productivity Model in Bus System," *Journal of Management Engineering,* Vol. 6, No. 2, April 1990. ©ASCE, Paper No. 24520; Sumanth, D.J. and Edosomwan, J.A., *Productivity Measurement Guide,* McGraw-Hill, New York, 1996, pp. 81–95.

6 UNIQUE FEATURES OF TPmgt

Total quality management (TQM) gained its notoriety with the institution of the national quality award in the United States—the Malcolm Baldrige Award. The first awards were given out in 1988 at the White House by President Ronald Reagan. Reengineering attained a prominent position as a management process and philosophy beginning in the early 1990s. Therefore, many should rightly wonder: "What's so novel about Total Productivity Management (TPmgt™)?" To answer this question, at least 15 unique features can be cited. They help to position TPmgt as a philosophy, concept, and systematic methodology that goes beyond the many significant, positive aspects of both TQM and reengineering.

6.1 INTERDISCIPLINARY EMPHASIS IN MANAGERIAL DECISION MAKING

TPmgt is not a single concept. It is a philosophy that integrates the emphasis of many concepts. As Figure 6.1 indicates, "TPmgt thinking" is an intersection of many well-established disciplines, including industrial engineering and systems theory, management science/operations research, accounting, and behavioral sciences such as psychology and sociology.

The theoretical constructs in TPmgt are based on proven concepts, techniques, and methodologies rooted in these well-established disciplines. For example, the Total Productivity Model (TPM©)—the nerve center of TPmgt—is built on the systems theory approach to identifying all input factors associated with the production of outputs of the total system at an operational unit level or

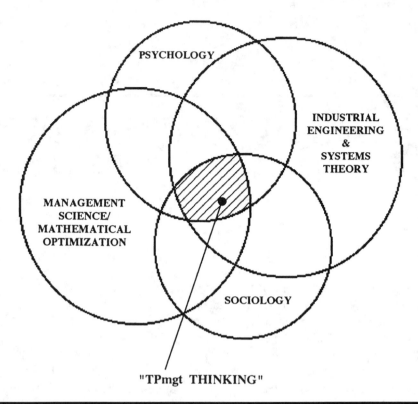

"TPmgt THINKING"

FIGURE 6.1   The interdisciplinary emphasis in TPmgt thinking. (©1996, D.J. Sumanth.) (Note: Quality science, productivity science, and manufacturing science are often considered part of industrial engineering and management science, although they have emerged as separate areas since the late 1970s.)

at the firm level. Similarly, the total productivity gainsharing (TPG) concept in the TPmgt methodology is based on the vast research done by behavioral scientists such as psychologists and sociologists, who emphasize the need to recognize people for their accomplishments at work. The fundamental idea behind TPG is to reward *all* the people working for an enterprise—as a team, based on the gains in total productivity. The Productivity Quality Team (PQT) module in the TPmgt implementation methodology emphasizes training company employees at all levels in solving problems with proven processes and tools from industrial engineering and quality science, such as process flowcharts, operation process charts, flow diagrams, Pareto analysis, control charts, cause-and-effect analysis, etc. The TPmgt philosophy understands and recognizes the importance of corporate vision and mission, as emphasized by many management theorists. That is why TPmgt starts its implementation with the development of the mission statement. TPmgt also provides a simultaneous engineering or concurrent engineering mindset in many of its implementation steps. For example, in doing a detailed TPM analysis, the TPmgt Team is comprised of representatives from various functional areas such as engineering, marketing, purchasing, operations/ manufacturing, quality assurance, finance, accounting, customer service, etc. This approach ensures a high probability of success in implementing ideas to achieve a company's mission, because all functional areas—marketing to production/operations to distribution—are considered *equally* important contributors to the total productivity of each operational unit and of the firm. Unlike traditional productivity thinking, where primarily the employees in the production/operations area are held accountable for improved productivity, TPmgt creates an organizational culture that holds all functional areas accountable for their individual contributions to total productivity. TPmgt deliberately and thoughtfully integrates the well-proven concepts of many disciplines and all functional areas. Therefore, it offers a strong, realistic theoretical foundation upon which varied superstructures of management can be built.

6.2 "PEOPLE-BUILDING" EMPHASIS WITH A BEHAVIORAL THRUST

To understand, develop, and nurture organizations/companies or enterprises, and even nations and countries for that matter, we must first understand human beings.[1] Dr. Armand Feigenbaum, the American expert who wrote the first book on total quality control which set into motion the Japanese company-wide quality control and eventually the American TQM, also emphasized the importance of people when he said:

> In successful companies, men and women understand, believe in and are a part of the work process. Without a committed human resource foundation, automation in the factory and computerization in the office will simply produce more bad parts faster than before or generate more unstable documents more quickly.[2]

Most problems we see in companies/enterprises are "people problems." Many managers seem to rely heavily on technology rather than people. They somehow forget that it is the people who make it possible to design, develop, and implement technologies, and it is the people who help to get the most out of such technologies. As I said in 1991,

We must know how to manage people of diversity in *perception, behavior, and style,* to be able to work better with *multi-cultural, multi-racial, and multi-national people* and to shape an organizational culture that fosters high response rates of service in the enterprises of services of all types.[1]

Unlike TQM and reengineering, TPmgt emphasizes "people-building"—literally helping to *"build up people"* working in an enterprise in terms of their self-esteem, self-worth, dignity, and respect. Of the six standard functions of managers and supervisors (planning, organizing, motivating, directing, controlling, and communicating), the two most difficult ones for them are motivating and communicating. These two areas are even more challenging for many technical professionals. Yet, the three major themes managers must understand and deal with in order to succeed in the 1990s are:[3]

1. **Using organizational capability to achieve key goals**
   - Translate elegant concepts into practical actions
   - Manage people for competitive advantage—focus on *their* importance
   - Effective management of change
   - Shift focus from strategic planning and intent to strategic unity
2. **Managing paradox, not polarity, as a way of life**
   - Allocate managerial emphasis based on integrative capabilities
3. **Developing staff leadership through partnerships**
   - Unity of voice
   - Mutual respect
   - Leadership at the staff level

Notice that all these three themes emphasize people. As global satellite systems bring people around the world closer, they become more knowledgeable of their individual rights. Managing the employees of the early 21st century will be very different from managing in the 1980s and the 1990s. These employees need recognition and respect as much as monetary rewards. Tom Peters, in his classic work, *In Search of Excellence,* points out the "8 lessons from America's excellent companies," and number 4 among them is "Productivity through People" (Figure 6.2).

"People-Building"

TPmgt not only emphasizes "people-building" at all levels of the organization, as well as organizational stability, but also creates a natural setting to support and sustain people.

```
┌─────────────────────────────────────────────┐
│                                               │
│     1.  A bias for action                     │
│                                               │
│     2.  Staying close to the customer         │
│                                               │
│     3.  Autonomy and enterpreneurship         │
│                                               │
│  ◆  4.  Productivity through people           │
│                                               │
│     5.  Hands-on, Value-driven                │
│                                               │
│     6.  Stick to the knitting                 │
│                                               │
│     7.  Simple form, lean staff               │
│                                               │
│     8.  Simultaneous loose-tight properties   │
│                                               │
└─────────────────────────────────────────────┘
```

FIGURE 6.2 The "8 lessons from America's excellent companies." (Source: Peters, Thomas J. and Waterman, Robert H. Jr., *In Search of Excellence: Lessons from America's Best-Run Companies,* Warner Books, New York, 1984. ©Thomas J. Peters and Robert H. Waterman, Jr., 1982.)

Job Security

At a time when restructuring and improperly implemented reengineering have eliminated thousands of jobs in many companies, why should we say that job security is important?

A survey[4] reported in the *Miami Herald* in 1993 (Figure 6.3) indicated that the number one reason taking the fun out of work is "fear of job loss." It is just common sense to recognize that an employee who is constantly fearful of losing his or her job cannot be expected to be very productive. This survey also pointed out that while managers constantly emphasize productivity, they are creating bureaucracies that result in "unnecessary paper work" and "unproductive meetings." Layoffs cause poor morale and employees waste their positive energies on negatively contributing activities such as rumors, gossip, and bickering. It is very interesting that the results of this survey are so similar to those of the Barry study cited in Chapter 2.

In October 1984, I had an emotional encounter with a homeless person. I was about to enter a grocery store when an old, feeble-looking man called out to me and said, "Sir, would you come over here for a second?" Thinking he might ask for some spare change, I went over to him, but instead, he looked at my eight-year-old son and said with tears in his eyes, "You know, I had a boy of that age;

WHAT TAKES THE FUN OUT OF WORK

Corporate cutbacks have placed added burdens on remaining workers. A recent survey of 1,100 white-collar workers revealed their most prevalent sources of stress.

Fear of job loss	47%
Unnecessary paperwork	42%
Bosses who don't listen	37%
Unproductive Meetings	31%
Rumors	17%
No common goal	12%
People hiding behind voice mail	8%

FIGURE 6.3   The importance of job security and managerial effectiveness. (Source: *Miami Herald,* March 8, 1993.)

a few months ago, I lost him in a car accident." I was curious to know more, so my son and I sat with him as he told his story. He was laid off from a big steel company in the Midwest after having worked there for 18 years. He was so emotionally devastated that he took to alcohol. Losing a job can be as traumatic as losing a loved one. Due to his alcoholism and his inability to cope with his job loss, his wife left him. As if that were not enough, he lost his son in a hit-and-run accident. By now, I was unable to hold back my tears. I wished that his story would end there, but then he opened his right palm and lifted up his shirt to show his cancerous wounds. He had lost his son, his livelihood, his marriage, his health, and most importantly, his human dignity. His right to work was denied. His loss of job did not cause his son to die or his health to deteriorate, but surely it contributed to his sense of hopelessness and worthlessness as an individual. People's lives are destroyed in the name of *labor* productivity improvement, but in the context of *total* productivity management, a people-building process is advocated. Companies can be very selective about whom they want to hire, but once they hire an employee, top management should consider it a *moral responsibility* to provide a proper environment—one where there is motivation, encouragement, and reward. Since my encounter with this homeless man, I have been closing my letters with "People-buildingly Yours," hoping that this little phrase will remind the recipients about the importance of treating people in a positive, constructive manner. At the end of each day, I ask myself: "Have I been a people-builder, or have I been a people-destroyer?"

Lincoln Electric Company is an excellent example of an American company that consistently follows "morally right management principles" when many others have taken the easy route to showing profits and higher earnings per share by getting rid of employees using everything from two weeks severance to early retirement packages. In its almost 100-year history, Lincoln has never laid off any employees. On the contrary, during the 1982 recession, when most companies in Cleveland were laying off, Lincoln not only provided its employees at least a 30-hour work week, but even gave hefty annual bonuses of several thousand dollars! When many U.S. companies were busy laying off thousands, CNN reported on December 7, 1991 that Lincoln Electric was giving an average bonus of $18,000 because its profits continued to go up. How can the company do such an extraordinary thing? There are at least three reasons:

1. Lincoln Electric's mission is oriented toward all its stakeholders, particularly its employees. There is job security at all levels. Once the initial probationary period is over (and it is a demanding one), every employee is guaranteed at least 30 hours per week employment. Just about everyone starts at the operator level and learns about the products firsthand. Everyone in the company has strong product knowledge.
2. The Lincoln financial incentive system is directly related to performance in terms of quality, cost, and time. The company's product warranty is significantly better than that of its competition.
3. Top management's planning and communication are simply superb. The span of control defies conventional wisdom. It is as much as 100:1! Employees have representatives who meet with the president regularly. Top management has created an atmosphere where process technologies are the most innovative in the industry the company represents. The company's industrial engineers cost out processes to the minutest detail. Many process technologies are patented by the creativity of employees who enjoy professional recognition in addition to job security and an excellent financial incentive.

The obvious question is why other U.S. companies don't do what Lincoln Electric does. Many say that Lincoln is a small company, which makes it easier. But the fact is the company has deliberately, through the wisdom of its management, kept the total number of employees down to about 3,000. There has been hardly an increase in 25 years while sales revenues have soared. The company has virtually eliminated its Japanese competition within the United States. Not only that, Lincoln is even competing with the Japanese in their own territory.

Employee Creativity

The TPmgt philosophy of management emphasizes *both* human and technical dimensions at the same time, because they are *not* mutually exclusive. Human beings are more creative than the most complex machines. Even the most sophisticated robots do not have more than a five-year-old's intelligence. When we believe in the creative power of people and provide an organizational environment to nourish the potential of the human mind, of which most people utilize only about 10%, people do wonders for their companies! In one of my seminars on PQT (one of the modules in the TPmgt implementation), I used a simple exercise to demonstrate the power of creativity. I asked each person to list (in one minute) the number of ways two can be joined together. On average, each listed about six things. But when a group of five people were put in a brainstorming session where no one's ideas were criticized, the synergy of creativity produced a list of 43 different ideas (Figure 6.4).

WAYS 2 THINGS CAN BE JOINED TOGETHER

1. Welding	23. Assembling
2. Tying	24. Folding
3. Rubber Band	25. Fusing
4. Lace	26. Crashing
5. Place one over the other	27. Wetting
6. Glueing	28. Pictures
7. Inserting	29. Stamping
8. Screwing	30. Chain
9. Bonding	31. Marrying
10. Dissolving	32. Reaction
11. Blending	33. Packing
12. Nailing	34. Vacuum
13. Melting	35. Hammering
14. Magnetic	36. Static Electricity
15. Pressure	37. Padlock
16. Stapling	38. Pay
17. Chewing gum	39. Gravity
18. Mixing	40. Zipper
19. Separating	41. Velcro
20. Flanging	42. Evaporation
21. Pulling	43. Threading
22. Tape	

FIGURE 6.4   The results of a brainstorming exercise for the number of ways two can be joined together.

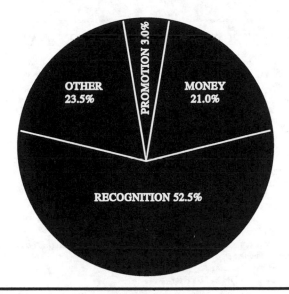

FIGURE 6.5   Importance of recognition and money in fostering creativity. (Source: "Productivity and Quality: IIE Evaluates Improvement by Productivity Engineers," *Industrial Engineering,* p. 57, May 1989.)

This is merely one example of what has been proven by many behavioral scientists—that a recognized and motivated group of individuals provide a positive performance environment for themselves and for the enterprise for which they work. A special report published by the Institute of Industrial Engineers showed that recognition and money accounted for 73.5% of the responses offering ideas to improve performance (Figure 6.5).

Matsushita, generally considered the largest consumer electronics company in the world, knows the importance of people. "Matsushita's Seven Objectives" (Figure 6.6), as the company calls them, all revolve around people. No wonder it has been such a successful company.

In summary, managers who design their companies around the "people-building" theme will be more successful than those who design with any other central focus, such as profits or technology. The TPmgt philosophy creates and sustains the people-building emphasis; therefore, the power of technologies designed by such people is long-lasting and totally productive. The people-building thinking in TPmgt ensures an enthusiastic work ethic, job security, organizational stability, and employee stability. Instituting innovations and creating technological or structural changes in such an environment are easier because of the "organizational resilience" for adaptability and accommodation.

"MATSUSHITA'S SEVEN OBJECTIVES"

1. NATIONAL SERVICE THROUGH INDUSTRY

Our purpose shall be not solely to gain wealth nor display industrial strength, but to contribute to the progress and welfare of the community and nation.

2. FAIRNESS

We shall be fair and just in all our business and individual dealings. Without this spirit no man can win respect nor can he respect himself no matter how wise or capable he may be.

3. HARMONY AND COOPERATION

Alone we are weak, together we are strong. We shall work together as a family in mutual trust and responsibility. An association of talented men is but an unruly mob unless each member is imbued with this spirit.

4. STRUGGLE FOR BETTERMENT

It shall be our policy to encourage trust and self-reliance that each may gain self-respect through his own endeavor and to struggle hard for betterment. Without this spirit, true peace and progress can not be achieved.

5. COURTESY AND HUMILITY

We shall respect the rights of others. We shall be cordial and modest. We shall praise and encourage freely. Without this spirit there is no social order.

6. ADJUSTMENT AND ASSIMILATION

Progress can not be achieved unless we adjust to the everchanging conditions around us. As the world moves forward, we must keep in step.

7. GRATITUDE

We shall repay the kindness of our associates, our community, our nation, and our foreign friends with gratitude. This spirit of gratitude will give us peace, joy and unlimited strength to overcome all difficulties.

FIGURE 6.6 People at the center of attention in Matsushita. (Courtesy of Matsushita Corporation.)

6.3 PRODUCT/SERVICE UNIT ORIENTATION

TPmgt explicitly emphasizes that companies must stress "product line thinking" rather than a functional focus. Several reasons can be offered for this thinking:

1. Every company or enterprise starts with an idea for a product that will suit the needs or wants of a particular customer segment in the market.
2. Customers are interested in the quality, price, and delivery of the product. They rarely, if ever, ask a question such as, "How is the total productivity of the engineering and manufacturing functions in your company, so that I can make a decision about buying your product?" Customers, on the other hand, ask, "What is the price of this product?"
3. Companies survive or thrive because of their products, not their functional areas. The latter support the former. They are the means to the ends, namely, the products.
4. Products are born, they grow (in sales), they mature, and they die—just like any living organism. New products replace old ones. A company's organizational and managerial systems are geared toward product lines. Creating functional areas first—to generate new products—is nothing but foolishness.

As companies grow in size, bureaucracy sets in, and "empire building" becomes a natural way of protecting turf and territories. After some time, the functionalism becomes an end in itself, so much so that the very purpose and mission of the enterprise are lost in the confusion. The more empire building, the greater the resistance to breaking down the barriers between departments and functions. When we talk about the critical organizational issues of today, most of them revolve around the rigidity and inflexibility surrounding functional areas, which resist change for natural reasons. The key is to prevent this inflexibility to begin with by emphasizing right from the time a company is started that it exists to offer products that customers need or want, not to create functional compartments that stifle communication, cloud the focus of the true mission, and ultimately threaten the very survival of the organization.

In TPmgt, the TPM analysis is done by operational units (which can be products, service units, customer groups, or divisions) to focus management's attention on those things that are directly viewed by customers as important. The TPM does not encourage measurement of total productivity by departments or functional areas, unless they are totally autonomous or independent, such as in the case of a research and development center.

There are many advantages to the *product line thinking* in the TPmgt concept:

1. All organizational efforts are directed and focused toward products, with one goal in mind: to make or offer them the way the customers expect them to be—high quality, low price, on time, and delivered with a delightful attitude on the part of the provider.

2. Because of the customer orientation through product line thinking, TPmgt creates a natural work environment, characterized by a common purpose, goals, teamwork, team recognition, and team rewards. The pre-TPmgt steps in the TPmgt implementation process create a unique emphasis on feedback from all customer groups, both external and internal.

3. Reorganizing functional areas becomes easier when product line thinking replaces a functional focus. There is a natural environment in which to constantly reengineer all the business processes which do not contribute to the desired goal of each product delighting the customer. People tend to be less territorial when they know that products which please customers are more important than their turf battles.

4. Because of the product line orientation, the emerging activity-based costing approach can be applied more readily than conventional cost accounting with its conventional functional orientation. This again provides a natural environment for value analysis to weed out all those activities and business processes that do not contribute value to the products (and, ultimately, to the customers).

6.4 "CUSTOMER CHAIN THINKING"

TPmgt, as a systemic concept, views customers in a very broad context, as shown in Figure 6.7, which indicates the importance of *all* the constituents impacted by an enterprise. Because of the TPM format, a company can and must

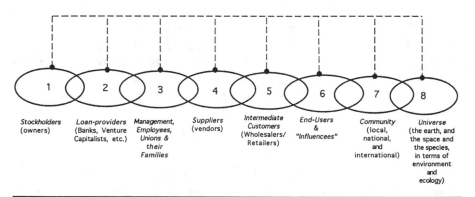

FIGURE 6.7   Systemic view of "customer chain thinking." Dashed lines indicate the responsibility relationships between all the players.

include the direct and indirect costs of all related effects in its decision making and associated actions. Often, such effects are ignored even in TQM because of lack of a proper quantitative measurement system.

Two recent events are examples of incidents that affected one or more of the eight links in customer chain thinking. Exxon paid several million dollars to compensate for the environmental damage and clean up the Alaskan coast following the Valdez oil spill. Union Carbide compensated hundreds of families for the deaths of relatives following the chemical disaster in Bhopal, India. It is quite straightforward to include these real dollar costs in the TPM, which would clearly show a dramatic drop in total productivity. The TPM constantly reminds a company that its decisions and actions have a quantifiable impact on total productivity and hence profitability. Thus, customer chain thinking is a designed strategy in TPmgt.

Link #6 in Figure 6.7 requires a bit of explanation. The "influencees" are all the people whom the end user of a product or service influences *after* the purchase experience. For example, someone who is very displeased with service at an auto dealership may significantly influence the decision of family members or friends not to patronize the dealership.

Everyone in the customer chain is important. The relative importance may vary depending upon a number of factors, but *all* eight types of customers must be satisfied and/or delighted. Most companies fail to view their role in such a manner, but when they do, they realize the power of customer chain thinking as an excellent strategic planning concept within the TPmgt framework. This is a unique quality of TPmgt compared to TQM and reengineering.

6.5 SYSTEMIC PERSPECTIVE FOR INTEGRATION

One of the most important and unique features of TPmgt is its ability to bring together and integrate all the necessary elements and subsystems, not only in a physical sense but also in a philosophical sense. The discussion on customer chain thinking in the previous section is just one example of this feature. Recall from Chapter 3 that:

$$ TP = \frac{O_1 + O_2 + O_3 + O_4 + O_5}{H + M + FC + WC + E + X} $$

Unlike the traditional labor productivity concept, the TPmgt concept recognizes that six input resources jointly and simultaneously work together to generate five types of outputs. If, for example, human productivity (corresponding to the "H" input factor) is low in a particular month, the logical questions to ask would be:

- Which one of the four subinputs of human input (management, professionals, clerical staff, workers) was the cause?
- Was there an increase in any of these four subinputs because of one or more of the other input factors (M, FC, WC, E, or X)? For example, perhaps workers had to put in overtime because materials did not arrive on time due to a vendor strike, and the other expense input (X) increased because the purchasing clerk had to procure the materials from another vendor after a number of expensive trips to the substitute vendor.

Clearly, the purchasing department in this case will have to devise a better vendor rating system in the future to avoid the negative impact on total productivity as a result of its managerial systems.

Consider another situation involving a retail store. During the busy holiday season, the cashiers were too slow and several customers chose not to return, thereby reducing the $O_1 + O_2$ components of the output dramatically. The reason the cashiers were slow was lack of sufficient training on the cash registers. The company had cut corners to reduce the training expense (which is a part of the X input), which resulted in not only a dramatic drop in total productivity but, more importantly, the loss of some valuable customers who may never return and who, according to well-established studies, may actually tell eight to ten others about their bad experience.

The point is that in the traditional productivity perspective, companies tend to be "penny-wise and pound-foolish." In TPmgt thinking, all five output factors (O_1 through O_5) and all six input factors (H through X) are considered in a systemic perspective that integrates their emphases together, not in isolation. This ensures a fair and equitable assessment of various input resources and outputs in order to optimize the total productivity of a company and its product lines.

One of the most important aspects of TPmgt is the fact that it integrates the emphases of both technology and people (Figure 6.8). Often, this integrative emphasis is lacking in organizations because of the myth that technology can cure productivity problems. Elizabeth Dole correctly recognized the importance of blending the best of both worlds—people and technology—when she said:[5]

> If the full potential of technology is to be realized, our human resource policies must take into account an imaginative blending of technology and human capabilities.

Deborah Reich[6] echoed the importance of the interaction between people and technology when she observed that:

> Investments in information technology systems, one example of advanced technology, now absorb more than 40 percent of all

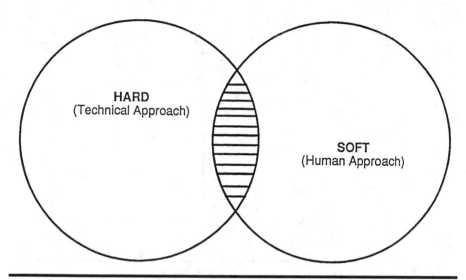

FIGURE 6.8   The integrative concept in TPmgt. (©1984–1989, D.J. Sumanth.)

investments in new plants and equipment, compared with 20 percent in 1980 and 6 percent in 1950. But dollar investments alone are not enough. According to a recent study, 75 percent of companies implementing advanced manufacturing technologies believe they do not achieve the performance they anticipated because of unforeseen problems in the interaction between people and new technology.

She also pointed out that:

> ...a research team from Massachusetts Institute of Technology, studying the American automobile industry, reported that implementing high-technology without complementary changes in human resources strategies did *not* produce significant improvements in quality or productivity. In a low-tech General Motors plant with traditional labor-relations practices and human resource systems, the team found that it took 34 hours to produce a car that had an average of 1.16 defects per car. After spending $650 million on high-technology at a similar plant, GM found that it took almost the same amount of time to produce a car and there was an increase in defects to 1.37 per car. In contrast, New United Motor Manufacturing (NUMMI), a joint venture between Toyota and GM in Fremont, CA, incorporated only moderate investments in new technology, but used fundamentally

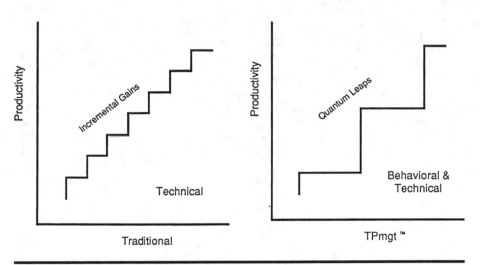

FIGURE 6.9   Traditional versus TPmgt emphasis. (©1988, D.J. Sumanth.)

different approaches to managing human resources and work systems. At NUMMI, it takes 60 percent as much time to produce a car
and the defect rate is .69 per car. Clearly, newly automated organizations demand multifaceted solutions to deal with the human resources issues resulting from the implementation of new technology.
These issues include employment security, training for new skills,
changes in work organization, and worker autonomy.

The TPmgt philosophy focuses on blending human talent with technologies
to create powerful socio-technical systems that are creative, innovative, and
flexible to adapt to change.

Productivity gains in general and total productivity gains in particular can
occur in quantum leaps with the TPmgt emphasis as opposed to the incremental
gains that accompany a traditional technical emphasis (Figure 6.9).

6.6 INDEPENDENCE FROM CULTURE

TPmgt has been applied, tested, and implemented throughout the world, cross-
ing geographic, ideological, and cultural boundaries. This concept works because of some fundamental beliefs that characterize it, and these beliefs are
universal in nature. They include the following:

1. TPmgt is centered around building people up, not destroying them.
2. TPmgt emphasizes the technical and behavioral aspects of organizational design and management systems as equally important and, in today's technology-driven organizations, people as the most important asset.
3. TPmgt's TPG system rewards all the stakeholders, not just the owners or the employees.

Because the TPmgt philosophy and methodology revolve around the enormous positive abilities of people, who, at a basic level, are the same throughout the world, the concept is appealing to people of diverse backgrounds. The TPM has been implemented in more than 300 companies in countries ranging from the United States to India and the United Kingdom to Guatemala and in companies ranging from a small flower distributor to a mega manufacturer of high-tech products distributed in 165 countries. The TPmgt concept has been tested in companies ranging from manufacturing to service, tourism to transportation, and non-union to union-based operations.

There are more similarities than differences among people of all cultures, when we look at it in a fundamental sense. Therefore, TPmgt, which is so people oriented, works despite cultural differences. This is not to claim that all facets of TPmgt are of equal success in all cultural settings; it would be naive to think so. However, experience with TPmgt suggests that cultural adaptation of the concept has not been a major challenge when the implementors understand the concept at least reasonably well. It is virtually impossible for every enterprise to understand any concept or philosophy fully. Unlike TQM, which lacks a uniform implementation process and a standardized quantitative mechanism, TPmgt has one uniform implementation procedure (as outlined in Chapter 4) and one standardized quantitative model—the TPM—to measure, evaluate, plan, and improve the competitiveness of an enterprise continuously.

6.7 ABILITY TO UNDERSTAND THE TECHNOLOGY– TOTAL PRODUCTIVITY SYNERGY

The TPmgt concept offers a systematic approach to understanding the technology–total productivity (T-TP) connection. An understanding of technology, in the most basic sense, is as primitive as humans themselves, from the time they improvised their cooking technology from stones to firewood, charcoal to kerosene stoves, and electric stoves to microwave ovens, but the management of technology as it is evolving today is a much more complex discipline. The implications of technology at the individual, enterprise, community, society, and global levels are of far-reaching significance, particularly with reference to the application of the total productivity perspective to integrate business and technology strategies.

As we move from 1990 toward the 21st century, the role of technology strategy is becoming more omniscient than ever before in the history of mankind. Many researchers at the first five international conferences on management of technology[7] pointed out the need to integrate technology strategy into business strategy to achieve better results in competitiveness. While some have attempted to do so in companies, the "mindset" of this integration has not become a reality. Little, if any, significant, empirical evidence exists in relating well-established business indicators to technology. Yet, in the fast-moving, pragmatic enterprises of the business world, strategic planners need a systematic linking mechanism between technology strategies and business strategies. In the ultimate analysis, after all, strategic planners have to "sell" their technology strategies to a profit-oriented top management.

Some commonly used business performance indicators include profitability, liquidity, sales turnover ratios, *quality,* and *productivity.* The latter two are interrelated, and they are becoming increasingly important in view of the customer-oriented management philosophies that focus on "quality competitiveness" in today's global markets. While it is a more exhaustive exercise to examine the linkage of all the above-mentioned business indicators to technology, it is considered a more manageable approach, at least for the purpose of this section, to attempt to concentrate on one of the most important business indicators, namely, productivity.

Traditionally, the impact of new technologies on productivity is seen in terms of their effects on efficiency and labor productivity. For the most part, whenever new technologies are considered for adoption, the economic payback period is often computed based on the savings in labor. Sometimes the effects of materials and capital are taken into account, but generally speaking, they are not explicitly expressed. Unfortunately, as pointed out in earlier chapters, even basic terms such as "efficiency" and "productivity" are not clearly understood, let alone the effect of technology on them. Efficiency and productivity are not the same. Highly efficient companies are not necessarily highly productive. Yet, a survey of Fortune 1000 companies in the United States revealed that about 80% of those companies use efficiency and labor productivity measures to reflect an enterprise's performance.[8]

Labor productivity—and, for that matter, any partial productivity measure—is a misrepresentation of reality when studying the impact of any technology, because such an indicator suffers from an inability to explain the impact of technology on *all* the resources and *all* the output produced. There is a natural interaction between the use of various input resources, as well as an effect on the output, whenever a new technology is introduced. Considering the impact of technology on only partial productivity measures such as labor productivity or capital productivity gives a distorted picture. It is the joint and simultaneous impact of all the inputs on the output that must be considered when studying the effect of any new technology before and after its installation in an enterprise.

The T-TP Framework

The impact of technology is more easily rationalized in the total productivity perspective. As discussed in Chapter 3, total productivity is the *ratio* of total tangible output produced to total tangible input consumed. The denominator in the ratio includes all the resource inputs: human, material, fixed capital, working capital, energy, and all other input. There has been a growing awareness among "productivity experts" of the importance of considering this holistic measure, as evidenced by a large proportion of the latest research devoted to it.

The total productivity perspective takes into account the effects of quality, reliability, profitability, and other performance indicators. For an easier understanding of the T-TP linkage, a conceptual framework (Figure 6.10) is proposed.

The T-TP framework works as follows:

1. The transformation of all the inputs (human, material, fixed capital, working capital, energy, and others) into outputs (products and/or services) is denoted by the usual "black box." In this transformation process, the *technology cycle*[9] (Figure 6.11) forms a central hub.
2. In any of the five phases of this cycle, the "technology user" makes a rational assessment of the given state of product technology, process technology, and management technology, which are interrelated through information technology.
3. The productivity engineer or technology manager applies the TPM[10] to determine the total productivity level for each product or service. The weighted sum of total productivity levels for all the products and/or services gives the total productivity for the enterprise/company as a whole.
4. The total productivity level is compared to the break-even point of total productivity for each product or service. Total productivity above the break-even point indicates a favorable, profitable situation. The reverse indicates an unfavorable, loss situation.
5. The impact of existing and/or new technologies is reflected by the changes in total productivity levels. Also, to determine the impact of

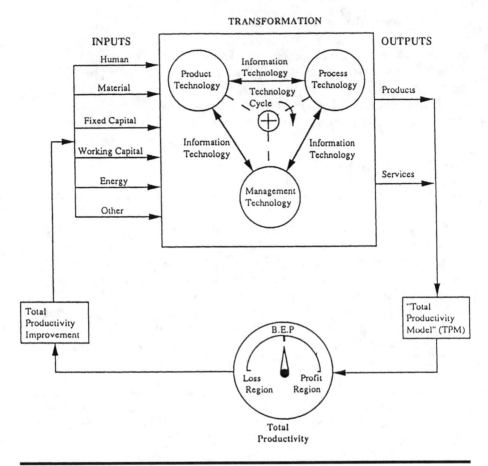

FIGURE 6.10 Conceptual framework for technology–total productivity linkage (the T-TP connection). (©1989, D.J. Sumanth.)

the technologies on each individual input factor, the incremental gains in the corresponding partial productivities are computed. For example, the direct impact of a given set of technologies on human resources is determined from the human productivity changes, on material resources by material productivity changes, and so on. Of course, the interactive effects can also be analyzed through a sensitivity analysis or factor analysis.

6. The productivity engineer calculates the impact of the technology changes on profitability and thus helps to link the profit-oriented business strategy

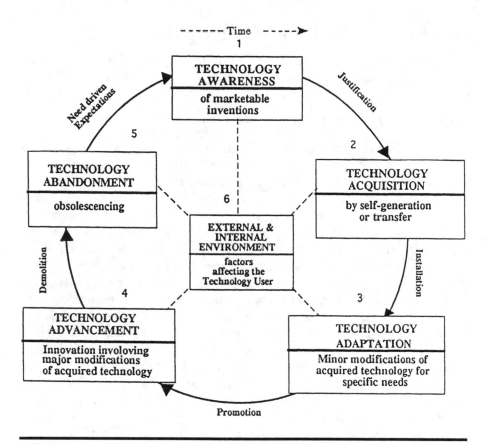

FIGURE 6.11 The technology cycle, showing the five basic elements of technology management at any level (product, service, function, work center, plant/division, corporation, industry, national, or international) to deal with an existing or new technology. Dashed lines represent analysis. (©1988, D.J. Sumanth.)

with the customer-oriented technology strategy. New targets are set to improve present levels of total productivity. To achieve these targets, a set of 70 different productivity and quality improvement techniques are available (see Chapter 3). Appropriate techniques are implemented using the existing or new technologies.

7. To determine the extent of improvement in total productivity as a result of the new technologies and/or improvement techniques, the TPM is applied again, and the whole monitoring process continues through the T-TP framework.

Case Studies Using the T-TP Framework

While the T-TP framework can be applied to any type of enterprise, two case studies are presented here as examples.

Case Study 1: Electric and Water Utility

A Dutch Antillean utility company with about 200 employees was exposed to the T-TP framework in the 1980s. The firm had two plants—one for electricity and one for water. All of the electricity was generated by one plant, while part of the water demand was met by a water plant managed by another company.

The electric power plant used very old Dutch diesel engine technology until 1980. A major new Dutch diesel technology (with a heat recovery system) was implemented in 1987. The capacity of the new engine using this technology was 2.3 megawatts. In 1988, a drastically different Finnish diesel technology was introduced (with a 9.6-megawatt engine). In 1989, an 11.6-megawatt Dutch diesel engine with "heavy fuel" technology was installed. In this case, the product technology did not change, but the process technology, management technology, and information technology were changed as part of a deliberate technology strategy to reduce the cost per kilowatt-hour. As a result of the new diesel technologies, which have a 15 to 20% lower fuel consumption inherently and a heat recovery of 80% for running the boilers in the water plant, the total productivity of the electric power plant increased by about 60% since 1985. Of this, nearly 27% of the contribution to total productivity was from the effective and efficient use of diesel and lubricating oils. The remaining 33% of the improvement in total productivity was due to new management technologies such as TPmgt.

All employees, from the managing director to the worker level, were introduced to the TPmgt concept over a period of one year. The personnel manager and the managing director used restraint in hiring new employees, even though the demand for electricity was increasing at an average of 12% per year since 1985. Instead, Productivity Quality Teams were formed to improve quality and productivity. The cost per kilowatt-hour decreased starting in 1985 (Figure 6.12). The company had a strong union, and the TPmgt process involved the union leader and the union stewards right from the start. A new "professionalization" thrust was created at the supervisory, department head, and top management levels to improve communication, motivation, and morale. This company has a clearly developed mission statement, with participation of all levels of management and union workers. The management technology in this company has been drastically different since 1985, thanks to the top management team, which was comprised of the managing director, the personnel manager, and the financial manager.

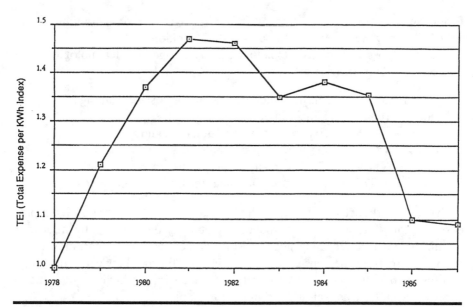

FIGURE 6.12   Total expenses per kilowatt-hour for an electric and water utility firm that implemented the TPmgt concept.

In this company, the business strategy was integrated into the technology strategy, with a focus on total productivity. It was clear that new technologies had a significant impact on *total productivity* and hence *total cost per kilowatt-hour*. The significant impact on total productivity and total cost per unit was primarily the result of the new process technology.

Case Study 2: Transit Maintenance Facility

The T-TP framework was applied in the maintenance facility of a transit operation to study the effect of new process technologies (automation based) on total productivity.

The transit facility, located in Bradenton, Florida, does maintenance of various types of fleets. The study considered three major service types: transit, para-transit, and emergency medical services (EMS). The physical plant of the transit operation consisted of 22 municipal buses, serving 10 fixed routes county-wide. The para-transit operation involved 20 special-purpose buses, fitted with special equipment to transport the physically handicapped, the elderly, and the disabled. The EMS consisted of 12 modular full-service ambulances and 6 auxiliary rescue vehicles. Prior to June 1985, all three services were run as public agencies.

From June 1985 to July 1986, they were run as private-sector operations, and in July 1986, they were returned to public administration.

Several types of process technologies and management technologies were introduced in this enterprise:

June 1985	On-line microcomputer for cost accounting
January 1986	Synchronous electric bus lifts
	Expert system for engine diagnostics
April 1986	On-line microcomputer maintenance
July 1986	Clerical maintenance management system
January 1987	Batch-compiled maintenance management system

The total productivity index graphs indicated that the most significant process technology to affect total productivity actually dropped for the first four months before it started rising steadily. This was because of the "learning curve."

This case study demonstrated a very definite linkage between technology and total productivity. The most significant effects in this facility were due to process technology as well as information technology.

Significance of the T-TP Framework

Among the many advantages and salient features of the T-TP framework, the most significant ones are:

1. Better operational understanding of the relationship between technology and total productivity
2. Interdisciplinary emphasis for greater teamwork
3. Top management's ability to see a direct linkage between technology and familiar indicators of enterprise performance, thereby making it easier to integrate business strategy with technology strategy

The T-TP framework is probably a first attempt to show the direct connection between technology and "total productivity." More research and empirical evidence are encouraged to validate the results of application of this framework.

6.8 ABILITY TO UNDERSTAND AND AFFECT THE QUALITY–TOTAL PRODUCTIVITY LINKAGE

With the traditional labor productivity measure, it is difficult to see the impact of quality. However, with the TPmgt concept, it is technically feasible to understand

and interpret the effects of quality on total productivity levels. In fact, recent research by Arora and Sumanth proposes a framework[11] to do so by considering the quality costs in the TPM setting. This research pointed out that the total productivity framework:

1. Can provide a company with a systematic way to evaluate and determine whether or not efforts to improve quality are productive at any time
2. Can be used as a benchmark for strategic management decisions, such as whether to allocate funds for quality improvement or for other strategies which may prove to be more productive at a given point in time
3. Demonstrates the fact that quality improvement helps to boost total productivity, though not indefinitely, for a given product or service unit
4. Shows that quality is one of the most strategic variables to affect total productivity for a product line or for a company as a whole

Recall again from Chapter 3 that

$$TP = \frac{O_1 + O_2 + O_3 + O_4 + O_5}{H + M + FC + WC + E + X}$$

Let's suppose the quality of material in a manufacturing firm improves significantly in a particular month. This might reduce human input (H) because the material does not have to be reworked by operators. Also, because the machines do not have be to run to compensate for inferior quality work, fixed capital input (FC) would decrease. If the reworked material inventory is reduced because of better quality material, working capital input (WC) would shrink as well. In all likelihood, energy input (E) and other expenses input (X) would also decrease. Further, when operators do not have to slow down their rate of production and are able to maintain a smooth pace as a result of working with high-quality material, the value of finished units (O_1) and partially completed units (O_2) generally goes up. Thus, the overall effect would be a substantial increase in total productivity (TP).

Now let's suppose the same company decides to purchase expensive quality control equipment, for example, automated inspection equipment. FC would increase because of additional training for operators working with the new technology, and X would most likely increase. E might increase, and there may not be any visible improvement in O_1 and O_2. Thus, in this situation, TP might actually drop slightly in the short run, but as the training is completed, the number of final inspectors needed might decrease, thereby reducing H. Eventually, as operators become more proficient in working with the new technology (learning curve effect), O_1 and O_2 would increase incrementally.

Depending upon the nature of quality improvement and the input and output factors affected, total productivity can either increase or decrease. If we consider both the "primary" and "secondary" effects of quality changes on one or more of the input and output factors, we can determine the overall impact on total productivity for any given time period. The bottom line is that the impact of quality can be assessed quantitatively with the TPM, and since total productivity is related to profitability, we can safely say that quality changes in the TPmgt perspective are fully quantified and are related directly to profitability. This is a unique feature of TPmgt, whereas no such statement can be asserted confidently with TQM.

6.9 ABILITY TO INTERLINK THE DIMENSIONS OF COMPETITIVENESS

As discussed in Section 3.6, the three critical dimensions of competitiveness today and into the 21st century are:

- Quality competitiveness
- Cost competitiveness
- Time competitiveness

The concept of TPmgt approaches these three dimensions of competitiveness simultaneously rather than serially or in isolation. All three components are required to face the challenges of global competitiveness. Expectations of clients/customers/constituents have risen so dramatically in recent years that quality and cost are taken for granted today. Because people expect to get high-quality products at the best price possible, the *time* dimension is often the deciding factor when quality and cost are assumed to be equal for competing products or services.

As mentioned in Chapter 3, there are 70 different techniques at a company's disposal to attain the targets of total productivity set in the *planning* phase of the *productivity cycle*. Unlike the myth that productivity can be improved by just a few techniques, like quality management, computer controls, robotics, incentives, etc., a set of nearly 70 proven techniques is available in TPmgt.

Cycle time reduction, time-based manufacturing, and similar techniques have become increasingly prominent today in improving the time competitiveness dimension and are differentiating the winners from the losers and the thrivers from the survivors.

The unique ability of the TPmgt philosophy to *interlink* all the critical dimensions of competitiveness differentiates it from other management approaches.

6.10 UNIQUE FEATURES COMPARED TO OTHER MANAGEMENT PHILOSOPHIES

It would be overly simplistic to claim that one particular management philosophy is the "best" from all perspectives. Perhaps it is more realistic to say that in a world of many management philosophies developed over the millennia, some are more *relevant* for certain periods of history, characterized by the cultural, economic, political, moral, and ecological concerns of the time. With this perspective as the backdrop, TPmgt can be considered as a management philosophy that is relevant in our current environment. It is important to note that TPmgt recognizes and incorporates some proven features of many major management philosophies, including those of Frederick Taylor, W. Edwards Deming, Joseph Juran, Philip Crosby, Armand Feigenbaum, Kaoru Ishikawa, Genichi Taguchi, and Masaaki Imai.

The Taylor Philosophy

Frederick Winslow Taylor's management philosophy centered around a scientific approach to analyzing and improving work. The industrial engineering profession is a direct result of his contributions to methods analysis and work measurement. Taylor's "scientific management" approach (Figure 6.13) is often misunderstood and misrepresented, but he was one of the first to recognize the importance of good labor–management relationships. In fact, in his seminal work,[12] he declared that his "whole object was to remove the cause for antagonism between the boss and the men who were under him." While many may criticize Taylorism, "the Japanese are the most fervent believers in industrial engineering in the world. At Toyota, even the foreman is often an IE, or studying to become one."[13] Taylor's scientific method of defining a problem, collecting data, generating alternatives, evaluating the alternatives and selecting the best possible solution, implementing the solution, measuring the results, and repeating the whole process remains very much the same today and is incorporated in all problem-solving approaches, including those in TQM. It is inconceivable to do reengineering without analyzing business processes through well-established industrial engineering techniques such as process flowcharts, operation process charts, and flow diagrams.

Taylor's 4 Principles of "Scientific Management"

1. Deliberately gathering together of the great mass of traditional knowledge by the means of time and motion study.

2. Scientific selection of the workers and then their progressive development.

3. Bringing together of this science and the trained worker, by offering some incentive to the worker.

4. A complete redivision of the work of the establishment, to bring about democracy and cooperation between management and the workers.

FIGURE 6.13   The often misunderstood Taylor. (Source: Boone, Louis E. and Bowen, Donald D., *The Great Writings in Management and Organizational Behaviour,* Random House, New York, 1987, p. 33.)

TPmgt differs from and incorporates Taylor's philosophy in many ways, including the following:

1. TPmgt emphasizes all the input factors, not just labor.
2. Taylor concentrated on labor productivity; TPmgt centers around total productivity.
3. The scientific method is applied in the PQT module of TPmgt for problem solving within teams that are accomplishing specific goals set in the TPmgt implementation process (see Chapter 4).
4. Methods analysis, work measurement, and standardization—the three major approaches applied by Taylor—are only 3 among the 70 different techniques available to improve total productivity.

The Deming Philosophy

I was privileged to meet with Dr. Deming and take his three-day seminar in 1979. He used as his lecture notes what was to become his seminal work,[14] which included his philosophy through his famous "14 Points" (Figure 6.14). This seminar was one of Dr. Deming's first in the United States, before he

1. Create constancy of purpose toward improvement of product and service with a plan to become competitive and to stay in business. Decide whom top management is responsible to.

2. Adopt the new philosophy. We are in a new economic age. We can no longer live with commonly accepted levels of delays, mistakes, defective materials, and defective workmanship.

3. Cease dependence on mass inspection. Require, instead, statistical evidence that quality is built in. (*Prevent* defects rather than *detect* defects.)

4. End the practice of awarding business on the basis of price tag. Instead, depend on meaningful measures of quality, along with price. Eliminate suppliers that cannot qualify with statistical evidence of quality.

5. Find problems. It is management's job to work continually on the system (design, incoming materials, composition of material, maintenance, improvement of machine, training, supervision, retraining).

6. Institute modern methods of training on the job.

7. The responsibility of foreman must be changed from sheer numbers to quality ..[which] will automatically improve productivity. Management must prepare to take immediate action on reports from foreman concerning barriers such as inherited defects, machines not maintained, poor tools, fuzzy operational difinitions.

8. Drive out fear, so that everyone may work effectively for the company.

9. Break down barriers between departments. People in research, design, sales, and production must work as a team, to foreseee problems of production that may be encountered with various materials and specifications.

10. Eliminate numerical goals, posters, and slogans for the work force, asking for new levels of productivity without providing methods.

11. Eliminate work standards that prescribe numerical quotas.

12. Remove barriers that stand between the hourly worker and his right to pride of workmanship.

13. Institute a vigorous program of education and retraining.

14. Create a structure in top management that will push every day on the above 13 points

FIGURE 6.14 Deming's 14 Points. (Source: Deming, W. Edwards, *Quality, Productivity, and Competitive Position,* Center for Advanced Engineering Study, MIT, Cambridge, MA, 1982, pp. 16–17.)

became widely recognized after being featured in the NBC White Paper "If Japan Can...Why Cant' We?" on June 24, 1980.

TPmgt incorporates, to some extent, Deming's Points #1, 2, 3, 5, 8, 9, 12, and 13 but differs from his philosophy in several ways:

1. Deming's concept of productivity is the traditional labor productivity—output per man-hour. None of his examples included total productivity the way TPmgt proposes.

2. TPmgt incorporates the essence of Deming's many philosophical viewpoints with regard to treatment of employees and understanding of systems, but it goes beyond these to create a quantitative framework through the TPM.

3. TPmgt includes clearly understood and uniformly interpreted numerical goals for management and employees because such goals actually help to improve morale. People improve their self-esteem and self-worth when they know they have actually achieved the goals and targets they have set themselves or which have been set for them. Of course, since TPmgt has a reward mechanism through TPG, the goals are oriented toward product lines and customers rather than departmental self-aggrandizement.

4. TPmgt does not subscribe to Deming's Point #11. In TPmgt, work standards are applied not to "police" the work force but rather to help employees see how they can improve their work methods, which they are more familiar with than anyone. Further, work standards are an enormous help in balancing workstations in assembly lines (industrial engineers call this line balancing) so that total throughput is increased and bottlenecks are eliminated. Lincoln Electric applies time standards to every operation, and these standards are tied to a piecework incentive system which has been very successful for decades. Whenever possible, work standards should be established by work groups or teams or by study analysts, in full cooperation with employees. A major caution here is that a team might decide to eliminate a business process altogether as part of achieving a management goal, in which case all the work standards associated with the operations in that business process would naturally be eliminated. Work standards must always be viewed as *means* for continuous improvement, not ends in themselves to monitor employees. Without work standards at each workstation, it is difficult to do accurate capacity planning, facility expansions, and manpower planning. The key is to include time-study analysts and industrial engineers as part of work teams and utilize their expertise to achieve the management goals as defined in Chapter 4.

5. Statistical quality control (SQC) is one of the major concepts at the heart of Deming's quality management philosophy. However, in many cases, companies can overdo this to the point of losing sight of the forest due to looking only at the trees. The time and effort needed to institute and

run SQC may often be so costly that the SQC effort should be limited to those situations which truly require it. Otherwise, SQC might become an end in itself rather than a valuable means to an end. TPmgt recognizes this practicality.

Deming is a legend. His contributions to quality management are unquestionably great. The differences cited with respect to TPmgt do not contradict Deming but rather supplement his philosophy where his concepts lack a quantitative framework.

The Juran Philosophy

Dr. Joseph Juran, another quality pioneer, made legendary contributions to quality management. Like Deming, he began teaching quality concepts to the Japanese beginning around 1950. His book *Managerial Breakthrough*,[15] published in 1964, set the stage for his management philosophy. Juran's breakthrough procedure is as follows:

1. Convince others that a breakthrough is needed.
2. Identify the *vital few* projects.
3. Organize for a breakthrough in knowledge.
4. Conduct an analysis to discover the cause(s) of the problem.
5. Determine the effect of the proposed changes on the people involved, and find ways to overcome resistance to these changes.
6. Take action to institute the changes, including training of all personnel involved.
7. Institute appropriate controls that will maintain the new, improved quality level but will not restrict continued improvement—perhaps through another breakthrough sequence.

Juran's *quality trilogy*—quality planning, quality control, and quality improvement—defines his concept of quality management. TPmgt fully acknowledges the importance of the quality trilogy. In fact, in defining the practical dimensions of quality, TPmgt adopts Juran's quality of design, quality of conformance, and quality of performance. TPmgt recognizes and reiterates that quality can and should be designed into a product or service at the time of design itself. For example, designing products for producibility and maintainability will significantly improve the chances for quality of performance (reliability and maintainability). When we said quality improves total productivity in the long run, we defined quality in terms of Juran's three dimensions—quality of design, quality of conformance, and quality of performance.

TPmgt also has many unique features when compared to the Juran philosophy of management:

1. TPmgt is a philosophy as well as a concept and, more importantly, is a 12-step process (Chapter 4) with a quantitative mechanism to measure, evaluate, plan, and improve total productivity.
2. TPmgt recognizes that "breakthroughs," as understood by Juran, are necessary all the time and must be incorporated as part of strategies for management teams to achieve the management goals.
3. From the TPmgt perspective, quality planning, quality control, and quality improvement must be implemented at both strategic and tactical levels.

The Crosby Philosophy

Philip Crosby, another quality guru, originated the concept of zero defects and became very well known for his work *Quality Is Free.*[16] I spoke to him at length one on one in 1993 at the Fourth International Conference on Productivity and Quality Research. His philosophy of quality management is that quality must start with the goal of zero defects. He considers the concept of AQL (acceptable quality level) irrelevant, particularly in today's environment. According to Crosby, defects result from lack of knowledge and lack of attention. He argues that if everyone pays attention to detail and prevents defects to begin with, quality is indeed free. The cost of redoing a job, whether a product or service, is often greater than the cost of doing it right the first time. His most recent work[17] reiterates this theme in many ways.

TPmgt agrees with the simple but valuable thought that "doing it right the first time" is a sure way to manage quality—and for that matter, total productivity—in a very effective manner. Crosby might appear to oversimplify issues, but there is much depth to his philosophy that "quality is free." We can appreciate his philosophy through the total productivity formula:

$$TP = \frac{O_1 + O_2 + O_3 + O_4 + O_5}{H + M + FC + WC + E + X}$$

If employees and managers do their tasks right the first time, there will be no rework. Eliminating rework of tasks reduces the time and effort put into human (H), material (M), machinery (FC), energy (E), and other (X) resources. Further, instead of expending these valuable resources on rework, they can be used to produce additional outputs (O_1, O_2, O_3, O_4, and O_5). Thus, total productivity (TP) can be substantially increased by doing everything right the first time.

Using the total productivity formula, we can illustrate dozens of examples where total productivity dropped significantly because someone did not do his or her job right the first time.

TPmgt differs from the Crosby philosophy in many ways, including the following:

1. TPmgt has a quantitative framework to back up what it claims.
2. TPmgt includes Crosby's main point, namely, aim for no defects and do it right the first time. The total productivity model can be a vehicle to monitor Crosby's philosophy in an analytical manner.
3. While Crosby's thinking conceptually relates quality to profitability in an *indirect* manner, TPmgt links them *directly* through the TPM.

The Feigenbaum Philosophy

Dr. Armand Feigenbaum originated the total quality control (TQC) concept. In fact, he first published this concept in 1951 under a different title. His TQC set the stage for viewing quality in *all* the functional areas of a company instead of just in manufacturing or operations. His concepts were the foundation for the present TQM philosophy. His book *Total Quality Control*[18] was indeed a landmark work, spinning off many ideas in modern TQM.

He pointed out that 15 to 40% of a plant's capacity often exists just to take care of rework. He firmly believes that quality, in the long run, is less costly.

As with Crosby's management philosophy, TPmgt accepts and absorbs Feigenbaum's thinking without any intellectual argument, for the most part. TPmgt goes a step beyond to say that the TQC effort is justified much better to top management when the costs associated with it are captured in the TPM, which further helps to link the TQC effort to dollars and cents in terms of profits.

The Ishikawa Philosophy

Dr. Kaoru Ishikawa popularized the quality philosophies of Deming, Juran, and Feigenbaum. In 1968, he began using the term company-wide quality control to distinguish the Japanese approach to TQC from what Feigenbaum was proposing.

Ishikawa's *thought revolution in management*, as he put it, was accomplished through the following six concepts:[19]

1. Quality first—not short-term profit first
2. Consumer orientation—not producer orientation; think from the standpoint of the other party

3. The next process is your customer—break down the barrier of sectionalism
4. Using facts and data to make presentations—utilization of statistical methods
5. Respect for humanity as a management philosophy—full participatory management
6. Cross-functional management

TPmgt differs from Ishikawa's management philosophy in the same way it differs from Feigenbaum's. With dramatic drops in product development cycles, companies have to seek profit. A company can "have its cake and eat it too" with the TPmgt philosophy, because right from the time a concept is initiated for product design or service design, the total productivity model begins to monitor the total productivity value and hence profits. In other words, TPmgt considers the welfare of *all* the stakeholders.

The Taguchi Philosophy

Dr. Taguchi views quality as a much broader concept than most other quality gurus. He says that "the quality of a product is the (minimum) loss imparted by the product to the society from the time the product is shipped."[20] He calls this the "Quality Loss Function." Taguchi's methods were first introduced in the United States in 1980–82.

Taguchi's "Off-Line Quality Control" concept involves engineering optimization of a product or process through three steps: system design, parameter design, and tolerance design.[21] His approaches to parameter design have become somewhat controversial.

TPmgt differs from the Taguchi philosophy in many ways, but the most important distinction is the manner in which the quality costs are captured. The Taguchi approach is to do so in terms of a loss function, whereas TPmgt captures the costs in the TPM. The Comprehensive Total Productivity Model (CTPM©) captures many of the quality costs incurred in the social dimension.

The Kaizen Philosophy

In 1989, I had the opportunity to meet Masaaki Imai, who wrote the first major book on *kaizen*. We chatted briefly about our topics of interest. I was quite impressed by his message on *kaizen* and the passion with which he delivered it. After our discussion, I read his work with more in-depth insights.

To quote Imai, *kaizen* "is the unifying thread running through the philosophy, the systems, and the problem-solving tools developed in Japan over the last 30 years. Its message is one of improvement and trying to do better."[22]

According to Imai, "there are two contrasting approaches to progress: the gradualist approach and the great-leap-forward approach. Japanese companies generally favor the gradualist approach and Western companies favor the great-leap approach—an approach epitomized by the term innovation:

	Kaizen	*Innovation*
Japan	Strong	Weak
The West	Weak	Strong

...Innovation is dramatic, a real attention-grabber. *Kaizen,* on the other hand, is often undramatic and subtle, and its results are seldom immediately visible. Whereas *kaizen* is a continuous process, innovation is generally a one-shot phenomenon."[23]

Imai goes to great lengths to contrast *kaizen* with the Western style of management. In a nutshell, he considers *kaizen* to be process oriented as opposed to results oriented, the premise being that if the process is improved, results will come. *Kaizen,* according to Imai, is also people oriented. He proposes what he calls the "*kaizen* umbrella" to denote the inclusion of many concepts, including customer orientation, TQC, quality control (QC) circles, total productive maintenance, *kanban,* just-in-time, zero defects, productivity improvement, cooperative labor–management relations, new product development, etc.[24]

The *kaizen* and TPmgt concepts have many elements in common philosophically, but TPmgt goes far beyond *kaizen* in the following ways:

1. *Kaizen* considers about 10 major improvement techniques, such as robotics, QC circles, just-in-time, zero defects, etc., whereas TPmgt considers 70 techniques, as pointed out in Chapter 3.

2. *Kaizen* falls short of a measurement system such as the TPM in the TPmgt concept.

3. Whereas *kaizen* is primarily *process oriented*, TPmgt is always *product oriented*. If products are not made with customers in mind, there is no need to improve processes. The reengineering approach to eliminate business processes goes to a radical level of process improvement when compared to *kaizen,* which relies on small incremental steps toward improvement.

4. TPmgt relates all activities pertaining to products with respect to quality, cost, and time back to total productivity and, hence, to profits. Managers can see which improvements are yielding a greater profit contribution.

5. *Kaizen* is portrayed in contrast to innovation. TPmgt believes first in innovation and then in small-scale improvement. Today's customer expectations in terms of time competitiveness cannot be met by merely incremental improvements.

6.11 COMPREHENSIVENESS OF PROBLEM-SOLVING APPROACHES IN TRAINING

Another unique feature of TPmgt is its recognition of the fact that there are nearly 40 different problem-solving *tools* available (Figure 6.15) to attain all the dimensions of competitiveness. TQM, on the other hand, recognizes, and uses for the most part, only "the seven statistical tools" and the "seven new QC tools." Occasionally, TQM also uses the four or so "advanced statistical tools." Since TPmgt is an interdisciplinary approach, it uses not only the tools of TQM but also at least 18 others which are commonly employed by industrial engineers. Thus, with TPmgt, companies have a much bigger "toolbox" to use for solving problems.

6.12 COMPREHENSIVENESS OF PRODUCTIVITY AND QUALITY IMPROVEMENT TECHNIQUES

In Chapter 3, 70 different techniques were listed for improving total productivity, in contrast to about 15 for TQM. More importantly, the TPmgt concept provides quantitative models such as the Analytical Productivity Improvement Model (APIM),[25] a flowchart for which is shown in Figure 6.16.

The basic strategy in the APIM is to select an optimum set of techniques from among the 70 available such that the company will maximize total productivity (and hence profit), subject to constraints on maximum funds available to do the total productivity improvement, maximum implementation time allowable, and minimum payback period in which to recover the investment of implementation funds. This is a sophisticated but practical quantitative model to select productivity improvement techniques for any given time period(s).

This approach to improving total productivity and hence competitiveness is unique to TPmgt. Other management concepts, including TQM, lack such a systematic process to select appropriate techniques for total productivity improvement.

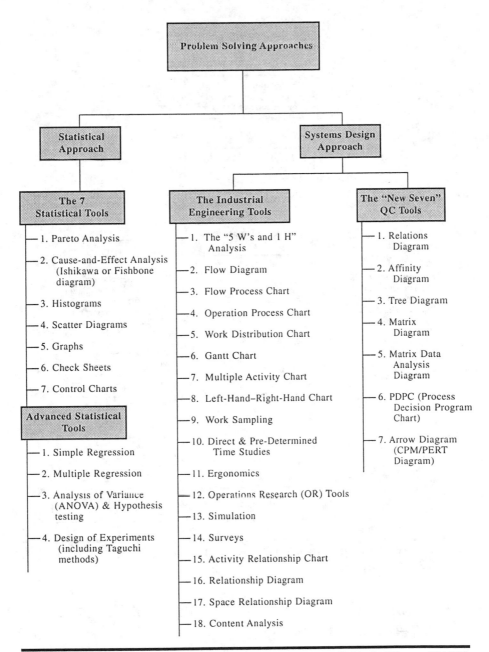

FIGURE 6.15   A wide variety of problem-solving tools available in TPmgt. (©1991, D.J. Sumanth.)

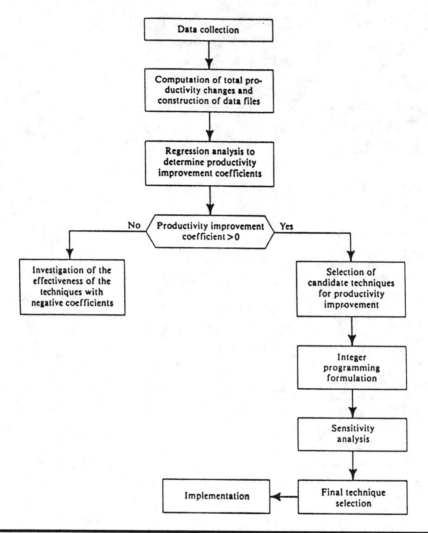

FIGURE 6.16   Flowchart for the Analytical Productivity Improvement Model (APIM) in the TPmgt concept.

6.13 ABILITY TO QUANTIFY THE IMPACT ON THE BOTTOM LINE

The effects of quality, productivity, technology, and continuous improvement efforts on total productivity, and hence profits, are uniquely captured by the TPM. Total productivity and the break-even point of total productivity, when plotted together, will indicate to a company whether all the so-called improvement efforts are indeed paying off in terms of profitability. Top management teams find this aspect extremely beneficial in deciding whether or not to continue funding programs or projects at any given time. In large firms, often many projects are under way and many new concepts are implemented. Any of these projects and concepts that do not contribute to achieving the management goals set in the TPmgt implementation process (Step 2, see Chapter 4) for any given time period should be discontinued. Otherwise, these non-value-adding projects and concepts will have a negative effect on organizational resistance, adaptability, customer responsiveness, and, of course, profitability. TPmgt uniquely prevents the initiation of inappropriate projects and concepts and helps to stop them from continuing if already begun.

6.14 REWARD SYSTEM BASED ON TOTAL PRODUCTIVITY GAINSHARING

Another unique aspect of TPmgt is the incorporation of a reward system for *all stakeholders* through TPG, as discussed in Chapter 3.

TPG ensures that all employees are rewarded through a total productivity bonus at least once a year. Owners or shareholders are rewarded at the end of each fiscal year through dividends on their shares. Customers are rewarded through price discounts as appropriate each year. This may occur more than once a year in some companies. The community is rewarded through sponsorship of worthy civic causes, scholarships and awards, and any number of other activities. Suppliers are rewarded through faster payment. Families of employees are rewarded through company-paid vacations or other similar benefits.

The TPmgt concept views employee motivation as a variable that is positively affected by what a company does for both the employee and his or her family. Delighted employees enchant their customers. The key is to create a work environment in which everyone in the company enjoys their work. TPG helps create such an environment.

6.15 THE PRACTICE OF "MANAGEMENT IS A MORAL ISSUE"

For many years, I have used the slogan *"management is a moral issue"* on my business cards. The meaning of this phrase is simple. Just as it is immoral to kill, steal, etc., it is equally immoral for a company to hire someone and then, after

"Just as it is immoral to steal, murder, or rape someone, it is equally immoral, in my opinion, to layoff some one from work, because, doing so amounts to stealing the opportunity to give the best of that individual's talent, time, and tenacity of purpose. No one forces you to hire someone to work for your organization. No one prevents you from taking all the time you want before you hire someone. But, once you hire a person, it is your moral responsibility and obligation to coach, mentor, nourish, train, retrain, locate, relocate, discipline and encourage that person, to be the most cherished, undepreciable, and competitive resource you have—in good times or bad times."

FIGURE 6.17 *"Management is a moral issue."* (©1989–90, D.J. Sumanth.)

years of dedicated and loyal service during which the company benefited from the individual's talents, fire the person (see Figure 6.17 for a more formal statement). Many U.S. enterprises have a tendency to treat experienced employees as though they are "dead wood." The fundamental reason why someone reaches this stage is largely attributable to the improper environment created by management. For example, if a manager ignores an employee who has been energetic, enthusiastic, and competent, the employee likely will become withdrawn and his or her performance will suffer. Soon, he or she does not participate as before, does not contribute as much, and loses interest.

TPmgt believes strongly in treating all people as a company's greatest asset. *The human asset must be treasured, not trashed.* The Japanese and the other Eastern countries, because of their people-oriented culture, understand the *art* of managing people with respect, recognition, and reward. In Western culture, particularly the United States, employees have become a disposable commodity. They seem to be nothing more than a number. Today's organizational culture seems to have been shaped by individual and family values, characterized by intolerance, impatience, lack of empathy and a caring attitude, and low self-image. The billions of dollars spent on fighting crime, teenage pregnancy, homelessness, etc. are a symptom of the social degeneracy we are facing today. A whole generation may be corrupted by managerial thinking which goes against goodness, wholesomeness, and decency. Today, people are hurting emotionally more than ever seen. Unfortunately, corporations only "add fuel to the fire" by mercilessly downsizing, restructuring, and destroying the morale of the people working for them. Everyone seems to have become so self-centered that basic trust, respect, and purposefulness have lost their meaning. Ironically, corpora-

- Sabotage
- Financial Embezzlement
- Stealing Company's Assets (products, components, machines, tools, etc.)
- Physical Abuse (of Supervisors, Fellow Employees, etc.)

FIGURE 6.18 Employee firings due to employees' fault. (©1990, D.J. Sumanth.)

tions can save huge sums of money if they learn to apply the TPmgt philosophy, which readily acknowledges the impact of layoffs, rehiring, and retraining on total productivity and hence on profit. There are many reasons for firing employees due to employees' fault (Figure 6.18), and management's fault (Figure 6.19), but there are also alternatives to firing employees (Figure 6.20).

As a result of implementing the TPmgt philosophy, a major insurance company in Florida has not laid off one employee since 1981. In fact, today this company has about 2,000 employees compared to about 1,600 in 1981. The company has grown substantially in revenues and has declared shareholder dividends regularly while most others in the insurance business have barely survived. This company has proved that if you put people ahead of everything else,

- Lack of clear Vision /Mission/Purpose
- Short-term Profit-Orientation rather than Long-term Customer-Orientation
- Lack of Consistent Commitment
- Excessive Bureaucracy
- Lack of "Employee Empowerment"
- Improper Incentives
- Greed
- Rigid Organizational Structures
- Lack of International Outlook
- Lack of Self-Confidence

FIGURE 6.19 Employee firings due to management's fault. (©1990, D.J. Sumanth.)

> - Second Chance
> - Professional Counseling
> - Rehabilitation
> - Increased Responsibility (!)
> - Personal Attention
>   (Mentoring, Coaching, Disciplining)

FIGURE 6.20   Alternatives to firing. (©1990, D.J. Sumanth.)

it pays off in a big way—through better utilization of *all* resources. After all, there are at least 11 alternatives to layoffs (Figure 6.21).

6.16 SUMMARY

Chapter 2 justified the need for TPmgt. The intent of this chapter was to highlight the unique features of TPmgt when it is stacked up against the major management philosophies of the 20th century. For a synopsis of the 15 features covered in this chapter, refer to Table 6.1.

> - Attrition
> - Retraining
> - Relocation
> - Market-Enlargement
> - Product/Service Diversification
> - Market-Development
>   (for know-hows related to existing products/services)
> - Vertical Integration
> - Early Retirement (last resort)
> - Reduced Hours/Alternative Tasks
> - Full Employment
> - Employment Freeze

FIGURE 6.21   Alternatives to layoffs. (©1990, D.J. Sumanth.)

TABLE 6.1 Uniqueness of TPmgt Compared to TQM and Reengineering

Feature	*TPmgt*	*TQM*	*Re-engineering*
1. Interdisciplinary emphasis on management decision making	Formal	Informal	Informal
• Simultaneous/concurrent engineering thinking	Built in	Acquired	Acquired
2. "People-building" emphasis with behavioral thrust	Unequivocal	Ambiguous	Little, if any
• Job security at all levels	Extremely high	Not guaranteed	Very low
• Organizational and people stability	Very high	Low–medium	Very low
3. Product/service unit orientation (instead of functional focus)	Substantial	Some	Some
4. "Customer chain" thinking	Designed strategy	Designed strategy, for the most part	Designed strategy, for the most part
5. Systemic perspective for integration	Excellent	Very good	Fair
6. Independent of culture	Always	Sometimes	Always
7. Ability to understand and impact the T–TP linkage	Analytical (quantifiable)	Subjective	Subjective
8. Ability to understand and affect the quality–total productivity linkage	Analytical (quantifiable)	Subjective	Subjective
9. Ability to interlink the dimensions of competitiveness (customer satisfaction, market share, profit, liquidity, etc.)	Directly measurable (through "Excellence Index")	Indirectly measurable (through individual indicators)	Poor
10. Unique features when compared to:			
• The Taylor philosophy	Many	Many	A few
• The Deming philosophy	Many	A few	Many
• The Juran philosophy	Many	A few	A few
• The Crosby philosophy	Many	Quite a few	Many
• The Feigenbaum philosophy	Many	A few	Many
• The Ishikawa philosophy	Many	A few	A few
• The Taguchi philosophy	Many	Quite a few	Many
• The *kaizen* philosophy	Many	Very few	Many

TABLE 6.1 Uniqueness of TPmgt Compared to TQM and Reengineering (continued)

Feature	TPmgt	TQM	Re-engineering
11. Comprehensiveness of the problem-solving approach in training			
• Team training with statistical tools	Yes	Yes	Yes
• Team training with industrial engineering tools	Always	Occasionally	Often
• Usual number of tools provided in training	36–40	7–18	7–18
• Emphasis on quality	Yes	Yes	Yes
• Equal emphasis on both quality and total productivity	Yes	No	No
12. Comprehensiveness of the productivity and quality improvement techniques available			
• Number of techniques taught explicitly	54–70	10–15	10–15
• Ability to select these techniques for optimal results	Always scientific	Occasionally analytical	Rarely analytical
13. Ability to quantify the impact of quality, productivity, technology, and continuous improvement efforts on the bottom line	Analytical approach (through the optimal TPM)	Quality costs approach (suboptimal)	Cost reduction approach (suboptimal)
14. Reward systems based on TPG	Available	Not available	Not available
15. The practice of "management is a moral issue"	Always	When economically convenient	Rarely

QUESTIONS TO PONDER

6.1 Why is an interdisciplinary emphasis important in today's organizations?

6.2 Conduct a study of companies/organizations in your industry that have demonstrated a strong and verifiable commitment to "people building." How does your own enterprise compare against these examples?

6.3 How does job security affect the competitiveness of today's enterprises? Investigate this question with both a literature search and personal interviews with appropriate people. Develop a strategy for managing your company's personnel for maximum positive impact on total productivity.

6.4 Study Lincoln Electric, Wal-Mart, Delta Airlines, American Bankers Insurance Group, Wendy's, and Matsushita. What common features can you identify among these companies? To what extent do these companies come close to the TPmgt philosophy?

6.5 Validate the study that identified the number one reason for what takes the fun out of work (Section 6.2).

6.6 Conduct a study of ten companies/organizations that have a product/ service unit orientation rather than a functional focus. What lessons can be learned from this study?

6.7 Study five companies that strongly defend the functional focus. What can you learn from this study? Contrast these results with those from Question 6.6. Discuss the main findings.

6.8 Who are the "customers"? Identify and develop a profile of your customers. Develop a customer service strategy based on this analysis.

6.9 Identify at least five examples of situations where a lack of systemic perspective caused a significant increase in avoidable costs. How would you have managed these situations if you had been the first one to notice them?

6.10 How does culture affect total productivity? Defend your answer with some research data. What conclusions can you draw from this research?

6.11 Identify real-world examples where investment in technology did not produce expected results because of poor understanding and treatment of the people who use such technologies. What are your recommendations to do better?

6.12 Does technology always improve total productivity? Give reasons either way.

6.13 What are the three dimensions of competitiveness? Discuss their significance in your particular situation.

6.14 Contrast Deming's 14 Points with those offered by other gurus such as Crosby. Discuss the differences in depth.

6.15 Update the list of problem-solving tools in Figure 6.15. State the sources of the additional tools that you identify.

6.16 Develop an alternative methodology to the APIM discussed in Section 6.12. State its pros and cons as opposed to the APIM.

6.17 Conduct a study of productivity gainsharing systems. Identify at least five enterprises that use one or more of these systems. What barriers, if any, exist to adopting one of these productivity gainsharing systems in your enterprise?

6.18 What *critical* factors ensure success with a productivity gainsharing system?

6.19 Do you personally believe that "management is a moral issue"? Give reason(s) for your answer.

6.20 After reading this chapter carefully and answering the preceding questions, what is your overall impression of the uniqueness of TPmgt? Critique the uniqueness in an objective and unbiased manner.

REFERENCE AND NOTES

1. Statement made by David J. Sumanth at a seminar on April 8, 1991.
2. See *Industrial Engineering,* p. 4, Nov. 1990.
3. Ulrich, D. and Lake, D., *Organizational Capability: Competing from the Inside Out,* John Wiley & Sons, New York, 1990, pp. 14–20.
4. What Takes the Fun Out of Work," *Miami Herald,* March 8, 1993.
5. "A Conversation with Elizabeth Dole, Secretary of Labor," *Labor Relations Today,* Vol. IV, No. 4, pp. 4–5, 1989.
6. Reich, Deborah, "Joint Technology Design Committees," *Labor-Management Initiatives* (newsletter), 1993.
7. These conferences, sponsored by the International Association for Management of Technology and hosted by the University of Miami, have been held in Miami every two years since 1988. The 1996 conference was co-sponsored by Case Western Reserve University. For more information, contact Dr. T.M. Khalil, Department of Industrial Engineering, University of Miami, Coral Gables, FL 33124 (fax 305-284-4040).
8. Sumanth, D.J., *Productivity Engineering and Management,* McGraw-Hill, New York, 1994, Chapter 7.
9. Sumanth, D.J. (ed.), *Productivity Management Frontiers I,* Elsevier Science, The Netherlands, 1987.
10. See Chapter 3. For more details, see Sumanth, D.J., Productivity Measurement and Evaluation Models for Manufacturing Companies, Ph.D. dissertation, Department of IE, Illinois Institute of Technology, 1979 (available from University Microfilms International, Ann Arbor, MI).

11. For a detailed treatment of this framework, refer to Arora, D.P.S. and Sumanth, D.J., "A Strategic Framework Linking Quality and Productivity," *Int. J. Materials and Product Technology,* Vol. 7, No. 4, pp. 331–347, 1992.

12. Taylor, Frederick W., *The Principles of Scientific Management,* Harper & Row, New York, 1911, pp. 20–28.

13. Schonberger, Richard J. and Knod, Edward M. Jr., *Operations Management: Improving Customer Service,* 4th edition, Richard D. Irwin, Homewood, IL, 1991, p. 201.

14. Deming, W. Edwards, *Quality, Productivity, and Competitive Position,* MIT Center for Advanced Engineering Study, Cambridge, MA, 1982.

15. Juran, J.M., *Managerial Breakthrough,* McGraw-Hill, New York, 1964.

16. Crosby, P.B., *Quality Is Free: The Art of Making Quality Certain,* McGraw-Hill, New York, 1979.

17. Crosby, P.B., *Quality Is Still Free: Making Quality Certain in Uncertain Times,* McGraw-Hill, New York, 1996.

18. Feigenbaum, A.V., *Total Quality Control,* 3rd edition, McGraw-Hill, New York, 1983.

19. Kaoru Ishikawa (translated by David J. Lu), *What Is Total Quality Control? The Japanese Way,* Prentice-Hall, Englewood Cliffs, NJ, 1985.

20. *Taguchi Methods® Quality Engineering: Executive Briefing,* American Supplier Institute, Dearborn, MI, 1988, p. I-15.

21. Ibid., p. I-36.

22. Imai, Masaki, *Kaizen: The Key to Japan's Competitive Success,* Random House, New York, 1986, p. xxxii.

23. Ibid., p. 23.

24. Ibid., p. 4.

25. A detailed presentation of this model is given in Sumanth, D.J., *Productivity Engineering and Management* (college custom series), McGraw-Hill, New York, 1994, pp. 320–329.

7

FRONTIERS BEYOND TQM AND REENGINEERING

7.1 THE TQM WAVE—WHERE IS IT HEADED?

The total quality management (TQM) philosophy of management has three basic ingredients:

- Customer focus
- Continuous improvement
- Employee involvement

Let's trace its evolution very briefly. There are many variations in explanations of the basic philosophy of TQM depending upon who is writing about it. Quality, unlike productivity, is such an open-ended concept that people define it differently, understand it differently, and therefore measure and improve it differently. Quality is like a wind. When it is blowing, you can feel it, but it is difficult to capture or measure. Productivity is always defined as the ratio of output to input, regardless of the nature of the output(s) and input(s). Quality is more elusive than productivity. We can describe the dimensions of quality but cannot seem to define it precisely, even for operational purposes. For example, in the early 1980s, companies in the United States and elsewhere were satisfied to define quality as conformance to valid requirements, but defining requirements is as much of a challenge as defining *valid* requirements. In the late 1980s and early 1990s, when quality was defined as meeting and/or exceeding customer expectations, the big questions were who our customers are and how their expectations can be identified.

The *quality wave* has been traveling across the oceans of the quality revolution but became more visible beginning with Dr. Walter Shewhart in the 1920s up to the end of World War II.[1] In the early 1930s, the *inspection wave* changed to quality control. This wave changed in amplitude and frequency as Dr. Deming[2] and Dr. Juran[3] gave it a new emphasis in the 1950s. Then, with Dr. Feigenbaum's[4] total quality control (TQC) concept, implemented widely in Japan by Dr. Ishikawa[5] as company-wide quality control (CWQC), the quality wave reached new heights from the 1960s to the early 1980s. Dr. Noriaki Kano,[6] one of Ishikawa's disciples, gave a number of seminars at the University of Miami in 1988. During those nine weeks of quality education and enlightenment, I came to understand that TQM is today's version of TQC/CWQC with eight basic concepts (Figure 7.1).

The importance of quality was rediscovered in the United States after the famous NBC White Paper "If Japan Can, Why Can't We?" aired in 1980. The late Dr. Deming, who was featured in that NBC special, was praised for his contributions to the Japanese quality revolution, and American companies began to seek his wisdom. When I first met Dr. Deming in 1979, he impressed me with the forthrightness of his message, his humility in attributing many of his insights to Dr. Walter Shewhart (who first proposed the Plan Do Check Act [PDCA] Cycle and pioneered many statistical quality control ideas), the depth of his understanding of quality as a passionate subject and, most importantly, his genuine interest

```
┌─────────────────────────────────────────────────┐
│                                                 │
│   1.  Management is Everyone's Job              │
│                                                 │
│   2.  PDCA  Cycle                               │
│                                                 │
│   3.  Product and Process Standardization       │
│                                                 │
│   4.  Education and Training                    │
│                                                 │
│   5.  Reoccurence Prevention                    │
│                                                 │
│   6.  Prevention by Prediction                  │
│                                                 │
│   7.  "Control by Facts"                        │
│                                                 │
│   8.  Statistical Quality Control (SQC)         │
│                                                 │
└─────────────────────────────────────────────────┘
```

FIGURE 7.1   Basic concepts of TQM as today's version of TQC/CWQC. (Source: Notes from Dr. N. Kano's lecture at the University of Miami, September 20, 1988.)

in the *welfare of employees*.[7] Dr. Juran, another quality guru who had a profound influence on Japanese quality management, began to reenergize America's penchant for quality through the Juran Quality Institute. It was a privilege to hear him speak at an American Institute of Industrial Engineers conference where he was bestowed the society's highest honor, the Gilbreth Medal. Juran's *Handbook on Quality* has been a classic since the 1950s; it is a major source of practical information on quality concepts, philosophies, and methodologies. Philip Crosby,[8] another quality stalwart, has been teaching his philosophy that "quality is free" when we do things right the first time. During a chat with him after he had addressed the Fourth International Conference on Productivity and Quality Research in February 1993, I was fascinated by his simple yet profound philosophy of quality management. During the late 1980s, scholars like David Garvin[9] suggested his "eight dimensions of quality" (Figure 7.2) and Manley[10] his product quality attributes and product maintainer's quality attributes (Figure 7.3).

The United States launched and popularized the TQM movement with the introduction of the Malcolm Baldrige Award in 1988. The first American large manufacturing company to win this prestigious award was Motorola, which set a target of *Six Sigma* for the quality of its products. The national quality movement has inspired many states to establish their own awards: for example, the Governor's Florida Sterling Award, the Minnesota Quality Award, and the New York Quality Award, to name a few. The Motorola quality story has come to represent the turnaround in American quality. Today, Motorola not only competes aggressively with its Japanese counterparts but is far ahead of them in many areas. Xerox, a pioneer in duplication technology, has more than regained lost market share from its Japanese competitors since CEO and chairman Dr. David Kern launched a major quality strategy in the early 1980s. All three major American auto companies are competing head on with the Japanese and are winning the competitiveness race as truly world-class players. We have indeed come a long way from those nervous days of the early 1980s when doomsday discussions were heard across the United States, from business schools to boardrooms.

The ten-year period from 1986 to 1996 was *TQM time* for many organizations. Perhaps no other quality management philosophy has received as much attention as TQM. In many ways, the principles or precepts of TQM have been applied at least partially by enterprises of all kinds and sizes. Indeed, TQM has been a giant management wave that has had a major influence on orientation toward customers/constituents/clients, both internal and external. Hundreds of articles and books[11] related directly or indirectly to TQM have been written.

Despite the plethora of publications on TQM, conflicting views abound in the literature about its effectiveness.[12] Whatever the findings of studies on TQM,

1. **Performance**
2. **Features**
3. **Reliability**
4. **Conformance**
5. **Durability**
6. **Serviceability**
7. **Aesthetics**
8. **Perceived Quality**

FIGURE 7.2   Garvin's eight dimensions of quality. (Source: Garvin, David A., "Competing on the Eight Dimensions of Quality," *Harvard Business Review,* pp. 101–109, Nov–Dec 1987.)

Manley's Product Quality Attributes

1. Functionality
2. Economy
3. Safety
4. Reliability
5. Usability

Manley's User's and Product Maintainer's Quality Attributes

1. Mean Time to Failure
2. Evolvability
3. Maintainability
4. Mean Time to Repair

FIGURE 7.3   Manley's quality attributes. (Source: Manley, John H., "Manufacturing Systems Engineering Education Quality Issues," Testimony to the U.S. House of Representatives, April 18, 1989.)

one thing seems to be clear—TQM has influenced thinking about quality as a strategic tool to improve competitiveness within and between industries, companies, and enterprises of all types.

The very nature of the ambiguity surrounding the word *quality*, in particular its open-endedness, makes it difficult to critique the concept. Thus, there is no one definition of or methodology for TQM.

7.2 THE REENGINEERING *DYNAMITE*

Michael Hammer and James Champy popularized and gave new meaning and emphasis to the term "reengineering."[13] They define reengineering as:

> the *fundamental* thinking and *radical* redesign of *business processes*
> to achieve dramatic improvements in critical contemporary measures
> of performance, such as cost, quality, service, and speed.[14]

The four key words here are *fundamental, radical, processes,* and *dramatic.* Hammer and Champy go on to denote the importance of these words in their definition.[15] The word *fundamental* emphasizes that "reengineering takes nothing for granted. It ignores what *is* and concentrates on what *should be*." *Radical* redesign implies "getting to the root of things: not making superficial changes...." Business *processes* are defined "as a collection of activities that takes one or more kinds of input and creates an output that is of value to the customer."

Hammer and Champy also point out what reengineering is *not* in five different ways:[16]

1. Reengineering "is *not* the same as automation."
2. Business reengineering is *not* to be confused with so-called software reengineering.
3. "Reengineering is *not* restructuring or downsizing."
4. Reengineering "is *not* the same as reorganizing, delayering, or flattening an organization, although reengineering may, in fact, produce a flatter organization."
5. "Nor is reengineering the same as quality improvement, total quality management (TQM), or any other manifestation of the contemporary quality improvement." They consider quality programs as incremental continuous improvements, whereas reengineering seeks breakthroughs.

In short, they say that reengineering "is about beginning again with a clean sheet of paper...and is the search for new models of organizing work."

Hammer and Champy give many examples of companies that have applied reengineering, including Ford, Kodak, and IBM Credit,[17] to name a few.

Hammer[18] identified the following guiding principles of reengineering:

1. Organize around outcomes, not tasks.
2. Have those who use the output of the process perform the process.
3. Subsume information—processing work into the real work that produces the information.
4. Treat geographically dispersed resources as though they are centralized.
5. Link parallel activities instead of integrating their results.
6. Put the decision point where the work is performed, and build control into the process.
7. Capture information once and at the source.

Many others[19] have also written extensively on the topic of reengineering.

Although Hammer and Champy caution that reengineering is not restructuring or downsizing, the net result of many so-called reengineering efforts has been downsizing, with undesirable social consequences. The strengths and weaknesses of reengineering can be viewed from three perspectives: socio-economic, cultural, and political. The following discussion suggests that reengineering can be a long-lasting way of managing a business if all three perspectives are understood and monitored carefully before, during, and after implementation.

The Socio-Economic Perspective—One positive aspect of reengineering has been the empowerment of teams for radical thinking, resulting in innovative ideas for eliminating redundant processes. There have also been dramatic reductions in costs. On the other hand, resistance to change can be difficult to overcome. One can oversimplify it or deny that resistance to change can be *managed* to reengineer business processes, but the reality is that a reengineering effort often occurs without appropriate consideration of the human dimension. The result is deflated morale, which is difficult to reinflate. It is even more difficult to reestablish top management's credibility. For example, if the initial promise of a reengineering effort was to utilize human talent to eliminate redundant processes without displacement of people, but some of the key people responsible for the success of the effort were let go after the reengineering effort was completed, the integrity of top management's intentions would be questioned by the employees. Once management's integrity is questionable, employees will not believe management the next time, no matter how sincere the words sound, because their trust has been betrayed.

Handling change is like handling dynamite. It should be used in a constructive rather than destructive manner, after researching the effects. Many organizations handle concepts like reengineering without fully understanding them. Ill-informed consultants and executives explode the social fabric of an enterprise by destroying the morale, creating job dissatisfaction, and eliminating the joy of work. The fundamental question to be asked is: *What is the social cost of a poorly engineered system, process, or enterprise as a result of misunderstanding and misinterpreting a concept due to lack of wisdom and/or patience?* Most people can acquire knowledge, but only a few seem to know how to exercise wisdom, and fewer still demonstrate a true understanding of human existence and human welfare. The cost is billions of dollars worth of human suffering because of shallow thinkers and timid leaders who look at the impact to their pockets instead of from the perspective of their conscience. The Total Productivity Management (TPmgt™) perspective puts people's welfare at the center of a business system's success and not at its periphery, to be thrown out in the first wave of economic exigency. One can argue that if reengineering were not implemented in some organizations, more jobs would have been lost, because the cost of doing business is too high. But whose fault is that? Is it not management's fault at the leadership level? What it boils down to is leadership with integrity, long-term planning, and stakeholders' success as opposed to stockholders' success.

The Cultural Perspective—Generally, the organizational culture changes dramatically in a company when the reengineering philosophy is introduced. Just the word *reengineering* can conjure up apprehensiveness, even if it is unwarranted. That's just human nature, and changing it requires a mature understanding of the cultural context. Culture, in a basic sense, is a result of certain beliefs, values, and views. Just as each of the more than five billion individuals in the world has unique fingerprints and DNA, it seems logical to say that in an organization employing a few thousand people, there would be at least a few hundred different "cultures" responsible for shaping the organizational culture. When the radical thinking of reengineering impacts employees' paychecks and pensions, the natural result is culture shock. If an organization designs a careful plan of action with the assistance of change management experts, reengineering can indeed result in some dramatic improvements in customer service, costs, and speed of service without destroying a positive organizational culture. *When a system is disturbed, it must be reset. Resetting it takes knowledge of the old and new system parameters.* If companies have the time and patience to reset systems with careful planning, the result can be dramatic. Unfortunately, however, patience often gives way to quick results, and reason is replaced by rashness.

The Political Perspective—In developing countries, where unions are controlled by political affiliations and political parties, it may be treacherous to undertake reengineering if it means getting rid of jobs and people. Although Hammer does not intend for reengineering to mean downsizing, his basic concept requires that you start with a clean slate. While it is feasible to reengineer any business process, the factors sustaining ongoing and new reengineering efforts must be clearly identified, and all necessary anchors must be dropped at the right place at the right time. If the political stability of an informal organization within the formal organization is threatened by a reengineering program or process, there can be major resistance. Resistance makes an organization rigid—the very thing reengineering tries to avoid!

7.3 THE TPmgt *TOTAL* PACKAGE?

In Chapter 6, we discussed the 15 unique features of TPmgt and how they contrast with TQM and reengineering. On the one hand, if I claim that TPmgt is superior to TQM and/or reengineering, you may agree, disagree, or be indifferent. On the other hand, if I say that TPmgt can supplement these two philosophies and concepts, you may think that I am not being forceful enough in defending TPmgt. I feel intellectually responsible to do neither for the following reasons.

First, claiming that any philosophy, concept, or methodology is earth-shattering, new, or unique in differing from known management theories is not only intellectually arrogant, but outright naive. After observing micro-level to macro-level systems for nearly 30 years in 45 countries, and after carefully analyzing the history of ideas and nations, I believe that we have acquired very little new wisdom today when compared to the many truths, laws, and principles that have been formulated, tested over millennia, and found to be timeless. With all the technical know-how we have today, we still cannot figure out many engineering aspects of the 4,000-year-old Egyptian pyramids, the markings on the landing strips in Peru, the musical notes produced by the pillars of an ancient Indian temple, and many similar accomplishments of the past.

To me, research is truly *re-search*. It is simply re-searching the old truths and then packaging them in a form relevant to our times. For example, the concept of monolithic construction of a canoe is nothing new. Thousands of years ago, so-called "primitive" people produced such boats by carving out one huge tree trunk. Ancient Mayan and Aztec cultures put together stones weighing several tons without using any mortar. They fashioned such a fine finish between the stones as to create a natural adhesive similar to the "slip gauge" concept.

Second, life in general and organizations in particular are much more complex than we tend to portray them. Despite much research on change management, starting with some of the seminal work of Kurt Lewin in the 1940s at MIT, we still have a long way to go in understanding the process of change, the nature of resistance to change, and the means to measure and monitor such resistance. Regardless of the claims of a particular concept or theory, its effectiveness often is measured by research methodologies ranging from the most simplistic, anecdotal evidence-oriented to the relatively more analytical, statistically based surveys for time periods of modest length. For example, it would be very helpful to have *longitudinal* studies on TQM so that we could evaluate its effectiveness more objectively. Obviously, it is not only expensive to conduct such studies but also somewhat impractical because of the rapidity with which organizational systems and their variables are changing today.

If each individual behaves like a random variable, an organization that employs a few hundred to thousands of people clearly is very complex. What individuals or enterprises adopt as ideas, concepts, and philosophies may not necessarily be right for them. Just because the majority is doing something does not necessarily make it right. The right things are often more difficult to do. If TQM, reengineering, TPmgt, or any concept is to be successful, top management must be committed, patient, and so on. But is that really the case? A majority of organizations would like to take the easy, quick route. That's not bad in itself. If an enterprise has deliberately created what I call "organizational resilience," then it may be justified in expecting faster responsiveness in everything from production systems to customer service. Most companies, however, have not been able to remove all the redundant variables from their systems—organizational and/or managerial.

Perhaps "tertiary thinking" is more realistic and pragmatic for arriving at appropriate solutions, as opposed to "binary thinking." TPmgt belongs to the tertiary thinking category, where it is not necessary to view TQM or reengineering as traditional, obsolete, or unfashionable or label them as the ultimate management philosophies of our time.

Therefore, TPmgt, in the spirit of tertiary thinking, can be the best of both worlds—TQM and reengineering—in that it has an interdisciplinary approach to managing organizational and managerial systems by blending the hard, technical side with the soft, human approach. Because TPmgt has had only one definition since it was first coined in 1981, and because of the consistency with which the methodologies for measuring, evaluating, planning, and improving total productivity and comprehensive total productivity have been developed, integrated, and tested around the world since 1979, there is a robustness and strength in the philosophy, concept, and methodology presented in this book. Therefore, the evolution to TPmgt can be viewed as shown in Figure 7.4.

The best way to summarize the TPmgt concept is to represent it as shown in Figure 7.5. The core or hub of TPmgt is comprehensive total productivity thinking,

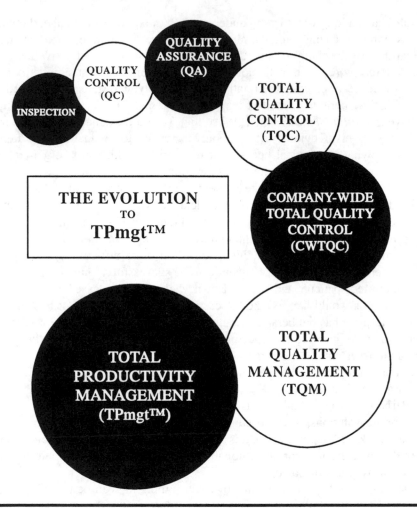

FIGURE 7.4   The evolution to TPmgt. (©1993, D.J. Sumanth.)

wherein all the tangible and intangible factors associated with outputs/outcomes and inputs are captured in a manner that all levels of management can understand and utilize to take action for improvements. *Total productivity gainsharing* provides the reward mechanism to motivate employees at all levels and to sustain that motivation on a consistent basis. *Productivity Quality Team* training for all personnel provides the tools necessary to help attain the goals and objectives set based on the vision and mission of the organization. The results are quality competitiveness, price competitiveness, and time competitiveness, which are what sustain profitability on a consistent basis. By iterating the four phases (measurement,

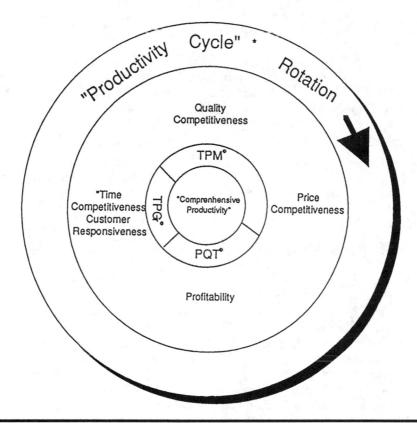

FIGURE 7.5 A snapshot of TPmgt. (*©1979, D.J. Sumanth.) "Comprehensive Productivity" = (Total Productivity) × (Intangible Quality Factor Index). (©1987–90, D.J. Sumanth.)

evaluation, planning, and improvement) of the *productivity cycle*, a company ensures the *continuous* nature of the TPmgt process, with a sense of achievement but tempered by a sense of humility that competitiveness is a moving target. Patient leadership is a key to making any philosophy or concept work. TPmgt is no exception, although its design enables it to flow naturally. It is designed to fit the natural phenomenon of organizational systems, rather than forcing them to behave unnaturally, thereby resulting in uncontrollable output/outcomes. To tame a system, its natural characteristics must be understood. TPmgt has been designed to harness the natural power of people and the technologies they create.

Clearly, continued empirical validation of the claims of TPmgt is not only warranted for the sake of scientific integrity, but also necessary for future insights from newer and even diverse applications worldwide.

QUESTIONS TO PONDER

7.1 From your own research, update the TQM bibliography in the open literature with works of some significance. Synthesize your observations and offer some insights as to the nature of the success and failure of TQM.

7.2 Repeat Question 7.1 for reengineering.

7.3 Repeat Question 7.1 for TPmgt.

7.4 Conduct a detailed study contrasting TQM, reengineering, and TPmgt.

7.5 From a history of management thought, what other management philosophies have been influential in the 20th century? Back up your answer with references to well-respected sources.

REFERENCES AND NOTES

1. Eberts, Ray and Cindelyn, *The Myths of Japanese Quality,* Prentice Hall, Upper Saddle River, NJ, 1995, p. 72.
2. Deming, W. Edwards, *Out of the Crisis,* MIT Center for Advanced Engineering Study, Cambridge, MA, 1986; see also Walton, Mary, *The Deming Management Method,* Perigee Books, New York, 1986.
3. Juran, Joseph M. and Gryna, Frank M., *Quality Planning and Analysis,* 3rd edition, McGraw-Hill, New York, 1993; see also Juran, Joseph M., *Managerial Breakthrough,* revised edition, McGraw-Hill, New York, 1994.
4. Feigenbaum, Armand V., *Total Quality Control,* 3rd edition (revised), McGraw-Hill, New York, 1991.
5. Ishikawa, Kaoru, *Introduction to Quality Control,* 3A Corporation, Tokyo, 1990.
6. Kano, Noriaki, Lectures on Total Quality at the University of Miami, Sept. 1988.
7. Dr. Deming discussed his views on this and his "profound knowledge" in his last book before he passed away in December 1993, *The New Economics: For Industry, Government, Education,* MIT Center for Advanced Engineering Study, Cambridge, MA, 1993.
8. Crosby, Philip B., *Quality Is Free: The Art of Making Quality Certain,* McGraw-Hill, New York, 1979; see also his most recent work, *Quality Is Still Free: Making Quality Certain in Uncertain Times,* McGraw-Hill, New York, 1996.
9. Garvin, David A., *Managing Quality: The Strategic and Competitive Edge,* The Free Press, New York, 1988; see also Garvin, David A., "Competing on the Eight Dimensions of Quality," *Harvard Business Review,* pp. 101–109, Nov.–Dec. 1987.
10. Manley, John H., "Manufacturing Systems Engineering Education Quality Issues," Testimony to the U.S. House of Representatives, April 18, 1989.
11. A few of these books on TQM are as follows: Berry, Thomas H., *Managing the Total Quality Transformation,* McGraw-Hill, New York, 1991; Bounds, G., Yorks,

L., Adams, M., and Ranney, G., *Beyond Total Quality Management: Toward the Emerging Paradigm,* McGraw-Hill, New York, 1994; Brocka, Bruce and Brocka, M. Suzanne, *Quality Management: Implementing the Best Ideas of the Masters,* Irwin Professional Publishing, Burr Ridge, IL, 1992; George, Stephen and Weimerskirch, Arnold, *Total Quality Management: Strategies and Techniques Proven at Today's Most Successful Companies,* John Wiley & Sons, New York, 1994; Omachonu, Vincent K. and Ross, Joel E., *Principles of Total Quality,* St. Lucie Press, Delray Beach, FL, 1994; Ross, Joel E., *Total Quality Management: Text, Cases and Readings*, 2nd edition, St. Lucie Press, Delray Beach, FL, 1995; Sashkin, Marshall and Kiser, Kenneth J., *Putting Total Quality Management to Work,* Barrett-Koehler, San Francisco, 1993.

12. Sumanth, D.J. and Ladak, Nizar K., A Study to Evaluate the Effectiveness of Total Quality Management (TQM) Practices in US Companies, Working Paper, 1995.

13. Hammer, M. and Champy, J., *Reengineering the Corporation: A Manifesto for Business Revolution,* Harper Collins, New York, 1993.

14. Ibid., pp. 32 and 46.

15. Ibid., pp. 32–35.

16. Ibid., pp. 48–49.

17. Ibid., pp. 39–51.

18. Hammer, M., "Reengineering Work: Don't Automate, Obliterate," *Harvard Business Review,* pp. 104–112, July–Aug. 1990.

19. For example, see Harrington, H. James, *Business Process Improvement,* McGraw-Hill, New York, 1991; Manganelli, Raymond L. and Klein, M.M., *The Reengineering Handbook: A Step-by-Step Guide to Business Transformation,* AMACOM, New York, 1994; Morris, Daniel and Brandon, J., *Reengineering Your Business,* McGraw-Hill, New York, 1993.

8   BENEFITS OF TPmgt

Over the years, as the Total Productivity Management (TPmgt™) concept has been applied in many parts of the world, some common perceptions have emerged as to its benefits. Of many such benefits, the following are the most significant:

1. Customer responsiveness
2. Quality competitiveness
3. Total cost competitiveness
4. Team building and accountability
5. Technology planning
6. Investment analysis
7. Acquisition and merger planning
8. Resource budgeting and allocation
9. Automatic profit targeting
10. Compatibility with well-established data collection formats

They are not necessarily listed in order of importance, and each is discussed in detail in this chapter.

8.1 CUSTOMER RESPONSIVENESS

TPmgt, as we learned in Chapter 3 (Figure 3.10), considers customers as the seat of a three-legged stool, with the three legs being quality, total productivity, and technology/innovation. That is to say, all activities in an enterprise are to be oriented toward a mission which, in turn, revolves around meeting customers' needs and wants well beyond their expectations.

Dr. Michael LeBoeuf[1] provides some startling statistics about customers:

- The average American company will lose 10 to 30% of its customers each year because of poor customer service.
- Over the years, 68% of the lost business can be attributed to poor customer service.
- Why do customers quit?
  o 3% move away
  o 5% develop other friendships
  o 9% leave for competitive reasons
  o 14% are dissatisfied with the product
  o 68% quit because they experienced indifference from an owner, manager, or an employee
- Only 4% of dissatisfied customers complain. The other 96% just go away, and 91% never come back!
- A dissatisfied customer tells 8 to 10 others; 20% of dissatisfied customers will even tell 20 others.
- It takes 12 positive service incidents to make up for every negative one.
  o Of customers whose complaints are resolved in their favor, 70% will do business with you again.
  o Of customers whose complaints are resolved on the spot, 95% will do business with you again.
  o A customer whose problem has been resolved will tell five people.
- It costs six times more to attract new customers than to keep existing ones.

Most people can relate to one or more of the situations to which LeBoeuf refers. Yet, we also see a pervasiveness of indifference to customers more often than a prevalence of "customer delight."

There is no question that customer demands and expectations vary, particularly in today's "60-second-service" mindset. In fact, there are at least 16 characteristics of customers (Figure 8.1) anywhere in the world. Thus, customers are complex individuals, and meeting and exceeding their expectations, let alone delighting them, takes much effort, planning, and formal strategizing.

The TPmgt concept provides a natural means to achieve extremely high levels of customer responsiveness because of its ability to see the effects of lack of customer responsiveness on the trends in total productivity and in comprehensive total productivity levels. When a downward or flat trend continues in either, one of the first areas examined by the TPmgt Team is customer responsiveness.

1. **Value-seekers**

2. **Bargainers**

3. **Educated about Products/Services**

4. **Expressive**

5. **Analytical**

6. **Argumentative**

7. **Knit-picking**

8. **Indecisive**

9. **Assertive**

10. **"Give-me-space" minded**

11. **Lavish**

12. **Appreciative**

13. **Diplomatic**

14. **Manipulative**

15. **Grateful**

16. **Pesky**

FIGURE 8.1 The 16 characteristics of customers. (Source: Sumanth, D.J., *Customer Service Management (CSM): A Necessary Approach for Survival into the 21st Century*, Monograph, 1996, p. 5. ©1996, D.J. Sumanth.)

Usually, there is a strong correlation between total productivity, comprehensive total productivity, and customer responsiveness. As customer responsiveness goes down, so do total productivity and comprehensive total productivity in the long run and often even in the short run.

The best place to analyze customer responsiveness is in the trenches, where customers are served, and in the service centers of the enterprise. Generally speaking, employees serving customers commit one or more of "the seven deadly

1. *Unenthusiastic* First Look

2. *"Take it or leave it"* attitude

3. Company's *Priorities*, not Customer's *Needs*

4. *"Sorry, we don't have it"* response

5. *"Check with us later"* response

6. *"Get rid* of the *aggravating* customer" mentality

7. Paying little attention to the last *10 seconds* of transaction

FIGURE 8.2   The seven deadly blunders in serving customers. (Source: Sumanth, D.J., *Customer Service Management (CSM): A Necessary Approach for Survival into the 21st Century,* Monograph, 1996, p. 5. ©1996, D.J. Sumanth.)

blunders" (Figure 8.2). All these blunders are *avoidable* if the employees serving customers are trained constantly in customer interaction and, more importantly, if they are shown how a lack of customer responsiveness on their part can drastically lower the demand for products/services and how that, in turn, can negatively impact the total productivity level and the profit level. When employees are given feedback in terms of how something can affect their job security, they will listen and respond positively.

8.2 QUALITY COMPETITIVENESS

A second benefit of TPmgt is quality competitiveness, that is, the ability of an enterprise to compete in the quality dimension. Many companies in the United States "woke up" and responded admirably to the challenge of quality competitiveness beginning in 1981, and this effort is now paying off. The latest GM commercial says that GM cars are rated the best overall according to J.D. Power and Associates surveys. GM's Saturn has been rated among the top five for the last three years, with quality close to Lexus and Mercedes. Today, the external and internal feel of an American car is close to that of a Japanese or German car, and in some cases even better. Service quality in American auto dealerships has not only significantly improved but, in some cases, exceeds that of Japanese counterparts. Today, for example, Ford Motor Company measures the customer service offered by its dealers so meticulously that a salesperson's job could be in jeopardy if customer service measurements do not meet or exceed expectations.

The quality gap has substantially narrowed among world-class companies. In fact, quality management education in the United States during the past ten years has helped enterprises to treat quality as a strategic variable. It has become a necessary though not a sufficient condition for corporate success. Educated consumers are so sophisticated in today's buyer's market that they don't waste their time on products and services perceived as having less than minimum quality.

Quality competitiveness translates into positive gains in total productivity and comprehensive total productivity levels and, hence, profit levels. For example, in Section 6.8 we examined how quality and total productivity are related. We also looked at how quality, total productivity, and profit are related. Since the Total Productivity Model (TPM©) and Comprehensive Total Productivity Model (CTPM©) monitor total productivity levels, TPmgt ensures the benefits of quality competitiveness.

8.3 TOTAL COST COMPETITIVENESS

Unlike the traditional labor productivity concept, TPmgt strives to improve the total productivity and comprehensive total productivity of a firm constantly. Therefore, there is a focus on reducing the total cost per unit (of products and/ or services) rather than merely labor or personnel costs. In fact, since TPmgt is systemic in nature, it utilizes people's creativity to concentrate on reducing the other costs, which are significantly larger for most products. For example, suppose a consumer electronics manufacturer, using traditional management thinking, tries to reduce costs by $500,000. The company lays off people, but its labor costs only account for 10% of total unit costs. With TPmgt thinking, the same company could motivate its employees to reduce material and capital costs, which account for 65% of product costs, by redesigning the product to eliminate some components, thereby dramatically reducing investments in equipment, facilities, distribution, and so on. The TPmgt approach better utilizes employee talents and skills in their areas of specialization. For example, in poorly managed companies, highly qualified technical personnel often use only 5 to 10% of their professional knowledge and skills and waste their valuable time on clerical tasks. Such companies and their human resource departments have done a poor job of matching talents to tasks. The result is poor morale, job dissatisfaction, low productivity, and, ultimately, high costs. Instead, in a TPmgt environment, technical people would spend 50 to 60% of their time on technical matters and only 20 to 30% on clerical work. An engineer who is paid $100,000 a year (including fringe benefits) and is doing 90% clerical work is essentially costing the company $90,000 annually, when a clerk could have been hired for about $20,000. In other words, the company has wasted $70,000 by utilizing an engineer for mostly clerical work. The net effect of this approach in a company with 1,000 engineers would be $70 million! This is just one example of not realizing the total cost to the company when TPmgt thinking is absent.

Because of the total perspective in TPmgt, and because of the quantitative models it uses, its focus on total cost is natural, consistent, and deliberate. By focusing on the total unit cost, TPmgt enables management to have a sufficient profit cushion while fixing the selling price (recall from Section 3.2 that Selling Price/Unit = Total Cost/Unit + Profit Margin/Unit). By reducing the total cost per unit consistently, there is greater room to slash the selling price as market conditions demand, without reducing profits.

Thus, TPmgt benefits a company consistently in ensuring total cost competitiveness and, hence, the ability to manipulate product/service price without sacrificing stakeholder benefits.

8.4 TEAM BUILDING AND ACCOUNTABILITY

A major benefit of TPmgt is creating a team environment and accountability in organizations. TPmgt creates an atmosphere of mutual respect, trust, and self-motivation, because it is designed to create a positive and nourishing socio-technical human environment by recognizing the importance of operating in the intersection of technical and behavioral approaches.

Although the team concept is not new, its effectiveness became more visibly dramatic in the early 1960s with the success of Japanese corporations which introduced quality circles. In 1981, William Ouchi, with his seminal work *Theory Z*, brought to light the importance of employee participation.[2] Today, team configurations range from simple homogeneous teams to cross-functional teams. When empowered, such teams become self-managing.

Dumaine[3] provides a number of examples of self-managed teams which have achieved rather impressive results. For example:

- **General Mills (Lodi, California, plant)**—Teams schedule, operate, and maintain machinery so effectively that no mangers are present on the night shift, and the plant's (labor) productivity is 40% higher than that of other plants.

- **3M Company**—Cross-functional teams in one of its divisions tripled the number of new products.
- **Aetna Life & Casualty Insurance Company**—Teams suggested ways to reduce and reduced the ratio of middle managers to workers from 1:7 to 1:30—while improving customer service.
- **Johnsonville Foods of Sheboygan, Wisconsin**—Teams of blue-collar workers helped show their CEO, Ralph Stayer, how to increase productivity by at least 50% since 1986.

More recently, the term *superteams* has been used. Superteams are said to have some specific characteristics, including the following:

1. **High level of dependency among three or more people**—A simple assembly line activity, where each operator is specifically concerned with control of only one operation, does not lend itself to superteams.
2. **Cross-functionalism**—When more than one function is involved in solving a problem, cross-functionalism is essential, and a superteam would be natural here.
3. **Corporate-wide role**—Superteams may be appropriate when middle managers are persuaded to lend their time, people, and resources to other functions for the good of the entire organization.
4. **Assistance with a new facility**—When teams are assigned to develop a new facility or office rather than marginally improving an existing one, superteams may be appropriate. "Team 99," which helped develop the Saturn car by establishing a whole new concept for manufacturing, distribution, and sales in a totally new location, is an example of a superteam.

TPmgt fosters an atmosphere conducive to teamwork. Through the ten-step process for TPmgt implementation (as outlined in Chapter 4), a structure and mechanism are created to focus on the management goals (based upon on the TPM/CTPM analysis), the mission, and the vision as a "Corporate Team." Further, through the reward mechanism established by *total productivity gainsharing* (TPG), employees at all levels are motivated individually and collectively to attain the corporate vision daily. What is measured and rewarded gets done. That's the nature of human endeavors. The TPM/CTPM help to measure achievement of the management goals, and TPG provides the reward for accomplishing those goals effectively. In a Dutch electric utility company, several teams were formed as part of the TPmgt implementation effort. One team, headed by the billing supervisor, came up with an idea to collect payments in two months instead of three. The team incorporated necessary software changes in the billing process and also changed the way bills were delivered to customers. The result was recurring, annual savings of nearly a quarter million dollars.

People do their jobs more responsibly and are more accountable when the goals they are to accomplish are communicated in clear terms, resources are made available, and they are empowered with mutual respect and trust. It is "icing on the cake" when they are measured not for punitive reasons but rather to help them find ways to improve their own work. Further, positive and consistent momentum is sustained when people know they will be rewarded.

8.5 TECHNOLOGY PLANNING

The CTPM, which extends the TPM (discussed in detail in Chapter 4), is a powerful tool to plan for new technologies. Recall from Chapter 4 that in the CTPM, the comprehensive total productivity index (CTPI) is given by:

$$CTPI = TPI \times IFI$$

where TPI = total productivity index and IFI = intangible factor index. This model can be applied to plan for new technologies when existing ones become obsolete.[4] During the transition period from the old to the new technology, a "discontinuity" occurs. The implications of technology discontinuities at the product and process levels are enormous:

1. **Product life cycles** — Product life cycles are directly affected by technology discontinuities, thereby making critical the decisions regarding advertising, marketing, outsourcing, capital equipment purchases, facilities layout, manpower allocation, and so on. A "wait-and-see" policy is often followed by enterprises as well as customers when there is a risk of rapid obsolescence due to technology discontinuities. Mistakes made by an enterprise in the timing of decisions can sometimes be catastrophic, with billions of dollars at stake.

2a. **Employee training and/or retraining**—When there are significant changes in product or process technologies, the need for training and/ or retraining becomes a significant challenge, particularly when the economic factors to compete in the market outweigh the social implications. In many companies, the first line of defense is to lay off employees, if the corporate mission is not emphatically oriented toward full employment.

2b. **Reorientation or re-education of customers**—When Lee Iacocca took over the chairmanship of the Chrysler Corporation, he instituted major product and process changes, but introducing new product and process technologies was not enough to attract new customers and retain existing ones; he launched a massive advertising campaign to promote the image of the "New Chrysler Corporation," and it worked.

3. **Corporate strategic planning**—Whenever technology discontinuities take place, the "shock" on the enterprise can be minimized if such discontinuities are part of the corporate strategic planning process. Of course, predicting such discontinuities is not easy, but not predicting them could put a company out of business. One example is the Osborne Computer Company, which did not time its product innovation properly and within less than two years was bankrupt. Notwithstanding the compounding effects of uncertainties in global, national, and regional environmental factors, the strategic planning process is more robust when technology changes are predicted ahead of time.

4. **Organizational structure**—Enterprises almost always "restructure" their organizations whenever major changes take place in product or process technologies. If such changes are not well planned, "cultural flexibility" suffers, creating negative forces in organizational management. One major U.S. corporation went from conventional communications technology to fiber optics, which resulted in a drastic restructuring of the organization. Deregulated airlines and banks went through a similar reorganization when their services had to be streamlined through better and newer equipment, automation, and so on.

5. **Vendors' inability to cope**—While large corporations can adapt their production systems to rapidly changing technologies, vendors often do not have the economic, technical, and managerial strength to do the same and still be profitable. When corporations choose "vertical integration" because of employment policies and economic factors of production, they put their vendors in a very vulnerable position. On the other hand, if external economic factors favor outsourcing parts and services to vendors, a company can be left with excess capital equipment and manpower. In either case, the implications of technology changes are not pleasant for either corporations or their vendors.

The CTPM Strategy for Technology Planning

When a new technology is a candidate to replace an existing one, the basic strategy in TPmgt is to ensure that:

$$\text{CTPI (for time period } t + T) > \text{CTPI (for time period } t)$$

where t = any time period, with t = 0 representing the base period, T = 1, 2, 3, ..., n where n = number of time periods from t.

Since the CTPM takes into consideration all the user-definable factors of output and input, and since profitability is directly related to total productivity, the above criterion for choosing a technology when a discontinuity takes place is comprehensive and practical from the point of view of "good business practice." It balances the technical, economic, social, cultural, and even political factors affecting an enterprise when major changes occur in product or process technologies.

Example

Consider a leading manufacturer of personal computers whose major product uses type A microprocessor technology. The company wants to introduce type B microprocessor technology, which has a much higher CPU speed and multitasking and multi-user capabilities. Therefore, the company is planning a new product technology, creating a discontinuity (Figure 8.3).

As a result of this new technology, some of the production processes would change drastically. Furthermore, the marketing and advertising would need to be refocused. The company wants to totally discontinue the old product (with the

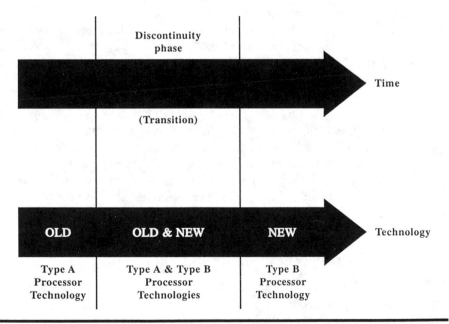

FIGURE 8.3 Transition of technologies through the discontinuity phase using the example of a personal computer manufacturer. (Adapted from Sumanth, 1988.[6])

type A processor) within a few months and offer service only to existing customers. Clearly, this situation poses a strategic challenge to the company's top management. The company builds a prototype and tests it on a select basis.

At this point, most traditionally managed companies would produce and market the new product aggressively. However, if the company were to rationally approach managing the discontinuity (from type A to type B processor technology), it would apply the CTPM. Suppose the company obtains the following values from the data collected:

$$TPI = 0.920$$

$$IFI = 1.225$$

Then,

$$CTPI = (TPI) \times (IFI) = (0.920) \times (1.225) = 1.127$$

This means that the introduction of the type B processor technology will initially reduce the total productivity level of the company by $(1 - 0.92) = 0.08$, or 8%, because of heavy capital expenditures to change the production processes at the company's plants and the consequent high fixed capital input. Total productivity is given by $TP = O/(H + M + C + E + X)$, where O is the tangible output and H, M, C, E, and X are, respectively, human input, material input, capital input, energy input, and other expense input. With the new technology, the company's C will rise drastically and, as a result, total input is expected to increase faster than total output, causing total productivity to drop by 8%.

On the other hand, with type B technology, the IFI is expected to increase by 22.5% because of sizable improvements in (1) product quality, (2) product reliability, (3) customer satisfaction, and (4) stockholder satisfaction. The first three are certainly important from the customer's viewpoint, and the fourth is important to the company's top management and board of directors. Considering that the personal computer market is highly competitive, with clones from Japan, Taiwan, and other countries infiltrating the market, the company correctly observes that the 8% drop in total productivity due to the type B technology is well compensated for by the 22.5% gain in the IFI. From the break-even point of total productivity, the company is expected to operate at a comfortable total productivity level. Therefore, the company decides to use the type B technology and aggressively market the new product in order to generate more output and higher total productivity.

Strengths of the CTPM Strategy

Unlike traditional management thinking, TPmgt thinking, which incorporates the CTPM, has many notable strengths:

1. **Holistic approach**—All enterprises are human-made organisms. Recognizing this, the CTPM considers the joint and simultaneous impact of all resources whenever new technologies are introduced. The CTPM's uniqueness lies in the fact that quality, reliability, effectiveness, efficiency, marketability, and all other performance measures are captured in an integrated manner rather than in isolation, thereby recognizing their importance individually as well as collectively.

2. **Ability to consider both tangible and intangible factors**—Both the tangible (easily quantifiable) and intangible (traditionally unquantified) factors in the impact of technology are considered in the CTPM. For example, the interests of customers, employees, vendors, stockholders, and society are all factored in, thus minimizing the risks of customer alienation, employee dissatisfaction, stockholder unhappiness, and the like.

3. **Relationship to profitability**—Because the CTPM has the total productivity component, which is directly related to "productivity-oriented profit," it can easily be understood and appreciated by management. A company's management can easily pinpoint the contribution of a newly acquired technology to profits.

4. **Integratability**—The CTPM framework forms a core philosophy around which business, technology, manufacturing, and marketing strategies can be woven, thereby providing a unified direction at all levels of management in an enterprise.

5. **Ability to accommodate other techniques**—Quantitative models such as simulations, mathematical programming, and statistical process control can be applied to monitor the adaptation of new technologies. The CTPM provides a natural and intuitively appealing mechanism to do "what if" analyses using such techniques.

6. **Impact analysis**—Data can be collected at different levels of interest: corporate (firm), plant/division, product/service unit, department, work unit, or task. Thus, the impact of new technologies can be assessed at several levels of interest: top management, middle management, and operational management.

7. **Linkage to gainsharing systems**—Employee incentives and gainsharing systems can be tied to the CTPM rather than traditional suboptimal bases. Teamwork becomes more natural in the CTPM environment than in the traditional labor-productivity-driven setting.

8. **Management of overall competitiveness**—Instead of reacting suddenly to external environmental factors, the CTPM offers a managerial tool to more broadly understand the role of technology and to generate competitive strategies in a more holistic but systematic manner.

The CTPM goes beyond being just a tool. It offers a different philosophy of management that provides an objective perspective to evaluate any alternative— not just technology—when decisions must be made. In today's corporations, where being the largest does not necessarily mean being the best, there must be refreshing approaches to evaluate alternatives at all levels of an enterprise. This methodology, though in abbreviated form for the sake of space, offers such an approach to minimizing the dangers of being caught unprepared in technology discontinuities, which are not only here to stay but which will occur with greater frequency in the years to come. As Horwitch[5] rightly points out, we must have a strategic perspective even in a rapidly changing, technologically complex world. In fact, management of technology is going to be an important field in the years ahead, and the seeds for such thinking have already been sown by the National Research Council.[6] New approaches must also be devised to assess the performance of managers, who will be increasingly associated with the management of technology in general and discontinuities in particular.[7]

In summary, one of the significant benefits of TPmgt is the ability to do technology planning. In today's enterprises, technology is a major driver of competitiveness. TPmgt offers a robust model—the CTPM—to accomplish technology planning in a quantitative manner.

8.6 INVESTMENT ANALYSIS

Another major benefit of TPmgt lies in its unique ability to do investment analysis, with a non-traditional outlook. Investment in this context refers to two types: capital equipment investments and financial investments.

Capital Equipment Investments

The need for improved productivity is forcing many manufacturers to automate their existing facilities to a higher degree. Computer-integrated manufacturing (CIM) systems, robotics, flexible manufacturing systems (FMS), and computer-aided manufacturing/computer-aided design (CAD/CAM) are some of the state-of-the-art technologies currently being implemented in manufacturing firms. In service organizations, including hospitals and financial institutions among others, communications technologies via computers are becoming increasingly common.

The introduction of costly capital investments requires a more complete cost-justification system than the ones available today. The complexity of such equipment dictates the need for a more detailed and rational approach to justifying capital equipment purchases. Traditionally, industrial engineers would predict the profitability of an investment through net present value, payback period, and break-even analyses, which lack a total systems view of the investment from the standpoint of all resources. They usually consider only labor savings, for the most part.

A study by Sumanth and Del Pino[8] demonstrated that better investment decisions and evaluations are possible with the TPM, whereby the predicted impact of any proposed equipment on profitability is assessed from the viewpoint of total productivity and its relative position with respect to the break-even point. Equipment is selected only if the break-even point of total productivity is surpassed.

The data used in this study were assumed to be for a particular operational unit, comprising one or more pieces of equipment. The cost justification of an entire equipment configuration can also be performed with the same method, considering interacting equipment as one operational unit. To allow for "what if" analysis, spreadsheet software is used. The spreadsheet is divided into two parts: *proposed method* and *traditional methods.*

In the proposed method section of the spreadsheet, total inputs, total outputs, partial productivities, and break-even point of productivity are computed automatically. As an additional feature, the user may view graphs of the inputs, outputs, partial productivities, total productivity values, and break-even points, as given by the TPM.

In the traditional methods section of the spreadsheet, payback period, net present value, and break-even points are calculated automatically.

The TPM cost justification provides a more detailed and rational analysis than traditional payback period and net present value analysis. For example, in the study referred to above, it was shown that the break-even point for the capital acquisition decision was expected in 1.73 years using the payback period method and in the third year of operation using the net present value method. Using the TPM analysis, the break-even point was found to occur in the second year. One traditional method overestimated the break-even point and the other underestimated it—both of which were incorrect.

Since the TPM considers the impact of not only direct labor but all forms of human, material, capital, energy, and other inputs, it can be applied to any configuration such as FMS, CIM, assembly lines, robots, just-in-time systems, and so on by considering them as operational units.

Financial Investments

The TPM can also be used in a non-traditional way to elevate financial portfolios for enterprises as well as for individuals. Using the TPM in much the same way as a bank would (see case study in Chapter 5), total productivity and the break-even point of total productivity for each investment portfolio can be computed. Within a given portfolio, the TPM can be applied to individual investment categories (e.g., mutual funds, bonds, individual stocks, etc.). Then, by determining their *intrinsic total productivity potential* (ITP^2), those with the highest ITP^2 can be selected for maximum possible return. For a given set of investment objectives (e.g., growth, income, growth and income, etc.), an optimum mix of investments can be chosen to maximize the total productivity of the portfolio. Of course, the CTPM can be used here as a further improvement over the TPM.

In summary, the TPmgt concept lends itself to making critical decisions with respect to both capital equipment investments and financial investments. Financial planners, finance managers, and financial controllers all have a unique tool in the TPM or CTPM to help companies (or individuals) save huge sums of money.

A 1984 survey by the National Electrical Manufacturers Association found that 91% of responding business executives use conventional justification procedures as their major consideration in approving factory automation.[9] The conventional techniques for capital equipment justification can be replaced or supplemented by the TPM or CTPM, which are the brain behind TPmgt thinking.

Before companies invest vast sums of money, they can now apply an additional tool—the TPM or CTPM—to determine the profit potential before making decisions that often prove to be extremely expensive using only traditional investment analysis and financial indicators.

8.7 ACQUISITION AND MERGER PLANNING

The second half of 1995 saw the merger of two mega banks—Chase Manhattan and Chemical Bank—to create the largest bank in the United States. Perhaps the largest merger ever, worth some $19 billion, took place on January 4, 1996 between two entertainment giants—Walt Disney Company and Capital Cities/ABC. Northrop Grumman, a major defense contractor, is acquiring the electronics division of Westinghouse for nearly $3.5 billion. As companies acquire and merge, the employees working for such companies are usually the victims. Company stock may go up but, unfortunately, at the expense of the employees' well-being. Most companies doing acquisitions or mergers would be quick to point out that they do not like laying off thousands of employees and that restructuring is often painful. The question is: Can acquisitions and mergers be less painful and without layoffs? The answer is yes, if proper planning is done by top management.

Traditionally, when acquisitions and/or mergers are done, top executives look at strategic strengths primarily from a financial standpoint. For example, they look closely at figures for the last three to five years for fixed and liquid assets, return on investment, liabilities, net worth, debt/equity ratio, current ratio, liquidity ratio, acid test ratio, net income, earnings per share, market value, market share potential, age of assets, dividends declared, and such other financial measures. They also assess the availability of management and the work force, the level and type of training and retraining needed, short-term or long-term effects on presently owned assets and/or enterprises, availability of funds, etc. In addition, financial analyses are often performed, including net present value, payback, and cost–benefit analyses.

Acquisition and merger planning is usually a carefully executed process. Depending upon how big the acquisition is, help is often sought from a CPA or a big accounting firm. Despite this careful process, however, thousands of newly acquired businesses become unprofitable in a relatively short time and are either liquidated or sold. Obviously, there seems to be something missing in the analysis, and the traditional selection criteria are not sufficient to assure a greater probability of success for owners or investors. One of the problems is that these measures or selection criteria do not indicate the inherent potential for improving the "total productivity" of an acquired business. In many instances, companies appear to do extremely well in terms of sales growth and financial ratios and yet do poorly in terms of operational effectiveness and efficiency. Also, labor productivity may be rising rapidly in a company, but profitability is going downhill. Clearly, neither the financial ratios nor the traditional labor productivity measure is, by itself, a successful predictor of the economic health of an enterprise. A more holistic, systems view is not only meaningful but also realistic in today's competitive environment.

Within the TPmgt framework, top management will be able to look additionally at the ITP^2. If the ITP^2 is a positive value in a growth mode, then that would ensure the profitability of the company. Likewise, if two companies are planning to merge, they will be much more "business wise" if the ITP^2 value and growth rate are positive for each company as well as for the potentially merged entity.

To illustrate this concept, consider Table 8.1, where three candidates are evaluated for a possible acquisition or merger. On the basis of the criterion mentioned above for acquisition or merger, company A happens to be the best choice to acquire or merge with, because it has a positive ITP^2 value and a healthy 5.2% growth rate before acquisition (or merger) and a 6.1% growth rate after acquisition (or merger). Company C has a healthy positive ITP^2 growth rate, but it is not sufficient to break the negative ITP^2 threshold. Thus, company C is the worst candidate, company B is a moderately successful one, and company A has the best potential for success.

TABLE 8.1 The TPmgt Approach to Analyzing Candidates for Acquisition or Merger

	Candidate Companies		
	A	B	C
At present			
ITP^2 value: annual average 1990–95	0.176 $/$	0.012	–0.102
ITP^2 growth rate: average (%/year 1990–95)	5.2%	–2.5	7.3
After acquisition or merger			
ITP^2 value: projected annual average 1996–2000	0.213 $/$	0.083	–0.055
ITP^2 growth rate: projected annual average 1996–2000	6.1%	–0.2	8.2

Note: ITP^2 = intrinsic total productivity potential = (TP – 1.00) (see Chapter 3 for further details).

Case Study[10]

The TPM approach for selecting a company for acquisition/merger was first successfully applied in 1985 by one of my graduate students, Cesar Gonzalez, who wanted to acquire a company from among three alternatives—a clothing manufacturer, an auto parts sales and service merchandiser, and a dry-cleaning business.

The TPM computations were done for 12 months of data for each of the three candidate companies. The gains in total productivity were assessed and compared against the break-even point of total productivity. For the clothing manufacturer, the total productivity trends showed a slight upward movement, but the total productivity profile was very close to the break-even point profile, indicating a low potential for both profit and total productivity. For the auto parts merchandiser, the total productivity trends showed downward movement and were too close to the break-even point profile. For the dry-cleaning business, the total productivity trends showed a continuously upward movement, with a large gap from the break-even levels of total productivity. Also, when the trends in the five partial productivities (human, material, capital, energy, and other expense inputs) were analyzed against this total productivity profile, all showed a consistently high productivity potential. Based on this analysis, the dry-cleaning business was the best choice and indeed was purchased. The methodology used is summarized in Figure 8.4.

The capability of the TPM to help in the process of investment selection is a unique addition to the body of knowledge available in the literature. After the

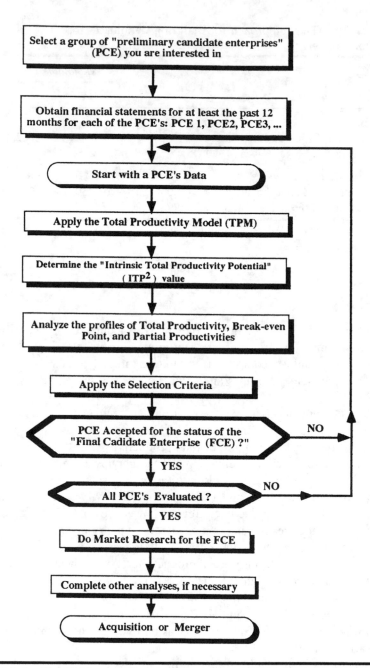

FIGURE 8.4   The TPM approach to selecting enterprises for an acquisition or merger. (Adapted from Sumanth and Gonzalez, 1988.[10])

dry-cleaning business was selected based on application of the TPM, the TPM was installed during the first month of operation (the application of the TPM is discussed in Section 5.4).

In summary, one of the most interesting benefits of TPmgt is its ability to select candidates for acquisition or merger with greater confidence. This analysis can indeed help prevent layoffs after an acquisition or merger, unlike the traditional analyses which are quick to look for ways to get rid of people and can cause social turmoil.

8.8 RESOURCE BUDGETING AND ALLOCATION

One of the most common activities any enterprise undertakes is budgeting. Allocation of resources is anywhere from an annual to a daily activity, depending upon a company's strategic (long-term), intermediate, and tactical (short-term) planning processes.

Traditionally, budgeting in private and non-private companies has primarily taken one of two basic forms:

- Zero-based budgeting
- Incremental budgeting

In zero-based budgeting, all expenses are initialized to zero, and the questioning process centers around the need for each resource—human, capital, material, etc. The idea is to ask the fundamental question: Why do we need that activity or that process? Clearly, this budgeting concept has a major advantage in that it promotes self-examination—a sort of reengineering mentality—to ensure that activities do not necessarily have to be continued in the next budgeting cycle the same way they were done in the current cycle. Many well-known companies use zero-based budgeting with laudable success.

Incremental budgeting, on the other hand, is the most popular approach, although not necessarily the most accurate. In this approach, budgeted expenses are incrementally increased or decreased from the current budgeting period, using more or less "seat-of-the-pants" thinking and "gut feelings." Often, this budgeting approach escalates costs and causes the type of problems seen in poorly managed enterprises.

In either of these approaches, budgets are prepared as projected income and expense statements and projected balance sheets. They are done at varying levels of detail, depending on whether they are consolidated at the product, process, plant, division, firm, or group level.

A major benefit of the TPmgt concept is the ability to supplement (or substitute) traditional budgeting approaches by developing a "TPM-based budget." Basically, a TPM-based budget is a projected TPM spreadsheet for the time period(s) of the budgeting cycle. The major advantage of this approach to budgeting is that the integrity of the total productivity improvement effort is not jeopardized, as a separate agenda is set up in the name of traditional budgeting compliance.

Resource allocation has traditionally been based on budget allocations. For the most part, such resource deployments have totally overlooked the impact of shuffling people, facilities, and equipment on morale, quality, productivity, and competitiveness of the products or operational units. The result is suboptimization, premature dismantling of systems that are on their way to expected performance levels, and most importantly, disenchanted, disgruntled, and thoroughly demotivated employees. These days, it is probably better to say "resource reallocation" rather than resource allocation, because restructurings are so common. Frequent organizational restructuring is akin to a child playing with a toy, getting bored, playing with another toy, getting bored again, and then coming back and playing with the first toy! Because organizational culture is a composite of individual human traits, it is reasonable to say that an organization's stability in leadership is directly proportional to the managerial maturity of the individuals comprising the organization, particularly those at the top management level, where important decisions are made with respect to policies and strategies covering resource allocations.

TPmgt is driven by the corporate vision and mission. Since it orients the vision and mission toward customers, the budgeting and resource allocation processes will be directed, rather naturally, toward only those management goals which, in turn, are based on the TPM and/or CTPM analysis (see Chapter 4 for details). Perhaps it would be a beneficial exercise for companies to do resource allocation based on management goals rather using "hit-or-miss" approaches.

In short, TPmgt benefits a company by its ability to do budgeting and resource allocation in such a way that the vision and mission are attained more spontaneously and naturally.

8.9 AUTOMATIC PROFIT TARGETING

One of the greatest benefits of TPmgt is the ability to set targets for profits from a total productivity standpoint, as discussed in Chapter 3, where the TPM was presented.

Considering the important relationship between profit and total productivity, a company can set a profit target in a non-traditional but practical manner. For

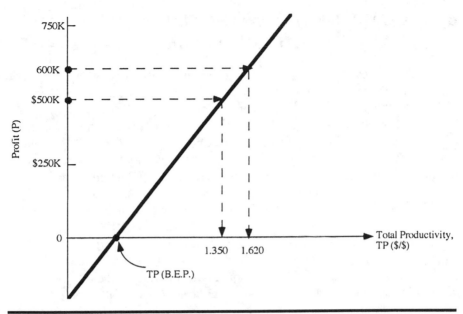

FIGURE 8.5 Profit targeting in TPmgt through the P-TP curve.

example, referring to Figure 8.5, if a company wants to achieve a profit of $500,000, management can use the *profit–total productivity (P-TP) curve* to project a value of 1.350 for total productivity.

If a company targets a profit level of $600,000 for the next quarter, management can use the P-TP curve to see that the company has to attain a total productivity level of 1.620 $/$. A company can work backwards in this exercise as well. For example, if a company knows its total productivity is 1.350 $/$ and wants to increase it to 1.620 $/$, it can easily establish that the estimated profit will increase from $500,000 to $600,000. Thus, whichever way a company chooses to look at it, the P-TP curve has a tremendous advantage over conventional means of estimating profits because it shows that profits will increase when total productivity improves and vice versa. Traditional approaches assume that profits will increase with sales, but improved sales revenues do not necessarily guarantee increased profits; improved total productivity, on the other hand, can indeed guarantee increased profits.

Irrespective of the shape of the P-TP curve in reality, profit targeting is an important feature of TPmgt. It is probably one of the greatest benefits of TPmgt when compared to other concepts. Neither TQM nor reengineering is able to relate profit to total productivity in such a manner as the P-TP curve does.

8.10 COMPATIBILITY WITH WELL-ESTABLISHED DATA COLLECTION FORMATS

One of the greatest benefits of TPmgt is the ability to use existing data with very little modification of the format in which it is available. This is possible because of the way the TPM and the CTPM were designed.

In most applications of the TPM, only two key people were brought together, one from accounting and one from information systems. In every TPM applications, information was put together within one to three months, depending upon the size of the company. For example, in implementing TPmgt in a major insurance company, the first TPM reports were generated in just two months. Even applying the CTPM in a medium-size manufacturing company took only 2.5 months.

To summarize, this chapter has reviewed the ten major benefits of TPmgt for any type of enterprise. The 17-year proven track record of the TPM, the 15-year implementation record of productivity quality teams, and all the other elements of the TPmgt concept make it possible to replicate this kind of success in companies throughout the world.

QUESTIONS TO PONDER

8.1 Analyze in depth each of the ten benefits of TPmgt presented in this chapter to determine the extent to which they are realized (partially or fully) in your enterprise. What inferences are you able to draw from this analysis?

8.2 Do an in-depth study of customer responsiveness in your organization. Consider all types of customers in your study. Prepare a list of recommendations for top management to position your enterprise to be better able to respond to customers' needs and wants.

8.3 Organizational culture has been changing dramatically due to the global nature of business today. In implementing teams, whether homogeneous or cross-functional, what factors are dominant to sustain their effectiveness? What are the do's and don'ts for self-directed teams?

8.4 Quality competitiveness has become taken for granted in many corporations, particularly in a highly oligopolic market. Conduct a quality audit in your enterprise or an enterprise of your choice to determine the nature and extent of quality as a philosophy and concept. Do a correlation analysis between quality and return on assets, return on investment, and other financial performance indicators.

8.5 How can total cost competitiveness be used as a strategy to aggressively compete in terms of price when new competitors enter your market? Research companies that have been successful in using total cost competitiveness to drive out the competition. (As a hint, start with Lincoln Electric Company in Ohio.)

8.6 Many companies have not yet reached the stage where technology planning has been truly integrated into their business planning.

a. Examine and learn from companies that have been able to achieve such integration.

b. Analyze your own company or one of your choice and develop a practical strategy for such integration or a strategy to improve integration based on what you have learned from other successful integrators of technology and business planning.

8.7 Design an implementation strategy for your enterprise or an enterprise of your choice wherein investments are evaluated using TPmgt thinking as described in this chapter as a supplemental approach to the traditional methods. What advantages and disadvantages do you see in this approach?

8.8 In planning for new acquisitions or mergers, how can your company (or one of your choice) implement the TPmgt approach? What obstacles do you anticipate in adopting this thinking for acquisitions? What positive reasons could justify this approach?

8.9 Compared to traditional zero-based budgeting, what are the advantages of TPM-based budgeting? Why? What challenges must be overcome to implement this approach?

8.10 One of the greatest pluses of TPmgt is its ability to do automatic profit targeting. For your organization (or one of your choice), do a detailed analysis with "what if" scenarios for various levels of total productivity and profit. Create graphical nomographs for easy use.

8.11 Based on the results of Question 8.10, what major benefits can you identify? How do they stack up against the traditional approach(es) to establishing target levels for profits?

8.12 In implementing TPmgt, what challenges would be faced in collecting data, and how can they be overcome? Describe an easier strategy for collecting or compiling data to ensure a successful TPmgt process.

REFERENCES AND NOTES

1. LeBoeuf, M., *How to Win Customers and Keep Them for Life,* Berkeley Books, New York, 1987, pp. 13–14.

2. Ouchi, William G., *Theory Z: How American Business Can Meet the Japanese Challenge,* Avon Books, New York, 1981.
3. Dumaine, B., "Who Needs a Boss?" *Fortune,* pp. 52–60, May 7, 1990.
4. Adapted from Sumanth, D.J., "Challenges and Opportunities in Managing 'Technology Discontinuities' on S-Curves," in Khalil, T.M. et al. (eds.), *Technology Management Frontiers I,* Interscience Enterprises, Geneva, Switzerland, 1988, pp. 271–279, and the invited case study prepared by D.J. Sumanth entitled "A Productivity Perspective to Manage Technology Discontinuities" in Edosomwan, J.A., *Integrating Innovation and Technology Management,* John Wiley, New York, 1989, pp. 187–192.
5. Horwitch, M. (ed.), *Technology in the Modern Corporation: A Strategic Perspective,* Penguin Press, Elmsford, NY, 1986.
6. In 1987, the National Research Council created an important document titled *Management of Technology: The Hidden Competitive Advantage* (National Academy Press, Washington, D.C.). As a result of this seminal work, the field of management of technology evolved rapidly. Today, a number of major universities have graduate programs in this field.
7. This view has been echoed by many, including Dearden, J., "Measuring Profit Center Managers," *Harvard Business Review,* pp. 84–88, Sept.–Oct. 1987 and Roberts, E.B. and Fusfield, A.R., "Staffing the Innovative Technology-Based Organization," *Sloan Management Review,* Vol. 22, No. 3, pp. 19–34, 1981.
8. Sumanth, D.J. and Del Pino, L., "Equipment Selection and Justification through Total Productivity Model," *Proceedings of the 8th Annual Conference on Computers and Industrial Engineering,* 1986, pp. 91–94.
9. Reported by Sullivan, W.G., *Industrial Engineering,* p. 45, March 1986.
10. More details on this case are presented in Sumanth, D.J. and Gonzalez, C., "A Productivity Engineering Approach to Select and Run a Business Profitability," *International Industrial Engineering Conference Proceedings,* 1988, pp. 333–338.

9

UNIVERSALITY OF TPmgt

9.1 FUNDAMENTAL SIMILARITIES IN MANUFACTURING AND SERVICE ENTERPRISES

The universality of Total Productivity Management (TPmgt™) is such that its philosophy, concepts, and methodologies have been successfully applied in enterprises that provide both goods and services, as shown through the case studies in Chapter 5. This universality is due to the fact that the similarities between manufacturing and service enterprises outweigh the differences, as discussed below.

1. Both are production systems—They require people (*human* resources); materials, stationery, office supplies, and the like (*material* resources); computers, other equipment, and tools (*fixed capital* resources); cash and inventories (*working capital* resources); electricity, water, air-conditioning, and other utilities (*energy* resources); and expenditures for advertising, marketing, accounting, legal counsel, travel, research and development, security, etc. (*other* resources). These six basic resource types are part of the Total Productivity Model (TPM©), the brain behind TPmgt.

2. Both have internal, intermediate, and ultimate customers/clients/users—For example, in an automotive plant, the internal customers for the store clerk are the machine shop workers, whose customers in turn are the assembly workers; the ultimate customers of the assembly workers are the dealerships and people who buy the cars.

In a service enterprise such as a fast-food restaurant, the internal customer of the grill cook is the sandwich assembler, whose client in turn is the register clerk; the ultimate customer is someone who orders a meal at the counter. Whether a small consulting firm or a multibillion-dollar manufacturer, the customer/client/user concept is the same.

3. Both require that the enterprise sustain itself in a fiscally sound fashion—This implies that a for-profit company must strive for consistent profitability; similarly, a non-profit enterprise must operate to at least break even.

4. Both must address safety, social, environmental, and ethical issues in a responsible manner—A small fast-food restaurant has a responsibility to take measures to prevent food poisoning, just as as a multinational oil company has a responsibility to take measures to prevent an oil spill.

5. Both have to constantly seek what customers need and want, how they are meeting or exceeding expectations, and how they are adapting to the constantly changing customer base economically, politically, socially, and demographically—A gas station that increases its prices unreasonably for short-term gains during a fuel shortage might lose its customer base when the supply is restored. Previously loyal customers would likely switch to another station that did not take unfair advantage of the situation. Similarly, a major computer manufacturer might lose significant market share if it is slow in bringing out a new technology when its competitor introduces the new technology six months ahead of customers' expectations.

Based on the above considerations, we can formulate some fundamental principles to manage total productivity in both manufacturing and service organizations, as discussed in the next section.

9.2 PRINCIPLES OF TPmgt

Principles are long-standing truths based on analysis of countless real-life situations, theory, practice, knowledge, wisdom, and judgment. Twelve such principles for total productivity management to produce world-class products and services with superior quality, low unit costs, and fast turnaround time are as follows:

1. Quality/perfection
2. Customer orientation
   - Global marketing
   - Leading competitor
   - International outlook

3. People orientation
4. Learning curve
5. Standardization/simplification
6. Emulation (benchmarking)
7. Miniaturization
8. Cooperative research and development
9. Product mix planning
10. Secrecy
11. Mutual benefit
12. Consistency

The relative importance of these principles depends upon several factors, including the type of business, the corporate culture, and the guiding philosophy of an organization.

Principle 1: Quality/Perfection

Seek perfection in the quality of design, the quality of conformance, and the quality of performance.

First, quality must be built into a product or service at the design stage. Defects should be prevented instead of correcting them later. Second, product or service components should be made according to their specifications in the design stage; at the very least, quality control should be the responsibility of every operator, and process control charting should be installed. Ambitiously high levels of quality should be the goal. Finally, the finished product or service should *totally* delight the customers. Quality improvement always leads to total productivity improvement in the long run. Therefore, *perfection should be pursued as a symbol of true quality.* Quality of design is a major responsibility of designers, quality of conformance that of production/operations personnel, and quality of performance that of reliability and design personnel. Responsibility for quality control and reliability, which traditionally has been assigned to a separate department, really belongs to the operators.

The reward system must be based on quality. The myth that quality implies slow production must be set aside. Managers should strive for perfection and set an example for their subordinates. It's time to return to the craftsmanship mindset. It is better to do something right the first time than to fix the defects later, after incurring additional costs in terms of money, goodwill, and customer confidence. Some companies boast of 100% product inspection at the final stage of a process, but what good is it if defects could have been prevented by operators checking their own work rather than waiting for inspectors to catch the defects in the final inspection? That would be "penny-wise and pound-foolish." Products and services should be designed to conform to not just national standards but rather world-class standards. This strategy will force companies to aim for the highest standards. For example, a U.S. company that manufactures electric motors should compare the U.S. standards of quality against, say, those of Japan (the Japanese International Standard) and Germany (the DIN Standard). If the U.S. standard for a particular motor falls short of the Japanese, the company should adopt the latter standard. Thus, motors made by the American company could compete in terms of quality in Japanese markets as well. ISO 9000 and ISO 14000 further this approach to producing to standards of world-class quality.

Organizations should strive to be leading edge in terms of quality just as they do in product or process technology. An appropriate motto might be: "Excellence is my starting point, perfection my ultimate goal." Harris Corporation has become a world-class competitor in the electronics market. The company beat out AT&T for a $1.6 billion contract with the Federal Aviation Authority (FAA) to install state-of-the-art communications equipment in the FAA's 22 route centers. The standard for the Harris air-traffic control system voice network is to be out of service no more than three seconds per year, which is a reliability specification of 0.9999999.[1] Under the leadership of Art Wood, the University Credit Union (UCU) in Miami has strived for perfection. The author has never had one experience of an incorrect transaction or statement in 18 years! The UCU really seems to know how to balance perfection with a personal touch.

Principle 2: Customer Orientation

Listen to customers intently, learn from them diligently,
give them what they desire instead of what you can offer, and
never displease them. Leave a positive impression in their minds
about you, your products/services, and your organization.
Strive to delight them rather than just satisfy them.

Research by Tom Peters and Robert Waterman, Jr. shows that one of the eight characteristics of excellent companies is closeness to customers and a willingness to learn from them.[2]

Companies and their management often forget that were it not for their customers, they would not be in business. When businesses start up, they are usually very customer oriented, doing everything they can to please the customers. Once a business begins to grow, however, a sudden arrogance and complacency seem to take over, as reflected in management's poor attitude toward the customers. This is a common, shortsighted approach taken by many ill-managed enterprises.

Some professions have more direct contact with their customers than others. A professor's constituents are students, a nurse or doctor's clients are patients, a government agency's customers are taxpayers, and so on. By practicing the customer orientation principle, everyone can adopt a more responsible attitude toward their customers.

A personal experience of mine is a good example of this principle in action. I was shopping in a well-known store in Tokyo and couldn't find the item I wanted. I asked the salesperson, but she did not speak English. She called her supervisor, who said that the store did not carry the item. The supervisor asked the salesperson to accompany me to a nearby competitor's store to make sure I found what I wanted. This type of treatment is very rare. The company *wanted* to delight me, the customer, instead of just saying, "Sorry, we do not carry that item"—a common response in many stores. The point is clear. Create a memorable positive feeling in the customer's mind.

Many successful U.S. companies practice this principle. Sears and Wal-Mart have a policy of taking back merchandise with no questions asked. No wonder they are two of the largest retailers in the world.

As important as this principle is, it is difficult to practice. But, as the saying goes, "When the going gets tough, the tough get going!" Even when it is challenging to delight an irate customer, it is worth trying to do so.

There are three subprinciples under Principle 2: global marketing, leading competitor, and international outlook.

Subprinciple 2.1: Global Marketing
Design and build products for global markets.

In today's world, the main strategy is to "go global." It's everywhere we look and everywhere we go. There is a McDonald's in every country. Motorola competes with NEC and Toshiba from their own territory in Singapore and is also going strong in India. Hewlett-Packard expanded its operations to Brazil. Coca-Cola now does business in the world's two most populous countries, China and India. Global marketing has become a reality with the information technology revolution, the Information Superhighway, and the Internet.

Travel Related Services (TRS), an arm of American Express, was facing an onslaught of competition from thousands of banks offering VISA and Mastercard in the late 1970s. Lou Gerstner, president of TRS at the time, launched a global marketing strategy for the company with market segmentation, aggressively developing a broad range of new products and services and investing in technologies to increase productivity and reduce costs. As a result, TRS's income increased dramatically, by 500% between 1978 and 1987—a compound rate of about 18! The business outperformed many so-called high-tech/high-growth companies. It had a 28% return on equity in 1988 and outperformed most low-growth and high-profit businesses.[3]

In 1986, MIT created the Commission on Industrial Productivity, with a mission to investigate the reasons for America's industrial decline and to come up with concrete prescriptions for regaining its strength. Two of the prescriptions were to "learn to live in a world economy" and that "American management must finally make the jump from cultural isolationist to international operator. This means coming to grips with exporting, foreign purchasing, and international joint ventures."[4]

All major Japanese auto companies have gone global. Suzuki partnered with Maruti to produce compact cars in India.[5] Suzuki opened a manufacturing assembly plant in Hungary in 1992. The company it formed, Autokonszein, has 51 Hungarian shareholders.[6] Mazda has had a joint venture in Thailand since 1992.[7] Mitsubishi became one of the first Japanese automakers to export a U.S.-made vehicle (Eclipse) to Europe, with 60% U.S.-made parts.[8]

Leading companies are constantly introducing products that are in demand worldwide. On September 19, 1990, Xerox Corporation announced that it would offer its office automation software, Globalview, for use in computers made by other manufacturers. The software would compete with products like New Wave Office from Hewlett-Packard and Officevision from IBM.[9] In 1989, an agreement was signed between six U.S. and former Soviet Union companies. The six participants to go global were Mercator, RJR Nabisco, Eastman Kodak, Chevron, Archer-Daniels-Midland, and Johnson and Johnson.[10] Citicorp began going global in 1902 by opening branches around the world, but only recently began to link them as a global business. It can seek the best rates and terms offered by its offices anywhere in the world. Michael Callen, who runs Citicorp's investment banking worldwide, says that this technology did not exist at the beginning of the 1990s. Today, Citicorp is testing automatic tellers that can serve a client anywhere in the world. Globalization helped Texas Instruments compete against Japanese memory chips. The company grabbed 5.2% of the world market for memory chips, and sales helped boost earnings by 69% to $368 million in 1988. American Express uses a global strategy in designing its ads. "Don't leave home without it" and "Membership has its privileges" are known around the world, but in Japan the ad says: "Peace of mind only for members." American Express predicted in 1989 that the company's international business would generate 40% of the growth in credit-card profits in the next two years.[11]

This principle applies not only to companies that produce goods and services, but to any organization that can generate substantial profits by competing internationally. Take the case of Northern Telecom Ltd., a leading manufacturer of digital switches for local phone companies and corporations. On November

8, 1990, it decided to buy control of British telecommunications equipment maker STC PLC for $2.8 billion. Chairman and Executive Officer Paul G. Stern explained that STC would give Northern Telecom a European beachhead and edge it closer to its goal of becoming the world's number one maker of telecommunications equipment.[12]

Bauer Aerospace, located in Farmington, Connecticut, is another example. At the end of 1990, the company was doing 60% of its sales in Europe and the Pacific Basin. Why would a company strive to compete at home when it can generate higher profits selling overseas? Exporting thus keeps companies eager to compete in international markets and achieve quality standards. "Overseas economies may be slowing, but their growth is likely to outstrip that of the United States in a very short time."[13]

Yet another major company that expanded globally in the late 1980s is Saab Automobile AB. It expanded its sales from Norway to Latin America, New Zealand, Eastern Europe, West Germany, and France.

Toys 'R' Us went global by announcing in 1987 that it would open stores in West Germany for the first time. The company's low prices later helped its European revenues to climb at triple the growth rate of total sales, heading toward $800 million in fiscal year 1987.[14]

Companies that believe in global marketing are proactive. Soft drink giant Coca-Cola went into East Germany even before German reunification.[15]

All the above examples show that a company should go global if it has the capacity to do so, because the increased profits can be dramatic.

Global marketing creates jobs. In 1984, one million Canadians owed their jobs to exports, which accounted for more than 30% of Canadian manufactured goods.[16]

Subprinciple 2.2: Leading Competitor

Be the leading competitor for as many products/services as possible.

In the area of telecommunications systems, AT&T stands out with a variety of products ranging from long-distance communications equipment to computer networks. AT&T's 1337 telephone-answering device is "...beating out Sony and other Japanese stalwarts," and its new Videophone has "...jumped ahead of foreign manufacturers..." Motorola's $1,200 MicroTac Lite Digital Personal Communicator is "the company's latest cellular phone, the lightest and smallest commercially available anywhere." U.S. companies will produce "the first mass-market multimedia home computer priced under $1000." Texas Instruments has come out with "Super Speak 'n' Spell, a learning device for children" for about $70.[17] All these companies strive to be leading competitors in their product groupings and their markets.

The airline industry's Boeing 777 has come out to compete with the announced Airbus A330-300. Although Airbus has made an entry into the airline industry and has established a good product, it is not the leader in its class. Boeing still heads the pack with its 777 Stretch, 777-200, and 747-400 models. It may come as no surprise that in the coming years Airbus, with its A330-300 and A340-200, might gain the lead in the commuter airline market.[18]

Honda and Mitsubishi, two unquestionable leaders in the automobile industry, got together and developed the "lean-burn engine" in order to move ahead of their competitors. The engine mixes swirling layers of air and gas and burns a leaner mixture than conventional engines.[19] General Electric developed a smaller headlight that is the size of a golf ball and emits a light whiter than conventional lights. These improvements will allow auto manufacturers to use new aerodynamic designs to further improve fuel efficiency.[20]

Procter & Gamble has developed the ultimate dietary self-indulgence—fake fat. It tastes like real fat but is not absorbed by the body![21]

IBM, Apple, and Compaq are three of the biggest manufacturers of computers, but that does not mean they are consumers' first choice. In 1990, a survey was conducted among 1,230 PC users at all levels to determine which computer company was most popular. "CompuAdd Service Corp., an Austin, Texas maker of IBM clones that has a U.S. PC market share of less than 1%, scored highest in overall customer satisfaction."[22]

Toshiba scored big in 1989 with its new laptop. "The title for the world's smallest real PC now goes to laptop market dealer Toshiba's new DynaBook model."[23]

In the summer of 1989, Sony came out with the Pocket Copier, a major advancement in Sony's handheld units. It was the size of a highlighter.[24]

A.C. Nielsen opened offices in Hungary, the Czech Republic, Slovakia, and Poland and expanded its tracking services in Japan, Australia, and Brazil.[25]

McDonnell Douglas Space Systems Company–Kennedy Space Center Division (MDSSC–KSC) is the leading competitor in payload processing at KSC; it holds the contract for payload ground testing, checkout, and all applicable support operations. Of course, as the leader in ground processing, the company must be careful not to become complacent in satisfying its contractual requirements. Being the leading competitor does not stop other companies from attempting to unseat a company. MDSSC has to constantly strive to satisfy NASA, the customer. As another major contractor discovered, no company is indispensable to NASA; when NASA is dissatisfied, contracts can be lost. To date, MDSSC has maintained a high customer satisfaction level. The company was a finalist in 1992 for the NASA George M. Low Quality Award.[26]

A leading competitor can make additional money from licenses. In 1991, Eastman Kodak licensed rival Fuji Photo Film of Tokyo to use its Photo CD technology in Japan. General manager Stephen S. Stepnes said: "No company had yet developed a competitive alternative to the Kodak system."[27]

Subprinciple 2.3: International Outlook

Keep an international perspective in management activities related to planning, research and development, marketing, operations/production, and technology transfer.

Most large companies have moved extremely fast in order to meet international expectations. By entering other markets, these organizations maintain an "international outlook." PepsiCo, for example, paid $1.4 billion to two major makers of snacks in order to obtain European technology and thereby compete in Europe. DuPont bought Howson-Algraphy, a leading maker of printing plates, for $445 million. Ford bought carmaker Jaguar for $2.5 billion, thereby enabling Ford to implement the English style of luxury into its American models. Emerson Electric paid $460 million for Leroy-Somer, a maker of electronic drivers and motors. Even AT&T got into the act by purchasing 20% of Italtel for $135 million.[28] These are all large investments, but the returns will be even greater now that these companies own new technology and are capable of expanding into new markets.

Coca-Cola joined with toymaker Mattel in the biggest cross promotion in its history. All Coca-Cola products will carry coupons that can be redeemed for Mattel toys.[29] In 1991, Procter & Gamble reported that it was planning to open plants in China. The perfumery was expected to produce 500 metric tons of product a year and the vulcanizing factory 28,000 tons of sulfide, which would cut the cost of Head and Shoulders by about 20%.[30]

Procter & Gamble (P&G) has learned much from marketing overseas. For example, in Japan, a relatively homogeneous society, there remains a classic market and a useful one for P&G. The company had huge losses after entering the market with Pampers disposable diapers. Competitors like Uni-Charm Corp. and Kao Corp. introduced fitted, thin diapers that won over mothers who had resisted disposables.[31] This taught P&G to market differently overseas.

Half way between Chicago and St. Louis, a new auto plant assembles sport coupes managed by both Chrysler and Mitsubishi. Mitsubishi and Volvo of Sweden plan to do the same in Amsterdam. The deal will mark the first large-scale Japanese joint venture in Europe. This enterprise could change the way Europe deals with Japan.[32]

In the cable TV industry, strong competition developed among U.S. companies to establish ventures in Europe, which was hungry for cable TV five years ago. Large cable companies believe that their international investments will eventually pay off in a big way.[33]

Levi Strauss is a leader in manufacturing jeans. "Twice a year, Levi Strauss & Co. calls together managers from its worldwide operations...(the)...conferees brainstorm, schmooze, and watch splashy television ads from around the world. If a marketing type from, say, Singapore finds an ad campaign appealing, he's encouraged to take it back home to sell more Levi's blue jeans."[34]

Hewlett-Packard (HP) searched for manufacturers of its Spectrum (RISC) machines, because Sun Microsystems and MIPS Computer Systems had licensed their RISC designs to other computer makers, producing higher volumes of the designs. Hitachi Ltd. agreed to jointly develop a chip to share with HP. In return, HP got to use Hitachi's advanced chip technology, which pushed Spectrum into high-performance markets.[35]

Companies without an international outlook can make some fundamental mistakes. For example, a first-class U.S. manufacturer of appliances went into the Japanese market. "Its outsized stoves and mammoth refrigerators won the prompt admiration of the Japanese buyers. But alas, the tight living quarters of the average Japanese home did not allow kitchen space for these standard American models. Even worse, the narrow width of Japanese doorways often denied entrance into the kitchen."[36]

Principle 3: People Orientation

Consider the people working for you as your greatest asset, and provide them job security and harmony in return for loyalty and consistent productivity improvement.

The importance of this principle cannot be overemphasized. Companies that practice this principle rarely fire or lay off their employees. The highly successful Lincoln Electric Company has had a "no layoffs" policy for almost 95 years. Even when economic factors beyond its control affect sales, the company guarantees a 30-hour work week to employees who are beyond their probationary period. Hewlett-Packard is another such company. American Bankers Insurance Group, headquartered in Miami, increased its employment from 1981 to 1994 by about 400 people without laying off anyone. Phil Sharkey, executive vice president of human resources, said that his company has initiated innovative reward systems and incentive systems to keep the nearly 2,000 employees motivated to constantly improve the quality of service, total productivity, and responsiveness to customers.

Prior to hiring people, companies screen applicants rigorously. Once hired, management should consider it a moral obligation to nourish, train, mentor, and coach employees. We often see people who have put in many years of service let go with nothing more than two weeks severance. The social cost of such layoffs is high. Managers can and should adopt a more caring attitude toward their employees, but many managers are inadequately equipped in terms of interpersonal communication skills. Such skills are essential for managing people effectively. Often, perceived or real problems of low work ethic can be minimized when managers recognize that their employees need a harmonious, flexible, and even inspiring working atmosphere. Managers must care for their employees on the job as well as off the job.

As pointed out in Chapter 4, there are six basic inputs to produce an output: human, material, fixed capital, working capital, energy, and other expense. Although each of these inputs is important in improving total productivity, the one common element in controlling them all is the human resource. No matter how sophisticated the technology, machinery, equipment, or tools, an organization cannot realize its full potential unless it has employees who are constantly motivated and encouraged, trained and retrained, and involved and inspired.

Motivation and Encouragement

How often do most people praise their fellow employees? How often do managers sincerely encourage their subordinates? We often take employees for granted. We say to ourselves, "They're getting paid for what they're doing here. Why should I have to go out of my way?" By nature, people want to be praised for accomplishing even the simplest things that may seem trivial to others. Recognizing people for their achievements, whether every-day or remarkable, fosters pride, self-worth, and dignity. Simple but sincere praise, given frequently and at appropriate times, creates high levels of motivation and encouragement that can reap rich and long-term dividends. Positive morale and job satisfaction help increase output and/or decrease total input.

An individual who is constantly encouraged and thus enthused will produce products and services of better quality and reliability at a lower cost than someone who is rarely recognized for his or her worth. On-the-job motivation and encouragement of employees are important in today's world to fill the emotional needs of many who have stressful relationships at home due to a host of social factors. An individual's personal life has a strong bearing on his or her performance at work.

If companies really want to increase their profitability, they should be concerned with the welfare of their employees both on and off the job. One general manager took the time to visit an employee who had been at home with the flu for three days. The employee was overwhelmed by such concern on the manager's part, and his loyalty and dedication to the company were reinforced considerably.

An employee who is happy at work will usually take that attitude home, which enhances his or her family environment. In turn, this creates a more consistently positive attitude at work, and such a positive attitude can have a direct impact on total productivity and profitability.

Employees should be given freedom to think and to act on their own within certain boundaries. Freedom is important. Freedom gives dignity and dignity gives freedom.

Positive motivation always works. Basic human nature is the same among people of all races, religions, and nationalities. Human beings are territorial, migratory, exploitative, exploratory, conceited, courageous, and complex by nature. We have not yet fully learned to theorize these attributes and to use them for the good of our fellow workers, friends, and mankind, but those who are sensitive to basic human nature are much more effective and efficient managers than those who are not. It is a good practice to ask every day, "Am I a positive motivator?" "Am I a people-builder?"

Training and Retraining

Just giving "pats on the back" is not enough to get the best out of people. Motivation and encouragement are necessary but not sufficient conditions for improving total productivity and quality. Employees need training in appropriate skills to do their jobs. Equally important is management's commitment to retrain employees who might otherwise be laid off.

In the spring of 1986, the Galvin Center for Continuing Education at Motorola opened its doors in Schaumburg, Illinois. In 1986, Motorola invested more than $40 million in training and education.[37] Saturn Corporation is committed to keeping employees well trained throughout their careers. Every new employee is expected to spend 250 to 750 hours in training. Of course, it should be noted that many Saturn employees have spent up to 25 years in GM plants. This extensive training is in addition to the knowledge and experience an employee brings to the company.[38]

Training should inculcate confidence in employees; after all, confidence breeds confidence. This is a key to managing people for improved quality and total productivity.

It is important to seek harmony in human relations at all levels of the organizational hierarchy. "Human relationships are such an important component in the success of a company, yet we tend to forget this and treat other people as if they were machines...." Every employee should believe that his or her job is as vital as the chief executive's.

It is also necessary to have a mission-driven training program. Frances Hesselbein, chief executive of Girl Scouts U.S.A., is admired by many because of her "visionary, creative, and hands-on management of a similarly tradition-bound organization—with a work force of 751,000 people in 333 autonomous subsidiaries nation-wide." Her simple yet successful strategy bears the following headings: (1) Smash the Hierarchy, (2) Use the Directors, (3) Tap the Grass Roots, (4) Create a Sense of Mission, (5) Overhaul Incentives.

Continental Airlines has brought a series of seminars from the Quality Service Institute to its employees. The seminars offer pop psychology, pep talks, and other strategies to Continental's employees to put them in touch with themselves. "We want people to attend, not because its good for Continental, but because its good for them," says Jan Lapidoth, president of the institute. The employees are grateful that Continental is equipping them with knowledge and skills.[39]

It is also important to provide a disciplined atmosphere during training. Discipline is the conscious conformity to a belief, objective, task, or activity. Nothing long-lasting can be achieved without discipline. But *disciplined harmony* does the impossible! At Hewlett-Packard, employees are in "harmony" by mingling with fellow employees of all ranks. At 3M, an employee choir travels all over United States to perform at corporate and community events.[40]

Involve and Inspire

Tandem Computers' president and CEO, James Treybig, believes that his employees are the company's #1 asset, and it is they who make the company successful. "When Tandem reached the billion dollar sales mark in 1987, he threw a big party, Texan style, for Tandem employees and anyone they wanted to bring along."[41]

When United Electric Controls was going through a period of increased competition, low profitability, and huge inventories, it created problem-solving action centers, suggestion programs, and committee memberships to allow employees to offer useful ideas. The program was successful.[42]

Monsanto Chemical Company's fiber plant in Greenwood, South Carolina, has involved its employees in making decisions and directing their own jobs. This freedom helped the company increase its return on equity from 15 to 20%. Also, quality showed improvement, and labor productivity increased by 47%.[43]

Digital Equipment Corporation in Colorado establishes work teams around the company known as self-managed groups. "This partnership approach changes how employees think about their jobs. They should be involved in decisions that affect their lives. Digital employees now are appraised by every member of their work team, not just their supervisors. The result is increased participation, commitment, and productivity."[44]

Principle 4: Learning Curve

Whenever possible, plan productivity levels and product costs on a learning curve.

An often ignored phenomenon in many companies is the existence of a learning curve. Whenever the time to complete a task is reduced by a constant proportion for every doubling of output quantity, the learning curve is in effect. To illustrate this principle, let's assume the time required to produce each of 50 units is 2 minutes. When production doubles to 100 units, the time per unit drops to 80% (the learning curve) of the previous time, that is, 80% of 2 minutes, or 1.6 minutes. When the production level doubles again to 200 units, the time per unit ratio drops to $0.80 \times 1.6 = 1.28$ minutes. Thus, the total time to produce the second 50 units is less than that for the first 50 units. The total time to produce the next 100 units is much less than that for the previous 100 units, and so forth.

Of course, the learning curve is not in effect in all types of operations, but wherever it is, it is wise to make use of it in targeting unit costs. Aircraft companies use this concept to quote contract prices for aircraft, particularly for the Department of Defense. A large electronic calculator maker uses a target-costing approach based on the learning curve, thereby disciplining itself to improve total productivity and reduce its product unit cost.

An example of the learning curve, offered by Ralph Barnes,[45] is from an assembly operation:

Hours	Average Output	Average Time
8	200	0.30
40	250	0.24
80	337	0.18
300	390	0.16
1,000	436	0.14

These numbers show that the average time per unit is decreasing due to the learning curve effect.

Surprisingly, managers find it difficult to recognize where the learning curve is in effect within their companies. For example, Scott Taylor, president of Bretts, a small retailer in Mankato, Minnesota, was interviewed by *Stores* magazine and asked about the learning patterns of the business. He responded that the company is still in a learning period because the business system is complicated to learn, and when you want to get information out, it takes a lot of time. He also added that both the company and the customers are still learning from each other, which is another difficult part.[46]

Some analysts prefer to ignore the learning curve. In November 1991, Edith Weiner, president of Weiner, Eldridge, Brown, Inc., said that businesses should stop worrying about the learning curve. She added, "Executives must come to value and master the forgetting curve. Forgetting is much more difficult than learning."[47] However, the learning curve, if recognized, can improve human productivity and reduce unit labor costs dramatically.

Principle 5: Standardization/Simplification

Design products/services with a deliberate strategy to standardize and simplify component elements.

An Italian scooter manufacturer practices this principle meticulously, so much so that its scooters can be assembled with just two special tools. By standardizing and simplifying product design, input factor costs can be reduced. According to Richard Bourgerie, former vice president of business and productivity planning at Allied-Signal Automotive: "Say that the number of parts in a component are reduced by 50 percent. If it's manually assembled, that part can be assembled in less time. If the assembly process is automated, then there are fewer variables, which means more consistent quality. And in either case, there's less investment in either human labor or capital goods."[48]

Standardization and simplification lead to a smaller variety of component elements and, hence, huge savings in inventory costs. Also, the availability of parts is greatly enhanced, resulting in lower stockout costs and higher customer satisfaction.

Standardization and simplification of forms can save material, human, and fixed capital inputs. Despite electronic communication, paperwork still abounds, although sometimes it is unavoidable for contractual and legal reasons. Redundant paperwork and non-standardized forms waste many hours and directly result in lower total productivity. Traditional industrial engineering methods, including methods analysis and work simplification, are excellent tools to minimize paperwork. Standardization and simplification are often the result of keen perception, close observation, and good common sense.

Principle 6: Emulation (Benchmarking)
Take the best of at least three competitors' technologies in product/service design and production processes and improve upon what the competition has achieved.

Many companies, particularly those in the United States, are reluctant to emulate the designs, production methods, and management styles of their competitors. They are caught up in the "not invented here" syndrome. At the other extreme, many non-U.S. companies have not hesitated to "copy" the technological know-how of other companies in general and Western companies in particular.

When technology gaps between the company emulating and the company being emulated are substantial, this principle may not seem too practical, but under conditions of close rivalry, emulation may become necessary.

Emulation is not always easy, particularly when trying to figure out the processes used to produce a product or service. A company can easily buy three competitors' products and have its research and development engineers dismantle them component by component, but determining what equipment, tooling, and processes were involved in making the components requires many hours of research.

The Japanese luxury automakers are a good example of the application of this principle, particularly in the early stages of development of their cars. Ichiro Suzuki, chief engineer on the Lexus project, said that the LS 400 design team set a goal of equaling or exceeding the performance of German luxury cars. Takayasu Matsui, chief designer of the Infiniti, admitted that some aspects of the car were emulated.[49] Toyota and Nissan engineers admitted to purchasing Mercedes-Benz and BMW cars and disassembling them piece by piece to unravel how they were assembled, because the Europeans had been leading competitors in the U.S. market at the time.[50]

According to Ronald Henkoff, the superfast robotic production line that makes pagers at Motorola's Boynton Beach, Florida, plant incorporates assembly methods developed by Seiko, Honda, etc. The pagers are so good that they rank among the top sellers even in Japan.[51]

Another buzzword for emulation is benchmarking, that is, "sharing the findings with other companies." US Xerox and Fuji Xerox, Ford and Mazda,[52] Ameritech, IBM, Procter & Gamble, and Florida Power & Light[53] are a few examples of companies that follow the emulation (benchmarking) principle.

The Italian textile industry used this principle to rebound from a bad year in 1991, according to "ACIMIT (Associazone Construttori Italiani di Macchinario per l'Industria Tessile: Italian Assn. of Textile Machinery Producers), a nonprofit national association of 240 firms whose output represents about 90% of the Italian textile machinery and accessories production."[54]

William R. Bruce, vice president and general manager of the Infiniti division of Nissan Motor Corporation in the United States, decided that to have an edge over Lexus, his best shot was to focus on customer service in dealerships. He emulated some details from Mercedes' service, such as washing the car while in service or maintenance. Following McDonald's example, he developed a standard architecture for all Infiniti dealerships so that customers would always feel that same quality service anywhere in the United States.[55]

Software and hardware manufacturers also apply this principle. After the Pascal language was invented, Borland came out with a version of Pascal called TurboPascal, which sold more than 1.5 million copies. Microsoft then entered the race with Quick Pascal, a version designed to be compatible with Borland's package.[56] "For years, Big Blue watched heavyweights Fujitsu and Hitachi take away customers by selling their IBM compatible mainframes at cheaper prices. Now, the U.S. giant has decided to play the same game. It is reengineering its mainframes to mimic Fujitsu and Hitachi's machines."[57]

Principle 7: Miniaturization

Attempt miniaturization wherever possible by using microprocessor-based technology in products and processes.

The use of microprocessors creates products and processes with built-in or intrinsic productivity and quality levels that may not ordinarily be achieved. In the last few years alone, we have seen microprocessor technology applied in systems ranging from automotive fuel-injection systems to improve fuel utilization, to microwave ovens to improve energy consumption and heat penetration, to calculators and computers that have made slide rules obsolete, just to name a few.

By using microprocessors in products and processes:

* The number of components in traditionally large logic circuits can be reduced.
* Power consumption can be lowered.
* Reliability can be increased.
* Flexibility can be enhanced.

A typical microprocessor unit, which is a complex integrated circuit, can replace several thousand transistors, diodes, resistors, etc. on a single silicon chip less than one-sixteenth of an inch square. Therefore, cumbersome traditional printed circuit boards can be eliminated in many electronic products and processes.

By drastically reducing the number of mechanical, electrical, and electronic components through the use of microprocessors, reliability can be built into a product or process. Reducing the type and size of components can also save money in terms of inventory and replacement parts.

Miniaturization also reduces space requirements, freight costs, and other material-handling costs. Total productivity is improved dramatically through this principle. Some important advantages of applying it include reliability, modularity, and reduced storage, shipping, and distribution costs.

With the introduction of supercomputer technology, the miniaturization principle will take on significant meaning with respect to total productivity. While this principle may seem obvious in today's high-tech environment, many companies are still reluctant to incorporate the latest microprocessor technologies into their products, processes, and services. Still others use microprocessors but don't know when to replace them with more appropriate ones. For example, in some cases, an existing system can be updated for about "half the cost of purchasing a new PC." A process improvement in material handling, by incorporating an automated storage/retrieval system, can "reduce 70% of the manual retrieving time." In large corporations with many plants, a satellite storage system can be used to reduce on-floor space and link information from plant to plant.[58]

New and improved microchips are constantly revolutionizing the way products are designed, built, and serviced. Cellular phone companies and others are exploring chips that analyze the characteristics of strange noises and then generate mirror-image sound waves that wipe out the original noise waves, thereby making the cellular phones more reliable. These chips can help route 6 to 20 times as many calls over cellular channels. In 1992, Motorola said that at two chips per phone, its sales would jump 50% that year, by about $70 million. Acer America, located in San Jose, California, is producing PCs with chips that can be programmed to turn text into voice mail, send a fax transmission, and function as a digital answering machine, all for about the cost of an ordinary modem. Digital signal processor (DSP) chips will replace tapes in answering machines, so that the messages stored can be played back at any speed without distorting the speaker's voice. AT&T uses the DSP chip in its Videophone 2500, which compresses and transforms millions of pieces of video data per second into picture transmissions sent over phone lines, resulting in sharper images. In Detroit, engineers are working on an "active suspension system." If a car hits a bump at 55 miles per hour, before the tire finishes rebounding from the bump, a chip gauges the force of the impact, lifts the wheels to minimize the bounce, and then tweaks the shocks to absorb more of the remaining jolt. Active Noise and Vibration Technologies and Fiat are working together to build a "muffler-on-a-chip" for cars. Noise Cancellation Technologies plans to test its electronic muffler on a tour bus from Connecticut to Walt Disney World.[59]

By using microprocessors, companies can eliminate excessive components, reduce power consumption, increase reliability, and enhance flexibility.[60] Debbie and Randy Fields of Mrs. Fields improved reliability and flexibility of franchise operations by incorporating an innovative computer software system called Retail Operations Intelligence (ROI). "ROI is a computer system that links the 650 Mrs. Fields' cookie emporiums and bakeries to its company headquarters in Park City, Utah. This system allows store managers, district managers, and regional directors across the country to have daily contact via computer with Debbie and the rest of the company's top administrative staff."[61]

In late November of 1989, K-Mart looked as if it would be stuck with 36,000 Victorian-style Christmas dolls, each priced at $29.97. Luckily, a company computer guided managers through a series of daily markdowns that ended with all but a few of the dolls gone by Christmas—none marked down more than 25%. This computer also spotted demand for a $1.97 ornament in time to order many more, resulting in an increased bottom line of $250,000. All of this was done by Intel's 80286 microprocessors.[62]

Merrill Lynch & Co., with the help of Joseph Freitas, director of investment banking systems, integrated a $500,000 computer system based on Intel micro-processors. The system, called Mezzanine, keeps tabs on documents and distrib-utes them. A banker anywhere on the network is able to access the information electronically. Reports entered on any PC are instantly made available to other PCs on the network. The new network gives Merrill Lynch an edge over its competitors.[63]

In 1989, Motorola released a new single-chip AM-stereo receiver. "The new chip crams all of the circuitry for a complete high fidelity AM-stereo radio on a sliver of silicon." The radio is slightly bigger than a paper clip and will cost suppliers less than two dollars. It is an excellent example of miniaturization.[64]

With computers, Electronic Transaction Corp. (ETC) verifies availability of funds for checks written to giant retailers. "Just in 1991, ETC verified $35.3 billion in checks for major companies, getting the most out of using microprocessors."[65]

Principle 8: Cooperative Research and Development

Aggressively pursue product research and process research, and work closely with academic institutions and generic research establishments to develop ideas for productivity improvement.

Research and development (R&D) is important in improving total productivity. Yet, many organizations ignore it because of the cash outlays required and the slow return on investment in many cases.

Companies need to accept R&D as a long-term tool rather than a quick way of increasing profits. A company may be able to prosper without an R&D function, but before long the consequences will become apparent. Quick profit gains without the backbone of a steady R&D effort are like huge waves—they recede as fast as they advance.

By practicing this principle, organizations should be able to develop and implement many new ideas for productivity improvement at a lower cost than if they had conducted the research by themselves. Managers should take advantage of the resources available at universities, research centers, and generic research establishments such as COGENT (Cooperative Generic Technology Centers), where generic technologies in specific areas are being developed.

Managers must also keep an international perspective in everything they do in R&D, particularly in today's fast-moving organizations. There is very little room for complacency, tunnel vision, and a "follow-the-leader" attitude. Managers must keep abreast of the latest information in product designs and process technologies, through reading, continuing education, study trips, etc.

Roger Schmenner[66] analyzed 171 of the more than 1,000 plant closings by Fortune 500 manufacturers during the 1970s. He found that the most commonly cited reason for the plant closings was inefficient or outdated process technology. Even though the survey is over 25 years old, the reason is still valid today.

Rapidly changing technologies in today's competitive world affect organizations of all sizes. Many companies have their own R&D departments, though not to the extent called for by this principle. The main goal behind this principle is to help companies and industries maintain their leadership positions or gain an edge on their global competitor(s).

In Japan, cooperative ventures act as catalysts to private R&D by bringing new firms into research systems and multiplying the effectiveness of their small research budgets. Japanese experience in cooperative R&D shows that a successful cooperative research system requires a delicate balance between government support and industry leadership.[67]

Japan has had joint ventures for some 65 years with the Ministry of International Trade Industry (MITI) and Nippon Telephone and Telegraph (NTT). MITI spawned a number of consortia that have made tremendous technological advances: ICOT (Institute for New-Generation Computer Technology), created to study parallel processing; SORTEC (Synchotron Orbital Radiation Technologies), devoted to working with x-rays, lithography, and other state-of-the-art methods; and OTRC (Optoelectronics Technology Research Corp.), a 13-company venture that carries out optical integrated circuit research and development.

Many U.S. companies also follow this principle. SEMATECH (Semiconductor Manufacturing Technology Initiative) and Semiconductor Research Corp. have "...established a Centers of Excellence program, which selects outstanding universities and works closely with them to attract and maintain top-notch faculty and provide graduate students with superior technological knowledge and experience." The Consortium for Scientific Computing in Princeton, New Jersey, is composed of 13 major universities and institutions, which are contributing to making the most advanced and most powerful superconductors.[68]

The United States and Japan have also collaborated to produce superconductor film, with Bell telephone companies, Rutgers University, and NEC of Japan participating.[69]

Bilateral cooperation is common between major universities and industry. MIT received a $12 million grant from Taiwan to start an educational exchange program wherein MIT students and faculty would study and work in Taiwan, and Taiwan executives and students would attend the Sloan School of Management at MIT.[70] "When officials at the Detroit Steel Products Company wanted to learn about potential European markets for their automotive products, they called the Krannet Library at Purdue University. Researchers at the Technical Information Service found 100 articles indicating that the company's prospects in Europe might be good."[71]

Even small companies can team up with big ones. AT&T and Pyramid, a subcontractor, won a contract potentially worth $1.4 billion to supply computers to the IRS. If all went well, Pyramid would have an order worth $200 to $300 million for its mid-range computers for five years.[72]

Researchers from Bellcore teamed up with AT&T to develop new ways of providing service. Recently, they developed the smallest laser ever built, one-tenth the thickness of a human hair! The laser will be used to transmit conversations.[73]

Many Japanese companies set up labs in U.S. universities to benefit from cooperative research. In January 1989, Hitachi Chemicals Ltd. built a laboratory on the campus of the University of California at Irvine. Hitachi will most likely benefit greatly.[74]

Principle 9: Product Mix Planning

Create a mix of products or services that will result in the largest possible gains in total productivity and market share on a consistent basis.

The total productivity of a firm is the weighted sum of the total productivities of its individual products or services. By targeting a group of products or services that show consistent gains in total productivity, a company can improve its total productivity as a whole at the fastest rate possible. A company that concentrates its marketing and production efforts on products that account for most of its business and are produced at the highest efficiency possible has an excellent chance of being competitive for a very long time.

Product mix must be planned on a long-term basis (more than one year), whenever possible. Of course, in some industries, such as the toy industry, it is not always feasible to do such planning easily because of the relatively short "shelf life" of some products. Planning is essential for success because it minimizes corporate and individual stress. It is wise to plan for a product mix that can achieve the highest gains in total productivity and market share. Greater market share has a spillover effect in that it creates greater demand and, hence, more employment. Bakers' Bakery had one central facility to produce all the baked goods for its several outlets in Nebraska. This made it difficult to provide a product mix that responded to customers' expectations. Slowly, but surely, the individual stores were expanded to produce their own baked goods, thereby providing a mix of service, quality, and variety.[75]

This principle may be the most widely used of all, particularly to increase market share. Many companies produce a large variety of products. Procter & Gamble produces soaps, candles, paper goods, food items, and healthcare products. AT&T has a broad product mix, including telephones, computers, telephone-answering devices, and video phones, to name a few. Hewlett-Packard also produces a variety of products, such as palm-top computers, printers, handheld calculators, electronic instruments, and the like. Most such companies diversify their product mix to increase their total revenue base as well as their total productivity.

The service sector can also benefit from product mix. Many analytical models have been developed to maximize a bank's product mix in terms of profitability. One model considers the essential intermediate functions of a bank and uses multiple inputs and outputs to compute a scaler measure of efficiency. The efficiency metric, a proxy for management quality, is computed using a linear programming technique called data envelopment analysis. The efficiency model is based on the notion of using the metric as a variable in an equation to predict bank failures. The variables included in the model capture the importance of management in a bank's survival, namely the input allocation and product mix decisions necessary to acquire deposits and to make loans.[76]

Big companies always know what their best-selling product is, and they are constantly developing it or making changes to it. Procter & Gamble extended its successful Pringles snacks by adding new flavors and testing them.[77] Gary Muzyka, shelf management coordinator for Big Y, a grocery chain in Springfield, Massachusetts, uses his Apollo space management software from Information Resources, Inc. to determine the packet and product mix within each category of grocery items in stock.[78] Another grocery chain, Fred Meyer, found that by using Nielsen's Spaceman III software, it could better allocate sales, unit movement, and profits. Given the expense of real estate, the best products have to be in the best location, and it is imperative to optimize the space and inventory that a store has. The Barbie doll, Mattel's flagship toy, is being introduced into comic books by Marvel Comics, which already boasts six million copies in circulation, with readers mostly between 6 and 17 years old.[79]

Mattel is a vivid example of a how a single product can generate vast revenues for a company. The Barbie doll is described by Mattel's chairman as a money-maker. The company devotes significant time to changing existing models and creating new ones. For Mattel, there are two immutable rules in selling toys: (1) Nothing is forever. (2) Except Barbie.[80]

In December 1990, Pepsi and Coke were competing to see who could come out with the first bottle made out of recycled materials. The bottle would attract consumers concerned about the environment and would be less costly.[81]

"On a flight from Japan to the U.S. three years ago, David M. Friedson was playing with a new device that removed fuzz from clothing. A woman seated behind him looked at it curiously and asked if she could buy one. That was all Friedson, the president of Windmere Corp., needed to hear. He added the 'Clothes Shaver' to Windmere's lineup of blow dryers, curling irons, and other personal care appliances, and this helped boost the company's revenues by 54% that year."[82]

Managing product mix is also important. In 1990, Ford was facing a series of new federal regulations for fuel efficiency for domestic cars. At the time, a foreign car was defined as having 25% or more foreign-made parts. In order to maintain profits from the Crown Victoria and Mercury Grand Marquis, which were good sellers but were unable to meet the new regulations, Ford added extra foreign-made parts to make them available to consumers as imports.[83] During 1990, Honda had a problem with its product mix. It was exporting a conservative model that had limited appeal in Japan. To enhance the less flashy coupe, Honda added decals depicting an American eagle. The technique failed miserably.[84]

Principle 10: Secrecy

Novel ideas and productivity improvement strategies,
particularly those developed in-house, must be kept secret.

Often, managers forget this principle, mostly unconsciously and unintentionally. They give away secrets of products and processes to suppliers, vendors, visitors, and even competitors without realizing what they are doing. Product design and process technology are two important areas that must be protected carefully.

One of the largest computer companies in the world practices this principle very well. It maintains filing cabinets with different colored tags corresponding to different security classifications, makes every employee sign a confidentiality statement, and maintains a tight policy on secrecy. European and Asian companies tend to practice this principle better than U.S. companies do. This principle can be crucial in both defense-related and civilian industries.

It can be costly to violate the secrecy principle. When photos of GM's new Saturn showed up in magazines, the company offered a $30,000 reward for information.[85] Reebok lost an attempt to block the sale and distribution of a baseball glove which it claimed used its pump technology. "Reebok accused its partner in developing the technology, Design Continuum, of improperly sharing its trade secrets with Spalding."[86]

Defense contractors have to take special precautions to ensure that their technologies are protected. McDonnell Douglas employees who work on Department of Defense projects are required to have top-secret clearance and are debriefed at the end of each mission. All personnel traveling overseas sign a form specifying the reason for the trip, persons with whom they may interact, and what technical documentation they are taking with them. Processing and integration information on the space lab missions, which is public knowledge, does not require special precautions, but all personnel require official authorization to be on the premises and special clearance for access to classified information.[87]

In 1991, two scientists formerly with Merck and Schering-Plough tried to sell secret formulas and products they had stolen while working there. The formulas were worth $1.5 million in cash and bonds. Fortunately, with the FBI's cooperation, the two men were eventually captured and convicted.[88] IBM also suffered from a secrecy violation when a former IBM manager went to work for Seagate Technology. When Seagate began using an advanced disk-drive design copied from IBM, IBM filed a lawsuit against both the manager and Seagate and won a preliminary injunction. The jury prohibited Seagate from employing the manager in a position in which he was involved in the development, manufacture, or design of products involving IBM technology. This disk drive had taken IBM 20 years and $200 million to develop.[89]

This principle emphasizes that companies should keep production strategies, processes, and new products from their competitors until they are ready to roll onto the market. A case in point is Daimler-Benz, which manufactures all of the Mercedes-Benz line of automobiles. While the company was testing a minivan that it planned to launch in 1993, neither competitors nor consumers knew what the engine design would be or what options would be available.[90]

"Ricoh Corp. unveiled a digital mimeograph that prints with the resolution of the best laser printers. The prototype duplicator has a special plug for hooking up a computer so a document can go straight from a PC screen to a stencil."[91] The word "unveiled" here implies secrecy until the product was released.

Digital Equipment Corp. (DEC) wanted to compete with other major computer manufacturers. In the fall of 1989, it planned to release its most important new product—the biggest Vax ever. Code named Aridus, it was expected to allow DEC to compete with IBM for the first time.[92]

Near the summer of 1990, General Motors was planning to release a convertible version of the Chevrolet Beretta. Major competitors would not know the automobile's features until it was released.[93]

Principle 11: Mutual Benefit

For each action taken, ask how it benefits everyone—the company owners, management, employees, customers, and suppliers.

Organizations must strive to rethink their philosophies of management to practice this principle, which is one of the most important yet the most neglected one. Many so-called productivity improvement programs fail because this principle is not practiced sincerely.

Many managers assure their employees that their jobs will be secure even with productivity gains. However, when reality warrants a reduction in the work force, assurances and promises are quickly forgotten. Naturally, employees and unions mistrust management under such circumstances. If managers find retraining or relocating options when productivity improvements take place, employees and the unions would react positively, creating mutual trust and better labor–management relations.

Rewards must be given for productivity gains. It is simply fair, equitable, and just to reward those responsible for gains in total productivity. Of course, the reward system must be designed carefully. The absence of productivity gainsharing will almost always result in unenthusiastic, unhappy, and disloyal employees who may not show any commitment to future programs.

Productivity gainsharing is a subprinciple of the mutual benefit principle. E.I. Du Pont's fiber department implemented gainsharing to help employees participate in the profits and losses of the department. The company sets a goal as a percentage level. If the level is met, the employees receive additional pay; if the goal is not met, the employees do not.[94] South Metropolitan Gas Company (South Met) implemented the gainsharing technique in 1889, making it one of the first companies to implement and maintain the profit-sharing scheme in the U.K.[95] Chrysler Corporation's Acustar profit-sharing technique resulted in a

20% decline in absenteeism, a 30% drop in grievances, and a big reduction in defective parts.[96]

Lawrence S. Phillips, PVH's chairman, offered an incentive of $1 million to each of his ten senior executives if the company's earnings per share grew at a 35% compound annual rate during the four years ending in January 1992.[97] The Motorola manufacturing plant in Guadalajara, Mexico, increased its productivity because the new management motivated and recognized the employees. Dick Wintermantel, the newly assigned manager for the Guadalajara plant, noticed that employees had a clear definition of their mission, but lacked a vision at all levels of production. In addition, poor morale and a high inflation rate were affecting the country. Wintermantel came up with the program "Transformation for Excellence," which basically consisted of making the vision of the company public in the work area as well as the surrounding community.[98] At Ross, employers recognized employees with "you did a great job," and employees were also compensated with cash awards. President Dick Gast was motivated to give these awards by the company's slogan: "At Ross You're Working in the Company of Excellence."[99] When family issues were affecting productivity at the Marriott Corporation, the company created a "Work and Family Life" department, an on-site child care center, and other benefits such as a family care spending account and family seminars.[100] United Electric Controls offered chuck wagons, golf games, and many other types of incentive programs designed to inspire employee involvement and to boost company spirit. The company's labor productivity increased significantly.[101] Levi Strauss & Co. developed a personal computer system (OLIVER) for its employees to view their total compensation package. This enabled employees to keep track of their remuneration and also motivated them to be productive.[102] Thomas Denton, vice president for human resources at Barnes Hospital in St. Louis, put it best: "...the beauty of gainsharing is that the money you pay out is essentially free if you structure the plan the right way. You are only paying the employees a portion of a gain that did not exist before. There is no downside risk, since there's no payment if there's no gain."[103]

Principle 12: Consistency

It is better to be good consistently than to be perfect occasionally.

Productivity improvement must be an ongoing, day-to-day process instead of a one-time project. Both people and enterprises tend to "jump on the bandwagon" whenever a new concept, or an old one in new form, is introduced, without truly analyzing its relevance. We seem to adopt something new simply because it is the "fashion" of the day. Often, companies behave this way for prestige rather than out of real need.

Productivity and quality improvement are necessary conditions at all times. When quality and productivity are improving at a comfortable pace, there may be a tendency to gradually ignore them and focus on other issues. Such an attitude can result in a crisis situation a few years down the road. It is wiser to be consistent in productivity and quality improvement efforts.

In any organization, whether for-profit or non-profit, there is a need to consistently offer the best product or service at the lowest possible cost in the shortest time possible. Only consistent, honest efforts can ensure this result, irrespective of the importance associated with the terms "productivity" or "quality." "Total productivity thinking" must be as much a routine in an organization as the production, selling, and accounting functions are. TPmgt is a consistent process, and those who practice this principle can stay ahead of the competition. Consistency and continuity command courage. One has to be bold to keep this management process going, with unwavering commitment and determination.

This principle emphasizes that the previous 11 principles must be practiced consistently. All employees and managers must strive to "improve the improved." Procter & Gamble uses the continuous improvement approach to maintain consistency in commitment. The company has a quality policy that resembles this principle. Even though it is not geared toward productivity, it helps the company increase its productivity, because an increase in quality always leads to increases in total productivity in the long run.

When Motorola received the Malcolm Baldrige Award in 1988, it was in the early stages of an ambitious plan that will hopefully be realized some time soon. The goal is to achieve Six Sigma quality—99.9997% defect-free products, or 3.4 defects per 1 million units in its product line.[104] Today, the company is at around 5.6 Sigma.

AT&T Credit Corp. applied the consistency principle in its lease process function. "In 1986, AT&TCC set up 11 teams of 10 to 15 newly hired workers in a high volume division serving small businesses. The three major lease processing functions were combined in each team. No longer were calls from customers shunted from department to department. The company also divided its national staff of field agents into seven regions, and assigned two or three teams to handle business from each region. Thus, the same teams always worked with the same sales staff."[105] This change increased the company's productivity and eliminated excessive time spent on other activities.

9.3 RULES FOR MAXIMUM SUCCESS WITH TPmgt

During the past 17 years, TPmgt has been applied in various parts of the world. Based on the lessons learned from these experiences, the following ten rules are proposed to ensure success when applying the TPmgt concept, philosophy, and methodology, either partially or completely.

Rule #1: Treat People with Mutual Respect and Trust

People want to be treated with dignity and to do a good job. Unfortunately, sometimes economic, social, cultural, political, and/or environmental factors get in the way. In TPmgt thinking, the worth of every person is valued. Each individual adds value to the organization. Without mutual respect and trust, it is difficult to get the best out of people, to create team spirit, and to develop the synergy that fosters creativity.

Mutual respect is a necessary condition for total productivity improvement. Everyone is an important part of the company's existence, survival, and profitability, and everyone wants to be respected, regardless of his or her rank, position, educational background, social status, culture, gender, or ethnic background. The Golden Rule translates into a practical principle: "Treat others the way you would like them to treat you."

At Bendix's Safety Restraints Division (for air bags), operators are trusted for their integrity and for their responsible nature. There is no inspection department. Workers are trained to be "production technicians," not merely line workers. They are responsible for their own quality, productivity and machine set-ups. One worker commented: "I could not sleep at night if I wasn't sure that we were doing the right things."[106]

Rule #2: In All Your Products and Services, Be an Innovator, Not an Imitator—Be a Leader, Not a Follower

This second rule of success for TPmgt says that companies must be innovators, not imitators. They must be proactive, not reactive, even though it is more difficult to innovate than to imitate. Organizations that constantly innovate and improve, without depending on their competition to set the tone, tend to improve total productivity more rapidly.

Sony, whose Walkman became a big hit in the mid-1980s, is a good example of an innovator. You can walk into any electronics store in the United States or Japan and find dozens of varieties of Sony's Walkman. It changed the entire concept of the radio. The 3M Company produces more than 60,000 different products. Innovation is 3M's main key to success. Citibank's Citigold, introduced in 1993, has been a major success because it is unique in the banking industry.

Another aspect of this rule is that organizations must be leaders, not followers. A product leader usually has an advantage in capturing market share first. Further, a product leader that enters the market with a product or service before the competition does can indeed claim being the pioneer in that type of product or service, at least until another company comes out to compete. The leader has a mental advantage in the marketplace. Enterprises that are product leaders have a greater opportunity to create higher demand and command greater market share. As a result, they utilize their capital equipment and resources much more effectively and efficiently. A company with a 90% capacity utilization can distribute its depreciation costs over a larger number of products than a company with just 50%. The greater the market share, the greater the demand and capacity, which translates into greater long-term growth and profitability.

Rule #3: Apply "3-P Thinking" in Everything You Do

The third rule for success in TPmgt is the *3-P formula*:[107]

$$S = P_1 \times P_2 \times P_3$$

where S = success, P_1 = planning, P_2 = preparation, and P_3 = patience.

In any successful venture, planning, preparation, and patience are important ingredients. Suppose that planning and preparation are 100% (1.0) and patience is 100% (or 1.0). Then, $1.0 \times 1.0 \times 1.0 = 1$, or 100%. That is, the perceived notion of success will be 100%. Often, when implementing a new concept, many companies quickly become enthusiastic and implement the concept hurriedly. They do not consider all the variables that can enter the picture. They want quick results, so their preparation may be fairly good, but their planning and patience are deplorable, particularly their patience. They don't want to wait even a few days, let alone a few months, before seeing the results. When the results are not realized, they blame the concept and the implementor(s), but do not ascribe the failure to lack of thinking through the 3-P's carefully.

In the context of TPmgt implementation, companies should consciously think through the 3-P's. First, they have to know what TPmgt is all about. What are its elements? What are its positive and negative features? Is the company environment ready for it? All this is part of the planning process. Next, companies have to meticulously prepare for the implementation, making sure that all the necessary facilities are available, with proper resources and training. Finally, they must have patience for the implementation to be successful. Often, companies waste hundreds of millions of dollars on a new concept, simply because their 3-P's were very low. The concept is not necessarily at fault. Instead, they have to carefully do the *planning* and the *preparation* and then wait *patiently* for the results.

Some companies plan ahead only as far as two or three years and think they are doing a great job. Yet other companies, in the Far East, for example, plan ahead 50 years, some even 200 years! The Japanese healthcare product and technology leader, Nikken, has a 100-year business plan, and Mr. Masuda, its founder, talks of the 22nd century already! It may seem unrealistic to plan this far ahead, but those companies that plan on such a long-term basis take into consideration many possible scenarios within the realm of their knowledge and imagination. By being prepared for the worst scenarios, an organization can minimize the chance of a narrow win and minimize the maximum risk.

In implementing TPmgt, it is important to carefully think through the 3-P's before following through. This is a difficult but important rule for maximizing the success potential with total productivity management.

Motorola became the first Baldrige Award winner in 1988. It did not set a target of winning the award. A process that began in 1981 happened to result in the award, and Motorola continues to baffle its competitors with the continued success of its products. In 1981, the company put into effect a plan to improve its products and processes by a factor of 10 over five years. The company discovered that what works to achieve continuous improvement on the manufacturing side can translate 100% to the non-manufacturing side as well.[108]

Rule #4: Implement Total Productivity Gainsharing

The ninth step in the implementation of TPmgt is total productivity gainsharing. Many companies follow everything in the TPmgt implementation process, but hesitate when it comes to implementing the gainsharing aspect. That is precisely why TPmgt fails to achieve its full potential, because the very essence of the concept is an equitable gainsharing process to reward all who have been a part of the success. Without total productivity gainsharing, TPmgt can still be successful, but with it, the maximum potential of TPmgt is realized. If top management is not completely committed to total productivity gainsharing with the employees, the full benefits of TPmgt will not be realized. The pre-TPmgt steps of the TPmgt implementation process (outline in Chapter 4) ensure up front that companies do not implement TPmgt if the "environment" is inappropriate.

Rule #5: Be Optimistic in Managing Change

While implementing the TPmgt system, there is certainly going to be a change. People tend to resist change, because it usually brings surprises. Fortunately, change also brings positive results when it is effected properly according to Rule #3 (the 3-P formula). Change is difficult to cope with when the 3-P's are not in place. Skepticism about implementing TPmgt can turn out to be a self-fulfilling prophesy. Optimism is a forerunner of great achievement and an important part of making the TPmgt concept work. If an enterprise plans its implementation carefully, executes the plan meticulously, and has the patience to see the entire process through rather than coming to a hasty judgment and abandoning it, then TPmgt is poised for success.

Rule #6: Manage Technology in a Holistic Sense

Many companies do not understand the importance of managing technologies, and they end up paying a high price for it. This is particularly true in companies where expensive capital equipment is involved. Every dollar must be spent wisely when investing in equipment, yet companies do not plan carefully for a technological change. The field of management of technology is relatively new; it was formally defined in 1987 by the National Research Council. A company has to manage technology from the right perspective in today's world, particularly when the enterprise is multinational or global. The Total Productivity Model, which includes the cost of usage of technology as one of the input factors, can help in choosing the right technology at the right time for a given target level of profit, as described in some of the case studies in Chapter 5 and the discussion of the technology–total productivity relationship in Chapter 6.

Rule #7: Insist on Interdisciplinary Emphasis, Not Functional Bureaucracies

Today's technological, social, and economic factors cannot be treated in isolation because they are too complex. With TPmgt, everything can be viewed through a systemic lens. Social factors are just as important as technological factors, and both are just as critical as economic factors. As organizations become more complex and diversified in terms of products and resources, emphasis on an interdisciplinary approach to managing becomes more significant.

A well-known example of highly interdisciplinary thinking is "simultaneous engineering" (or "concurrent engineering"), used by Ford Motor Company during development of the Taurus. Unlike the traditional design approach, where product engineering is isolated from market research, production engineering is isolated from product engineering, and so on, representatives from marketing, design, production, distribution, vendors, and customers acted as an interdisciplinary team right from the very conception of the Taurus. They looked at all aspects of building the car. They reviewed market research reports which identified customer preferences and tastes. Next, design engineers came up with designs that were aesthetically pleasing and functionally excellent. Production engineers examined those designs and made necessary changes to produce the car. Distribution analyzed what would make the car sell. Everybody worked as a team right from the beginning. As a result, total turnaround time from conception to production was reduced by a considerable margin, and the car became one of the best-selling models in the United States. It won the Car of the Year Award from *Motor Trend* magazine the year it was introduced.

Interdisciplinary thinking is a necessity in complex organizations, particularly in today's dynamic, technologically complex, interdependent environment. TPmgt emphasizes interdisciplinary thinking. Bureaucracy has crept into organizations as a result of a functional emphasis. This structure is irrelevant and counterproductive for today's enterprises, which simply cannot afford such regimentation. Involving teams of people from all relevant disciplines and functional areas within a company will ensure good results with TPmgt.

Rule #8: Have Many Team Builders Instead of a Few Superstars

When there is a question about a job design, often the workers doing the job come up with a better answer than the engineers who designed it. Workers who have been doing a job for many years know it better than anyone else. Employees must be recognized for their talent and be allowed to contribute their ideas.

Positive reinforcement should be an important part of the team-building process. If we tell people they are good and are capable of being better, they indeed will rise to that level of expectation. When we reason with people and provide them positive reinforcement, they do the job well. At work, we often complain about people not doing their jobs. But have they really been given the positive reinforcement they are looking for? Have they been given a "pat on the back" when they did a good job? Have they been given the necessary tools to overcome a problem?

Positive reinforcement is a very important factor in motivating teams and individuals. The synergy from teams is more significant than the contributions of a few superstars. The concept of expert systems is to harness the talents and experience of people who have worked on a particular project or product for several years. When we recognize the importance of "human expert systems," we are essentially recognizing the merit of experience. But how do you build experience? You have to create an environment where there is job security for everyone, not just for a few. A good way to do so is to create and nurture high-performance teams. By harnessing the group wisdom and experience of teams, we can avoid the need to fix the same old mistakes. Every defect has an impact on the real cost of quality. By forming and sustaining high-performance teams through motivation, TPmgt can be enhanced significantly.

Rule #9: Practice "Management by Example"

We should not expect from others that which we do not do ourselves. Managers often fail to get results from their subordinates because they themselves do not know how to do the job. They have not been trained properly. We can achieve more when we are consistent. In the context of TPmgt, we must strive for total productivity gains on a consistent basis instead of just once in a while.

If managers do not practice what they preach, how can they expect employees to achieve the management's goals? TPmgt believes in teamwork, shared responsibility, joint privileges, and shared rewards. For consistent success with TPmgt, everyone, starting with top management, must set an example as a good role model. People tend to emulate the behavior of others. One good example is worth a hundred slogans or tons of empty rhetoric. A servant model of managing people is probably the most effective yet most difficult to practice consistently. Supervisors have to be trained to be "servant-managers" or "servant-leaders"—with strong positive personal qualities, a penchant for servitude, and enormous faith in people's talents and abilities.

Rule #10: Aim High, So You Can Reach High

In everything an organization does in managing its resources, it must try to achieve perfection, so that the products or services it generates will appeal to its customers. We may think that we have to pay a high price for perfection, but often that is not really the case.

Perfection is difficult to define because everyone has a different perception of it. Someone who sets a goal of achieving "perfection" and achieves 50% of his or her imaginary "perfection level" probably does a better job than someone who achieves 80% of the normal level of achievement. My motto is: "Excellence is my starting point and perfection, my ultimate goal." When I strive for perfection, I am working from a starting point which is excellent, not just good or fair. This type of thinking is equally feasible for an enterprise, but it cannot be infused in a company overnight. Top management personnel must set an example of striving passionately for perfection and excellence.

In TPmgt, when we try to achieve the very best, human input may go up. On the other hand, material, energy, and capital input will be streamlined as a result of such thinking. Thus, we might save money on the other input factors even if human input is increased. In the long run, total productivity should actually increase to a level beyond the break-even point, thereby creating a profit situation. Therefore, if you want TPmgt to be truly successful, you have to be infatuated with the word "perfection."

QUESTIONS TO PONDER

9.1   If your enterprise is in manufacturing, identify the fundamental similarities between your company and one in the service sector. If your company is in the service sector, do the same for a company in manufacturing. What differences, if any, are dominant?

9.2   Analyze the extent to which the quality/perfection principle (Principle 1) has been applied in your company and the positive and negative effects it has had. If this principle has not been applied, develop an action plan for implementing it, to present to company officials.

9.3   Answer the above question for each of the other 11 principles presented in this chapter.

9.4   Consider each of the ten rules for maximum success with TPmgt. Which of these rules are the most critical for your enterprise? Discuss the reasons why.

9.5   Which of the 12 principles would be the most difficult to implement? Analyze and discuss the reasons why.

9.6   Which of the 12 principles would be the easiest to implement? Analyze and discuss the reasons why.

9.7   Which of the ten rules would be the most challenging to implement? Analyze and discuss the reasons why.

9.8   Which of the ten rules would be the easiest to implement? Analyze and discuss the reasons why.

9.9   What additional principles and rules would you add to those discussed in the chapter? Discuss your reasons for doing so.

9.10 Reflect upon the possibility of applying one or more of the 12 principles to yourself as an individual. If appropriate, practice them at a personal level. Keep a journal or diary for three months. Then, analyze your experience by writing down the three most important insights you have gained. Share them with at least five people.

REFERENCES AND NOTES

1. Kolcum, Ed, "Harris Eyes ATC Voice Network Award as Boost to Global Expansion Plans," *Aviation Week & Space Technology,* pp. 38–39, Jan. 20, 1992.
2. Peters, T.J. and Waterman, R.H. Jr., *In Search of Excellence: Lessons from America's Best-Run Companies,* Warner Books, New York, 1982, pp. 156–199.
3. Kolter, J.P., "What Leaders Really Do," *Harvard Business Review,* p. 106, May–June 1990.
4. Dertouzos, M.C., "America Can Regain Its Edge," *Boardroom Reports,* Vol. 19, No. 10, pp. 9–10, May 1990.
5. Mukerjee, Sad, "Around the World," *Automotive News,* p. 32, July 2, 1990.
6. Burner, Richard, "Hungary Plant," *Automotive News,* p. 34, June 1991.
7. Burner, Richard, "Mazda to Make Transmissions in Thai," *Automotive News,* p. 38, May 1990.
8. Chappell, Lindsay, "Mitsubishi Tags Eclipse for Europe," *Automotive News,* p. 3, July 2, 1990.
9. "Software Offer from Xerox," *New York Times,* p. D3, Sept. 20, 1990.
10. Gumbel, Peter, "Pact with U.S. Firms Is Pet Soviet Project," *Wall Street Journal,* p. A12, March 31, 1989.
11. Nain, Jeremy, "How to Go Global and Why," *Fortune,* pp. 70–76, Aug. 28, 1989.
12. Coy, P., "Northern Telecom Takes a Big but Careful Step," *Business Week,* p. 46, Nov. 26, 1990.
13. McNamee, M. and Mangnusson, P., "Think Globally, Survive Locally," *Business Week,* p. 51, Nov. 26, 1990.
14. Oster, P. and Reichlin, I., "Toys 'R' Us: Making Europe its Playpen," *Business Week,* p. 89, Jan. 20, 1992.
15. Protzman, Ferdinand, "Coke's Splash in Eastern Germany," *New York Times,* p. D1, May 3, 1991.
16. Phillips, R.A., "Why Improve Productivity," *Business Quarterly,* pp. 64–67, Winter 1984.
17. Bylinsky, Gene, "A U.S. Comeback in Electronics," *Fortune,* p. 77, April 20, 1992.
18. Ibid., p. 112.
19. Brown, Warren, "How Long a Wait for the Car of the Future?" *Washington Post,* p. H1, Aug. 11, 1991.
20. "Bright Lights in Tiny Packages," *Environment,* p. 23, July/Aug. 1989.

21. "Fake Fat as Filling as the Real Thing," *Business Week,* p. 130, May 6, 1991.
22. Verity, John W., "The PCs that Please the Users Most," *Business Week,* p. 132E, Nov. 12, 1990.
23. Verity, John J., "Toshiba's New Laptop May Be Small But It's The Real Thing," *Business Week,* p. 136F, July 17, 1989.
24. Freundlich, N., "The Smallest Copier Yet Prints on About Anything," *Business Week,* p. 48, July 3, 1989.
25. 1992 Annual Report of the Dunn & Bradstreet Corporation, p. 7.
26. Hoffman, S., Omark, R., Omark, S., and Wallace, L.J., The Application of the Twelve Productivity Improvement Principles to the McDonnell Douglas Space Systems Company–Kennedy Space Center Division, Class Project Report, June 26, 1992, pp. 23–24.
27. "Fuji Photo to Use Kodak CD System," *New York Times,* p. D3, Sept. 13, 1991.
28. Blanca Reimer, "America's New Rush to Europe," *Business Week,* p. 48, March 26, 1990.
29. U.S. Correspondence, "Coca-Cola Toys with Huge Mattel Promotion," *Marketing,* p. 16, Sept. 1990.
30. Bangsberg, P.T., "P&G Reported Expanding Production in China," *Journal of Commerce and Commercial,* p. D4, Jan. 16, 1991.
31. Schiller, Z. and Holden, T., "P&G Goes Global by Acting Like a Local," *Business Week,* p. 58, Aug. 28, 1989.
32. Kapstein, J. and Toy, S., "Mitsubishi Is Taking a Back Road into Europe," *Business Week,* p. 64, Nov. 19, 1990.
33. Magnusson, P., "American Cable Is Lassoing Foreign Markets," *Business Week,* p. 70, Aug. 14, 1989.
34. Shao, M. and Neff, R., "For Levi's a Flattering Fit Overseas," *Business Week,* p. 76, Nov. 5, 1991.
35. Lewis, G., "Hewlett Packard Makes Friends in the RISC Market," *Business Week,* p. 66, March 26, 1990.
36. Seal, G.M., "1990's—Years of Promise, Years of Peril for U.S. Manufacturing," *Industrial Engineering,* Vol. 22, No. 1, pp. 18–21, Jan. 1990.
37. Robinson, J., "An Expert in Every Port," *Design News,* Vol. 43, pp. 117–118, Feb. 9, 1987.
38. Cardenas, D., Letizia, C., Morton, G., and Trueba, L., Principles of Productivity Improvement at Saturn, Class Report, April 1994, p. 11.
39. Byrne, John A., "Profits from the Nonprofits," *Business Week,* p. 66, March 26, 1990.
40. "How to Create Harmony at Work," *Fortune,* p. 14, Nov. 19, 1990.
41. Filipowski, D., "The Tao of Tandem," *Personnel Journal,* p. 72, Oct. 1991.
42. Gunsch, D., "Employees Team Up with HR," *Personnel Journal,* p. 68, Oct. 1991.
43. Ellis, J., "Monsanto Is Teaching Old Workers New Tricks," *Business Week,* p. 67, Aug. 29, 1989.
44. Norman, Carol A. and Zawacki, Robert A., "Team Appraisals—Team Approach," *Personnel Journal,* p. 101, Sept. 1991.

45. Barnes, Ralph M., *Time Study Design and Management of Work,* 7th edition, John Wiley, New York, p. 548.
46. Robins, Gary, "Bretts—A Smaller Retailer's View," *Stores,* p. 23, Feb. 1992.
47. Weiner, Edith, "Business in the 21st Century," *The Futurist,* p. 14, March–April 1992.
48. Macaulay, S., "Allied-Signal's Pragmatic Visionary," *Production,* Vol. 100, No. 6, pp. 62–65, June 1988.
49. Maskey, Mary A., "Design Decisions: Memories of Big American Cars Come into Play When Stylists Penned the Lexus and Infiniti Luxury Models," *Automotive News,* pp. E38–39, March 27, 1989.
50. Sanger, David E., "Japan's Luxury Car Gains Pose New Threat to Rivals," *New York Times,* pp. A1, D5, Jan. 3, 1990.
51. Henkoff, Ronald, "What Motorola Learns from Japan," *Fortune,* pp. 157–164, April 24, 1992.
52. Zurier, Steve "Distributors Join Forces to Help Heidel Harris," *The Daily Distributor,* p. 1, March 1, 1992.
53. Ensolow, Beth, "The Benchmarking Bonanza," *Across the Board,* p. 16, April 1992.
54. Isaacs III, McAllister, "Italy's Machine Builders Bank on ITMA for Rebound," *Textile World,* pp. 40–46, March 1992.
55. Barrett, Amy, "After-Sales Service = Infiniti," *FW,* p. 49, April 14, 1992.
56. Weber, J., "Programming in Pascal Is Getting Even Easier," *Business Week,* p. 84E, July 10, 1989.
57. Gross, N., "IBM Clones a Strategy from the Clonemakers," *Business Week,* p. 42, Aug. 21, 1991.
58. Allen, L., "A Selection Guide to AS/R Systems," *Industrial Engineering,* p. 28, March 1992.
59. McWillimas, Gary, "Putting a Concert Hall on a Chip," *Business Week,* pp. 90–91, April 13, 1992.
60. Sumanth, D.J., *Productivity Engineering and Management,* McGraw Hill, New York, 1984.
61. Schember, J., "Mrs. Fields' Secret Weapon," *Personnel Journal,* p. 56, Sept. 1991.
62. Armstrong, L., "Teradata Gets Magic from a Gang of Microchips," *Business Week,* p. 124, Nov. 26, 1990.
63. Schwartz, Evan I., "The Dinosaur that Cost Merrill Lynch a Million a Year," *Business Week,* p. 122, Nov. 26, 1990.
64. Freundlich, N., "Stereos that Make a Walkman Seem Weighty," *Business Week,* p. 89, July 10, 1989.
65. Yang, Doris J., "Where Gloom and Doom Equal Boom," *Business Week,* p. 66, Jan. 13, 1992.
66. Schmenner, Roger, W., "Every Factory Has a Life Cycle," *Harvard Business Review,* pp. 121–129, March–April 1983.
67. Heaton, George, "Cooperative R&D in Japan," *Chemtech,* pp. 14–17, Jan. 1990.
68. Barron, Janet J., "Consortia: High-Tech Co-ops," *BYTE,* p. 269, June 1990.
69. "New Ventures in Electronics," *New York Times,* p. D16, April 5, 1989.

70. "M.I.T. to Get Taiwan Grant," *New York Times,* p. D5, Dec. 20, 1991.
71. Nicklin, Julie L., *The Chronicle of Higher Education,* Vol. 78, No. 24, p. A29, Feb. 19, 1992.
72. Wiegner, Kathleen K., "Teamwork," *Forbes,* p. 106, Aug. 19, 1991.
73. Smith, Emily T., "Supersmall Lasers May Be the Key to Supersmart Computers," *Business Week,* p. 73, Aug. 7, 1989.
74. Oran, Daniel P. and Gross, N., "Advanced Bio Class? That's Over in Hitachi Hall," *Business Week,* p. 73, Aug. 7, 1989.
75. Linsen, Mary Ann, "Bakers' Bakery Living Up to Its Name," *Progressive Grocer,* pp. 131–132, Sept. 1991.
76. Siems, Thomas F., "Quantifying Management's Role in Bank Survival," *Economic Review,* p. 29, Jan. 1992.
77. "Food: P&G," *Advertising Age,* p. 44, Sept. 30, 1991.
78. Michael, Gary, "Managing Space from the Top," *Progressive Grocer,* p. 81, March 1992.
79. Fitzerald, Kate, "Comic Book Barbie," *Advertising Age,* p. 48, Jan. 14, 1992.
80. Morgenson, G., "Barbie Does Budapest," *Forbes,* p. 66, Jan. 7, 1991.
81. Collingwood, H., "Coke and Pepsi Rush to Go Green," *Business Week,* p. 38, Dec. 17, 1990.
82. De George, G., "Windmere Tries to Comb Out the Kinks," *Business Week,* p. 44, July 24, 1989.
83. Carey, J., "More Fords Will Be Imports," *Business Week,* p. 36, July 3, 1989.
84. Miller, Karen L. and Treece, James B., "Honda's Nightmare: Maybe You Can't Go Home Again," *Business Week,* p. 36, Dec. 24, 1990.
85. "Ex-Aide Held in GM Theft," *New York Times,* p. D7, Oct. 22, 1990.
86. "Reebok is Denied a Ban on Glove," *New York Times,* p. B5, Aug. 2, 1991.
87. Koopman, M. and Reile, G.M., The Application of the 12 Principles of Productivity Improvement at McDonnell Douglas Space Systems Company–Kennedy Space Center Division, Class Project Report, June 1992, p. 9
88. Carley, William M. "The Sting," *Wall Street Journal,* p. A1, Sept. 6, 1991.
89. "IBM Wins Injunction Against Seagate's Use of Disk-Drive Design," *Wall Street Journal,* p. B5, Jan. 6, 1992.
90. Hoensscheidt, W., "Mercedes Minivan Cruises Toward '93 Debut," *Automotive News,* p. 35, May 7, 1990.
91. Port, O., "Coming Soon to a School Near You: The Mimeograph," *Business Week,* p. 97, July 31, 1989.
92. Sicking, M.A., "DEC Has One Little Word for 30,000 Employees: Sell," *Business Week,* p. 86, Aug. 14, 1989.
93. Conelly, M., "Delays Rain on New Chevy, Dodge Ragtops," *Automotive News,* p. 1, May 7, 1990.
94. Joyce E., Santora, "Compensation," *Personnel Journal,* p. 72, Dec. 1989.
95. Lindop, Esmond, "The Turbulent Birth of British Profit-Sharing," *Personnel Management,* p. 44, Jan. 1989.

96. Casey, Mike, "Chrysler Plant Pays Big Bonuses," *WARD's Auto World,* p. 61, May 1990.

97. Knowlton, Christopher, "11 Men's Million-Dollar Motivator," *Fortune,* p. 65, April 9, 1990.

98. Banning, Kent and Wintermantel, Dick, "Motorola Turns Visions to Profits," *Personnel Journal,* p. 51, Feb. 1991.

99. Koch, Jennifer J., "Ross Employees Are in the Company of Excellence," *Personnel Journal,* p. 108, June 1990.

100. Solomon, Charlene M., "Marriott's Family Matters," *Personnel Journal,* p. 40, Oct. 1991.

101. Gunsh, D., "Award Programs at Home," *Personnel Journal,* p. 85, Sept. 1991.

102. Laabs, Jennifer J., "OLIVER: A Twist on Communication," *Personnel Journal,* p. 79, Sept. 1991.

103. Droste, T., "Gainsharing: The Newest Way to Up Productivity," *Hospitals,* p. 71, June 1987.

104. Cook, Brian M., "In Search of Six Sigma: 99.9997% Defect-Free," *Industry Week,* pp. 60–61, Oct. 1, 1990.

105. Hoerr, J., "Benefits for the Back Office Too," *Business Week,* p. 59, July 10, 1989.

106. Vasilash, Gary, "Failure Isn't an Option," *Production*, pp. 38–39, April 1992.

107. Developed by D.J. Sumanth, ©David J. Sumanth.

108. Bergstrom, Robin, "You Go Flat Out," *Production,* pp. 38–40, Nov. 1991.

10   WHERE TO GO FROM HERE?

I have attempted to synthesize approximately 15,000 pages of my past 25 years of theoretical and empirical research and personal observations in this book. Needless to say, many facets of Total Productivity Management (TPmgt™) may be difficult to grasp completely through this work alone. However, it is sincerely hoped that the time-tested concepts, principles, and methodologies presented here will be further validated, with new insights replacing the old ones and old insights reinforced by new findings. Empirical testing is not only desirable but highly encouraged. It will be fascinating to hear from those of you who put this work to further tests.

In the meantime, as refinements continue to be made, the following blueprint for action is recommended.

10.1 BLUEPRINT FOR ACTION

For any enterprise—private or public, in any country around the world—TPmgt can be a timely, refreshingly different but relevant approach to managing all resources (human, material, capital, energy, and others) for maximum effectiveness and efficiency.

The blueprint for action to infuse TPmgt into an enterprise depends on where the enterprise is situated in the *organization culture status tree* (OCST). In recent times, total quality management (TQM) and reengineering have become two of the most commonly implemented management concepts. Let's consider the possible states of organizational culture with one, both, or neither of these two concepts in any given enterprise, as represented in the OCST in Figure 10.1.

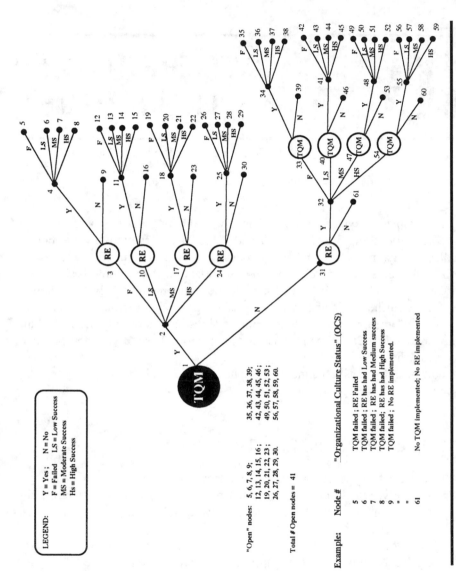

LEGEND:

Y = Yes;   N = No
F = Failed   LS = Low Success
MS = Moderate Success
Hs = High Success

"Open" nodes: 5, 6, 7, 8, 9;
                12, 13, 14, 15, 16;
                19, 20, 21, 22, 23;
                26, 27, 28, 29, 30.

                35, 36, 37, 38, 39;
                42, 43, 44, 45, 46;
                49, 50, 51, 52, 53;
                56, 57, 58, 59, 60.

Total # Open nodes = 41

Example:	Node #	"Organizational Culture Status" (OCS)
	5	TQM failed ; RE Failed
	6	TQM failed ; RE has had Low Success
	7	TQM failed ; RE has had Medium success
	8	TQM failed; RE has had High Success
	9	TQM failed ; No RE implemented.
	"	"
	61	No TQM Implemented; No RE implemented

FIGURE 10.1 The Organization Culture Status Tree of an enterprise that has (or has not) implemented TQM and reengineering (RE).

An enterprise may be at one of 41 possible states of organizational culture, represented by the 41 "open" nodes in Figure 10.1. Node 61 is the only one where the enterprise has implemented neither TQM nor reengineering. Thus, node 61 is a possible state where TPmgt might be introduced. Now let's consider another node. Tracing through the OCST, we find that the state of organizational culture at node 19 indicates that TQM was implemented with moderate success and reengineering failed. Let's suppose the enterprise wants to introduce TPmgt at this point. Clearly, the blueprint for action to infuse TPmgt must carefully consider the factors that resulted in the current state of affairs; otherwise, TPmgt is bound to fail miserably because the organizational factors contributing to the present state at node 19 have not been taken into consideration before introducing TPmgt. (Incidentally, the OCST can be used to plan the introduction of any new concept.)

From the OCST in Figure 10.1, we can see, for example, that an enterprise

- Will likely have high success with TPmgt if the enterprise is at nodes 8, 15, 22, 29, 38, 45, 52, or 59
- Will likely have the least success with TPmgt if its organizational culture corresponds to nodes 5, 12, 19, 26, 35, 42, 49, or 56

The OCST can be an extremely powerful tool for dealing with organizational change. Often, the contributing factors are not viewed in such an analytical manner. If they were, more companies would be more successful in implementing powerful management approaches such as TQM and reengineering.

By carefully analyzing the path corresponding to the node at which a company wants to introduce TPmgt, chances of committing the mistakes of the past are minimized, and the positive aspects of implementations of previous concepts are accentuated. By following the systematic, proven methodology for TPmgt implementation outlined in Chapter 4, and by paying attention to the ten rules for success with TPmgt in Chapter 9, a company increases its chances of a highly effective TPmgt infusion.

Another consideration in drawing up the blueprint for action is deciding whether to pilot test TPmgt or institutionalize it throughout the company in one big sweep. This is a critical decision before jumping into the implementation. In very small organizations (with 200 or fewer employees), it may be appropriate to go ahead with TPmgt on a company-wide basis. However, in a medium-size or large company, particularly one that is global in nature, it is not only pragmatic but also wise to introduce TPmgt on a pilot basis for about one-and-a-half years and then draw up a blueprint to infuse the concept throughout the company. One of the attractive aspects of the planned perspective of the TPmgt concept is that new tools, techniques, and concepts can be assimilated with core concepts (see Figure 4.2). Therefore, a company does not have to develop a new implementation scheme every time a new concept emerges. The same 10-step process (for Basic TPmgt) and 12-step process (for Comprehensive TPmgt) described in Chapter 4 can be iterated. This approach to implementation can save companies money in hiring consultants. A preferred approach is for the TPmgt Team to hire a consulting firm to implement a new concept within the TPmgt process and under close supervision of the TPmgt Team. The TPmgt Team should be the only official arm of the organization to communicate the TPmgt process to the employees. The outside consultants should not be given free rein to use their own pet programs to the detriment of a carefully designed and thoughtfully implemented blueprint for action developed by the TPmgt Team.

10.2 NEED FOR FORMAL EDUCATION AND TRAINING IN TPmgt

A common idea in corporations is to drastically cut education and training budgets when times are tough. They do not realize that one of the reasons times are tough is that they have ignored the constant education and training of their employees. In today's organizations, updating the knowledge and skills of the work force is an ongoing necessity, not a luxury. As pointed out in Chapter 3, there are at least 70 different techniques available to improve total productivity and/or comprehensive total productivity, and the list is growing by about ten every five years. No company can afford to ignore the fact that the competition is trying to outwit it. The learning organization, according to Peter Senge (Director of the Systems Thinking and Organizational Learning Program at MIT's Sloan School of Management), is one that treats its "learning disabilities" with a great deal of commitment, tenacity of purpose, and patience.[1]

An enterprise constantly engaged in learning newly emerging tools, techniques, and technologies is a progressive one, trying to stay one step ahead. As pointed out in Chapter 2, transnational strategic alliances are becoming quite common because of the realization that even companies that are leaders in market share and product perception can leverage their leadership through the knowledge of competitors. The Ford–Mazda and GM–Toyota ventures are two examples of such alliances that compete and cooperate simultaneously. This partnership is a two-way street and flourishes when both partners strive to acquire greater knowledge in their respective areas of strength. Companies can take full advantage of the continuing education opportunities at universities, institutes, and international conferences and forums. Benchmarking has opened

> *"If you give a man a fish, he will have a meal. If you teach him to fish, he will have a living. If you are thinking ahead, sow seed. If you are thinking ten years ahead, plant a tree. If you are thinking one hundred years ahead, educate the people. By sowing a seed once, you will harvest once. By planting a tree, you will harvest tenfold. By educating the people, you will harvest one hundredfold."*
> *– Anonymous Chinese Poet, c.420 B.C.*

FIGURE 10.2 The power of education and training.

the eyes of many companies and shown them how little they knew about their seemingly harmless competitors. Corporate ego must give way to learning humility. Companies implementing TPmgt can keep up to date with formal education and training in productivity management, productivity engineering, quality management, and technology management.

Training is also an effective approach to improving the morale of and retaining valuable human assets. As Ben Nelson of Harris Trust and Savings Bank points out: "Retention in training increases about 20 percent to 80 percent if the person has the chance to translate what he's been taught into meaningful action."[2] Another way to look at the need for education and training is through the Chinese proverb in Figure 10.2.

Supervisory effectiveness training, at all management levels, is one of the most important factors for ensuring success with TPmgt. Typical training topics are shown in Figure 10.3

1) Role Playing - Empathizing
2) Group Dynamics
3) Leadership
4) Organizing
5) How to deal with internal politics of the organization
6) Motivational Techniques
7) Delegation and Follow-up Techniques
8) How to respond to feedback
9) Interpersonal Skills
10) Social Networking
11) Management by Example
12) Management by Exception

FIGURE 10.3 Typical topics in supervisor effectiveness training.

10.3 EXPERT SYSTEM TOOLS FOR TPmgt

The heart of the TPmgt concept is the Total Productivity Model. The uniqueness of the TPmgt philosophy lies in the seamless integration of the measurement, evaluation, planning, and improvement phases of the productivity cycle.

A knowledgeable user of TPmgt can take advantage of the groundwork already done through research in developing expert systems to make "intelligent" decisions based on programmed knowledge. One of the earliest expert systems was developed by Sumanth and Dedeoglu.[3] A more elaborate system was developed by Sumanth and his graduate research assistant Viswanatha Rao in 1989.[4]

More research is needed in this direction, to perfect expert systems in TPmgt to a point where they are integrated as a decision support system into existing computerized strategic planning models.

10.4 VIDEOTAPE AND SEMINARS ON TPmgt

The first videotape set on TPmgt, featuring the author, has been produced by a leading educational communication company in India. The PAL version of the set, titled "Total Productivity Management (TPmgt) for Continuous Competitiveness," is available from:

Corporate Communication Systems (India)
No. 5 Park Avenue
Ameerpet
Hyderabad 500 016
INDIA

This tape set is divided into five VHS cassettes. Most well-known Indian corporations have applied the concepts from this series. For NTSC format VHS tapes, as well as information on seminars on TPmgt, contact:

Dr. David J. Sumanth
8501 SW 151 St.
Miami, FL 33158-1963
Fax: 305-252-2707

QUESTIONS TO PONDER

10.1 Do a self-analysis of your enterprise, and list the ten most important factors that caused the failure of a major management concept recently attempted. What could have been done to minimize this failure?

10.2 Through a comparative analysis of your company and three major competitors, discuss the reasons for success and failure in TQM. What lessons can be learned from this analysis, and how can you effect strategies to apply these lessons?

10.3 Repeat Question 10.2 for reengineering.

10.4 Repeat Question 10.2 for benchmarking.

10.5 Develop an OCST for your company or organization, going back perhaps five years. Which node are you now at to implement TPmgt?

10.6 Continuing your answer to Question 10.5, list and elaborate on the factors that contributed to the current state of organizational culture.

10.7 After answering Question 10.6, develop a blueprint for action on TPmgt.

10.8 Study some of the expert systems available in the literature related to productivity management in general and TPmgt in particular. Prepare a comparative table of the features of these systems.

10.9 Based on your answer to Question 10.8, explore the possibility of developing your own expert systems for TPmgt.

REFERENCES AND NOTES

1. Senge, Peter M., *The Fifth Discipline: The Art & Practice of the Learning Organization,* Doubleday, New York, 1990.
2. Major, Michael J., "Innovative Quality Programs at Work," *Bank Marketime,* p. 24, Oct. 1993.
3. Sumanth, D.J. and Dedeoglu, M., "Application of Expert Systems to Productivity Measurement in Companies/Organizations," *Computers & Industrial Engineering,* Vol. 14, No. 3, pp. 241–249, 1988.
4. Sumanth, D.J. and Rao, V., An Expert System, Linking the 4 Phases of the Productivity Cycle, Working Document, University of Miami, 1989.

APPENDIX A:
HISTORICAL INTRODUCTION
TO QUALITY*

Year/Period	Significant Contributor(s)	Landmark Work/Event
384–322 B.C.	Aristotle	Describes quality (*qualitas* in Latin) in the book *Metaphysics* as the difference between items and as goodness or badness.
About 1000 A.D.	Craftsman guilds (associations)	Apprenticeship training to become master craftsmen.
1500s	French weapons industry	Provides instructions on important measurements and some details concerning inspection.
1700s	French armor and weapons industry	Switching emphasis from one-of-a-kind to standardization was considered important.
Late 1700s and early 1800s	Eli Whitney	Applies concept of interchangeability to manufacturing muskets.
		Rudimentary beginnings of *quality control* (QC) techniques applied, including in-process gauging, testing and inspection, inspection standards, quality, and workmanship standards.

---

* This list is by no means exhaustive, but it does provide a convenient historical snapshot of quality.

Year/Period	Significant Contributor(s)	Landmark Work/Event
Mid 1800s	—	Rapid industrialization leads to labor shortages. Responsibility for quality wrested from the worker/supervisor and given to an independent agent (inspector).
Early 1900s	—	Mass production and automation introduced. The speed of machinery (output) begins to replace the skill of the craftsman (quality).
		Specialization of the QC functions introduced.
1924	Western Electric's Bell Telephone Labs	Inspection Engineering Department formed (members of the Labs included H.F. Dodge, D.A. Quarles, W.A. Shewhart, G.D. Edwards, R.B. Miller, E.G.D. Paterson, H.G. Romig, M.N. Torrey, and P.S. Olmstead)
		Walter A. Shewhart introduces control charts for *statistical quality control* (SQC).
1925	Harold F. Dodge	Develops basic concepts of *sampling* and *inspection by attributes.*
1927	The Western Electric Group	Average Outgoing Quality Limit sampling tables developed.
1920s	Walter A. Shewhart	Application of Shewhart's SQC charts.
1931	Walter A. Shewhart	Publishes his seminal work, *Economic Control of Quality of Manufactured Product.*
1930s	—	Dissemination of Shewhart's ideas.
1930s	Joseph Scanlon	Concept of QC through employee motivation and involvement (*Scanlon Plan*) to improve the overall quality of work life.
1935	E.S. Pearson	Develops *British standard for application of statistical methods to industrial standardization and quality control.*
1939	H. Romig	Presents *variable sampling plans.*
1940	American Standards Association	Application of SQC to manufactured products. American War Standards on Quality Control and Control Charts developed.

Year/Period	Significant Contributor(s)	Landmark Work/Event
1942	Army's Office of the Chief Ordinance: G. Edwards, H. Dodge, G. Gause	*Standard inspection procedures* developed (contained sampling tables based on Average Quality Level (AQL).
1942	Edwards Deming	Teachers SQC to 31,000 engineers, inspectors, and others involved in wartime production.
1943	A. Wald (Statistical Research Group, Columbia Univ.)	Develops the theory of *sequential sampling*.
1946	—	*American Society for Quality Control (ASQC)* formed.
1946	Kaoru Ishikawa	Begins popularizing SQC in Japan.
1946	Engineers and scholars	Form the Union of Japanese Scientists and Engineers (JUSE).
1947	Edwards Deming	Visits Japan (his first visit).
1949	—	"Quality control faded from use," said Deming, mournfully.
1949	JUSE	Quality Control Research Group formed to teach QC in Japan.
1950	U.S. military	*MIL-STD 105-A, B, C, and D* developed.
1950	Edwards Deming	Begins to teach QC in Japan.
1951	Joseph Juran	*Quality Control Handbook* published.
1951	JUSE	The *Deming Prize* instituted in Japan by a formal resolution of the JUSE Board of Directors.
1954	NASA/U.S. War Department	Introduces "*maintainability*" as a discipline.
1955	Kaoru Ishikawa	Introduces control chart techniques in Japan.
1956	Armand Feigenbaum	Introduces *Total Quality Control (TQC)*.
1956	AT&T	Develops and publishes the first edition of the *SQC Handbook*.

Year/Period	Significant Contributor(s)	Landmark Work/Event
1957	Advisory Group on Reliability of Electronic Equipment (AGREE)	Basic concepts of reliability introduced in a major report.
1959	U.S. military	*MIL-STD 414 (Acceptance Sampling by Variables)* developed.
1960	JUSE	*QC text for Foreman,* Vol. A & B developed.
1961	Martin Marietta Corp.	On-time delivery of a perfect missile that is fully operational in 24 hours, using the *"zero defects"* philosophy.
1962	—	The magazine *Quality* is first published.
1962	JUSE	*QC Circle* movement begins. Publishes *Gemba to QC* magazine.
1967	ASQC	Begins publishing *Quality Progress* magazine and the *Journal of Quality Technology*.
1967	—	Walter Shewhart passes away.
1969		*First International Conference for Quality Control* held in Tokyo.
1970s	Armand Feigenbaum	Popularizes *Total Quality Control or Organization-wide Quality Control*.
	Kaoru Ishikawa	Popularizes *Company-wide Quality Control*.
1974	Lockheed Co.	Applies QC circle concept in the United States for the first time.
1976	Kaoru Ishikawa	*Cause-and-Effect Diagram* introduced. Also, Asian Productivity Organization (Tokyo) publishes his work *Guide to Quality Control*. This work is later published by Kraus International Publications in 1982.
1976–77	Genichi Taguchi	Promotes statistical methods for product design improvement (concept of "Loss to Society"). His concepts are considered to have been developed much earlier in 1953 (*Quality Engineering*).
1979	Philip B. Crosby	His book *Quality Is Free: The Art of Making Quality Certain* is published by McGraw-Hill.

Year/Period	Significant Contributor(s)	Landmark Work/Event
1980	NBC and writer Clare Crawford-Mason	The NBC White Paper *"If Japan Can, Why Can't We?"* features Deming. The quality consciousness level in the United States begins to surge after this program is broadcast.
1980	International Technical Information Institute (ITI)	Publishes an eye-opener: *How the U.S.A. & Europe Can Increase Productivity and Enhance Quality Control: An In-Depth Japanese Industrial Survey.*
1980–82	AT&T Bell Labs, Ford, and Xerox	Pioneers in introducing *Taguchi methods* in the United States.
1980s	Edwards Deming, Joseph Juran, Philip Crosby, and Genichi Taguchi	Are kept busy conducting seminars on quality in the United States and overseas.
1982	W. Edwards Deming	MIT Press publishes Deming's book *Quality, Productivity and Competitive Position.*
1985	Kaoru Ishikawa and David J. Lu	Prentice Hall publishes their work, *What Is Total Quality Control? The Japanese Way.*
1987	U.S. House of Representatives	Passes a bill to establish a *national award for quality.*
1987	ANSI and ASQC	*ANSI/ASQC Q04* (American National Standard for Quality Management and Quality System Elements).
1987	International Organization for Standardization (ISO)	Publishes the *ISO 9000 Standards* in Europe.
1988	ASQC, APC, U.S. government, and other companies	*Malcolm Baldrige National Award for Quality* instituted. First awards presented by President Reagan at the White House.
1988	American Supplier Institute	Launches seminars on *Taguchi Methods®.*
1988	U.S. Department of Defense	Defines *Total Quality Management* (TQM).
1989	FPL	Becomes the first company based in the United States to receive the *Deming Prize.*

Year/Period	Significant Contributor(s)	Landmark Work/Event
1989	University of Miami Institute for Studies in Quality	Formed by a grant from FPL. Seminars by N. Kano and H. Gitlow. A number of courses and degree/certificate programs initiated.
1992	European Economic Commission (EEC)	ISO 9000 series accepted as *European Standard for Quality.*
1993	—	Dr. Deming passes away after a very fruitful 93 years.
1996	Philip B. Crosby	His book *Quality Is Still Free: Making Quality Certain in Uncertain Times* is published by McGraw-Hill.

INFORMATION SOURCES

1. Sai, Yasutaka, "Productivity Programs in Japan," *JMA Newsletter,* No. 28, Oct. 1, 1986.
2. Carubba, Eugene and Gordon, Ronald, *Product Assurance Principles: Integrating Design Assurance and Quality Assurance,* McGraw-Hill, New York, 1988, Chapter 1.
3. American Supplier Institute, *Taguchi Methods®: Quality Engineering, Executive Briefing,* New York, 1988.
4. Banks, Jerry, *Principles of Quality Control,* John Wiley & Sons, New York, 1989, Chapter 1.
5. Hunt, V. Daniel, *Quality in America: How to Implement a Competitive Quality Program,* Business One Irwin, New York, 1992.
6. Hutchins, Greg, *The ISO 9000 Implementation Manual,* Oliver Wight Publications, Essex Junction, VT, 1994.
7. Eberts, Ray and Eberts, Cindelyn, *The Myths of Japanese Quality,* Prentice Hall PTR, Upper Saddle River, NJ, 1995, p. 279.

APPENDIX B:
THE TPM FORMULAS©

1. $O_{it} = (O_1 + O_2 + O_3 + O_4 + O_5)_{it}$

2. $I_{it} = (H + M + FC + WC + E + X)_{it}$

3. $OF_t = \sum\limits_{i-1}^{n} O_{it}$

4. $IF_t = \sum\limits_{i=1}^{n} I_{it}$

5. $TPF_t = \dfrac{OF_t}{IF_t}$

6. $TPF_t(BEP) = 1 - \dfrac{\sum\limits_{i=1}^{n} WC_{it}}{IF_t}$

7. $TPIF_t = \dfrac{TPF_t}{TPF_o}$

8. $TP_{it} = \dfrac{O_{it}}{I_{it}}$

9. $\quad TP_{it}(BEP) = 1 - \dfrac{WC_{it}}{I_{it}}$

10. $\quad TPI_{it} = \dfrac{TP_{it}}{TP_{io}}$

11. $\quad PPF_{jt} = \dfrac{OF_t}{IF_{jt}}$, $\{j\} = \{H, M, FC, WC, E, X\}$

12. $\quad PPIF_{jt} = \dfrac{PPF_{jt}}{PPF_{jo}}$

13. $\quad PP_{ijt} = \dfrac{O_{it}}{I_{ijt}}$, $\{j\} = \{H, M, FC, WC, E, X\}$

14. $\quad PPI_{ijt} = \dfrac{PP_{ijt}}{PP_{ijo}}$

NOTATION FOR THE TPM FORMULAS

F = Firm

i = *Operational unit* number; i = 1, 2, 3, ..., n

n = Total number of operational units considered for productivity computations in the firm

t = time period; t = 0, 1, 2, 3... (when t = 0, it is considered to be the
base period with respect to which all the productivity indices are
computed)

j = Input factor

H = Human input

M = Material input

FC = Fixed capital input

WC = Working capital input

E = Energy input

X $\quad$ = Other expense input*

O_1 $\quad$ = Value of finished units of output

O_2 $\quad$ = Value of partially completed units of output

O_3 $\quad$ = Dividend income

O_4 $\quad$ = Interest income

O_5 $\quad$ = Other income

OF $\quad$ = Total tangible output for the firm

IF $\quad$ = Total tangible input for the firm

TPF $\quad$ = Total productivity for the firm

TPF(BEP) = Break-even point of total productivity for the firm

TPIF $\quad$ = Total productivity index for the firm

TP $\quad$ = Total productivity for an operational unit

TP(BEP) = Break-even point of total productivity for an operational unit

TPI $\quad$ = Total productivity index for an operational unit

PPF $\quad$ = Partial productivity for the firm

PPIF $\quad$ = Partial productivity index for the firm

PP $\quad$ = Partial productivity for an operational unit

PPI $\quad$ = Partial productivity index for an operational unit

Note—In all calculations of the output and input values, the output and input values for any period t must be expressed in constant dollars (or any other monetary unit) with respect to the base period, 0. This is done to identify "physical" or "real" changes in output and input as opposed to changes due to price changes. See Chapter 3 for the operational unit concept.

---

* Includes all those input costs that are not included in the other five input factors. Other expenses may include a few to several hundred items. Typical examples are travel, taxes, consulting fees, marketing expenses, information processing expenses, etc.

INDEX